CU00759606

FOOTBALL, CORRUPTION AND LIES

World football is in crisis. The corruption scandal engulfing FIFA is arguably the biggest story in the history of modern sport and a watershed for sport governance. More than a decade ago, John Sugden and Alan Tomlinson laid the foundations for subsequent investigations with the publication of *Badfellas*, a ground breaking work of critical sport sociology that exposed the systematic corruption at the heart of world football. It was a book that FIFA and Sepp Blatter tried to ban.

Now re-issued to combine the original contents of *Badfellas* with new chapters covering the current crisis, this book points to the ways in which FIFA's new administration can learn from the Blatter story. The prequel traces the course of Sugden and Tomlinson's game-changing investigation into FIFA, while the sequel updates the FIFA story from 2002 onwards and provides a chronology of crises and scandals within the FIFA narrative.

Demonstrating the vital importance of critical investigative methods in sport studies, *Football, Corruption and Lies: Revisiting 'Badfellas', the book FIFA tried to ban* is essential reading for anybody looking to understand Blatter's rise and fall.

John Sugden is Professor of the Sociology of Sport at the University of Brighton, UK. He is well known for his work on the sociology of boxing; sport and peace building in divided societies; his studies – with Alan Tomlinson – of the world governing body for football, FIFA; and for his investigative research into football's underground economy. Currently, John is a leading member of the Sport and Leisure Cultures subject group and Director of the University of Brighton's flagship worldwide community relations project, Football4 Peace.

Alan Tomlinson is Professor of Leisure Studies, School of Humanities, at the University of Brighton, UK. He is a renowned scholar and researcher on the social history and sociology of sport, leisure and popular culture. Alan has researched the history and politics of FIFA since the mid-1980s, and is a pioneer of the critical social scientific study of sport. He is the author/editor of numerous books on sport, leisure and consumption, including *Consumption, Identity and Style* and *FIFA: The Men, the Myths and the Money* as well as being a long-term contributor to the soccer periodical *When Saturday Comes*.

'A brave, evidenced and sustained account of the governing body of world football, FIFA. If you care about the fate of the most popular game in the world and want to understand what could be done to move on from 2015 read this book. Two of the most intrepid voices, who both understand how football can operate in the humanitarian arena, have re-issued and extended a book of uncommon power and uncompromising argument.'

—Grant Jarvie, former acting University Principal and Chair of Sport, University of Edinburgh, UK.

'Long before the FBI swooped on FIFA, John Sugden and Alan Tomlinson were on the case. Combining critical sociology with gonzo journalism, they pursued corrupt and ethically bankrupt practices in association football's governing body with the stubborn tenacity of ethnographically-inspired investigative newshounds. This book documents the many twists and turns of a strange road trip, bringing their feisty 2003 book *Badfellas* back into the spotlight that FIFA's lawyers had tried hard to extinguish. Detailing recent developments leading to the fall of the house of Blatter and his associates, the authors unflinchingly appraise the challenges facing genuine reformers of football governance.'

—David Rowe, Professor of Cultural Research, Western Sydney University, Australia.

'Without the pioneering work and brilliant forensic journalism of *Badfellas* and their subsequent books, it is a frightening possibility that the discredited Blatter regime which blighted FIFA for so long, could still be in place. They started the ball rolling and all true lovers of the game should thank John Sugden and Alan Tomlinson for the part they played in exposing football's greatest ever scandal.'

—Mike Collett, Reuters Global Soccer Editor, UK.

'Long before FIFA became synonymous with an unsavory melange of corruption and greed, John Sugden and Alan Tomlinson were on the case. In their pioneering and prescient book *Football, Corruption and Lies: Revisiting Badfellas, the Book FIFA Tried to Ban*, Sugden and Tomlinson take us on a rollicking ride through the grisly annals of FIFA, full of shady characters, backroom deals, and Machiavellian mayhem. Blending gumshoe investigative work with toothy sociological analysis, they untangle the history of brazen chicanery that paved a platinum-plated path for 'Blattergate' in 2015. Through a rich sequel and coda that detail the great unravel at FIFA in 2015, they bring us full circle, all the while sifting the sins from the spin. Sepp Blatter and his phalanx of lawyers tried to ban the original *Badfellas* from distribution in Switzerland, where FIFA is headquartered, but their heyday is passed. Sugden, Tomlinson, and their ilk have won the day. Insightful and incisive, *Football, Corruption and Lies* is a must read for anyone interested in the history of FIFA's profligacy, the modern-day malaise in which it is mired, and possible pathways forward.'

—Jules Boykoff, Professor of Political Science, Pacific University in Oregon, USA.

'*Football, Corruption and Lies* is a brilliant rejuvenation of *Badfellas*. In its original form, the book was a courageous exposé of the septic nature of FIFA's leadership and governance. This updated rendition prompts reflection as to how such corruption flourished and, moreover, why it fell to a handful of academics and supportive journalists to reveal a festering underbelly of deceit, profiteering and bullying. The book's new sections, which evaluate the fall from grace of Blatter and his acolytes, are just as poignant. With the badfellas having been marched off by the FBI, FIFA is in no position to try to ban *Football, Corruption and Lies*.'

—Daryl Adair, Associate Professor of Sport Management, University of Technology Sydney, Australia.

FOOTBALL, CORRUPTION AND LIES

Revisiting *Badfellas*, the book FIFA tried to ban

John Sugden and Alan Tomlinson

Routledge
Taylor & Francis Group

LONDON AND NEW YORK

First published 2017
by Routledge
2 Park Square, Milton Park, Abingdon, Oxon OX14 4RN

and by Routledge
711 Third Avenue, New York, NY 10017

Routledge is an imprint of the Taylor & Francis Group, an informa business

© 2017 John Sugden and Alan Tomlinson

The right of John Sugden and Alan Tomlinson to be identified as authors of this work has been asserted by them in accordance with sections 77 and 78 of the Copyright, Designs and Patents Act 1988.

All rights reserved. No part of this book may be reprinted or reproduced or utilised in any form or by any electronic, mechanical, or other means, now known or hereafter invented, including photocopying and recording, or in any information storage or retrieval system, without permission in writing from the publishers.

Trademark notice: Product or corporate names may be trademarks or registered trademarks, and are used only for identification and explanation without intent to infringe.

British Library Cataloguing in Publication Data
A catalogue record for this book is available from the British Library

Library of Congress Cataloguing in Publication Data
Names: Sugden, John Peter, author. | Tomlinson, Alan, author. |
Sugden, John Peter. Badfellas. | Sugden, John Peter. Great balls of fire.
Title: Football, corruption and lies : revisiting "Badfellas,"
the book FIFA tried to ban / John Sugden and Alan Tomlinson.
Description: [2016 Edition, First edition] | New York : Routledge, 2016. |
Includes bibliographical references and index.
Identifiers: LCCN 2016021728| ISBN 9781138681736 (Hardback) |
ISBN 9781138681774 (Paperback) | ISBN 9781315545615 (eBook)
Subjects: LCSH: Soccer–Economic aspects. | Sports sponsorship. |
Soccer–Corrupt practices. | Fâedâeration internationale de football association.
Classification: LCC GV943.3 .S84 2016 | DDC 796.334–dc23
LC record available at https://lccn.loc.gov/2016021728

ISBN: 978-1-138-68173-6 (hbk)
ISBN: 978-1-138-68177-4 (pbk)
ISBN: 978-1-315-54561-5 (ebk)

Typeset in Bembo
by Out of House Publishing

Printed and bound by CPI Group (UK) Ltd, Croydon, CR0 4YY

CONTENTS

PREFACE TO 2017 RE-ISSUE

This book is a re-issue of *Badfellas: FIFA family at War* (Mainstream Publishing, 2003). The preface to the 2003 edition is included here, preceding the fifteen chapters of the original *Badfellas*; that preface offers some background to the generation of the 2003 book.

We are republishing *Badfellas* because of the enormously expanded worldwide interest in the recent history and contemporary politics of the Fédération Internationale de Football Association (FIFA), and the relevance of the book to an informed understanding of the genesis of the Havelange-Blatter FIFA dynasty, which ran from 1974 to 2015, when Joseph "Sepp" Blatter finally found that his powerbase in the world football governing body had gone.

Re-visiting *Badfellas* is also necessary because, as the subtitle of our new edition states, FIFA's president and its lawyers sought to ban the book from distribution in Blatter's home country of Switzerland. This legal challenge certainly affected distribution policies and consequently the book was not adequately marketed, circulated or distributed at the time of publication. Many of the cast of characters that we brought alive in the book were to become long-term players in the scandals that marked Blatter's presidential tenures in particular, exploiting an organizational structure legitimated for FIFA by a lax Swiss polity; as such characters and names made world headlines, interest in their activities, excesses and abuses of power and privilege has markedly increased. A re-issue of *Badfellas* provides a distinctive and informative account of the provenance of such embedded malpractices within FIFA's culture of corruption, reaching to the highest levels; corrupt practices that have led the US Attorney General Loretta L. Lynch to describe, in December 2015, "the betrayal of trust" by those charged by the US Department of Justice's law enforcement action as "outrageous"; and the "scale of corruption", going back generations, as "unconscionable". The US indictments stated on 20 May of the same year that FIFA as a corrupt, racketeering "enterprise ... arose and flourished" as those in positions of governance in world football "became increasingly intertwined with one another and with the sports marketing companies" moving in on the sport media product. In this context, the indictment added: "The corruption of the enterprise became endemic." As we showed in *Badfellas*, in the opening chapter "Blattergate", "endemic corruption in FIFA practices and procedures" was the order of the day during the Havelange-Blatter régime.

The text of *Badfellas* is published in this re-issued edition as it was in 2003, with some slight editorial amendments to clarify meaning and context. These include sub-titles to the chapter headings, as signposts to the thematic content and narrative of the book. The new material in this edition provides our story of how and when we undertook the work that led to the original publication, in what we call a "Prequel: *Badfellas* begins". After the full text of the 2003 book we provide two further new sections: the "Sequel: *Badfellas* on the run"; and a concluding discussion, "The end of a dynasty: *Badfellas* re-formed?" In the former, we provide an update of the FIFA narrative of the last thirteen or so years, including FIFA's legal attack on *Badfellas*, a New York court judgement against FIFA, and the pivotal FBI-led arrests of FIFA-connected personnel in Zurich. In "the end of the dynasty", we reflect on the FIFA Congress of 26 February 2016 that elected its ninth president, and on the reforms that must be implemented if FIFA is to have any chance of restoring some credibility to its reputation, and regaining the trust of a disillusioned global public. This new material takes the opportunity, where particularly appropriate, to cross-reference the reproduced 2003 text itself.

Producing *Badfellas* for a popular market, we forewent the academic orthodoxies of referencing our sources, or including appendices, glossaries, and an index. We have kept the *Badfellas* text intact for this new publication, but in the new sections we have referenced primary sources, and secondary academic literature of particular relevance to the continuing FIFA story; and we provide an index, glossary of acronyms, and cast list relating to the whole book. The *Badfellas* text itself was based upon extensive research, including interviews, observation, document analysis, and a series of ethnographic excursions across the international football world. Since 2003, one of us has also written a further book on the troubled organisation (*FIFA: The Men, the Myths and the Money*, Routledge 2014, by Alan Tomlinson), and this has provided some of the updating materials for this new edition.

Sport has long been vulnerable to exploitation by crooks and charlatans, even before the process of commercialization and an increasing global media profile brought unprecedented amounts of money into it. Sport's inbuilt drama of the competitive dynamic and the production of a winner has long attracted gambling entrepreneurs to the track and to the stadium. The rewards that have become available for top performers have generated systematic strategies of performance enhancement, in drugs and doping regimes for instance, that have produced cultures of hypocrisy, cheating and lying in sport, within all levels of a sport's hierarchy. This vulnerability of sporting encounters and events to profiteering, to the fixing of results and outcomes, has been throughout the modern period a major cause of concern for sport's governing bodies. The sport-based international non-governmental organizations (INGOs) that grew at the end of the nineteenth and throughout much of the twentieth centuries have always had to cope with such issues, yet have themselves in numerous cases become the source of the problem. It is some of those occupying the highest positions at FIFA who have been shown to be the most accomplished of hypocrites, liars and corrupt racketeers.

So when the team of the US Department of Justice and the FBI brought its weight down on FIFA's networks in the indictments leading to the arrests of 27 May 2015 in Zurich, the global public began to show an intensifying interest in the FIFA story. We hope that this re-issue of the *Badfellas* study will help many of those disillusioned millions understand how the situation arose; and help all fans and followers of the game question the crooks and the charlatans who have taken FIFA so far away from its stated goals and objectives. Perhaps it should also be asked how and why the authorities in various countries – Switzerland in particular, but also "big" football countries such as Brazil, Germany, Italy, France, Spain and the UK – could choose to ignore FIFA malpractices for so long, when the story told in *Badfellas* made it so clear just how deeply and extensively a culture of corruption was taking hold at FIFA at its highest echelons.

John Sugden, Eastbourne, East Sussex, UK
Alan Tomlinson, Brighton, East Sussex, UK; and Campillergues, L'Hérault, France
March 2016

ACKNOWLEDGEMENTS

We are grateful to the University of Brighton for its support over the years, through which we have remained on the FIFA trail; to our colleagues and to media people and institutions that have shown an interest in our work; to Simon Whitmore, the most supportive of editors at Routledge/Taylor & Francis; and most of all to our families, who have shown particular tolerance of our fieldwork schedules in keeping on that FIFA trail.

PREQUEL

Badfellas begins: critical sociology and the purging of FIFA

In this opening chapter to this re-issue of *Badfellas: FIFA family at war* we identify and trace the beginnings of our multifaceted and enduring investigative mission to expose and expel the amoral, self-serving and rancid regime that has governed FIFA since the early 1970s. In doing so we outline the key features of a style of the critical and investigative sociology of sport approach that underwrote and framed most of our published interventions and research articles in this field, including the earlier edition of this book. *Badfellas* was first published in 2003, and for reasons we will expand on here but also go on to explain in a later section of this book, the FIFA president Joseph "Sepp" Blatter, and FIFA's lawyers, tried to ban the book in Blatter's and FIFA's own home territory, Switzerland. This was both a tribute to the book's revelatory impact, and a relatively scary experience for us as authors; after all, if FIFA's Swiss lawyers could expend so much expensive time looking to silence two academic researchers, who Blatter himself referred to as the "English Professors", as we note in *Badfellas*, how far would they go if they got to the Swiss courts and beyond? This was a strategy of aggression by a powerful organization whose top man was clearly rattled by what we had to say. There is a scene in the side-splittingly awful film *United Passions* where an investigative journalist/researcher – a young-ish Irishman – takes on Blatter and his corrupt regime, and Blatter (played by the squirmingly embarrassed Tim Roth, wishing no doubt he was back under Quentin Tarantino's direction) simply brushes the intrusion to one side.[1] It was not quite like this in real life when the bailiffs arrived at our front doors in the summer of 2003, depositing the legal documentation that also threatened our publisher and led to the mysterious disappearance of the book from outlets and distributors. But more of that below, and later in the extended narrative that we provide after the complete *Badfellas* text.

In identifying the main milestones and episodes in this ongoing exploration we outline and evaluate what we believe to have been the distinctive and possibly

pivotal contribution of the critical academic perspective, allied to a persistently reso-
nant and hectoring scholarly voice, in the exposure of and subsequent demolition of
the incurably corrupted Havelange/Batter FIFA dynasty (HBFD). Our joint story
begins at the football World Cup in the USA in 1994. We went to USA '94 in part
as football fans to support the Republic of Ireland, given neither England nor any
of the other so-called "home nations" of the UK had qualified for that tournament.
We were also in the USA to promote our new book *Hosts and Champions: Soccer
Cultures, National Identities and the USA World Cup*.[2] Book launches were scheduled on both the east coast, at Secaucus, New Jersey; and the west coast, in west
Hollywood. Extensive debate had taken place internationally on the appropriateness
of the USA as a World Cup host and venue, and the place of FIFA and the motives
of FIFA's leadership were part of these debates. It was an area of research unpopu-
lated by critical scholars and it was clear to us that some seriously fruitful leads could
be followed in researching FIFA's role in the burgeoning cultural economy and the
globalization of the game.

Later the same year we gave related academic presentations at the North
American Society for the Sociology of Sport (NASSS) annual conference in
Savannah, Georgia, and one of us had also been invited a little before the NASSS
event to a pre-Olympics conference in Atlanta, two years before the centennial
Summer Olympic Games were held there. Georgia Tech, a prominent beneficiary
of the planning blitz necessitated by the Olympics, was hosting an event on World
Sport Management. There was a buzz in the conference halls of Atlanta as some of
us were seen to be taking potshots at apologetic Olympic shibboleths; and in the
middle of the conference hall of the next Olympic host city, the English investigative
journalist Andrew Jennings, co-author of the explosive *The Lords of the Rings: Power,
Money and Drugs in the Modern Olympics*,[3] was making waves that would swell into
the perfect storm of revelations of Olympic corruption within the spheres of governance and the International Olympic Committee (IOC); revelations, related to
Salt Lake City's winning of the 2002 Winter Olympics, that would mobilize the US
legal system and rattle the rafters of a corrupt and unaccountable IOC. And much
of the foundation for this trail of research and revelation was attributable to the
ground-breaking work of Vyv Simson and Jennings.

Jennings was also one of the keynote speakers at the NASSS symposium later in
the year. *The Lords of the Rings*, published in 1992, and drawing on earlier collabora-
tions with Patrick Nally, claimed, possibly for the first time in such a sustained and
in-depth investigation, that the upper echelons of global sport governance were
riddled with cronyism, graft and corruption – a proposition which may not raise
as many eyebrows in 2016 as it did back in 1992. Unsurprisingly, Jennings' keynote
lecture echoed the themes of the book, by now familiar to us as critical scholars,
but as we listened to his speech what struck us most forcefully was his acerbic
and pointed critique of the academic community for not contributing anything of
substance to challenge the received wisdom churned out by those who occupied
the commanding heights of global sport's governing institutions. Instead, Jennings
argued persuasively, hitherto the academic sport community had, at best, produced

tepid and descriptive accounts of the machinations of world sports' major ruling institutions and their leaders. At worst, argued Jennings, we scholars had conspired with the PR machinery of these organizations to reproduce glossy "coffee-table" official histories and fawning hagiographies that glorified the accomplishments and masked the failings of the IOC, the International Amateur Athletics Federation (IAAF, now renamed the International Association of Athletic Federations), and what was our own main object of interest, world football's governing body, the Fédération Internationale de Football Association (FIFA). Our own new book included a chapter on the history of FIFA, and was laying the foundation for a more informed approach to the critical and interdisciplinary study of such a body, following a pioneering piece in the 1986 book *Off the Ball: The Football World Cup*.[4] However, these were relatively small strides forward; we felt the sting of Jennings' critique, but also sensed the openness of the field.

In 1994 the IOC and its then leader, the Spaniard Juan-Antonio Samaranch, was Jennings' main villain and investigative target. It would be a number of years later before he turned his guns fully on the organization which was to be our main concern in the coming decades. While we were still interested in the activities of the IOC and its leaders, at the same time we were becoming increasingly concerned about the manoeuvrings of world football's governing body, FIFA, which at the time was led by another Hispanic doyen, the Brazilian multi-millionaire João Havelange, one of Simson and Jennings' rapacious protagonists in *Lords of the Rings*. Jennings' accusatory tirade was uncomfortable for us to listen to in our positions as prominent members of the sport-focused academic community; nevertheless, it struck a chord and his chastisement was still ringing in our ears the following day as we sat in a small diner in the coastal resort town of Tybee Island, Chatham County, Georgia's most easterly point, well away from the madding crowd of the conference. We had a blank sheet of paper between us, and two coffee mugs brim full, taking advantage of the diner's generous offer of free refills. Several hours and half a gallon of coffee later we had agreed to pick up the gauntlet thrown down by Jennings in his previous day's harangue, and outlined the bare bones of a research proposal to undertake a critical scholarly investigation of FIFA. This Jennings-prompted and caffeine-stimulated outline proposal would mature to become the basis of our trailblazing book *FIFA and the Contest for World Football: Who Rules the Peoples' Game?*[5] Jennings continued his determined pursuit of Samaranch and the IOC's ruling elite in two further books,[6] whilst we sallied forth on a new quest of our own and took off after Havelange and FIFA. Inspired in part by Jennings, we needed to borrow from his investigative journalist's toolkit to accomplish our task. Theoretically and methodologically, though, we could also trawl some neglected sources within the academic tradition, packing additional and different research weapons and resources in our hunter's armoury, ones not easily or routinely available to – or perhaps understood by – investigative journalists.

There were to be several stages/phases to our FIFA research. At the outset it should be borne in mind that we began undertaking our ground-breaking research at the pre-dawn of the internet age when the electronic search engine was an artefact of science fiction/fancy. In the early 1990s, recruiting Professor Google as a research assistant was not an option for us or anybody else. As such we had to rely on what may now be considered old-fashioned methods of research scholarship including using libraries, visiting accessible archives to track down records and other relevant documents, even writing to and telephoning potential contacts and sources, before eventually interviewing people who were the guardians of other relevant hoards of data. At the outset of our investigations, in order to clear the ground we knew FIFA needed to be subjected to a detailed and historically grounded institutional analysis which had not been done by anybody else until then. In doing this we were able to specify the key features of and figures in FIFA's organizational architecture; from the base of this institutional analysis we were able to identify and trace the impact of overlapping flows of globalization on FIFA's organizational evolution. This phase of our investigation included interpreting and taking account of the genesis of FIFA's crucially important worldwide governing and administrative sub-structure built around the powerful continental confederations – which as we discuss later would go on to play a huge part in the construction, undermining and ultimate collapse of the HBFD. This done, we turned our attention to understanding the relationship between these confederations and the overarching ruling body, mapping FIFA's labyrinthine network of committees and sub-committees, charting their interconnecting corridors and in so doing seeking to analyse and interpret the nexus of hierarchical and horizontal power relations that bound the whole edifice together. In completing this essential ground-clearing and mapping exercise we were able to recognize and catalogue FIFA's most centrally important roles; identify the role bearers, who were the gatekeepers that looked after the keys to the vaults that held the secrets to the organization's modus operandi; as well as getting to know the names of those that exercised these responsibilities. Once this stage of our investigations was complete we were able to target those who occupied the institutional vantage points who we would need to gain access to in order to get the fully informed panoramic picture of how this complex and secretive multi-dimensional organization carried out its affairs. This done, we were then able to embark on the "close-up and personal" and arguably more telling ethnographic phase of our investigations. We are both experienced qualitative researchers and as such knew our biggest challenge would be gaining access to FIFA's corridors of power by getting to know and winning the confidence and trust of the gatekeepers identified in our institutional analysis.

How we set about achieving this is explained in fuller detail in our research articles on the investigative tradition, in an article in the *International Review for the Sociology of Sport*, and in a chapter in our book *Power Games*.[7] The approach we took to researching FIFA summarized in this article became the bedrock of a much larger portfolio of critical social science research that came to be associated with interdisciplinary social scientists working in the area of Sport and Leisure Cultures at the University of Brighton. The fully articulated manifesto in *Power Games* grew to be known as "the Brighton method", and guided our entry into the dauntingly unlimited field. When we embarked on this ethnographic phase we knew we faced a massive set of challenges, not the least of which being how to get to the heart of the FIFA operation. With the most modest of budgets, raised by personal consultancies and earnings to complement seed-corn monies awarded from our University's research funding, how could we set about tracking down and getting access to the cast of powerful and secretive characters who are spread worldwide?

Presciently, we figured out very early on in our research journey something that the FBI would itself come to understand and exploit to devastating effect some years later: that is, FIFA follows a rhythmic calendar of annual, biannual and quadrennial events, including regional and world football competitions, committee meetings and congresses to which FIFA's governing classes are invited, indeed expected/required to attend, taking advantage of lavish travel and generous hospitality allowances and expenses. This travelling circus of beneficiaries also included the sport media pack and associated FIFA roadies and groupies. We reasoned that all we had to do was target the appropriate FIFA and/or Confederation events, and turn up ourselves, staying in proximity to FIFA's five star hotels of choice, and once there worming our way into the institutional cracks and crevices. If it sounds like we were lurking in the shadows in the hope/expectation that FIFA's ruling elite and its *cognoscenti* entourage would eventually come close enough for us to make some initial contacts, you are listening well. However, the earlier work on FIFA in *Off the Ball* and *Hosts and Champions* had established a presence, at several national associations, and by letter and correspondence at FIFA House itself. There was a kind of calling card in this, one that could be brandished as we began to build and roll out our research snowball.

The event we selected to commence our ethnographic investigations, to get close to and observationally familiar with the workings and practices of FIFA people and events, was the African Cup of Nations when it was held in South Africa in January 1996. While there we were able to meet and get to know a small number of, but nonetheless important, FIFA watchers and assorted FIFA apparatchiks and insiders who, after we'd given them a flavour of what and who we were interested in, could put us in touch with others whom they believed might be willing and/ or able to help us forge ahead with our enquiries. Once we had gained a small measure of access, using tried and tested ethnographic fieldwork principles, like energetic, inquisitive moles we "snowballed" around and dug beneath FIFA's corridors of power, picking up contacts, informants and confidants on the way and burrowing deeper into FIFA's world, building an extensive Filofax of well-placed contacts and informants. Later the same year one of us attended the Asian Football Confederation's (AFC) equivalent event, the Asian Cup, in Abu Dhabi, United Arab Emirates, meeting more international and local journalists, numerous football administrators from across the continent, and gaining invaluable contacts with movers and shakers from the Gulf states, powerful figures from Saudi Arabia to Malaysia, including a prominent powerbroker from South Korea, and the general secretary of the AFC. Saudi Arabia beat the hosts in the final but the more important result for us was that an "in" had been earned for another archive and case-study visit, to the AFC's headquarters in Kuala Lumpur.

With an excitingly expanding list of names and contacts in our notebooks from our time at the African and Asian events, and more contact established with individuals encountered on a research trip to FIFA House itself, our research snowball trundled on to the Egyptian capital Cairo where the FIFA World Under-17 Football Championship was being hosted in 1997, affording us more opportunities to get to know and interview FIFA insiders, including the biggest fish of all, the incumbent FIFA President João Havelange. The full transcript of our interview with the FIFA supremo is published as an appendix to *FIFA and the Contest*. The then director of FIFA communications, who conducted the research tour of FIFA House with one of us, not only facilitated our Havelange interview, but was later able to assist us in securing media accreditation for the World Cup finals that were to be hosted in France the following year. By now, too, we had a pedigree of accreditation, after the African and Asian events, and were writing occasional pieces for the football magazine *When Saturday Comes*, and features for the UAE's *Gulf Times*, the *New Statesman* and the *Financial Times*. It was a challenging balancing act, combining the role of detached and disinterested academic researcher with that of the critical commentator on sport politics writing on issues of immediate interest for a wider public.

Before the World Cup began in France 1998 we had gathered a sufficient amount of material to finish writing and publish *FIFA and the Contest*, the book that for us and perhaps others too would become the foundation for and guidebook to future FIFA investigations. Even before this book was published we had realized that the FIFA story would be an ongoing saga, so in June 1998 we set off to Paris to begin gathering more evidence for future investigations and publications. As a base, funded by a publisher's advance, we rented a modest apartment for the duration of the competition, overlooking Montmartre Cemetery in the French capital. This accommodation was shared briefly with Andrew Jennings, as he began his own investigations into FIFA. It was an ideal location for us to bed down in, and in the build up to the 1998 FIFA presidential election we kept up our daily surveillance of members of the FIFA Executive Committee (ExCo) who were lodging in more salubrious surroundings in the five-star Hotel Le Bristol in the centre of Paris.

When we arrived in Paris, after dropping off our bags in Montmartre, we set off to the World Cup Media Centre to pick up our media accreditation passes. The book *FIFA and the Contest* was out – we had launched it at a well-attended London event – and we were now fully accredited members of the media pack for one of the world's biggest sport mega-events. It was a four-year journey from Tybee Island, but we knew that we now had an unprecedented opportunity to take the research still further, to expand our networks and sources and study the transition of power at the top of FIFA from as close as you could hope to get, in the Equinox Hall where Havelange's successor as FIFA's eighth president would be chosen in a runoff between FIFA general secretary/chief executive Sepp Blatter, and UEFA president Lennart Johansson. It was no time to sit back with our passes and just watch the football; there were further contacts to be had, networks to unravel.

While we were waiting to have our accreditation passes issued at the media centre we spotted a journalist looking through a copy of *FIFA and the Contest*. We also felt obliged to introduce ourselves as the authors of the book. The journalist was Michael (Mike) Collet, senior football correspondent for Reuters, the international press agency. He recalls the encounter, which led us into a protracted conversation in a coffee booth discussing the ins and outs of FIFA politics and the likely outcome of the forthcoming election of the next president: Mike was, in his own words, "bowled over by your knowledge and point of view on FIFA". At the Equinox Hall for the election that elevated Blatter to power, Mike had *FIFA and the Contest* on hand, as a reference/source for background to the news stories that he would be wiring across the world over the next days. In our time in Paris we would get to know Mike well. In fact it was he, along with some other journalist colleagues, who reaffirmed for us the interest that there would be in *Great Balls of Fire: How Big Money is Hijacking World Football*,[8] an accessibly framed version of the major themes of our relatively formal and stylistically heavy academic study. To recraft this for a wider audience, Mike and others were saying, would be a valued contribution; the rationale for this being that the core story within the pages of the academic study was too important to be left gathering dust on library shelves, in books priced for university libraries rather than the concerned football fan or professional. This reinforced our commitment to get the popular version moving, also rendered distinctive by some new material from the election and Blatter's early days in the presidential post; with this in mind we roamed around France '98 gathering material to update and popularize *FIFA and the Contest*.

The following year, our second FIFA book was published. It appeared in hardback only, with some illuminating colour photographs, so was still not as accessibly priced as we believed the story and the subject profile warranted. However, we first realized that this more accessible publication was having a powerful impact in the upper echelons of world football in 2001 when, after the UEFA Champions League Final between Bayern Munich and Valencia in Milan, we attended on the following morning a UEFA Executive Committee post-match press briefing at which we witnessed the then UEFA president, Lennart Johansson, brandishing a copy of *Great Balls of Fire* in the faces of his executive and the assembled media. "You must all read this!" he bellowed. This shows you how the "world of FIFA" really works, he added. Knowing that the HBFD corruption saga was set to run on, it was after this episode that we felt compelled to continue our investigations into the self-styled FIFA "family". By this time the parallels/parodies between FIFA and the networks of organized crime such as the mafia were inescapable – and we'd demonstrated the *omertà* principle of collective and individual silence at work in a number of cases in *Great Balls*. The FIFA narrative was becoming so scandal-ridden in Blatter's presidency that we felt a further update of the popular version of the story was needed, to cover the depth and range of examples of abuse, incompetence and corruption in the practices of FIFA and its institutional partners, particularly the confederations representing the world's regions.

And so, sitting on the pavement of a bar in Milan, in another coffee-inspired moment, our third FIFA book was incubated: and when, on that Italian morning, thinking of a title for this book, we simply inverted the emphasis in the title of *Goodfellas* – the successful Hollywood depiction of the Las Vegas mafia and its modus operandi. The new book would be *Badfellas*, and, in tribute to the mafia's nickname "The Family", the subtitle of the book would be *FIFA family at war*. We finished work on that manuscript in August 2002, and within a year the county court bailiff of Brighton was busy tracking us down at our home addresses "to give some court papers" to us "in regard to the above action" (quoting just one of the deliveries), this being "Re: Foreign Process v. Mr Alan Tomlinson". Blatter and FIFA's lawyers, Nobel & Hug of Zurich, were serving an injunction on us, the publisher, and Amazon Germany, seeking to block distribution of *Badfellas*. We pick up the threads of this story later in this book, in the "Sequel" section following the full *Badfellas* text.

Events would move beyond parody when, twelve years later – or roughly three more cycles of Blatter's presidency – in May 2016, the FBI arrived in Zurich. Using United States RICO (Racketeering-Influenced Corrupt Organizations) laws, federal legislation that had been designed purposefully to bring down New York's notorious Gambino mafia crime family, FBI agents and Swiss police swooped and arrested a number of senior FIFA-related personnel, mostly officials from confederations and their associates, at the exclusive Baur Au Lac hotel in a dawn raid two days before the FIFA presidential election. Full details of the FBI's badfellas bust are covered in the "Sequel" that constitutes the penultimate chapter of this book.

Just as Lennart Johannsson and his colleagues at UEFA had realized (regarding the septic nature of the contents of *Great Balls* and the damage it could do to the reputation of football's governing body), Sepp Blatter and his cronies in FIFA House soon realized that *Badfellas* contained even more dynamite that could – if widely disseminated – explode and destroy the HBFD. Thus, FIFA's lawyers got hold of *Badfellas* as soon as they could, and instituted the court processes described above, a form of bullying tactic ensuring as much as possible that distributors were scared off and the book's distribution and circulation minimized. Reading Blatter and his lawyers' interpretations of the book, though, convinced us that our investigations into FIFA could not be ignored, and were bearing fruit. When he was asked about vote-buying after his 1998 victory, Blatter said "the match is over", and silence and survival became the order of the day for many within FIFA who had opposed Blatter's elevation. But outside the inner circles of FIFA, we argued, "there may still be enough people who, in the words of the FIFA motto, 'care about football' enough to carry forward the investigation. This game may be longer than Blatter thinks."[9] We are pleased that this has proven to be the case, and that the impact of works by David Yallop[10] and ourselves from the beginning of Blatter's regime has proved enduring.

Of course without the backing and budget of a wealthy newspaper or related sport media organs, or access to resources equivalent to those at the disposal of some journalists and international police agencies, there were limits to what we could achieve alone to expose wrongdoing and undermine FIFA's house of corruption. But investigative work is a long game, as we said in the immediate wake of Blatter's passage to power. And as Susan Strange reminded us in her brilliant book

Casino Capitalism: "Money's fructifying, enabling power for good was matched by its terrible disruptive, destructive power for evil."[11] The HBFD story is one bearing out this frightening anomaly as FIFA continued to publicly profess its universalist redistributive mission, whilst providing increased opportunities for corrupt individuals to make off with the family silver. Strange is also right to call on academics to contribute research that helps people and institutions "think about the feasible options of what might be done". *Badfellas* began as a long-term investigative project; we believe that there are still vital lessons in the book that will aid and inform any debate about what might be done, not just in and about FIFA, but in relation to other sport organizations that could be diverted from the path of corruption.

However modestly resourced then, we approached our subject with a sociologically informed critical perspective using perhaps a more subtle range of research skills and critical/analytical powers than those routinely deployed by journalists and crime fighters; and we have had the pressure of neither the news deadline, nor the responsibility of the administrator or official. We have been able to sift, select material, wait for the sources to speak again, give the lobbyists something to say, offer the broader picture to the newscasters. We contend therefore that in *Badfellas* we brought something distinctive and important to the FIFA investigators' table. Not just to the journalists, or an angry UEFA president, but also to the reformers. Dr François Carrard, the Swiss lawyer who chaired the reform process that hauled the IOC back from its excesses of corruption, took on the task of chairing FIFA's 2016 Reform Committee, and has stated that our research and books on FIFA have been on his radar: "I am quite aware of your numerous contributions relating to various sports as well as football and more particularly FIFA. They are important contributions."[12] Well, we hope so. We are convinced that when the last vestiges of the HBFD are finally eradicated from world football, and the post-mortem takes place, the story told in this book will be held up as an outstanding example of the powerful impact that can be made when journalists, law enforcement agencies and academics collaborate in the cause of fighting corruption and promoting progressive social and political change in the world of sport administration and governance.

Notes

1   *United Passions* was co-funded by FIFA itself, to the tune of around £17 million (US$29 million), and on its release in the US over the weekend of 6 June 2015 took $918. It is recognized as one of, if not the, lowest-grossing films in Hollywood history. See www.espnfc.com/fifa-world-cup/story/2496658/fifa-film-united-passions-among-worst-in-us-history, accessed 10 March 2016.

2   John Sugden and Alan Tomlinson, eds, *Hosts and Champions: Soccer Cultures, National Identities and the USA World Cup* (Aldershot: Arena/Ashgate, 1994).

3   Vyv Simson and Andrew Jennings, *The Lords of the Rings: Power, Money and Drugs in the Modern Olympics* (London: Simon & Schuster, 1992).

4   See Alan Tomlinson, "Going global: The FIFA story" in Alan Tomlinson and Garry Whannel, eds, *Off the Ball: The Football World Cup* (London: Pluto, 1986); and Alan Tomlinson, "FIFA and the expanding football family" in Sugden and Tomlinson, *Hosts and Champions*.

5 John Sugden and Alan Tomlinson, *FIFA and the Contest for World Football: Who Rules the Peoples' Game?* (Cambridge: Polity Press, 1998).

6 Andrew Jennings, *The New Lords of the Rings: Olympic Corruption and How to Buy Gold Medals* (London: Pocket Books/Simon & Schuster, 1996); Andrew Jennings and Clare Sambrook, *The Great Olympic Swindle: When the World Wanted its Games Back* (London: Simon & Schuster, 2000).

7 John Sugden and Alan Tomlinson, "Digging the dirt and staying clean: Retrieving the investigative tradition for a critical sociology of sport", *International Review for the Sociology of Sport*, Vol. 34, No. 4 (1999): 385–97. For the extended version of this article and argument see their "Theory and method for a critical sociology of sport" in John Sugden and Alan Tomlinson, eds, *Power Games: A Critical Sociology of Sport* (London and New York: Routledge, 2002).

8 John Sugden and Alan Tomlinson, *Great Balls of Fire: How Big Money is Hijacking World Football* (London and Edinburgh: Mainstream, 1999). Hereafter referred to as *Great Balls*.

9 John Sugden and Alan Tomlinson, "Sepp mire", *When Saturday Comes*, Vol. 138, August 1998.

10 David Yallop, *How They Stole the Game* (London: Poetic Publishing, 1999).

11 Susan Strange, *Casino Capitalism* (Manchester: Manchester University Press, 1997): vi–vii.

12 Personal correspondence/communication to Alan Tomlinson, 30 November 2015.

BADFELLAS

FIFA family at war

John Sugden and Alan Tomlinson

[first published 2003, by Mainstream Publishing Company (Edinburgh) Ltd]

PREFACE (TO 2003 EDITION)

Badfellas is a significantly updated and amended version of *Great Balls of Fire: How Big Money is Hijacking World Football*, published in hardback by Mainstream in 1999. Since that book was written there have been some seismic happenings within the cloistered and Byzantine world of FIFA, and we were persuaded that we needed to provide a still more contemporary account of this never-ending story. We have opted for a new title, first because of the amount of new material that this book contains, and secondly because the change more accurately reflects the book's focus and contents. It remains a story about how big business has infiltrated and all but taken over the commanding heights of the world's most popular game. But because it is chiefly centred upon a cast of characters who call themselves the FIFA family and who, at least in style and mannerism, approach their guardianship of world football like the *Cosa Nostra* takes care of the family business, we think that *Badfellas* is more appropriate. We are not suggesting that those who work for, represent or have significant dealings with FIFA really are *mafiosi*. Nor is it our intention to imply that FIFA-types are all bad people all of the time. We are suggesting, however, that some might be bad for football some of the time and others most of the time.

The idea for *Great Balls of Fire* started with conversations with journalists and friends working in other areas of the media after publication of our academic book, *FIFA and the Contest for World Football: Who Rules the Peoples' Game* (Polity Press, 1998). Journalists opened the book on their laps during the boring bits of the FIFA Congress in Paris in 1998, and were clearly finding it of some value as a source of information. Some media publications were heavily derivative of our research and scholarship, outside of the conventions of academic attribution, and this undoubtedly prompted some territorial aspirations in us. We had also edited a book – *Hosts and Champions: Soccer Cultures, National Identities and the USA World Cup* (Ashgate, 1994) – that had provided insights into, and generated international responses on, the vibrant football cultures that were ripe for further development and exploitation by those in charge of world football.

Media colleagues especially, but practitioners and academics too, convinced us that some of the themes that ran through the earlier books needed to be developed and made accessible to a wider, popular audience. We have continued to be encouraged and informed by colleagues and confidants in the media.

The core of the book (Chapters Two to Thirteen) remains largely the same as *Great Balls of Fire*, mostly a character-driven contemporary history of world football's governing body. We believe that the analysis and interpretation presented therein still holds. We have made some minor alterations, however, where we have discovered new material that throws additional light on these subjects, and where time and context have suggested shifts of tone, tense or emphasis. The bulk of the new information and argument is presented in two new chapters – Chapter One, 'Blattergate', and Chapter Fourteen, 'The Terminator' – as well as parts of Chapters Eleven and Thirteen ('Tout Heaven' and 'Bidding Wars'), and the final chapter, 'Fifaland'. We have used the events surrounding the 2002 FIFA Congress and presidential election in Seoul, and England's adventures in Japan during the World Cup Finals, as frameworks within which to present the key characters, episodes and turmoil that made Joseph S. Blatter's first four years at the FIFA helm so eventful. In doing so Alan Tomlinson took up the trail in Seoul and the South Pacific, and other parts of FIFA's global network, particularly in the margins where the powerbrokers muster their loyal subjects; and John Sugden went to Tokyo and other Japanese venues, where the FIFA family members continued to be pampered and hold on to their places in one of the best clubs in the world.

In Chapters One and Fourteen, where appropriate we adopt a third-person narrative style for some individual encounters and experiences. We hope that this does not appear too indulgent. Throughout our research, we worked together on the FIFA trail, following FIFA's family fortunes. At times Tomlinson has been called John, and Sugden has been called Alan, by one or other of our respondents or informants. We conducted over 100 formal interviews in the course of this research, and engaged in many more hundreds of conversations and untold thousands of observations, and we report the bulk of these using the collective pronoun. If some interviewees thought that one of us was hiding in the bushes or under the sofa, they will be mistaken and we are confident that they will accept this authorial device.

Why should the way world football is run matter? In the last 25 years FIFA has overseen (or turned a blind eye to) football's transformation from the people's game to the plaything and cashcow of big business and multinational capital. Behind the rhetoric of world development and national representation, from its offshore fortress in Switzerland, without transparency, democracy or accountability, FIFA has brokered this transformation.

Having spent much of the last decade watching at close quarters the behaviour of FIFA's leading luminaries, we have grown to be deeply suspicious of those who purport to speak 'for the good of the game (FIFA's motto). As events within the cloisters of the International Olympic Committee (IOC) have reminded us, the administration of international sport is vulnerable to exploitation by tin-pot, pompous and vainglorious carpetbaggers. Football is not an exception.

The guardians of world football have a duty to care for a precious cultural product. While they do not trumpet quite so gloatingly the hypocritical ideals of the Olympic movement, FIFA has a moral obligation to abide by democratically established sporting ethics such as equality, representation, responsibility, fairness and accountability. If they want to run football like a business, they should at least follow a code of good practice. As it stands, FIFA plays by its own rules.

The profit-driven logic of the contemporary game, if unchecked, will see world football turned into a meaningless global circus, with fewer and fewer genuine fans either capable of or interested in getting inside the big top to witness no more than an increasingly dehumanised spectacle. They may as well stay at home and fiddle with their PlayStations.

This book is not an epitaph for the people's game. We have written it because we believe that information is power. Pointing to the truth about who is doing what to your game, we believe that we can make a valuable contribution to the growing resistance and reaction against the total commodification of football. In the UK, the Monopolies and Mergers Commission's ruling that Rupert Murdoch's BSkyB could not buy Manchester United is a good example of what can be achieved when enough well-informed people take to the barricades.

We believe that world football should be run by able and honest men and women who put the game first and the bank balance, personal power and prestige, and the high life some way down the list. It's time the people got their balls back and did something to get rid of the freeloaders by putting their power behind those who call for reform. We hope this book will help, and in our concluding chapter we make our own recommendations for change.

As far as possible, we have drawn on our own, exclusive research materials. We are grateful to many people for informing our project. Many are 'insiders' who were understandably reluctant to see their names in print. We have done as much as possible to respect their anonymity. To those who have been willing to be named and quoted we are particularly grateful. Despite the issues and concerns articulated in the following pages, we are genuinely grateful for assistance received from personnel in all of the six regional confederations that administer world football, and from those within FIFA itself. While the FIFA family jealously guards its secrets, during the course of our research it became clear that some members recognise the need for wider and more honest dissemination of information.

We are grateful, as ever, to our colleagues at the University of Brighton, where the Sport and Leisure Cultures group in the Chelsea School Research Centre has provided invaluable stimulation. Key fieldwork trips for the new material in the book have been funded by the Chelsea School's research budget. Without this support, in time and resources, it would have been impossible to have stayed in touch with the FIFA family saga in the way that we have managed to do. Undergraduates and postgraduates in the School have listened to some of our ideas and analyses and provided thoughtful and useful responses.

Special thanks go to Alys and Rowan Tomlinson, who contributed to images and text that have informed the writing and the book, and to Ron Maughan who contributed images for the book's cover. We are also grateful to Bill Campbell and his colleagues at Mainstream Publishing for their faith in the project. Finally, thanks to Chris, Alex and Jack Sugden, and Alys and Rowan Tomlinson for sustained family encouragement and support, and to Bernie Kirrane, Jo and Sinéad.

John Sugden and Alan Tomlinson,
Eastbourne and Brighton,
March 2003

1

BLATTERGATE

Blatter consolidates power

'I am not a bad man', said Joseph 'Sepp' Blatter on stage in the convention centre of the Hotel Seoul Hilton, South Korea, the Wednesday before the weekend kickoff of World Cup 2002. 'Many, many thanks. You cannot imagine what it means to me having been during months accused by a certain press saying what a bad man I am'. 'I am not a bad man', he'd also stated at a press conference a little earlier: 'Look into my eyes'. 'I am not a crook', said US President Richard Nixon, one grey November day in Washington in 1973.

In Seoul this sweltering May day in 2002, the FIFA president sought to stem the tide of his own Watergate. Documents were disappearing from the files at FIFA House, and integrity and credibility draining daily from the veins of the world governing body. Blatter had just been re-elected as president of the governing body of world football, FIFA. There'd never been a FIFA Congress quite like this one. It had come close in 1998, when Blatter won the presidency against European (UEFA) football boss Lennart Johansson. This time round Blatter faced a challenge from boss of the African football confederation, Cameroonian Issa Hayatou. The world media were hungry for this, and Blatter was spread across the headlines of the world press, featured in *Time* magazine – in mainstream rather than sports items – all asking whether he could survive the serious allegations over his stewardship of FIFA.

'*For the good of the game*', FIFA's slogan, was looking like a laughing stock as Blatter reeled in the face of accusations of administrative malpractice, financial mismanagement and outright organisational deception and fraud. The English press, the *Daily Mail* in particular, went beyond a reliance on media releases and mere speculation, and attacked relentlessly the FIFA president and his network of cronies, crooks and charlatans who have made personal gains from their lofty positions. Much of the attention focused upon the question of whether Blatter was even fit to stand for re-election for the FIFA presidency. The media revelled in the dramatic atmosphere of charge and counter-charge as the FIFA edifice looked more and more shaky.

But the dapper Blatter never quite lost his confident step. He knew that there was little chance of him losing the election. What surprised the parvenus to the FIFA scene was the margin of Blatter's victory. There were 197 national associations present in the hall and entitled to vote, and 195 valid votes cast. A two-thirds majority (130) was needed for an outright first-round victory: Blatter got 139 of them, Hayatou a mere 56. The Cameroonian's supporters estimated that only 19 votes had come from the membership of his African confederation. Blatter more than doubled his 1998 winning margin, despite the charges of corruption and the extraordinary spectacle of the FIFA family feuds in headlines across the world.

Media people in the hall gasped in shock when the results were announced. Of course for most of the vote-holders the election had little or nothing to do with principles of integrity. Top UEFA people recognised that 'we fought a fucking hard campaign to expose Blatter, but too many countries were worried about what would come out if Blatter came down. So many have profited and done well out of Blatter'. UEFA knew that for the moment, the game was up.

Many of the new FIFA watchers seemed bemused, but the result was highly predictable for anyone familiar with the FIFA story and the manner in which the organisation has worked for well over a quarter of a century; the FIFA delegates in the congress hall were less surprised at the outcome than were the gullible media outsiders. They represented football's worldwide family, the more than 200 national football associations from FIFA's six confederations. In the year leading up to the election, Asia had 45 member associations, Africa 52, South America 10, and the Central and North American and Caribbean confederation 35. Oceania (Australia, New Zealand and the South Pacific islands) had 11 full members; and the powerful European body, UEFA, 51. The bosses of the confederations were the powerbrokers of the FIFA family, seeking to mobilise bloc votes of their member associations. The presidents and their general secretaries, and the men from the national associations themselves, knew that Blatter was the master manipulator of FIFA's pseudo-democratic structure. In the FIFA congress, the delegate from the Cook Islands (population 17,000) has as much power and influence as the delegate from Germany, Brazil or the USA. Blatter had worked this system for over twenty years, first as general secretary, then for four years as president. He would know how to splinter the African vote, just as he'd done four years earlier, following the example of his old mentor, Dr João Havelange, when he gained power in 1974 and held on to the throne until his retirement in 1998.

Havelange – the fittest 85-year-old you might ever encounter – was there in Seoul, observing the legacy of his presidency. The Big Man of the FIFA family, Havelange reminded his flock that the presidency demanded strong qualities. Hedging his bets, he didn't give Blatter his total blessing as, rather than taking the stage, he gave his still-presidential nod. His former protégé had made a mess of too many aspects of the family business, and was certainly incurring Havelange's wrath. But Blatter's former mentor was still confident that the smooth Swiss charmer had done the business on the campaign trail.

Chuck Blazer, general secretary of the Central and North American and Caribbean confederation (CONCACAF), was also certain that Blatter would glide to a second term. The weekend before the congress, we had asked him whether his confederation could continue to deliver a bloc vote of its members on any issue, especially the presidential election. He confirmed the delivery of 35 votes for Blatter: 'It can continue to deliver bloc votes where a common interest is concerned. This is certainly the case in the Presidency and there are other issues as well, but this is one of the few which is voted on by the membership in full'.

Blazer's boss, confederation president Jack Warner, from Trinidad and Tobago, was looking as confident as ever, despite press revelations of his dubious business privileges in FIFA deals in the region. Suave Peter Velappan was also present. Velappan was one of the men who'd turned against Sir Stanley Rous back in '74, casting his Malaysian vote in favour of Havelange. Velappan was now general secretary of the Asian confederation, 45 votes less easy to manipulate as a bloc. The FIFA executive committee member Dr Mong Joon Chung, from Korea, was one of the outspoken critics of Blatter's style and practices. But the man from the Gulf, Mohamed Bin Hammam Al Abdulla of Qatar, was a key Blatter supporter. Bin Hammam has been accused by Somalian Farah Addo of offering bribes for votes back in Paris in 1998. Addo claimed, in a story broken by the *Daily Mail's* investigative reporter Andrew Jennings, that 18 of Blatter's votes came from African delegates persuaded to break ranks, helped along by bundles of cash dispensed in Paris's Le Meridien hotel on the eve of the election. If those votes had gone to Johansson, he'd have been ahead of Blatter by five votes in that first poll. Bin Hammam also facilitated Blatter on the campaign trail, with the provision of private jets to help him in his busy schedule.

European associations were split down the middle. Some big football powers, including England, supported Hayatou, but many – such as France, Germany, Spain – were still hand-in-hand with Blatter. It was recognised (though only whispered) in European football's corridors of power that Hayatou was never in the running. Numerous football associations were for Blatter, and not just because of past favours and the spiders' webs of patronage and dependency. They were also adamant that no African (for that, read black man, and the myriad of alternatives to that term that floated in some nations of Europe, particularly the newer nations in the east of the continent) could be contemplated as FIFA president. And it wasn't just at the heart of Europe that such prejudice was simmering. Delegates from South America, Asia, Arab Africa and the Gulf would not want a black African at the head of the FIFA family.

South America, Brazilian Havelange's original power base, was behind Blatter all the way. Julio Grondona from Argentina, chair of FIFA's finance committee (which was fast beginning to look comic), was a long-term survivor of FIFA politics. Johansson had found South America a fruitless campaign trail in 1998. It was to be no different for Issa Hayatou this time round.

Little Oceania was now well-represented in the hall, a dozen member associations in a confederation only granted full status in 1996. Glasgow-born New Zealander Charles Dempsey, the only man ever to resign from the FIFA executive committee, had slugged it out with the toughest Fifacrats for over thirty years. He'd attended every FIFA congress and extraordinary congress from 1968 to 1999, and been Oceania's representative in consultations with FIFA throughout that time. Charlie recalls talking to Englishman Sir Stanley Rous when Havelange took the throne at the Frankfurt congress, and describes Sir Stanley's sense of despair in defeat. He was fond of Sir Stanley, who'd been a great supporter of Oceania's ambitions and aspirations, and had given Charlie a bit of advice that he'd stuck by in his 10 years as general secretary and 18 years as president of the confederation: 'Never give up a confederation once you've got it'. Charlie acted on this advice through thick and thin, until his resignation in 2000 following a blaze of controversy six months earlier concerning his vote, and the outcome of the bids to get the 2006 World Cup finals. Charlie knew the way things were beginning to work; he knew what was driving the new forces in FIFA. He knew how Rous had lost, and that Havelange had paid the fares of delegates from Fiji and Papua New Guinea.

Charlie was out of the front line now. But Oceania unanimously elected him as honorary president in December 2000, at its Vanuatu congress. Charlie knew that most of his old confederation's delegates would back the incumbent president, for Blatter was delivering on enough promises. Adrian Wickham from the Solomon Islands, for instance, wouldn't waste much time listening to Issa Hayatou's case. He'd recently got onto the FIFA executive committee, and a nice lump of cash from FIFA – US$668,000 – had just renovated and upgraded the Solomon's national stadium in Honiara. He liked Blatter's '*Goal*' initiative to help small footballing nations like his own. He wasn't about to waste all that good work by backing calls for reform and accountability and the like.

Charlie had attended the Champions' League final back in his boyhood home of Glasgow a couple of weeks before the Seoul congress. He'd been in good form, a sprightly 81-year-old still living his football and golfing passions to the full, talking at his old school; the local lad made good in the New World, the Man from FIFA. Now he was back in the fold and looking forward to the Seoul trip, where he was to be acclaimed by congress as an honorary member of FIFA. He could withdraw from his role on the disciplinary committee, which hadn't called upon him anyway, and pick and choose the perks of the FIFA Club, spending more time at his beloved golf clubs in Auckland with his still-vivacious octogenarian wife Annie.

The day before the congress, Blatter had looked vulnerable at an extraordinary congress where he'd planned to answer his critics. English Football Association chief executive Adam Crozier called Blatter's performance an 'absolute disgrace from start to finish. There was no attempt at transparency in two hours of manipulation'. No opponents of Blatter were allowed to address the congress. Among the observers at this extraordinary staged event was the *Daily Mail*'s Andrew Jennings. Delegates from Blatter's client countries, such as Iran, Libya and Jamaica spoke fulsomely of the president's leadership, insulted UEFA president Johansson, bad-mouthed Scot David Will (FIFA vice-president and chair of an internal audit committee set up to probe FIFA finances), and praised Blatter's financial acumen. The Libyan delegate, Muammer Al-Gadaffi Assadi, son of the dictator, was jeered as he tried to discredit African-based critics of Blatter. David Will was prevented from speaking, and confirmed that 'only one side of the financial information was given. Blatter just refused to let me speak and I'm very angry.' Korean Dr Chung was permitted to speak only in the form of a welcoming address on behalf of his home country, a World Cup 2002 co-host, but did say that 'only one person is responsible for the division of FIFA'.

Blatter was unapologetic, but defensive: 'I am not ashamed of what I have done. I don't always act according to procedures that are normally accepted, but I have done nothing against the Statutes of FIFA.'

'No peace in our time here,' muttered one seasoned international journalist as the votes were cast.

The FIFA family wars had been intensifying over the previous eighteen months, since the collapse of long-term marketing partner International Sports and Leisure (ISL). Veterans of FIFA's executive committee agreed that Blatter wasn't cutting the mustard as president. He had fall-outs with the Asian confederation and lacked Havelange's style, presence, gravitas and charisma. Things came to a head earlier in 2001 when the marketing company ISL, FIFA's long-term partner, went bust. We talked to numerous ISL people in Lausanne as news of this was breaking, but all denied responsibility, shuffling away from the discussion and pointing towards the culpability of the long-term bosses.

Dick Pound, marketing maestro at the International Olympic Committee over the years, and about to unsuccessfully contest the IOC presidency, said that FIFA lacked business credibility. The IOC had already ditched ISL: 'We got out of our ISL relationship [a few years ago] ... they were way offside the core business.' FIFA could hardly do this whether it wanted to or not. ISL had been long known as the black-box bolstering FIFA finances. Blatter himself was of the same generation as ISL top bosses, all inspired by the vision and style of the late Horst Dassler of Adidas, whose brainchild ISL was. Some had left to form their own outfits. Jürgen Lenz headed up TEAM, the company behind the Champions League. At the time of the ISL collapse, the normally loquacious Lenz couldn't 'talk to you in good conscience', choosing 'to abstain from comment'.

ISL's parent company ISMM had been ordered to start bankruptcy proceedings by a Swiss court in April 2001. Vivendi-Universal, a Paris-based media group, had turned down an invitation to rescue the company by making a takeover bid. ISMM collapsed the following month, and arguments raged within FIFA concerning the financial implications of the collapse. ISL losses were put by the Swiss courts at a monumental $US1.25 billion. Monies went astray. Revenues due from broadcasters in Brazil were diverted to a secret bank account. Sponsorsip revenues of up to US$200 million were reported to have gone missing. A hundred million US dollars of television money owed to FIFA were said to be hidden away in a bank account in Lichtenstein. Blatter was claiming that the ISL collapse had cost FIFA a 'mere' US$30–32 million, but as Agence-France Presse reported at the beginning of 2002, 'independent marketing experts suggested an extra zero could be added to that figure'. FIFA general secretary Michel Zen-Ruffinen's estimate was US$116 million.

The scale of the ISL-based losses was at the heart of the debates within the FIFA committees and factions. Whatever the precise figure, FIFA needed to take out a $US420 million 'resecuritization' bond from Crédit Suisse First Boston to get its finances back on track. FIFA's business credibility looked to be at an all-time low when ISL's 'partner' KirchMedia itself went bankrupt in April 2002, though its creditors and FIFA agreed a deal to transfer the World Cup TV rights into a separate company, KirchSport.

Blatter's 'Venetian night of love', as he himself characterized his 'sweetheart deal' with Dassler's baby ISL over the years, had plunged FIFA into its most serious financial crisis ever – a crisis which had certainly been avoidable. Even FIFA's prodigal son, Guido Tognoni, recognised this: 'FIFA made with ISL a three-term commitment. Nobody was really challenging ISL in those days. Everybody knew that the links between ISL and FIFA are so strong that there was no chance and the links brought their status strong and there was no chance for another one, so you can make your own thoughts on that. ISL was the leading company in the world. They did a good job … What I put the question mark on is the procedure. I think that everybody should have the same chance to bid for rights, and it is questionable that this is the case.'

But Blatter hadn't got where he was without loyal deals. He had always been close to his old mentor, Horst Dassler. Tognoni reminds us that: 'Blatter was partly paid by Adidas in the early days because FIFA did not have money. Blatter says that he only had his office in the Adidas office, this was while FIFA was building a new one. Now it was doubtful, strange, why should the general secretary of FIFA live in an Adidas building for a certain time? You can also hire your own office.'

ISL had been Dassler's baby, and the long-established conduit for the less accountable FIFA-related monies. Blatter's loyalty was misplaced in the case of the over-stretched ISL, his faith in his family not paying off this time round.

On the initial collapse of ISL, European football powers were incensed. After the Champions League final in Milan, UEFA top brass announced that Blatter must explain; if he couldn't 'provide an explanation … he'd have to step down'. UEFA was in its long game. It wanted a special meeting with FIFA to explain the financial mess, and had a list of 25 questions to put to Blatter, on financial, management and related matters. The forthcoming FIFA congress in Buenos Aires would be critical. A vote of confidence was called for.

Blatter knew that this was a critical moment, vital for his survival if not credibility. The big European powers of UEFA had people in the wings, ready to challenge the shaky-looking Blatter in a presidential election in Seoul in 2002. Dr Chung, of Korea and Hyundai, was one of these. His countryman 'Mickey' Kim had failed to win the IOC presidency, and this cleared the way for Chung to put himself forward, if called, for the top job in football. If not Chung there was the charismatic Cameroonian, Issa Hayatou, recently handed an IOC membership.

In Buenos Aires Blatter faced a vote of (no) confidence. He stage-managed an astonishing escape-act, getting delegates from Jamaica and other small countries to speak out and remind the big Europowers (England, France, Germany) of FIFA's crucial constitutional fact – one vote, one country. The big powers might win the football and be first-world leading nations, but they had no more power in FIFA than the tiniest member. Blatter moved quickly to call a vote of confidence. FIFA's general secretary Michel Zen-Ruffinen flapped, reminding him that there'd been no roll-call, no proper procedure. Brushing aside his top administrator, Blatter won his vote of confidence on a show of hands that made militant trade unionism voting tactics look like pure democracy. The Europeans were outmanoeuvred in classic FIFA fashion, a turning point for Blatter in his fight for survival. 'Pure Blatter, brilliant', conceded Franz 'Kaiser' Beckenbauer. He might have lacked the presidential gravitas of Havelange, but Blatter was crafty. Chuck Blazer has said that 'his predecessor was a better politician', but the streetfighting skills of a lifetime in the business saw him through.

In October 2001, UEFA suddenly announced that it would not oppose Blatter standing for a second spell as president. Without European support, no African or Asian candidate would stand a chance. Chung, in Paris, told a close FIFA watcher that he'd no inkling of the UEFA deal. During the summer, a European executive committee member had hinted that peace was breaking out between UEFA and FIFA. One legal expert had advised executive committee members that should FIFA go terminally bust, they would be personally liable.

UEFA may have been backing Blatter to get his help in preventing French football icon Michel Platini from bidding to succeed the cancer-hit Johansson as UEFA president. But as the scale of the financial crisis at FIFA escalated, and Blatter's leadership style became increasingly despotic, the Europeans revised their position, and a challenge to Blatter's presidency was planned.

Blatter's salary had been a recurrent issue. One insider claimed that he was on a 6-year deal worth US$24 million, a deal projected beyond the period of his 4-year presidency. The head of the finance committee, Argentinean Grondona, must have drawn up the contract but the executive committee was never consulted on the deal. Chung took this up with Jack Warner, deputy chairman of the finance committee, in January 2002. A man who is born and bred to rule, scion of the Hyundai *chaebol*, he didn't mince his words: 'During the private dinner we had before the Buenos Aires Extraordinary Congress last year, I asked you how long it will take to restore the honour and dignity of FIFA ... your answer was "Never".' He continued:

> As you know well, in the face of its own scandal, the IOC set up an investigation committee, which actually pales in its extent compared with FIFA's own scandal. I feel that FIFA can follow the IOC example. Without such a legitimate probe, no one both on the inside and the outside of an organization would find it easy to believe the simple explanations from the top. I am convinced that your 'never' will change to 'soon' when we adopt the same open approach like IOC.
>
> I would like to emphasize that the management of FIFA's finance is flawed and the lack of transparency is at the root of current speculations. It is of critical importance that we provide a clear and transparent investigation of

FIFA's financial situation so that we can restore FIFA's honour and image in the world.

Strong stuff indeed, from a heavyweight global businessman. Chung focused on three points in particular: the inadequacy of audit company KPMG's review report on finances after the ISL collapse; the financial strategy, termed a 'securitization scheme', a 'sort of loan arranged against the collateral of future revenues'; and 'the story I heard about the president's salary … that it is more than 20 million dollars over 6 years, instead of 4 years.'

Chung's letter was one of numerous communications flying to and fro across FIFA's corridors of power between November 2001 and March 2002. Blatter wrote in early November to national associations, confederations and the executive committee, assuring them that the ISL losses would not exceed 51 million Swiss francs, and attaching a review report by the auditors, KPMG. KPMG's report, on an interim balance sheet, was at pains to point out that a review is not an audit. It is hardly reassuring. Though it stated that 'nothing has come to our attention that causes us to believe that the accompanying interim balance sheet does not comply with Swiss law and FIFA's articles of incorporation', the ISL question was not settled: 'The overall implications of ISL's bankruptcy for FIFA may only be assessed once bankruptcy proceedings are completed.' The auditors also drew attention to FIFA's recognition of revenue and expenses 'on a cash basis', including 299 million Swiss francs of 'future income recorded in 2000 from existing marketing contracts (excluding TV-Rights) for the 2002 and 2006 World Cups.' The balance sheet was well-balanced indeed – 465,157,894 Swiss francs of assets; and exactly the same figure for the equity and liabilities. However, it only balanced with the help of the monies clawed back from what was not yet earned. In December, 13 (all the European, all the African, and Korean Chung) members of the executive wrote to express their overall dissatisfaction at the review report, and posed questions on the ISL losses, lost income from cancelled events, FIFA's relationship with Brazilian broker Traffic (partly owned by Havelange and his son-in-law Ricardo Texeira), commercial contracts held by members of the executive committee, and the increasing profile of unaccountable presidential advisers.

'I am determined to continue to lead FIFA with policies of utmost transparency and open communication,' countered Blatter within days. Lennart Johansson responded immediately on the financial question, the inner administration and conflicts of interest of committee members: 'Why do you oppose the setting up of an internal investigation group? What are you afraid of? We will come back.'

On Christmas Eve, Jack Warner from Trinidad and Tobago wrote to Blatter to condemn the 'posturing and histrionics of some members', and their threat to Blatter's principles of 'solidarity and fraternity'. Warner looked back and forward: '… brokering and confederational politics take precedence over genuine discussion and debate and ... the elections of '98 have never been over and are being fought in the FIFA Executive Committee. It will never be won at the level of the Congress.' Warner was reassuring Blatter that in any vote among the full FIFA membership, his loyalty base was intact.

Argentinean Julio Gondona, chair of the finance committee, joined the fray in January to apologize for the late circulation of key papers, and to spout some FIFA rhetoric on restoring 'a sense of security to the entire FIFA family'. David Will responded scathingly to the two-page auditor's review – he'd anticipated a 200–300 page document – and remained focused on the key issue of the riskiness of drawing upon future anticipated income 'to cover current costs without the direct permission of the Congress'.

At the end of January the 13 members reasserted their demands for the setting up of an investigation committee. Blatter conceded, following Will, proposing 'an ad hoc internal audit committee' and an extraordinary meeting of the executive committee in March, dedicated to financial matters. There was a bit of work to do in between times, as Blatter reminded his colleagues: 'The plethora of commitments over the next few weeks ... the African Cup of Nations, the Muslim Aid Festival, the pilgrimage to Mecca, the finalist team's workshop in Tokyo, the Winter Olympic Games in Salt Lake City.' Blatter would be on the road, consolidating his hold on FIFA's worldwide base, reaching deep into unprincipled alliances the executive committee could hardly hope to penetrate.

The national associations heard from Blatter at the end of January, and were interested to learn that after the ISL collapse he 'personally took charge of FIFA's financial situation ... and FIFA is in a position to keep up the benefits due to the national associations, competition organisers and commercial partners without any reductions whatsoever'. He also told them that the recalcitrant 13 were acting out of line with FIFA Statutes. This was too much for Chung, Johansson and Hayatou, who felt the need to also write to all the national associations, explaining their dissatisfaction with the 'drip by drip confirmation in writing of what we suspected already last year in June', that the ISL fall-out may have been 500 million Swiss francs, ten times the amount claimed by Blatter. The three vice-presidents also wanted to know why ISL's bankruptcy administrator was not being pursued with reasonable claims, and why Blatter had not even referred to ongoing negotiations. In early February Blatter wrote to the executive committee, calling the reproaches in the letter 'erroneous, some of the accusations caluminous ... I can accept none of this.'

The Qatari Mohamed Bin Hammam, 'to defuse the volatile situation', asked Blatter, in February, to convene the extraordinary meeting, and to make known his salary and all financial benefits received by the other 23 members of the executive. This would of course deflect attention away from the revelations concerning his vote-fixing in 1998, and he mentioned in his letter to Blatter his concern about 'the damages caused to FIFA's dignity by irresponsible rumours distributed worldwide regarding Executive Committee members' financial situation'. At the beginning of March Bin Hammam wrote to CAF president Issa Hayatou and lifted the FIFA family wars onto a new global scale. A reproduction of this diatribe repays citation in full:

> It is with great sadness and shock that I am writing to you. It is regrettable to see what we believed to be a fair contest and duel between knights has now changed to a dirty war where all possible tactics including hitting under the belt, character assassination, smirching the reputation of people and throwing accusations and allegations left and right have become the order of the day.
>
> I will say a war started by an illiterate person who does not realize that he will suffer from the consequences sooner or later. At this juncture I would like to say that Mr Addo is not the only one who can fabricate news and throw accusations.
>
> Mr. President, what Mr. Farah Addo, CAF Vice President has claimed is painful, disturbing and full of venom and hate not only for me and those Arab names who have been quoted in his claims but even for Africa and its free men who don't deserve to be stabbed in the dignity and accusing them with bribery claims.
>
> Let me make a confession if we are going to start hitting under the belt, Mr. Addo has personally come to me in Zurich and claimed that you are in his pocket and you will do whatever he wants. He told me that he wants me to run for AFC Presidency and he wants me to support you to become FIFA President while he would take over CAF Presidency. He went on to say that imagine with three Muslims leading the global football confederation (FIFA) and two largest confederations (CAF & AFC) what power we will have in hand. This shows you what kind of sick illusion and racism is in the head of this man. President, I told him 'Islam has got nothing to do with this and for me as far as Blatter is a candidate I will always be with him, only if he steps down I can think of an alternative and Issa is my favourite.'
>
> Mr. President, as far as Mr Hassan Ali is concerned let me tell you the following. I know Mr. Hassan Ali as a very decent and religious man. God alone knows what kind of pressures he has faced to say what he said and write what he wrote (if he did say and write).
>
> Mr Hassan Ali had left Somalia under a strict and stern order from his political leaders to vote for Mr. Blatter. Besides Mr. Hassan Ali had not gained voting rights, so why should I even think of bribing him to vote for Mr. Blatter. I did not pay Mr. Hassan Ali any money, I did not pay his travelling ticket and I did not pay his hotel accommodation in Paris. However, upon his request I paid his room extras bill – French Franc 900!!
>
> Mr. President, I have helped Mr. Blatter immensely in his campaign in the 1998 election and some even claimed that I was the major reason for his victory not because I bribed people but because we planned the battle. We were right in the field while the others sitting behind their desk. Here I would like to tell you something you may never have heard about. We were in Paris and we were planning a trip to South Africa in a commercial flight, not belong or financed H.H. the Emir of Qatar. When the night before the travel I received a

frantic call from my wife with the shocking sad news that my son aged 22 years had met with a very serious accident and was fighting for his life and his condition was more towards death and was lying in the Intensive Care Unit in a Coma. I should immediately return to Doha. I regretted and apologized to my wife and told her that my son doesn't need me but needs the blessings of God and help of doctors while it is Mr. Blatter who is in need of my help now. So I sacrificed seeing my son maybe for last time. I did not leave the campaign of Mr. Blatter so as not to let him feel alone. This kind of help which never can be evaluated in any monetary terms I have extended to Mr. Blatter. I was working with the heart and with morality and ethics because the man who was against Mr. Blatter in the election was also a decent and respectable person. I was sorry that I didn't know Mr. Johansson the way I should have before the election when may be I could have taken a neutral stand.

Dear President, I know you from close, intimately and am well aware of your nature and the type of person you are and I know for a fact that you will never accept anything wrong from any party even if he is a close assistant to you in CAF. For that reason I beg you and your colleagues in CAF Exco to give instruction to establish an Investigation Committee to assess the various allegations Mr. Addo has made. Further, I put myself under your disposal and at this Committee's order. If you ask me why CAF should conduct this investigation, I will say because Addo's allegations are directed against African National Associations and African personalities. This what I request you to do personally because as far as allegations against His Highness, the Emir of Qatar and the late Prince Faisal which Mr. Addo would like to deny what he has received from him in terms of cash or kind, I believe the respective governments of their countries are in a much better position than anybody and are capable along with the Somali government to take care of.

Mr. President, we are men of integrity and let us deal with the subject in a sincere and honest manner not to spoil the reputation of each other.

Best regards,
Mohamed Bin Hammam Al Abdulla

It's all in this letter: threats of revenge, conspiracy theory, dictatorial government, human interest story, personal sacrifice, denial of corruption. By now the FIFA family was looking like a worn-out warring shambles of cabbals and feuding factions. Hammam also wrote on the same day to Blatter, asking for the executive committee to establish an independent committee 'to find out the truth' on the subject of *Daily Mail* investigative reporter Andrew Jennings's allegations of bribery and lying.

Hammam did not deny that in Blatter's 1998 campaign they'd been jetting off to South Africa, accompanied by 'Mr. Emanual (sic) Marada (sic) and Mr. Flavio and travelled by a commercial charter flight'. Not the Emir's plane, Hammam insisted, and not on the Emirate's expense account.

His companion on the flight was 'London-based journalist Emmanuel Maradas', organiser of the 'Blatter camp in Africa', as Mark Gleeson has put in *World Soccer*.

Of course such an independent journalist wouldn't be on a private charter either. By now, however much corresponding he was doing, the Qatari was big news, but beginning to be old news. A few weeks later FIFA's general secretary was ready to talk in detail about the extent of the endemic corruption in FIFA practices and procedures.

Michel Zen-Ruffinen had been groomed by Blatter as his successor as general secretary. He had arrived in FIFA House, keen and ambitious, from a background in law and international-standard football refereeing. He came from Blatter's own neck of the Swiss woods, the Vallée. Guido Tognoni, now back in the FIFA fold as 'special advisor to the president', talked in Zurich after he'd been sacked in New Year 1995 as FIFA's media and marketing guru. He spoke of Zen-Ruffinen with bitter resentment: 'He came to FIFA and after three days he says that he wants to become general secretary, that is his aim. He is crazy. We were a bunch of people who were working together, we thought he is kinky.'

Kinky or not, Zen-Ruffinen's rise was close to meteoric. Blatter had told Tognoni before the new deputy general secretary was appointed '… "We need better organisation in FIFA House. FIFA House has also to work when I am not in". I said, "Well, what happened during the last ten years, you were frequently away and the house didn't crash down, it worked fine."' Then something 'very strange' happened. In classic coup style, without having consulted anybody, Blatter announced that FIFA had a new 'organisational chart' that brought Michel Zen-Ruffinen in as deputy general secretary.

Tognoni didn't mince words: 'I was shocked, everybody was shocked in the management, everybody was shocked that Blatter took such a measure, taking the youngest one, the least experienced one and a lightweight, promoting him to deputy general secretary. I said to Blatter, "Can he give me orders?" and he said, "Yes." Then I said, "This I have problems to accept because he is not competent enough to give me orders, he has not the experience …" I said, "This creates a problem for me if this young chap has the competence to give me advice."'

It was a problem that Tognoni never managed to deal with, and when he was shown the door from what he saw as the best job of its kind in the world he had ample time to reflect on his relations with Blatter, his boss again now that he'd rejoined the bad guys. Blatter had canvassed for support, approached UEFA when he considered mounting a challenge to Havelange's presidency at the 1994 USA congress. Little support was forthcoming, but after Blatter's botched coup, Tognoni recounts 'nobody knows' who or why anyone 'was on the death list of the president … Blatter was supposed to be kicked out and then the people surrounding the president were thinking, "Well somebody has to do the job of general secretary, and I was seen as one of the Blatter fan club, one of the allies.' Blatter was kept in place, Tognoni booted out. Zen-Ruffinen, the golden boy and potential Blatter successor, was kept in and rewarded for helping Blatter survive. When Blatter became FIFA president in 1998, it seemed only natural that Zen-Ruffinen should succeed him as general secretary.

However, now things had turned sour. In the four years of Blatter's presidency, Zen-Ruffinen had been cut out of the loop of power, and could no longer stay silent on the manner in which Blatter was running FIFA. Blatter supporter Chuck Blazer claims that 'Blatter's administration is much more transparent' than that of his predecessor: 'More meetings, more information, distribution of committee chairmanships and positions, including his opponents. Financial information is much more ample and available.' Zen-Ruffinen's view from the heart of the FIFA administration was a million miles away from Blazer's glowing testimonial.

At the FIFA executive committee of 3 May 2002, just weeks before the upcoming presidential election, Zen-Ruffinen broke his silence on what he called 'various turbulences'. Here is part of the statement of the former referee turned whistleblower:

> FIFA is flawed by general mismanagement, disfunctions in the structures and financial irregularities. I therefore decided to stand up for the good of the game; it has been too long, that I was loyal to the president.
>
> Many FIFA representatives from places all over the world encouraged me with their full support to clarify matters in regard of the various harmful occurrences taking place in and outside of the headquarters of FIFA. They felt embarrassed to be seen as 'FIFA family members' after all the recent news which damaged the image of our organisation.

In his explosive document, Zen-Ruffinen asserted that Blatter took over both the administration and management of FIFA, against the statutes, working with a few select people in his inner group, the F-Crew (the *Führensgruppe*, the leadership group), and

> manipulating the whole network through the material and administrative power he gained to the benefit of third persons and his personal interests. FIFA today is run like a dictatorship. FIFA is not a decent and structured organisation anymore. It has been reduced to the Blatter Organisation.

Zen-Ruffinen describes a bloated family at FIFA House, with 150 staff now rather than 50, plus 80 refugees from the ISL debacle, located in FIFA Marketing AG:

> FIFA is in a bad shape today. FIFA is disorganised, staff is dissatisfied, frustrated and the FIFA administration is governed by the President and a handful of people of his choice. The finances only seem to be in order. In fact, FIFA today lives from income of the future.

Blatter's seven personal advisers are listed:

> Guido Tognoni, in charge of marketing matters/relations (FIFA Marketing AG) including broadcasting relations; coordination of legal affairs. Jérôme Champagne, dealing with the elections and campaigning for the President by networking with the national associations, blatantly interfering in their affairs.

Markus Siegler, in charge of corporate communications. Urs Linsi, CFO; Deputy GS not actually acting as such. Michael Schallhart, HR, appointed Director by the President. Two personal secretaries (Ms P – with Director title – and Ms S.)

All of those persons did and do directly report to the President and avoid the GS (general secretary).

The style of working of the F-Crew – the inner-circle of four of Blatter's 'closest collaborators', Champagne, Linsi, Siegler and Schallhart – is outlined. Described to Johansson in Buenos Aires in June 2001 as 'merely an internal consultation body', the F-Crew really went way beyond such an advisory role and began to deal with staff appointments, budget decisions and the like. The general secretary himself was nominally part of this grouping, but routinely found himself 'systematically circumvented'.

Zen-Ruffinen's document describes wide-ranging forms of maladministration, personal self-aggrandizement, conflicts of interest, financial irregularities and alleged cases of outright bribery and cronyism. The spiralling mess of the FIFA finances is plain to see. Zen-Ruffinen rubbishes the president's public claim that FIFA had the highest ratings for its procedures, from established financial bodies:

> For 1998 and earlier, the years for which the President was responsible as GS, no information is available anymore, even though documents must be stored for 10 years due to the law. Neither the former auditors of FIFA nor FIFA itself do have such information.

According to Zen-Ruffinen's summary of 1999, the first year for which he had responsibility as the new general secretary, the strategy of borrowing against future income – what Chung called 'rather like the situation of a patient who extends his life by emergency aid' – was already in place:

> At the end of 1999, the liabilities exceeded the assets of FIFA, i.e. FIFA was overindebted in the amount of CHF67.8 million. The situation could be improved since CHF144 million were accounted as income out of TV rights in the year 2000. However, what must be disclosed is that the balance sheet never appears to reflect a true and certain situation. Already in 1998 CHF65 million were booked as income into the year 1998 out of TV rights regarding the World Cup 2002 to be recognised as income only for the period 1999–2002. The auditors (KPMG) have clearly criticised the respective accounting policy.

This borrowing against future assets – 'securitization concept' – was used with increasing desperation by FIFA, especially after the 2001 collapse of ISL. Regardless of this, the disillusioned general secretary goes on to say, Blatter, acting alone, casually committed 250 million Swiss francs to the local organizing committee for the

2006 World Cup in Germany; committed 12 million Swiss francs to McKinsey & Company, and conducted numerous other dodgy financial deals with individuals and outside bodies, with little or no internal accountability back in the general secretary's office or to the executive committee.

Zen-Ruffinen's remarkable document raised the stakes in the FIFA in-fighting, and provided the basis for what was submitted to the Swiss prosecutor the following week.

It looked like this could be Blatter's toughest ride yet. The venom flying around the factions of the executive committee, and the stunning testimony of Zen-Ruffinen, culminated in the lodging of a criminal complaint by eleven members of the executive committee, on 10 May, just a couple of weeks before the Seoul Congress at which the presidential election would be contested. It was delivered by hand to the Public Prosecutor's Office in Zurich, filed on behalf of: Lennart Johansson, Stockholm; David Will, Brechin, Angus, Scotland; Antonio Mattarese, Rome; Issa Hayatou, Cairo; Mong Joon Chung, Seoul; Michael D'Hooghe, Bruges; Per Ravn Omdal, Eiksmarka, Norway; Amadou Diakité, Mali; Slim Aloulou, Tunisia; Ismael Bhanjee, Botswana; and Senes Erzik, Istanbul. The amassed forces of Africa and Europe were pushing the FIFA wars to unprecedented levels of intensity. The complaint concerned 'Suspicion of Breach of Trust' and 'Dishonest Management', as the charges are termed in the Swiss Criminal Code, which the complainants' attorney argued to be applicable as Blatter's activities were on behalf of FIFA, and the city of Zurich 'the centre of his professional activity as FIFA President'. The 'initial situation' of the complaint is expressed as follows:

> Since his election as FIFA President in 1998, there has been and has remained a latent suspicion that the Accused was practising favouritism with FIFA assets in order to build up an autocratic power base (which is contrary to the Statutes) and in order to secure his re-election on 29 May 2002. FIFA's financial situation has become opaque. Following the bankruptcy of the ISL/ISMM, Zug, Group in May 2001, and after the recent collapse of the Kirch Group, Munich, it became totally impenetrable. These two companies were mandated by the Executive Committee with the marketing of the TV marketing rights to the 2002 and 2006 WCs as a result of intensive efforts on behalf of the Accused. The FIFA Executive Committee's requests for information were either ignored, put off or fobbed off with global statements to the effect that the FIFA was in perfect financial health.

The Complaint document establishes that according to FIFA Statutes 'there is … no room for authoritarian, autocratic powers of leadership on the part of the FIFA President', and asserts that 'Mr Blatter's constant stalling and varnishing tactics could not but increase the mistrust of numerous member of the Executive Committee'. It details the way in which Blatter suspended FIFA's internal audit committee, so silencing potential witnesses (Zen-Ruffinen himself, and finance director Urs Linsi) when they were scheduled to give evidence to that committee, and refused to make files available for scrutiny. Batter was operating, the document claims, 'again with the aim of *keeping secret* the financial situation of FIFA and his own financial machinations'.

Blatter's 'persistent, systematic *secrecy* tactics', and his 'equally persistent *stalling tactics*' left the complainants with little option: 'Mr Blatter has forced the 11 Complainants to act ... there is a pressing suspicion that the Accused misused FIFA assets entrusted to his care for the benefit of third parties and thereby for his own benefit, in order to consolidate his personal position of power.'

Thirteen individual cases – 'individual putative offences' – are then catalogued:

- Payment of US$100,000 to former executive committee member Viacheslav Koloskov, president of the Russian football union, for no services rendered: 'The Accused sought to buy with FIFA money the vote of Mr Koloskov and the votes of further persons who are close to Mr Koloskov.'
- Payment of US$25,000, and promise of the same again, to Lucien Bouchardeau, a referee living in Nigeria, for information that could compromise or incriminate Farah Addo, who had confirmed that bribes were made to buy votes for Blatter in his 1998 presidential victory. Was this 'an incitement to false witness'?
- Payment to Cameroonian football hero Roger Milla, of 25,000 Swiss francs, 'to make his 50th birthday and the benefit game into a worldwide election campaign for the re-election of Sepp Blatter!'
- Bypassing FIFA's own travel organisation, and giving travel work for the Under-17 tournament to Jack Warner, accruing additional, unnecessary costs of US$32,135.
- Payment, in two tranches, of US$55,000 to Havelange, 'in order that he should provide the Accused with as many votes as possible from South America for his re-election in 2002'.
- Preferential treatment of ISL and/or Kirch, in their US$220 million bid for US TV broadcasting rights to the 2002 and 2006 World Championships, and simply ignoring a bid of US$100 million more from the firm AIM.
- Unjustified writing-off of a sum of US$9,474,000, owed to FIFA by the Central, North American and Caribbean confederation (CONCACAF) – 'patently obvious that a "friendly gesture" of that nature is apt to secure for the Accused numerous votes for his re-election'.
- Cash payment of 160,000 Swiss francs to the president of the football association of Liberia.
- Payment of US$1 million to CONCACAF, 'accounted for under the GOAL Project, although it was contrary to procedural rules for this project'.
- Payment, for at least a year, of monthly sums of US$5,000 to Rahif Alameh of Lebanon, as a 'personal adviser' to FIFA: 'However, Mr Alameh never did any work for FIFA. He was unlawfully favoured by the Accused with this sum.'
- Payment, 'without any justification', of US$80,000 to the Football Union of Russia, for each of the years 1999 to 2002.
- Mandating of special information technology project, to the firm SEMTOR, in which 'one of Jack Warner's sons occupies a leading position', at a cost of

US$1,950,000, when FIFA estimated a more realistic costing of around a third to half a million dollars.

- *'Personal emoluments of the FIFA President'*: Blatter stated on assuming the presidency that his salary was 1.4 million Swiss francs per year, but no corroboration was ever provided for this claim: 'There is a compelling suspicion that, with his secrecy tactics, Mr Blatter is seeking to cover up unlawful personal emoluments.'

This is an extraordinary list: vote-buying across the old Soviet satellites of Eastern Europe, all of the Americas and parts of Africa; nobbling witnesses; shredding evidence; favouring insider contractors; stage-managing activities for personal aggrandizement; ignoring the board (the executive committee).

As the family at war bared its feuds to the outside world, Blatter stuck to his guns. He knew where the grateful support would come from, and where the loyal votes lay. He had been planning for this for four years, and the key was his international schedule around the *Goal* development projects, a 'tailor-made aid programme', as Blatter himself put it: 'all about giving a chance: giving a chance to FIFA to channel the fruits of football's success back to the grass-roots of the game, and by giving those grass-roots a chance to taste some of that success'. It would not be a bad chance for Blatter, too, to remind the minnows of world football where their bread was buttered. They could certainly be relied upon to turn up at the Seoul Hilton and show their respects to the president.

The stage-management of Blatter's victory was accomplished with consummate skill. Appealing to FIFA's higher ideals, Blatter called up a procession of young schoolchildren, and hundreds of footballs. The footballs will go, he announced, to the most needy members of the FIFA family. And the neediest of the needy came in for special consideration. East Timor and Afghanistan, war-ravaged and stricken, would be the main recipients of this FIFA *largesse*. 'What could Issa Hayatou do to follow that?' asked Charlie Dempsey, waiting his turn for the president's call, and within minutes receiving an orator's acclaim from Blatter, and accepting his honorary membership to a standing ovation.

'Everybody's compromised,' Charlie observed to us a little after the event. You could tell that he knew what he was talking about. And it looked as if Dempsey was spot on as on the announcement of the result, Blatter urged the gathered assembly to get up off their seats and hold hands in an orchestrated standing ovation for the ecstatic victor, like nothing so much as a mediaeval monarch manipulating his court.

Blatter has claimed to BBC television's *Newsnight* that he is 'a footballer'. BBC man Peter Marshall had secured five minutes of Blatter's time, stretching it to twenty minutes and earning the wrath of Markus Siegler, Blatter's media minder – not too media-savvy in spluttering 'I am very pissed off.' In winning his second presidential election victory Blatter certainly displayed some impressive skills – a good body swerve, and tricky weaving on his feet. Certainly he needed some of these in his encounter with the *Newsnight* team. Issa Hayatou has a campaign slogan 'Vote for honest Issa', Blatter was reminded, and asked whether he could have a comparable one: 'I would say vote for honest Sep and vote for football ... I am a footballer, I'm a footballer ... I vote for football. I vote for the good of the game, and I always work, I'm honest in football.' Blatter wriggled his way out of the BBC challenge time and time again. Of Zen-Ruffinen, he protested that: 'Since two years ... he is collecting all documents which could be one day used against me. I told him at the very beginning, you are a man, I am a man, we should sit together and discuss the matter. This is also a part of his tactics to have everything somewhere written down, registered and this is not the right way to work together.'

No documents or records for Sepp's presidential style. Blatter also confirmed his 'personal' $25,000 gift to African referee Bouchardeau: 'This is my money ... of my own pocket. I felt sorry for him because he said he had to leave his country. I have paid more for other people, they are in need. I am a generous man, definitely I am ... much money I spent on humanitarian works, personally. I live alone, I am alone, I have no family, so therefore I give a lot of money to humanitarian community ... I have committed some errors. If you work a lot you commit some errors. But I am not in corruption and I am not what you say, mismanagement.'

Marshall summarised things for the uncomfortable interviewee: 'You admit you don't write things down always, you pay money out of your own account to people who come to FIFA. You don't always consult your committees when you should. Sloppy, isn't it?'

Blatter countered, 'No, it's not sloppy, because everybody inside FIFA and especially the general secretary, he knew everything, otherwise it would not be now known to the general public. And this is not sloppy, this is to have too much trust in the people you have educated, and then they have knife, and they come behind ...' Cloak and dagger stuff, up there on the hillside.

The FIFA motto, 'For the good of the game', is often parroted by the insiders in the FIFA elite, from their luxury rooms in the world's top hotels, or as they welcome you to the bunker-like FIFA House in Zurich's exclusive hilly suburb overlooking Lake Zurich, the Alpine summits across the water, and the self-satisfied gloss of the Banhofstrasse, with its top designer stores and morally dodgy banks. The FIFA elite is comfortable here. The wives of FIFA's top brass like the lobbies and the stores. The FIFA men like the loot and the secrecy. With honest, generous, lonesome Sepp always ready and willing with a smile and a chequebook, the Seoul victory securing his second term as president looked set to keep the FIFA family in the style to which it had become accustomed.

Given the number and scale of charges against Blatter, if he had been the CEO of a multinational company he would have lost his job and gone to jail. Instead he was re-elected with an increased majority. Blatter heaved a mighty sigh of relief as he led his FIFA family forward to its centenary celebrations in 2004, when the organisation would review its Statutes and no doubt tighten the grip that Havelange, Blatter and their autocratic ilk have taken on world football.

Havelange's achievement was to expand football across the globe by bringing the interests of world football and global sport closer than ever to business interests, fuelled by the ruthless ambitions of aspirant autocrats, international businessmen and politicians from newly independent emergent countries of the underdeveloped world, and then from the heartlands of the developed economies, the USA and Japan. Blatter has continued striking deals with such allies, particularly from small countries in Africa, Asia and the Pacific region. Everyone's had a bit more of the expanding action – in World Cup qualifiers, World Cup places, new tournaments for younger age-categories, the women's World Cup, the Olympics, the Club Championship. Under Blatter's presidency, FIFA has kept everyone happy with increased expense accounts for its inner circle, regular (unmonitored and unaccounted for) payouts of a million dollars to every one of its 204 or so member football federations, and reconciliation for troublesome members of the FIFA family.

We visited FIFA House back when Blatter was still general secretary. A cautious welcome was offered by him at the beginning of a guided tour by the director of communications, Keith Cooper. Media files, sponsor files, and a number of the most interesting documents were immediately branded as 'classified, confidential'. Cooper is no longer there; he is one of those purged by Blatter after Japan/Korea 2002 – and neither are the files. However, Blatter is consolidated in power by a group of henchmen and sycophants; the family values and the dynasty, for the moment, are intact. FIFA House is like a court of the *ancien-régime*. Running FIFA is a matter of mastering not the football rulebook, more Machiavelli's *The Prince*. Those fearing for the future of their beloved game have much to learn from the FIFA story, of which Blattergate and the FIFA president's Seoul triumph are just the latest episodes.

2

THE BLAZER-AND-SLACKS BRIGADE

FIFA's amateur roots

'Football's coming home' was the adopted anthem of the host fans at the 1996 European Nations Cup in England, the same mantra used by England's campaign team in their bid to host the 2006 World Cup Finals. Nice try, but world football came home to its organisational roots in 1998 when the French hosted the finals and took the trophy. And it came home to its romantic roots when Brazil took the World Cup for the fifth time in Tokyo four years later.

England claims to be the birthplace of football, but it was not one of the founder members of the world governing body, FIFA, when it was set up in 1904, nor did it make it to the first World Cup, in Uruguay in 1930.

The World Cup's creator was a Frenchman, Jules Rimet. From 1921 to 1954 he was president of FIFA. It was this self-made professional and religious do-gooder who dominated the growth of international football – not the English who, apart from for a few years in the early 1900s, stayed out of FIFA, refusing to have anything to do with a bunch of foreigners trying to mess with 'their' game.

Like so many senior sports administrators Rimet was trained in law. As an older man, the bearded, bowler-hatted and thoroughly bourgeois Rimet was an established figure among Parisian polite society. But he came from humble origins, born in 1873 into a modest family in rural France, and from an early age helped his father in the family grocer's shop.

From the age of 11 he was raised in Paris where his father had moved in search of work. He lived in the heart of the city, learning to survive and play football on the street. He was a conscientious and able schoolboy.

The young Rimet worked his way towards a full legal qualification, and was active in encouraging football among the poorer children of the city. He was a philanthropist who saw sport as a means of building good character. He was Christian and patriotic. His love of God and France came together in his passion for football. He believed in the universality of the church and saw in football the chance to create a world-wide 'football family' welded to Christian principles.

Like his countryman, Baron Pierre de Coubertin, the founder of the modern Olympics, Rimet believed that sport could be a force for national and international good. Sport and football could bring people and nations together in a healthy competitiveness, he thought. Sport could be a powerful means of both physical and moral progress, providing healthy pleasure and fun, and promoting friendship between races.

Rimet resisted the development of continental confederations and the empowerment of football confederations in Africa and in Asia. He argued that decentralisation would destroy FIFA, and that 'only direct membership will retain FIFA as one family'.

Heading FIFA during its expansive years after World War 1, Rimet gave FIFA a clear mission: to produce a global football family. But he found it difficult to overcome Europe's imperiousness. Europeans still looked down their noses at their poor South American relations, for example. At the first World Cup in Uruguay in 1930 only 4 of the 15 competing teams – France, Belgium, Yugoslavia and Romania – were from Europe.

Uruguay had shattered the world football establishment by winning the Olympic football championship in 1924 and 1928. These were the most dramatic achievements of the emerging football superpowers of South America. Football was also well established in Brazil and Argentina, where the game had been growing for getting on for half a century. It thrived initially in the ranks of nomadic British diplomats, planters and engineers who took balls and boots and The Football Association rule book wherever they went. The colonials' love of the game soon spread among the local, poorer classes.

The sport took hold most strongly around the River Plate and games between Argentina and Uruguay were played regularly from the turn of the century. The South American confederation, CONMEBOL, records its founding date as 1916, long before any other continental confederation. In its early days FIFA was so Eurocentric that no need was seen for any separate European organisation.

Uruguay's Olympic victories encouraged the country's diplomats to lobby for the first world football championships to be held. Rimet was flattered and excited at the prospect of spreading the FIFA gospel on the other side of the world.

Even in its inception the World Cup, for a chosen few, was one of world sport's greatest junkets. The Uruguayan authorities clinched the event by pledging to cover travel and hotel costs of all the competing teams. They also constructed the Centenario Stadium. The date chosen to launch the finals, July 1930, was a political decision rather than a sporting one: it was the centenary of the adoption of the Uruguayan constitution.

The hosts outplayed all rivals to add to their Olympic laurels. Argentina defeated a US team by six goals to one and, because the US included five Scots and an Englishman, the Argentineans claimed to have thrashed a side from football's birthplace. When 20,000 people huddled under newspaper loudspeakers in the middle of Buenos Aires to follow the match against the US, they were cheering more than just a football result. They were asserting their national identity against the Anglo-American oppressor. This was symbolic vengeance. Such dramatic victories fuelled the nationalist passions of supporters.

Argentineans herded onto the ferries across the River Plate, from Buenos Aires to Montevideo. They joined the crowds of Uruguayans flooding the main artery of the city, climbing through the city's central park to the massive and modernist Centenario Stadium. There were no sponsors' hospitality villages or armies of media and reporters to get in the way.

This first World Cup was a politically motivated statement by a national government. It was staged by a small country anxious to show its bigger neighbours how well it could perform on a global scale. There were national benefits in communication and transport. And in both staging and winning the event, Uruguay strutted the world stage as champions, world-beaters, modernisers. In Uruguay Rimet's FIFA laid the foundation for the next World Cups in Italy in 1934, and in his native France in 1938.

In between, in 1936, Hitler staged what became known as the Nazi Olympics in Berlin. He took his lead from Italy where Mussolini first mobilised sport in the service of fascist ideals. The fascists developed élite performers, exploiting big events for mass publicity. In Italy they did this with the World Cup and brought together private capital with public money to build new stadiums.

Mussolini's hard men adhered to the Italian principle and practice of *transformismo*, the use of bribery, coercion and threats as a way of combating opposition. As Italy bludgeoned its way to the 1934 World Cup title, ugly scenes in big games, weird refereeing decisions and fanatical crowd scenes showed that *transformismo* was rife on the field of play as well as in Italy's corridors of power.

Italy held on to its title in France in 1938. Only three non-European sides competed. Argentina, weakened by the loss of Italo/Argentineans to the big-spending Italian clubs and insulted at not being allowed to host the finals, decided to stay away. Uruguay also didn't turn up. Central and South America were scarcely represented.

With little serious opposition (the great 1930s Austrian side was crippled by Nazi Germany's annexation of six of its top players) the Italians won again, handsomely repaying their fascist leader and government for the resources poured into international sport.

The Second World War and its consequences changed the face of international football. Global communications improved dramatically, and the British were forced to realise that strong and vibrant cultures of the game existed beyond their island shores.

During both the First and the Second World Wars football had been a popular diversion for troops from many countries. British soldiers returned home with fresh memories of the skilful and enthusiastic way in which the peoples of the world played football. One such man returning from World War 1 was Stanley Rous, and in a career including physical education teaching, international football refereeing, football administration at The FA, and World War II charity work recognised by a knighthood, it was he who led the Home Associations back into FIFA in 1946. Rous's rationale was simple enough: 'If you can't beat 'em, join 'em and if you have to join 'em, you may as well lead 'em'. So it was that first in Arthur Drewry, a businessman from the eastern fishing town of Grimsby, and eventually through Rous himself, an Englishman stood at FIFA's helm during football's golden years. Drewry and Rous were FIFA presidents, like the four presidents before them, who took no salary for what was seen as a combination of voluntarism and vocation; this commitment to service in an essentially amateur mode to administer a relatively uncommercialised global game characterised FIFA's leadership until the last quarter of the twentieth century.

Stanley Rous, although not assuming the FIFA presidency until 1961, was an influential force in the game both before and after the Second World War, holding the post of secretary of The Football Association from 1934 to 1961. Rous took over at FIFA in his mid-sixties, the age at which most people retired, and he grasped this new challenge with typical energy and commitment.

Walter Winterbottom, the first man to be appointed as manager cum coach of the England team, said that 'in our own country he took us out of being an insular Association Football League and got us back into world football and this was tremendous'. Winterbottom also praised Rous's exceptional charm and diplomatic skills.

A son of the modest middle classes, Rous's father had planned for him to go to Emmanuel College, Cambridge, as Rous related in his memoirs. But, after service in Africa and Palestine during the First World War, he studied at St. Luke's College, Exeter, and then taught at Watford Grammar School. Rous was not born into the establishment but through football he became an establishment figure. For him, teaching and football were acts of public service. He played football at school, then in the Army during the Great War and at his training college after the war. Though he may have been good enough to play the game professionally, his commitment to amateur ideals denied him the chance to be paid for playing. Instead, Rous became a referee of international repute. This is where he made his first impact on world football. His rewriting of the rules of the game was immensely influential. In administration, he went on to modernise the English game, establishing a more efficient bureaucratic base, introducing teaching schemes for all levels of the game – coaching, playing, refereeing.

But this mission was about more than just football. Britain was in crisis after the Second World War, losing its Empire and looking for a role to play in the modern world. Educating football players as coaches and practitioners was one way of restoring British prominence.

The FA had left FIFA in 1928 and Rous believed that it was time for Britain to be reintegrated into the world football family. In a paper which he presented to The Football Association, first drafted in May 1943, he claimed that the activities of the FA's War Emergency Committee had boosted football's international profile by fostering relations with government departments and by establishing links with influential people through cooperation with the armed forces.

Recognising that Britain's formal political empire was about to shrink dramatically, he saw in football a chance to retain some influence over world culture. 'The unparalleled opportunity which the war years have given the Association of being of service to countries other than our own', pontificated Rous, 'has laid an excellent foundation for post-war international development.'

A self-styled moderniser, he remained trapped in an anachronistic set of values. 'We used to look upon it as a sport, as a recreation,' he once said in a BBC interview. 'We had little regard of points and league position and cup competitions. We used to play friendly matches, mostly. There was always such a sporting attitude and the winners always clapped the others off the field and so on.' Ruefully he added, 'That's all changed of course.'

From the old world of a parochial English middle-class, but negotiating the volatile world of post-colonialism, Rous 's life and philosophy were a bundle of contradictions. He could be both innovative and traditional, adventurous yet crabbily cautious, modern yet steeped in traditional values.

The late 1940s, 1950s and early 1960s were modern football's brightest years. In Britain, continental Europe and South America, stadiums bulged with massive and largely orderly crowds of fervent supporters making their weekly pilgrimages to cheer on local heroes. With high attendances and relatively modest salaries for players, domestic professional football was self-sustaining and provided a stable basis of the development of national representative sides.

On this foundation FIFA's World Cup flourished. During the decisive game of the 1950 World Cup finals in Brazil, the highest-ever crowd in the history of football (199,854) turned out to watch Uruguay beat the hosts 2-1 in the imposing Maracaná Stadium. Earlier in the tournament, England had been left in no doubt of the threat posed by foreign football when they were unceremoniously defeated by the USA, who won 1-0 (though not many people in the USA knew about the match or even cared). England then lost to Spain and went no further in the tournament.

That threat was driven home in 1953 when the majestic Hungarians, inspired by Puskas, beat England 6-3 at Wembley. It was England's first defeat at the national stadium and the already-dented façade of invincibility was shattered once and for all.

Hungary were unlucky 3-2 losers to West Germany in the 1954 finals in Switzerland. By the next World Cup in Sweden in 1958, the majesty of the Hungarians had been eclipsed by the rise of Brazil, and Puskas's mantle as the world's greatest player had been stolen by Pelé. Brazil won both that tournament and the 1962 World Cup in Chile, establishing themselves as the greatest team in the world.

In the early years of FIFA's World Cup there were few bidders for the job of hosting the event. Decisions regarding where the World Cups should be held were made in smoke-filled rooms by the FIFA president and a few cronies. Bidding later became more competitive, but was nothing like the frenzy of today. England based its successful 1966 bid entirely on existing facilities. FIFA president Sir Stanley Rous had been secretary to The Football Association when the decision was made, but was very close to the English president of FIFA, Arthur Drewry. At the 1960 FIFA Congress in Lisbon, England won a close vote over West Germany to host the 1966 finals.

When England won the trophy, the political symbolism of national sports victories was not lost on the prime minister, Harold Wilson, who made sure he was photographed with the victorious English players. And the idea that political gains could be had from hosting the finals was becoming stronger and more widespread.

Rous was concerned at the economic shenanigans and interpersonal pressures which surrounded the bids of Argentina and Mexico to host the 1970 finals. To curb this, he developed a planning cycle for the event. He called this 'the long look ahead', and designed it to give adequate notice to those committing themselves to such a major event. He wanted to give hosts the advantage of a 12-year lead-in, and at FIFA's 1963 Congress in Tokyo, a future list for post-England 1966 was confirmed: Mexico 1970; West Germany 1974; Argentina 1978; Spain 1982. Colombia got the same 12 years of notice, at the end of Rous's presidency, for the 1986 finals (they ended up having to pull out). Rous foresaw the co-hosting role, and proposed that FIFA's long-term plan should envisage zoning the finals, suggesting that the event could be split between three or four countries.

Television executives were wising up to the worldwide popularity of football and the World Cup. This worried Rous, for more pitches and stadiums would be needed. Press and TV facilities would be demanded and, in the age of expanding sport tourism, accommodation would be required and security expected. The emerging cultural and media industries were becoming more and more crucial to the event. This was not the comfortable colonial world of the baggy-panted international referee Rous, dispensing his schoolmasterly wisdom to the needy of the world. Sir Stanley was never comfortable with the intrusiveness of the broadcast media. It invaded the cosy spaces of his football bases in his London home down the road from The FA's Lancaster Gate headquarters, and in the sleepy villa in lush suburban Zurich.

Harry Cavan, senior vice-president of FIFA during Rous's reign, recalled that before Havelange arrived on the scene, Rous was 'probably the most travelled man in football in the world in those days. He had the right connections, he had the right influence and, above all, he had the ability and the skill to do the job. And of course he was clever. He was generally one or two moves ahead of most of the others.' But 'most of the others' were like-minded fellow Europeans. Rous was ill-equipped to deal with the charismatic Brazilian, João Havelange, and his ambitious and ruthless pursuit of the presidency in 1974.

When he stood for re-election as FIFA president, claiming that he wanted 'just a couple of years to push through some important schemes', Rous either had a confidence which was misplaced, or he had miscalculated the institutional politics of FIFA. Ten years on he put his defeat down to the limitless ambitions of his rival: 'I know what activity was being practised by my successor, the appeals that he'd made to countries.'

Rous's reflections are only half right. Yes, Havelange did run a ruthless and aggressive campaign which, as some believe, may have been seriously questionable. But it was the perception of football administrators in the Third World that Rous viewed them and their problems through Colonel Blimp's binoculars which did him most damage. In the years leading up to the 1974 election he had plenty of chances to challenge and change the perception of him as old-fashioned, imperious and even racist. That he chose not to, cost him his presidency.

3

GOODBYE COLONEL BLIMP

Shifting political landscapes

Sir Stanley Rous lived a stimulating but lonely life. For most of his career with the English FA and at the helm of FIFA his wife was an invalid, but he left her at home as he travelled the world spreading the gospel of the game. Work was Stanley's passion and football was his work.

Trying to piece together a picture of the Rous years at FIFA, we spoke to The FA librarian David Barber: 'Might the FA cellars or archives have any of Rous's FIFA papers?', we asked.

'Oh, no,' David said, 'we haven't room for that kind of thing. Anyway, Rose-Marie's got all Sir Stanley's papers.'

For most of his life after moving into the FIFA presidency, Rous's personal assistant and companion was Rose-Marie Breitenstein. In photographs taken of the globe-trotting FIFA president in the 1960s and 1970s, the slender and attractive Rose-Marie frequently appears by his side, his loyal and faithful right-hand woman.

We asked where in the world could we find Rose-Marie. 'You'll find her upstairs,' said the librarian. 'She's Graham Kelly's secretary.' We were hardly able to believe our luck. After a quick phone call, to the FA Secretary's office, Rose-Marie came to meet us in the library.

Now retired, she is the daughter of a Swiss businessman of Rous's acquaintance, an attractive woman who carries herself with finishing-school elegance. She speaks perfect English, but with the slightest Germanic inflection. Behind bright eyes, her memories of her days with Sir Stanley remain vivid. During regular visits to The FA, we sat enthralled as she gave us insider accounts of the career highs and lows of world football's first great moderniser.

Rose-Marie had dutifully filed away thousands of papers from Sir Stanley's FIFA years in the cellar of her London home. We told her what topics we were interested in and she would stuff the files into a shopping bag before bringing them down and leaving them with us next to the photocopier in the FA library.

Reading Sir Stanley's immaculate longhand annotations on drafts and original documents, we suspected he was becoming increasingly out of touch and out of place in a changing post-colonial world in which newly independent nations saw football as a means of gaining status and worldwide recognition. He could neither ignore nor control the political and commercial forces swirling around his beloved game.

Havelange planned his challenge to Rous on this basis. He plotted his campaign to seize FIFA's throne with military precision, planning to exploit the one-nation, one-vote system which FIFA employed for presidential elections. He could bank on the full backing of South America's ten members, including the big three of Brazil, Argentina and Uruguay. The emerging Central and North American and Caribbean block was dominated by Mexico, where Havelange had cultivated business and sporting links. He could expect considerable support from this quarter, but he would still need more votes if he were to overcome Rous and the Europeans.

The Brazilian worked out early that if he could win over FIFA's numerous marginal members, the world of football could be delivered into his hands. He saw that the support of the poor and developing football nations could be bought by the highest bidder. There would be promises to keep, but Havelange would worry about these once he became president.

He concentrated his campaigning on the African and Asian continents. He told them that it was time for a change, for a new and visionary leadership from beyond the privileged and haughty shores of the developed European world. It was time to break the stranglehold of the former colonial masters. He was helped by the resentment which was felt towards Rous, who was perceived as blimpish and out-of-touch in the far-flung corners of the FIFA empire.

Rous's plea that 'bloc' interests be avoided had little effect, and he soon encountered difficulties in monitoring the South Americans' activities and claims. In November 1969 his general secretary sent him, from Zurich to his London address, a full briefing letter for a forthcoming congress. This correspondence catalogued a long list of backstage manoeuvrings which were read as threatening to FIFA's central (but European-based) authority.

The FIFA general secretary, Helmut Käser, expressed surprise that the South American federation wished to change completely the administration at the end of a presidential term of office: 'There will be no continuity in administrative business … Possibly this is the South American way of thinking.' He added: 'As usual South America is pretending that FIFA is giving preference to European referees and that South American referees are neglected.'

'A very delicate matter' could arise, Käser pointed out, concerning referees for World Cup preliminary matches. The delicacy arose from a remark made by a member of the South American referees' committee that 'it is customary in South America to make "pilgrimages" to the referees' countries'.

On one trip to the Central and North American confederation in 1971, Rous called for the member associations to clean up their act – to make sure that financial resources were effectively and correctly used, to improve slack administration, make committees properly representative and to take more care in nominating referees.

This was quite a list – dodgy delegates, crooked refs, financial irregularities. This strong school-masterly ticking off hardly endeared Rous to the FIFA family in this part of the Americas. His style evoked stereotypes that were to be played upon with brilliance by Havelange.

As Havelange mobilised his support, Sir Stanley noticed that the Brazilian wasn't always playing with a straight bat. By early 1973 Havelange was turning up at confederation congresses. FIFA queries on this were brushed aside. CONCACAF president, Joaquin Sorvia Terrazas – one of those who had ignored Rous's ticking off – denied that Havelange had been invited to take part in or attend the congress, or that he'd been present at any of the meetings. 'Unfortunately', Terrazas told FIFA, Havelange's 'spontaneous visit to the Mexican Football Confederation coincided on the same dates as our Congress'. Passing off such a visit as a coincidence strains credulity.

Football officials in Argentina and Uruguay had proposed that Havelange become the South American candidate for the FIFA presidency. Accepting this, the dynamic businessman then moved fast. With the backing of most of the South American countries, he spent 1971 to 1973 in worldwide canvassing. Preparing for the 1974 FIFA election, he visited 86 FIFA countries, concentrating on Africa and Asia. Havelange made personal calls to FIFA members to talk up his manifesto. He made eight promises. He would increase the numbers of participants in the World Cup finals. He'd create a junior, Under-20 World Championship. FIFA would get a swish new head office. FIFA would provide materials to underdeveloped associations. It would help them construct and improve their stadiums. He pledged more courses for sports professionals, and the provision of extra technical and medical expertise to underdeveloped countries. He also promised to introduce an inter-continental club championship. With the exception of the promise to build new headquarters, all of these proposals can be read as developments which would bring most benefit to those at the margins of world football.

Lobbying effectively, and pledging these commitments, Havelange – 'a very clever man, a very skilled politician', in Ulsterman Harry Cavan's words – aimed to become FIFA's first non-European president. His candidature was cleverly pitched, harnessing the resentments and aspirations of South and Central American, southern European, Soviet, African and Asian footballing nations.

No candidate for any sports post had ever run a campaign like this. 'It was such a radical change to suddenly have this dynamic, glamorous South American character, brimming with *bonhomie*, travelling the world with the Brazilian team, travelling with the likes of Pelé,' recalled Patrick Nally, former business intimate of the late Horst Dassler of Adidas. It was Brazilian carnival time and Havelange led the main parade.

With Central and South America already in his pocket, wooing the African football nations became critical to the Havelange election strategy. Rous's FIFA made this easy for him. By the mid-1960s, even though the membership of the African confederation (CAF) had considerably increased from its modest base, African representation in the World Cup finals could be achieved only by a play-off between the winners of the African Cup of Nations and the Asian equivalent. Opposing such obvious discrimination, Dr. Kwame Nkrumah, then president of Ghana, supported CAF members to boycott the qualifying tournament for the 1966 Finals in England.

This action shocked FIFA and, at the pre-tournament congress in London, African representation in future finals was granted. The struggle for this concession was still fresh in the memories of many of the African delegates as they prepared for the 1974 Frankfurt congress. If it was not, Havelange lost no time in reminding them.

Through the political machinery which he had put together to manage his African campaign, Havelange shrewdly exploited the antipathy between the former British and French colonies. As the 1960s wore on more and more African countries gained independence; as this happened, unnoticed by Sir Stanley Rous, the balance of power within CAF shifted from English-speaking to French-speaking Africa.

One of Havelange's main collaborators in Africa was Jean-Claude Ganga from the Congo, who was the first secretary of the Supreme Council for African Sport which was founded in 1966. According to Oroc Oyo, the first secretary of the Nigerian Football Association after independence, 'Ganga mustered Africa for Havelange'. There was little love lost between Rous and Ganga and the latter appeared to be only too willing to use his influence to persuade fellow Africans to support Havelange.

'I remember the 1974 elections very vividly,' explains Oyo, who had trained under Rous at The FA. On the eve the 1974 elections Oyo was running one of Africa's largest and most influential football associations and was at the centre of the tug-of-war between Rous and Havelange. He recalls attending the CAF congress in Egypt in 1974. After the congress Havelange invited African delegates to a cocktail party hosted by the ambassador of Brazil in Egypt. 'All of us were invited. The plank of Havelange's campaign was to ostracise South Africa, because this was the clarion call of African football. This was a carrot which Dr Havelange brandished before Africa.'

Of all Rous's mistakes, Oyo believes that his misreading of South Africa was the most serious. FIFA suspended South Africa, not for the first time, in 1961, pending an investigation into the mainly white Football Association of South Africa (FASA). Rous visited the country in January 1963 along with Jimmy McGuire, the secretary of the United States Soccer Federation (USSF), and produced a report which suggested that the FASA 'was not − or by its rules should not have been − concerned with the government's policies and attitudes'. His official report concluded: 'FIFA cannot be used as a weapon to force government to change its internal sports policy. To do so would wreck FIFA's true purpose.' Rose-Marie Breitenstein recalls that Sir

Stanley believed that football conditions in South Africa were widely available to all, whatever their background or colour.

In truth, apartheid poisoned sport as it did every sphere of society in South Africa. In an attempt to appease the international community, in 1971 Premier Vorster introduced a 'multi-national' sports policy: officially sanctioned racial categories (whites, Indians, Africans and coloureds), under certain circumstances, could play against each other at an 'international level' and play touring international teams.

In South Africa in the early 1970s there were separate administrative bodies for Indian soccer, coloured soccer, African soccer, non-racial soccer and white soccer. And the whites lobbied aggressively to be recognised as the commanding voice for South Africa in the world arena. This was the bizarre zenith of sporting apartheid, even leading to an absurd proposal that South Africa would rotate the racial mix of the national team as it attempted to qualify for successive World Cup Finals. They would enter a black team for England in 1966, a white team for Mexico in 1970, presumably a coloured team for Germany in 1974 and so on.

Rous's dogged determination to stand by his antiquated views on the separation of sport from politics flew in the face of pan-African sensibilities and played into Havelange's hands. Mawad Wade, then secretary of Senegal's football association, admits to being one of those in the African confederation who helped Ganga with Havelange's campaign. 'Why? Because of apartheid in South Africa. I was talking to Sir Stanley Rous in the Sheraton Hotel in Cairo. I told him, "If you are elected, can you keep South Africa out of FIFA until apartheid goes down?" He says to me, "I can't promise you because I follow my country the United Kingdom." I say to him, "In this case, then, we will never vote for you."'

Wade got the answers he wanted from Havelange. 'I met Havelange in the same hotel,' recalled Wade. 'He says to me, "Okay, so long as I am in charge and apartheid still exists, South Africa will never come into FIFA."'

From his earliest days in the presidency, Rous sided with the white football establishment in South Africa. In the early 1960s the FASA faced a challenge from the multiracial South African Soccer Federation (SASF). In its January 1963 visit to South Africa, Rous's two-man commission held interviews with many sports organisations and received full submissions from the two football bodies. In its scathing critique of its multi-racial opponents, the whites-only body exploited Rous's naiveté, claiming most of its opponents were 'uneducated, and not fit to assume positions of authority in any sphere of life. I do not desire to enter into any political discussions, as I am aware that your body does not allow politics to enter into any of its deliberations.'

Rous and McGuire 'unreservedly' recommended that the suspension of the FASA be lifted. 'The members of the dissident Federation whom we interviewed, would, in our opinion, be quite unsuitable to represent Association Football in South Africa. We found that they desired to hinder and to act contrary to Government Policy, which clearly indicates their inability to foster and propagate the game of soccer in that country.'

The Rous-McGuire recommendation was supported in the executive committee by 13 votes to five. Despite this substantial majority Rous began to think that he was losing control over his executive. Rous wrote to Aleck Jaffe of the FASA: 'The votes against were all from the left wing and for the first time those members demonstrated their solidarity as a bloc.' His worst fears were confirmed the following year at FIFA's Tokyo Congress, when members took the unprecedented step of overturning the 1963 executive committee decision, and by 48 votes to 15 suspended the FASA for 'the practice of racial discrimination'. This should have been a warning to Rous about the growing might of the Third World vote, but he was either too blind or too arrogant to take heed.

South Africa was to haunt Rous throughout his presidency. At the Eighth Ordinary General Assembly of the African Football Confederation in Addis Ababa, in January 1968, the president addressed the assembly, warning delegates against the sports politics subversives in South Africa. Referring to a letter received from the South African Non-Racial Olympic Committee (SANROC), Rous enraged many African delegates when he said, 'In fact you should take no notice of their letter. I know these peoples. I have been in South Africa to meet them. In fact this group is more interested in communist politics than in football.'

In response, the Kenyan delegate spoke of 'the unwarranted attack of Sir Stanley Rous against the General Secretary and the AFC' on the South Africa question. 'We in Kenya wish to see that all means possible are used to bring about a change in South Africa so that our brothers there may enjoy the freedom of sports we have.' In the eyes of most of the African delegates, Rous was a racist.

As late as 1973 he was still working to bring South Africa back into the world footballing fold. He organised a postal ballot supporting a 'special dispensation' for the suspended association to stage a South African multiracial sports festival. SANROC, from its exiled base in London, wrote back condemning this as 'a dubious postal vote which is not in conformity with rules'. Yet again, Rous misread the international response to such a gesture.

The African confederation roundly condemned his action. Rous argued – in response to a query from Dakar – that 'this gesture was made as an experiment to overcome apartheid in sport'. The dispensation was withdrawn by Rous and FIFA, claiming to have been misled on the make-up of the teams, but the damage was done. His support for such racist schemes was to sink him in the following months.

Granatkin of the USSR telegrammed Moscow's 'categorical' opposition to FIFA's support for the event. It was not the last Rous would hear from the Soviets that year. His relations with the communists were further damaged through the position he adopted over the World Cup qualifying match between Chile and the Soviet Union, scheduled to be played on 21 November 1973 in Santiago's National Stadium.

Chile was governed by a military junta headed by General Pinochet, which had overthrown the democratically elected Marxist government of Salvador Allende in September of that year. Pinochet's régime had brutally eliminated political opposition and it was well known that dissidents had been rounded up and held captive at the National Stadium, where they were tortured and murdered. The Soviets argued that under these circumstances, the game should be played in a neutral country.

In October 1973 Rous sent a FIFA delegation to Santiago led by vice-president D'Almeida and general secretary Dr Käser. The FIFA officials were put up in one of the capital's finest hotels and provided with a chauffeur-driven limousine for the duration of their three-day visit.

It is obvious from their report that D'Almeida and Käser failed to look further than the guided tour provided for them by Chilean officials. 'In reply to our precise question concerning the stadium,' the report states, 'we were told that in a couple of days the stadium will be at the disposal of the sports organisations as it is expected that the interrogation of the remaining detainees will be terminated and most of them will have gone home.'

Between them, Käser and D'Almeida made what was effectively a concentration camp sound like a holiday resort. 'The stadium is at present being used as a "clearing station" and the people in there are not prisoners but only detainees whose identity has to be established.'

'The stadium is under military guard and entry is only with a special pass,' they went on. 'Inside the stadium itself the seats and pitch were empty and the remaining detainees were in the dressing and other rooms. Outside the stadium approximately 50 to 100 people were waiting for news of relatives who were still detained. Inside the outer fencing everything seemed to be normal and gardeners are working on the gardens.'

'The grass on the pitch is in perfect condition as were the seating arrangements,' D'Almeida and his colleague cheerily concluded. 'In Santiago, life is back to normal.' Let the game go ahead.

Without hesitation the FIFA executive accepted these recommendations. The Soviets were furious. From Moscow, Granatkin despatched a telegram to Rous at his London home:

WELL KNOWN THAT AS RESULT FASCIST UPHEAVAL OVERTHROWN LEGAL GOVERNMENT NATIONAL UNITY NOW IN CHILE REVEALS ATMOSPHERE BLOODY TERRORISM AND REPRESSIONS ... NATIONAL STADIUM SUPPOSED BE VENUE HOLD FOOTBALL MATCH TURNED BY MILITARY JUNTA INTO CONCENTRATION CAMP PLACE OF TORTURES AND EXECUTIONS OF CHILEAN PATRIOTS STOP ... SOVIET SPORTSMEN CANNOT AT PRESENT PLAY AT STADIUM STAINED WITH BLOOD OF CHILEAN PATRIOTS STOP ... USSR FOOTBALL FEDERATION ON BEHALF SOVIET SPORTSMEN EXPRESS DECISIVE PROTEST AND ... REFUSE PARTICIPATE QUALIFICATION MATCH AT CHILE TERRITORY AND MAKES FIFA LEADERS RESPONSIBLE FOR IT STOP

FIFA received many other outraged objections to its ruling. A personal letter to Stanley Rous from a youth football organisation in East Germany said that a Santiago match would be like playing at Dachau. The president of the East German football federation, Reidle, asked Sir Stanley how he could expect any nation to send their athletes to arenas 'saturated with the blood of noble and honest men'. Complaints rained in from Africa and Latin America. Sir Stanley ignored them all.

On 6 November the following cable from the USSR Football Federation was delivered to Rous's home:

DECISION ABOUT VENUE OF MATCH NOT ACCEPTABLE FOR SOVIET FOOTBALLERS WHO CONFIRM REFUSAL TO PLAY GAME IN CHILE STOP REGRET THAT DID NOT FOLLOW COMMON SENSE AND NOT RECONSIDERED ITS DECISION

Rous prepared to face the consequences through the ballot box. 'The Russian attitude may well have repercussions outside Europe, since their political muscle extends wide,' he recalled in his memoirs. 'While a sitting President has certain advantages there were several "political" issues militating against me, because I was not prepared to connive at ignoring its [FIFA's] own statutes.'

Rous believed he had a sizeable proportion of the African vote in his pocket. In 1971 Oroc Oyo, then the secretary of the Nigerian Football Association, promised him that Nigeria, perhaps the most influential country in West Africa and one of the continent's strongest football nations, would support him. However, as Oyo himself told us in 1996, 'I went to his room and pledged him Nigeria's support. Being British trained and since I had some tutelage under Sir Stanley Rous, I did not favour Dr. Havelange's drive, I was for Sir Stanley Rous. But unfortunately, when they went for that election in 1974 I had a brush with the Nigerian Football Association and I was sidelined.' The Nigerian delegation 'swallowed the bait of Dr Havelange and Ganga's Supreme Council and that was how he won the election', concluded Oyo.

Right up to the vote in Frankfurt, just prior to the 1974 Finals in West Germany, the Europeans did not realise that they had been outmanoeuvred and remained confident that Havelange's challenge would fail. Rous played what he saw as a fair match in the presidential election, but in the conclusion to his April 1974 last-minute campaign brochure, in a thinly veiled critique of Havelange's campaign, he said he would not stoop to vulgar electioneering, emphasising his belief in the 'president's role as world ambassador for football', and playing up his honourable motives and style: 'I can offer no special inducements to obtain support in my re-election nor have I canvassed for votes except through this communication,' Rous stated. 'I prefer to let the record speak for itself.' Unfortunately for him, the needle was stuck on this particular post-colonial record and the sounds were coming through too softly and too late.

Many Asian friends of Rous also sensed the tide turning. For all his respect for Sir Stanley's accomplishments, the young Peter Velappan, then secretary of the

Malaysian Football Association, was one of those to take Rous by surprise. Velappan recalls that the president was widely respected, but 'I think Sir Stanley did not take the election too seriously. He didn't believe in campaigning. But Dr Havelange and his people did a lot of groundwork, and specially promising Asia and Africa many benefits.'

The 79-year-old Sir Stanley Rous put his 12-year tenure of office and Europe's monopoly of the world body in the hands of 122 delegates, of whom 37 were African. It was a close-run contest, but Havelange edged over the required mark in a second ballot, with the Africans and Asians behind him.

According to Peter Pullen, a senior official in the Brazilian foreign office and a long-time associate of Havelange (Rose-Marie Breitenstein recalled him as 'Havelange's agent in England'), there was a hidden irony in this result. Some time before he launched his own campaign for the FIFA presidency, Havelange, in his capacity as president of the Brazilian Sport/Football Federation (CBF), had warned Rous of the increasing power of the Third World. Havelange counselled that Rous should consider changing FIFA's constitution in such a way that the votes of the more established nations of Europe and Latin America would weigh more than those of the newer members from Africa and Asia. Rous, thinking that he had the votes of the British Commonwealth nations in the palm of his hand, turned down Havelange's proposal – a decision that was to haunt him after the Frankfurt congress.

This result shattered Rous, whose response is recalled by his loyal PA, Rose-Marie Breitenstein, as 'certainly one of deep upset, and in some senses as a betrayal'. Over a century earlier, the prime minister, Disraeli, commented that Britain's colonies had become a 'millstone round our necks'. In 1974 Rous and European sports' other power-brokers harboured similar thoughts.

Letters of condolence poured into Rous from the upper echelons of world sports administration, such as Lord Killanin of the IOC, some referring to the 'dark forces' which had engulfed the world's top sport in the figure of the Brazilian bogeyman. People whispered that Havelange and his cronies had spent £500,000 on his campaign (equivalent to well over £4 million pounds 30 years on).

Havelange had warned Rous of what was to come. He claims that he did not want at first to contest the presidency, but others 'were very insistent'. So Havelange visited England to dine with Sir Stanley: 'I told him that of the two of us there would be only one winner, and as I was originally a swimmer I told him there would be only one medal. Either I would win the medal, or he would win the medal. He put his arms around me, as a grandfather would a grandson, and I think he didn't believe it.'

Rous, and he was far from alone in this, did not realise that in this historic moment the Grandfather was on the way out, the Godfather on the way in.

4

THE BIG MAN

Havelange and the transformation of FIFA

The most powerful men in the world never walk alone. So it was when Dr João Havelange, FIFA president, swept through the lobby of Cairo's luxurious Marriott hotel on the banks of the Nile. Flanked by bodyguards, trailed by an entourage of factotums, the 81-year-old strode athletically towards the hotel exit like a much younger man.

The Big Man was in town to open the Under-17 World Championship Finals, and to chair one of his last executive committee meetings before completing his 24 years at FIFA's helm. In his long-standing role as International Olympic Committee member he would, in a few days, be jetting back to Switzerland to cast his vote and give Athens the 2004 summer Games.

FIFA's executive brings together the heads of its worldwide family. As he took the chair in the main committee room of Cairo's modern exhibition centre, Havelange's piercing, steel-blue eyes scrutinised the executive, the men who lead a global football industry reckoned to be worth more than $250 billion.

There was Joseph 'Sepp' Blatter, FIFA general secretary, Havelange's one-time apprentice, long-term confidant and soon-to-be anointed successor. Dr Mong Joon Chung of South Korea was there, representing Asia's interests. Dr Chung was not just a football man. He was also a member of Korea's national parliament and head of Hyundai heavy industries, a man who sees within his football mission a greater prize: the unification of Korea, perhaps under his own political stewardship.

Cameroonian Issa Hayatou spoke for Africa, with the potential to control more than 50 African congress votes. Abdulah-al-dabal, Saudi Arabian football supremo, brought with him the power and influence of the oil-rich Gulf states and the will of Saudi's royal family.

Veteran FIFA committee man David Will, little-known Scottish lawyer, was there for the UK associations. The North and Central Americas and the Caribbean, CONCACAF, were represented by flamboyant entrepreneur Chuck Blazer, general secretary and controversial successor to the deceased Guillermo Cañedo, a veteran executive member, senior FIFA vice-president and Mexico media baron. Finding it pretty peaceful here in Cairo away from the threats of the Russian mafia was Viacheslav Koloskov, experienced head of the mighty Soviet football federation.

Julio Grondona, arbiter of South American interests and defender of Argentinean football during that country's recent political turbulence, was at the table. New Zealander and Scottish expatriate Charlie Dempsey CBE was also there. Dempsey calls himself just 'an old Glasgow street fighter', but he was tough and wily enough to get Havelange to recognise Oceania as a full confederation.

Perhaps Havelange's gaze rested longest on the man who would be king, his bitter rival, the burly Swedish truck boss Lennart Johansson, president of the European federation. Johansson led Europe's resentment at Havelange's manipulation of the world body for his own selfish ends. The Swede had threatened to open up the FIFA books, democratise world football and conduct FIFA business with a modicum of transparency.

While Pelé may be remembered as the most influential footballer of the twentieth century, off the field it is this other Brazilian who did most to shape the destiny of the world's most popular sport. After many failed attempts to get an interview with Havelange, we were eventually summoned to his temporary headquarters in a suite in another, even more exclusive, hotel, the Cairo Sheraton. We stepped nervously past two guards brandishing machine guns and negotiated our way past Havelange's glamorous personal assistant before being ushered in for an audience with the Big Man himself. Havelange is not really that big – no taller than five foot ten – but he has a big presence. He has the air and the physical charisma of the dictator and has not been slow to use this in his presidential role in FIFA.

'Havelange had such an aura about him,' recalls vice-president David Will, 'people were actually physically scared of him, were frightened of him, in a one-to-one situation. He's devastating. His control of himself is amazing.' A painful look crosses Will's face as he recounts a recent brush with the Big Man. 'We've had situations recently where he's been shouting at me, because I was supporting the voting procedure in the Congress.' Havelange never loses his composure, though. 'At the end, when we stand up to leave, he says "Sorry, David", shakes my hand and kisses me on both cheeks. He's in total control of himself.'

During our meeting, Havelange recalls with relish and self-congratulation how he made his way in the world. The son of a Belgian industrialist and arms trader, Jean-Marie Faustin Godefroid Havelange was born on 8 May 1916 in Rio de Janeiro. He joined his father's arms company as a youngster and learned the rudiments of business administration. His father died when he was 18, and he went to work and studied part-time: 'I wasn't earning very much, but I was learning something for life.' He worked for an iron and steel company which had a Belgian link, before working in law for a couple of years. He told us how, early in life, he decided that he could not work for anyone else. After six years, he went to the company director and told him that he was resigning and never wanted to work for another boss in his life: 'I have never had another boss in my life, except maybe my wife,' he said. He branched out on his own, building a business empire in the transport and financial industries of a modernising Brazil.

In 1997 he could boast that 20 million people a year were transported by his company, which he'd been with for 57 years (53 as chairman). He had also been a director of the biggest insurance company in Brazil: 'When I became president of FIFA,' he said, 'I had to take a step down in that company.'

Havelange displayed a deadly seriousness – even his attempts at humour were delivered with the grim earnestness of someone who finds laughter a sign of weakness. As he built Brazil's and then FIFA's football empires, he had little time for laughter. He would leave a trail of defeated rivals, victims and dependants, as he extended his influence beyond his home nation, the continent and across the entire globe.

Young Havelange was an athlete of some distinction. He had played junior football with Fluminense, the amateur sporting club for Brazil's elite. To join this club, it was necessary to belong to a family of means – which meant being white. When a famous mixed-race player, Carlos Alberto, sought to pass himself off as white by powdering his face in the locker-rooms, they called it the 'face-powder club'. Now, of course, Fluminense is a professional club, one of the most famous and successful in South America.

Professionalism would later bring more opportunities for non-whites and also herald the end for mediocre upper-class footballers like Havelange. Not good enough to play alongside the talented professionals, he redirected his energies to swimming. From the mid-1930s to the early 1950s he competed at the top of his two chosen performance sports, representing Brazil in the Olympics in Berlin in 1936 in swimming and in Helsinki in 1952 in the water-polo team. He said that 'water-polo served to discharge my aggressiveness and all my occasional ill-humour', and it is a common boast of his that he swims every morning of his life.

Havelange's memories of the Hitler Olympics are extraordinary. 'The first thing I remember is that the organisation of the transport was perfect, and the equipment and the facilities for 25,000 people were very well arranged.' He also recalls the convivial hospitality provided by the Nazis and the several visits some athlete guests made to hear the 70 musicians playing in the Berlin Philharmonic. 'From the start it was a pleasure to be in Berlin,' Havelange said. Like many others, he received the travel and privileges that Hitler's and Goebbels's friends in the Olympic movement laid on. Train tickets could be booked at a 75% discount, and the 20-year-old saw 25 different cities. He didn't suffer in Hitler's Germany.

Brazil declared war against Germany and Italy on 22 August 1942. It joined the defence of the South Atlantic against Axis submarines and also sent an expeditionary force to Italy in 1944, which conducted itself courageously in several bloody engagements.

Back home, Havelange spent the years of his peak sports performances building up business and social contacts in Brazil's capital, São Paulo. The young entrepreneur – son of an arms dealer, a chip off the old block – sensed some real business openings in the transport industry. The state had taken over public transport and this would be re-privatised after the war. Brazil had nuzzled up to the US during the conflict, giving its powerful ally the use of naval and air bases. In exchange, the two countries signed a number of agreements for economic development and for the production of Brazilian raw materials.

With the state in temporary control of the economy and a black market thriving, it was a good time to be a young businessman on the make. The city government requisitioned the transport system, creating a municipal company. This was not to Havelange's liking, nor in line with his individualist market philosophy. In his own words, the post-war years were for him ones of opportunity for fighting government interference in the market. 'Since I did not want to be a public servant, I and some friends founded the Viação Cometa in 1947.'

Highway construction was top of Brazil's post-war agenda of modernisation. When most of a country's people can't afford cars, how will they travel on the highways? In buses, of course. It didn't take Havelange long to see this crucial, expanding market. On the eve of the twenty-first century, it was still the vehicles of Viação Cometa that filled the urban hinterlands of São Paulo and Rio de Janeiro. Go and view the stunning movie *Central Station* to see how the moderniser's buses still dominated and scarred the Brazilian landscape half a century on.

By the mid-1950s Havelange had established a power base in national business networks. His time with the steel-making company Belgo-Mineira helped him learn how to oil the wheels of bureaucracy. Senior partners realised that if they wanted to speed their imported buses through customs, young João was the man to help them. Although no more than a minority shareholder, Havelange was chosen as director-president of Viação Cometa.

The sports world was fertile ground for big-business contacts, too. During his São Paulo years, Havelange had swum and played water-polo at the Espéria rowing club, cultivating and consolidating friendships with some of the country's leading industrialists. From his mid-20s onwards, he was displaying the qualities of the deal-maker and fixer that would serve him well throughout the following half century. No one else had combined sports and business networking and interests so closely, so early in the era of modern and global sport.

In Havelange's view, simply being Brazilian made him the man for FIFA's top job. 'It was an advantage for me when I became president of FIFA that since a small child I have lived together with all the different races and understood their mentalities. It is nothing new for me to be in FIFA's multi-racial environment,' he told us.

He makes it sound as though he was brought up in Rio's *favelas*, the notorious slums. 'I had the good fortune to be born a Brazilian, which is a multiracial society – Indians, blacks, Arabs, Jews, Europeans, Japanese, Korean, Latinos, everything. All the various races of the world joined together to make a multiracial world.' It sounds good, but he refuses to disclose how much social contact he has with Brazil's lower classes and the poorer immigrant groups. He warms to his theme. 'In São Paulo and Rio there are streets with Arabs on one side and Jews on the other and they live in the same street in perfect harmony.'

Havelange points out that Brazil is the eighth industrial power in the world, that São Paulo is an industrial city just like those in Germany. Yet the northern part of the country is less developed, he observes, a little like Africa. Havelange claims that Brazil is both a mid-point and a microcosm of the world: a leader of the non-aligned nations with aspects of the First, Second and Third World. This allows Havelange cleverly to position himself as representative of the developed world, as much as of the developing world – but with an empathy for the entire planet.

Trading on his achievements in the swimming-pool and his associated networks and contacts, in the late 1950s Havelange brought his business and administrative skills into Brazilian sport. His base in the Brazilian Sports Federation (CBD) gave him authority over all the country's major sports, including football. 'I brought to the federation the entrepreneurial skills and the business skills from my own company,' he told us. 'There were just [sports] coaches, but I brought in specialist doctors and administrators for the federation to give it a wider basis. This is what made the difference and why we won the World Cup in 1958, 1962 and 1970.'

He recognised the potential football had to promote Brazil's international image, and his own global profile in both sport and business. He used his experience of restructuring football in Brazil, with an expanded national and regional league and cup set-up underpinned by commercial intervention, as a model for the expansion of the world game when he seized FIFA's reins of power from Sir Stanley Rous in 1974.

His election to the presidency was a watershed moment in the history of world sport. Already a key member of the International Olympic Committee (IOC), Havelange eased the passage of Spaniard, Juan Antonio Samaranch, into the Olympic family and helped him to secure the presidency of the IOC. Similarly, Italy's Primo Nebiolo rose to the top of the increasingly influential International Amateur Athletic Federation (IAAF), confirming a new Latin dominance in world sport. Once at the FIFA helm, Havelange set about taking control of world football away from its established Northern European, Anglo-Saxon stronghold. To do this he would have to fulfil the promises he had made to the developing world during his election campaign.

When Havelange took over at FIFA, operating from its modest headquarters in Zurich, it was little more than a one-man operation run on a shoestring. The organisation had fewer than a hundred members and operated one tournament only, the World Cup finals, for which only 16 nations could qualify to take part.

After a quarter a century, when Havelange stepped down in Paris in 1998, on the eve of the first ever 32-nation senior competition, FIFA, according to its president's estimate, had more than $4 billion heading into its coffers. As a global industry, he reckoned football to be worth in the region of $250 billion annually, way in excess of General Motors' $170 billion. This huge expansion, including the addition of a series of world championships for male youth players and women, was achieved in partnership with transnational media partners and business interests including such global giants as Coca-Cola, Adidas and McDonald's.

Havelange, with the help of his close ally and confidant, the late Horst Dassler of Adidas, was the first to recognise the full commercial potential of sport in the global market. He opened the gates and the money flooded in, along with the media and marketing men with their own ideas about the scale, structure and presentation of the world's most popular sport.

Havelange was a consummate political operator who ruled FIFA in autocratic style. Henry Kissinger, having acted as spokesman for the USA's failed bid to host the 1986 World Cup, experienced the president's managerial style. 'It made me feel nostalgic for the Middle-East,' he said dryly. British sports minister Tony Banks declared that compared with Westminster, the politics of FIFA in the Havelange era were 'positively Byzantine'. Former FIFA media director, Guido Tognoni, said that on a clear and sunny day, 'Havelange could make you believe that the sky was red when it was really blue'.

People have talked about Havelange's almost supernatural powers of strength and concentration. 'He was a master of managing meetings,' Tognoni told us. 'He was also a master of giving people the feeling that they are important without actually giving power away. He was just a master of power.'

There is a physically competitive side to this use of power. 'He was always the toughest guy, and even when he was tired he didn't want to stop the meetings,' said Tognoni. 'He was always fully informed about everything – whereas the members, they were not professionals, they had to eat what was served.' After a reflective pause, Tognoni concluded that the Big Man 'had the power to do everything that he wanted'.

When Havelange rang FIFA House in Zurich, from his office in Rio, it was as if his physical authority came down the telephone line: FIFA staff have been known to stand to attention at such times. So too have presidents and monarchs, as Havelange in his prime dispensed patronage and spouted pledges of support to countries scrambling for the privilege of hosting the World Cup finals. Morocco and the USA were rival candidates to stage the event in 1994, for example. Both countries fought to outdo each other's hospitality. Havelange enjoyed an audience with President Reagan in the White House and received the Grand Cordon Alaouite from King Hassan of Morocco.

In the late 1980s, at a time when Switzerland was considering bidding for the 1998 tournament, the Swiss Football Association nominated Havelange for the Nobel Peace Prize, praising him for his achievement in turning FIFA into 'a world power binding all nations'. The announcement of this proposal generated a standing ovation from many delegates at the 1988 FIFA Congress in Zurich. The French and the Moroccans remained in their seats. Jacques Chirac claimed during his successful presidential campaign that he had been promised by Havelange that France would be given the 1998 World Cup before this had even been considered by FIFA's executive. Havelange, with Chirac in Paris, stated that, 'I would be happy to see the committee look favourably on France's candidature,' knowing that Morocco would run again, as well as Switzerland.

The FIFA president did not mark out France as a favourite in his early pronouncements on the race to host the 1998 Finals. In late 1988 – within five months of receiving his Nobel Peace Prize nomination – he praised Switzerland for its good transport network, telecommunications systems, hotel provision and stable currency. He told the Swiss what they wanted to hear – that it was 'able to organise an outstanding World Cup as in 1954, but brought up to date'. The stadiums would require to be extended and renovated, but 'given the financial strength of the country', he could foresee no problem there. Each of the bidders translated Havelange's remarks as a clear endorsement of their chances rather than those of their rivals.

Havelange welcomed the president of the French football federation to Zurich. The French felt that they had to move quickly to counter the Swiss Nobel proposal. Worse, the French FA feared problems in the relationship between their new prime minister and Havelange. The FIFA president had backed Barcelona over Paris in the race for the 1992 Olympics and he was seen as part of a Latin monopoly of world sports leadership. In East Berlin in 1985 when he was Mayor of Paris, Chirac – seeking the support of the East European lobby – accused Havelange of bias and threatened to use his influence in Africa to ensure that the Brazilian was not re-elected president of FIFA. Tensions had simmered between the two men since. Awarding the winter Games to the French venue, Albertville, was a clever IOC strategy which meant that Paris could hardly be awarded the summer Games too. The sequence of voting was reversed so that the decision about the winter Games was taken first – so scuppering the Paris bid and putting Barcelona in prime position.

The people of the Swedish city of Falun were the real losers in this story. They had several times sought to host the winter Games and had polled a promising 31 votes in the ballot for the 1988 games against the 48 votes of the eventual winner, Calgary. IOC members urged the Swedes to mount another bid. 'You will have my full support,' Havelange told them. In fact, Samaranch persuaded Havelange to change his mind and lobby for Albertville, which he did. Albertville romped home with 51 votes against Falun's 11.

At the time, Havelange's transfer of support from Falun to Albertville worked against the greater French interests, and the Brazilian could be seen to be blocking Chirac's ambitions. A successful outcome to the French bid for the '98 World Cup would be quite some consolation for this. Reminded by FIFA spokesman Guido Tognoni that it was FIFA and not a national prime minister that awarded the finals, Chirac nevertheless told the nation that France had 'a good chance of being awarded the World Cup finals. And I will do everything I can to ensure that we get them.'

There were still four years to go until FIFA was to make this decision. In France the media provided free advertising to the level of an estimated 25–30 million francs. After September 1991 the French football federation was ready, in the last stages of the bid, to spend six to seven million francs in courting the FIFA committee members who were to award the finals.

By November 1991 Havelange was 'very, very unhappy' about the Swiss candidature, saying that 'FIFA could not accept the temporary tubular steel grandstands proposed for stadia'. At the same time as he was dismissing the Swiss bid that he had so consistently encouraged in the previous five years, the French campaign was reaching a climax. In a piece of shameless vote-catching, Havelange was inducted into France's Legion of Honour – the country's highest decoration – by the country's president, François Mitterand. In a ceremony at the presidential palace, Mitterand praised the Brazilian as 'one of the great figures of today's sporting world'. Enraged observers thought otherwise, describing the award as 'disgraceful'.

Like many other sports leaders, Havelange said a lot about promoting world peace through sport. He claimed to have done much through football to bring China fully into the world's economic and political embrace. He declared high hopes for the positive impact on international relations in East Asia of the co-hosting arrangement between Japan and South Korea for the World Cup finals of 2002. One of his final ambitions was to organise an international 'friendly' match between Israel and the fledgling Palestinian state to be played in New York, the seat of the United Nations, to show, in his words, 'that football can succeed where politicians cannot'. This was initiated by Vice-President Al Gore, who approached Havelange during the 1994 World Cup finals in the USA. Havelange recalls that Gore was 'very upset' when the suggestion was not received with great enthusiasm, the FIFA boss initially saying, 'No, we are a sport, we are not politics in that sense.' Magnanimously, in his own telling, Havelange reconsidered and through the liaison of Prince Faisal he communicated with the Saudi King, Fahed, who 'offered to give the Palestine Football Federation a hundred million dollars to get them going. Now things have moved on and Palestine is a more clearly defined political entity.'

Within a year, he was seeking to arrange this game for the end of 1997, though it never took place. Palestine, however, was accepted as a full FIFA member at the June 1998 Congress. It was a defining moment when the Palestine delegate carried its flag around the Equinox Centre, welcomed along with a few other nations as the newest members of the FIFA family. There were no doubts as to where its vote would go in the election for the FIFA presidency later in the day.

Havelange claims that FIFA is truly democratic, with each member country having one vote. But the secret ballot, one-member one-vote system gives him a great deal of control. Vanuatu, the tiny island republic in the Pacific with a population of around 180,000, has the same voting rights in a FIFA congress election as does Germany with 80 million inhabitants; the Faroe Islands have the same voting weight as the mighty Brazil. For years this has worried more powerful football nations, as the outcome of elections can be assured from the accumulated commitment of tiny constituencies. Achieving the majorities necessary to change the rules, procedures or statutes of FIFA is exceedingly difficult.

In the 1970s, it was clear that if world football was to become truly global, it needed a man like Havelange. By fulfilling his 1974 election promises and making football a truly world game, he achieved much. The Brazilian himself is not slow to claim credit for the way he personally remodelled FIFA to do this. He matter-of-factly writes that in his time 'the FIFA administration may be considered perfect'.

FIFA claims to be non-commercial as well as democratic. Under Swiss law it has non-commercial, almost charitable status – despite the $4 billion claimed by

Havelange to be safely in its coffers – and escapes the usual company reporting requirements. This provided the perfect set-up for the Big Man's operations.

A FIFA document claimed in 1984 that Havelange was a 'football magnate who combined the qualities of far-sightedness and openness, an entrepreneur in body and soul', who 'in no time transformed an administration-oriented institution into a dynamic enterprise brimming with new ideas and the will to see them through, so that now the administration is managed in the form of a modern firm.' Guido Tognoni, though, said that 'people say that he was leading FIFA like an industry – but he was leading FIFA like a private enterprise, like a proprietor'.

'As if he owned it?' we queried.

'Yes, exactly,' replied Tognoni.

As late as the end of the 1990s, deals regarding the sale of the television rights for the World Cup Finals of 2006 were completed by Havelange, Blatter and their FIFA lackeys without reference to the executive committee. 'It's depressing', David Will recalls. 'I think we just have to keep chipping away at this. The first task is to have the committees properly chosen, and not to have committees packed with pay-offs. We don't know how the [2006 television] deal was made.' He sighs. 'Per Omdal [Norwegian fellow committee member] and I have seen the contracts, but we asked that the contracts be laid before the executive committee for final approval, and instead we were told at the executive committee that the contracts were signed that day.'

So Havelange's 'perfection' has come at a price. Pelé, amongst others, criticises him for over-expanding football in Brazil, to the point of crisis in the finances of the domestic game. Similarly, in exposing football to the overwhelming influence of market forces, Havelange has helped to hand the world game to people who view the sport as no more than an opportunity to make big money.

Havelange has faced a torrent of allegations. Investigative writer David Yallop, in his 1999 book *How They Stole the Game*, confirmed that during the year that Havelange gained the FIFA presidency, he submitted accounts to the Brazilian Treasury, claiming that the Brazilian Sports Federation, CBD, was in surplus, when in fact it had a deficit of $1.7 million, the equivalent of more than $5 million today. Yallop reports that during the 16 years of Havelange's reign at the CBD, from 1958 to 1974, over $20 million in today's values 'vanished without trace'. Some in the Brazilian junta wanted to put the blame on Havelange. The Big Man rode the storm, however, and in the end a state-owned bank paid the missing sums for 1974 into the federation's bank account, debited to the Social Assistance Fund. Yallop's investigations also show Havelange dealing in Rio de Janeiro's lottery and in the arms trade and related industries.

Throughout all of this, Havelange has kept his football empire together. It has had as its binding theme the idea of the family, inherited from Jules Rimet, but inflected in the modern era with a dose of the president's own philosophy, the imperative of *omertà* by which the real truth is what is most of all kept within the family.

Even as he planned for his retirement in 1998, Havelange worked ceaselessly behind the scenes to ensure that the régime which he had installed at FIFA would continue through the election of Sepp Blatter. We were there to see it happen, and to track Blatter's undignified fight to hold onto the position when challenged in 2002, his further presidential term of office securing the continuation of the Havelange-Blatter FIFA Dynasty (HBFD).

At FIFA's watershed conference in Paris's Equinox Centre in June 1998, the riches of world football were kept in the family when insider-candidate Blatter routed his rival. On confirmation of that result, the Big Man embraced his protégé and successor. The family treasures were secure.

In the huge exhibition hall in Paris where the future good of the game was passed on into the hands of the Havelange-backed candidate, we wondered for whose good the whole self-indulgent pantomime was staged – for football people, for regional cabals, for ruthless and power-hungry individuals?

Havelange believes that he has done nothing wrong. In response to the fierce criticism that followed his visit to Nigeria just as dissident Ken Saro Wiwa was heading for the gallows, the Brazilian gave away perhaps more than he intended to with regard to his own personal philosophy: 'I don't want to make any comparisons with the Pope, but he is criticised from time to time, and his reply is silence. I too am sometimes criticised, so explanations about such matters are superfluous.'

Silenzio, Señor Dr Havelange. It's official – *omertà*. We couldn't find it in the statutes, but here it is – FIFA's own brand of presidential infallibility. Above the law of nations, above conscience, he has simply been used to doing what he wanted to do. Even after his withdrawal from formal office, FIFA still bears Havelange's indelible stamp. On or off the throne, Havelange's imperious figure – FIFA's Big Man to the end – continued to cast a shadow over the football world.

As Havelange sat by the Emperor of Japan to applaud his country's fifth World Cup triumph in Yokohama Stadium in June 2002, he could reflect on a job well done. FIFA's crises were no longer his personal problem, and the internal shambles and corruptions of Brazilian domestic football were overshadowed by the victory of the national side. His abdication – played out as an honourable, disinterested action – had come in the nick of time, and the Big Man could continue to sanctify himself in the annals of football history.

5

THE PREDATOR AND THE PROTÉGÉ

Doing the business of FIFA

High above the Champs Elysées, as if proclaiming its conquest of France '98, the blue and white banners of Adidas fluttered atop the company's exclusive retreat in the heart of Paris. Mingling with the elite at the Adidas Club, we made small talk, nibbled delicate *hors d'oeuvre* and quaffed Bolly with them in their penthouse suite. We were there to hear the official announcement of Adidas's major sponsorship role in the Women's World Cup finals, USA 1999.

On and off the field there had been many battles fought during France '98 – between teams, between fans, between touts, among the media and among FIFA wannabes and has-beens. But possibly the greatest conflict was the war of the sponsors.

The FIFA hierarchy turned out in force for Adidas's party. Sepp Blatter was here to address the sycophants and hand over the official Adidas match ball to the captain of the American women's team. However, despite its pretty blue and pink – for girls – design on the exterior, the ball was identical to the one that few players had been able to kick properly during the early matches of France '98. Like the men's edition it had been laboriously hand-stitched by child labourers in the sweatshops of northern Pakistan. In our hyper-technological age, the sporting-goods industry's claim that a machine which makes and stitches leather casings for soccer balls cannot be made sounds farcical. Low labour costs in China and the Indian sub-continent seem a more plausible rationale for continuing the practice of hand-stitching. (We took one home for the lad, who eyed its pinkish exterior suspiciously before taking it down to the park for a kickabout with his mates. 'Too light,' he pronounced when he returned home. 'It kept getting stuck up in the trees, so we played with Tom's Mitre instead.' Adidas balls may get FIFA approval, but they get a big thumbs-down from Ratton Rangers Under-11s.) It was more of the same in 2002 as yet another new Adidas ball was introduced on the eve of the World Cup. That this was the first time the players had touched the new ball, and novices like Beckham and Roberto

Carlos couldn't kick it properly, was irrelevant to Adidas. In sporting goods stores around the globe queues were already forming as boys and girls lined up for their 'must have' new ball.

On a plinth in the entrance hall to the Adidas Club, next to the World Cup match ball, the latest example of the Predator football boot was on display. For some, its sleek looks brought to mind outrageous free-kicks from outside the penalty-box curling into the top corner of the net, beyond the reach of a flying, flapping keeper. For us, in this setting, the Predator reminded us of a man who, along with Havelange, played a major role in turning world football into big business – Horst Dassler.

Once he ousted Sir Stanley Rous, João Havelange had a big problem. He didn't have the money to keep his election promises. Unless he found filthy-rich financial backers, his African and Asian allies would prove to be fickle friends. Enter Horst Dassler, the German sporting-goods manufacturer and fixer.

'Can you give me any justification as to why a football boot manufacturer should wish to decide who should become the president of FIFA and control world football?' former British sports minister Denis Howell asked the president of the Adidas empire in 1983. The answer is obvious: to make a lot of money. In order to add to a fortune which, thanks to the Olympics, was already considerable, Dassler offered his sports networks and his vision of global marketing to the new boss of FIFA. Havelange's cash-flow problem was on the way to being solved.

Television was central to Dassler's plans. For Rous, the medium had been nothing more than an educational tool – you might use it for teaching the laws of the game, or as a coaching aid, but little more. With Dassler to guide him, Havelange saw television's potential as a money generator. Together they plotted to harness the broadcasters' increasing interest in football to the marketing interests of multinational companies.

Crucial to the success of their plan was the way in which Dassler and Havelange, through the mediation of Patrick Nally, secured Coca-Cola as a global partner for FIFA and its main asset, the World Cup. Nally had been involved, with the commentator Peter West, in the early growth of sports sponsorship in Britain. Through an advertising agency and then their own company, West Nally, they had established sponsorship deals with brewery companies, Green Shield Stamps, Benson & Hedges, Kraft, Ford, Esso and Cornhill Insurance.

Nally proved useful to Dassler. He was well established in the UK sports sponsorship market, with a unique portfolio of powerful clients. Dassler's British agent, John Boulter, the runner, involved Nally in promoting Adidas's Arena swimwear line. This was fronted by Mark Spitz, exploiting the American's astonishing haul of seven gold medals at the 1972 Munich Olympics. Adidas was expanding its textile and clothes range, and in late 1974 Boulter arranged for Nally to meet Dassler.

Dassler was head of Adidas's French arm, based in his retreat at Landersheim in the Alsace hills in France. The German had a unique vision: he could see that international sports federations were going to become very important, as old amateur beliefs gave way to professionalism and commercialism in Olympic sports. He knew an opportunity when he saw one. With Rous on the way out and Havelange on the way in he realised that FIFA and the World Cup were there for the taking. 'Sir Stanley suddenly woke up to the fact that he was about to be bumped off by this Brazilian,' said Nally. 'Dassler had seen the election of Havelange as being a big watershed – here you had the gentlemanly "old school" of Sir Stanley Rous suddenly ousted.' A new style of opportunistic leadership was in charge at FIFA House and Dassler was soon knocking on the door. Havelange, already aware of the German's skills in international sports networking, was quick to invite him in.

Dassler was trained in a tough school of sports business. The young Horst was dispatched by his father, Adi Dassler (founder of the company and, of course, the source of its name) to the 1956 Melbourne Olympics to market, by any means possible, the company's sports equipment, particularly the shoes with the distinctive triple stripe. Adidas achieved a near monopoly of brand marketing at that event, and Dassler admitted that he paid amateur athletes to wear the Adidas brand.

In cut-throat competition with Puma (founded by his uncle, in a bitter family competition), Horst Dassler also managed to persuade dockers in Europe and Australia to slow down the dispatch or import of any Puma goods. To the multilingual salesman, this blatant bribery was normal business practice. 'He became very adept at moving around and getting to understand people,' Nally remembers. 'He knew how to get things from people. In other words, he always knew who he could approach and offer money to and who he could approach and *not* offer money.' According to his one-time associate, Dassler knew whether an IOC membership was more attractive than a straightforward bung. Nally claims that Dassler even offered to broker an IOC membership for UK Sports Minister, Denis Howell. Shortly before he died, Lord Howell told us that this allegation was 'certainly not true', but recognised that Dassler's brazen approaches and sharp practices had few limits.

A small, squat man with a harried look, Dassler was driven by the suspicion that someone was always trying to do him over. He was also secretive to the point of paranoia. As Patrick Nally recalls, 'He would have spies. All of his sports people who were out there to look after the athletes would always spy on the opposition. They'd all be trained to bug telephones. They'd all be trained to go into other people's briefcases.'

Like an old soldier recalling his favourite campaigns, Nally talks about his time with Dassler with barely hidden pride. 'It *was* the shoe wars. You were out there to do what you could to the enemy,' he said. 'Dassler would keep information, you would get people drunk, you would be trained to investigate and find out what other people were up to.'

Dassler recognised how to control the riches of the growing sports market. He made deals with sports administrators in the international federations, and was aware of the big prizes that would flow from gaining and holding power and influence in the biggest organisations of all, the IOC and FIFA. He saw 'what Havelange needed to help him make his dreams a reality', said Nally. The man Havelange 'went to was Horst Dassler and the man Horst Dassler went to was me.'

Nally travelled the world for 18 months, negotiating with key figures in Coca-Cola. He was the first sports marketing man to view the entire planet as his market, rather than separate countries or regions. His main contact, Al Killeen, was number two in Coca-Cola. Killeen had been hooked on football ever since he had been persuaded by one of England's greatest-ever players, Sir Stanley Matthews, to pump some of Coca-Cola's money into coaching camps in Africa. However, the Coca-Cola company had a federal structure and did not usually make central decisions concerning worldwide policy and investments. Cunningly, Nally took Killeen to a match at Brazil's Maracaná Stadium, 'which absolutely blew his mind', recalls Nally. 'He couldn't believe these 110,000 screaming Brazilians that were there for the warm-up, before the real match.'

Killeen realised that if football could mobilise commitment and passion on such a scale, it had huge marketing potential for his product. Dassler got Havelange to impress the Coca-Cola people, at the company's world headquarters in Atlanta, by flying in on his private plane to meet them. Killeen fought to convince the board and, backed by the company's number one, J. P. Austin, pushed through his ambitious plan to tie Coca-Cola to the world's most popular game. Or was it the other way round?

All of the regional companies would contribute. They weren't asked, they were told. They had to contribute a small percentage of their income to a central pot in Atlanta which the Coke headquarters would then pipe to FIFA and its various competitions. 'Previously local countries and bottlers had made their own sports sponsorship policy,' explained Nally. 'Killeen was brave enough to dictate to the whole Coke world that they would back one sport – soccer.'

Havelange's eight-point manifesto, in his campaigning brochure, as mentioned in Chapter Three 'Goodbye Colonel Blimp, was both too broad and too vague, a long way from a development programme. Nally claims he had to make things up as he went along, under the tutelage of the wily Dassler. Horst introduced him to another German, teacher and sports administrator Klaus Willing. Together they produced a strategy which would accelerate global football development. It would also increase FIFA's and Havelange's power and, crucially, expand Coca-Cola's markets. They sent administrators, coaches, medical experts and trainers into countries around the world as part of the development philosophy. They wrote the regulations for the new World Youth Championship. Their development programme exported the knowledge of the strong football nations to another hundred countries. Prime targets were Africa and Asia, 'all those places where the votes were important', as Nally wryly noted. And places where the Big Man was indebted to those who had brought him to power.

Dassler also recognised that the FIFA administration as it stood was not equipped to make this programme work. Havelange had inherited a Dickensian set-up from Sir Stanley Rous. It operated from a small house in Zurich with 'Dr Käser, his secretary and the dogs', as Nally disparagingly caricatures it. The personnel had to go and a new HQ was needed.

Tommy Keller, who worked for Swiss Timing-Longines and ran the international rowing federation as well as the General Association of International Sports

Federations (GAISF), introduced Dassler to Joseph Blatter, an administrator work-ing for Swiss Timing. Dassler head-hunted him to manage the football development programme. Blatter was trained at Landersheim for a number of months. Shadowing the master, he learned how Adidas worked, before moving on to become Dassler's preferred choice in FIFA. When the new FIFA House was under construction, for-mer press boss Guido Tognoni recalls, 'Blatter worked from premises made available by Dassler.'

The manner of Blatter's appointment to FIFA demonstrated the characteristic Havelange style. The Brazilian announced the appointment ahead of the date set aside for FIFA's executive committee to make its decision. Blatter had impressed Havelange and other FIFA officials by administering the Coca-Cola sponsored World Youth Championships in Australia and stepping in and saving the local organisers from chaos. On the spot, Havelange telexed FIFA his decision that Blatter was the man for the job.

Havelange recognised how important the sponsors were to football's future development. The Big Man wanted to be in a position to take control of any such potential relationship. He could see that Blatter had the qualities that were needed: he was a skilful communicator, fluent in five languages; he could flatter and charm the right people; and, if necessary, he could undermine rivals.

The result of the Coca-Cola deal was an extensive FIFA programme giving Havelange the means to honour his election mandate – to develop Africa and Asia, create a World Youth Cup and bring more developing countries into the main tournament.

Blatter was there at the beginning of this new phase of football finance and global development. Dassler's protégé learned fast, and so well that he would have to commit himself to keeping FIFA family secrets for the rest of his working life.

For Patrick Nally, persuading such a big name as Coca-Cola into the soccer programme was crucial because it gave the game massive credibility and attracted the attention of other top-name brands. 'If you're into Coke, you're into the biggest blue-chip company on a global basis,' he explained. Bringing Coca-Cola into the sponsorship of world soccer 'became the blueprint for everyone who wanted to try and bring money into international federations through this source'.

The multi-million investment package put together for FIFA concentrated ini-tially upon the new Under-20s Youth World Cup, first held in Tunisia in 1977 and followed up by tournaments in Asia, the Soviet Union, South America and the Arabian Gulf. The inaugural Under-17s World Championship was held in China in 1985. Like the Under-20s competition, it too was hosted in regions which were peripheral to football's main Western European theatre but central to Coke's global marketing strategy. In Blatter's hands, Havelange's programme worked like a dream. Football expanded its playing base, Coca-Cola extended its market penetration and FIFA got richer and richer.

However sceptical the established football nations might have been about such events (some seeing them as tin-pot, in comparison to their own apprenticeship systems and fully developed professional leagues), the FIFA initiatives offered valuable international experience and competition which were to stand Asian and African footballing nations in good stead on the larger stages of the World Cup and the Olympic Games.

By using Coke's money to create such platforms for developing countries, Havelange fulfilled his electoral pledges. He also guaranteed a sound basis for his five subsequent uncontested presidential nominations. Developed world finance secured the future of the Brazilian and the expansion of football in the developing world.

Coke cash also supported a worldwide soccer skills programme, ensuring even more widespread publicity for the sponsor. The company was so happy with its new love affair with football that it pumped more than $10 million into the 1978 World Cup in Argentina.

The up-front negotiations with Coca-Cola were conducted by Nally, but the internal fixing was accomplished by Dassler and Havelange. 'He wanted all the politics handled through him and his team,' says Nally. This included grooming Blatter at the Adidas base and convincing Havelange to place Blatter at the centre of FIFA's future plans.

Nally and Dassler established sponsor clients' exclusivity in all aspects of merchandising and franchising. This was all controlled through FIFA House. By the first World Cup of Havelange's presidency, in Argentina in 1978, Nally had contracted six major sponsors to FIFA, including Coca-Cola, Gillette and Seiko, though he was still juggling the advertising billboards of companies contracted with different national teams. This was soon to be streamlined, in FIFA's template for what became the Olympic Programme scheme in the case of the Olympics. From then on, the only option open to sponsors was the complete marketing package. Dassler and Nally knew that the cost for companies was so high that many could not get near the scheme, but this suited them. It made it easier to work with those élite global brand names who could afford the stake. This new scale of football finance involved the acquisition and distribution – with minimal accountability – of huge sums of money.

Once he got the sponsors where he wanted them, Havelange had to feed them. One way was to increase the number of FIFA's competitions. The Youth and Under-17s tournaments were augmented by the Indoor World Championships and the Women's World Cup. Another way was to expand the senior World Cup itself. Nally's task was to create a marketing programme to fuel this expansionist programme. Dassler, in turn, committed vast sums to the FIFA president.

As the 1982 World Cup in Spain approached, Havelange needed big money to convince 'the Spanish to take the World Cup up from 16 teams to 24 teams as part of his commitment to get more Asian and African teams in,' said Nally. 'In Spain, in the Palacio de Congresso, in the gentlemen's toilets, Horst said the going rate with the Spanish organising committee wasn't going to be the $4 million which I'd already negotiated and agreed. We had to pay an additional [several] million Swiss Francs.' In men's roomsall over the world, the new élite of the FIFA family was reshaping football for ever.

Nally argues that the Coca-Cola connection gives sports organisations an aura of respectability, generated by the company's global image of corporate cleanliness. But behind the scenes, without Coca-Cola's knowledge, there is skulduggery. 'There's no government checking on them. There's no auditors checking them. Nobody's trying to see where the payment goes or what the individuals get,' explains Nally, 'so somehow the IOC and the IAAF and FIFA are totally beyond reproach.' And, so they think, beyond the law.

Being president of a rich and unaccountable international federation suddenly meant first-class air tickets, hospitality and awards around the globe. 'It certainly beats sweeping out the back of the garden at the weekend,' grinned Nally, 'if you're flying first class everywhere to major international events.'

How did Horst Dassler hold together an operation on this scale? He provided lavish hospitality, the 'compulsory Adidas dinner' at every international sports federation meeting. He invited sports administrators to Adidas's residential and catering complex at Landersheim, Alsace. And, mostly for Africans and Asians, he opened up his sports shop and restaurant with other hospitality, social and personal services, in Paris's Montmartre district.

Dassler and Havelange looked after loyal family members. Harry Cavan, Northern Irish football administrator and FIFA vice-president, had worked closely with Rous, but soon shifted loyalties to Havelange. Cavan had the eloquence of the Irish and the look and persistence of a door-to-door salesman. Dassler made him a 'shoe consultant'. Twenty years on, in the urinals of the top hotels of Europe, there would always be a FIFA comrade on hand to help the emaciated, shuffling and Parkinson-afflicted Cavan open and do up his flies.

The booming world of sport sponsorship and marketing worried Denis Howell when he was Britain's sport minister. Chairing a Central Council for Physical Recreation (CCPR) inquiry, he questioned the role of sports agencies. Mark McCormack's International Management Group (IMG), for example, staged events, represented performers, sports bodies and sponsors, negotiated television rights and even commentated on the event. To a streetwise Old Labour man raised in the municipal politics of Birmingham, this looked like too big a concentration of power: 'Such a situation is pregnant with conflict of interests and cannot carry public confidence.' McCormack, though, refused to meet with Howell's committee of inquiry to discuss these matters.

Howell and his committee also expressed some astonishment, when they learned that 'Adidas had undertaken an extensive programme of education in Africa on behalf of FIFA, the most powerful governing body in world sport'. The committee recommended that such initiatives should be monitored by agencies with public accountability. Howell, a top referee in the professional game in his younger days, wanted to ensure that FIFA and its partners were playing by the rules. His recommendations have never been taken up.

Dassler's empire was beyond the reach of the likes of England's quaint CCPR. Howell did not fully understand the scale of Dassler's grip on the organisation of world sport and the collusive nature of Dassler's relationship with the network of tame sports organisations. Dassler promoted the creation of the Association of Summer Olympic International Federations (ASOIF) as a counter to the influence of the independent General Association of International Sports (GAISF). He manipulated the Italian fixer, Primo Nebiolo, into its presidency, and later into the presidency of the IAAF. By 1986 the GAISF gained as its President the Korean Kim Un Yong (Mickey Kim), nine days after he became a member of the International Olympic Committee. Kim, a former agent of the Korean CIA and the hard man of international tae kwon do, would later gain notoriety in the bribery scandals that shook the IOC in the late 1990s.

Dassler infiltrated world sports organisations with a cadre of ruthless and greedy individuals like Kim. It has been reported that Nebiolo mustered $20 million for his IAAF from the organisers of the 1988 Seoul Olympics for changing times of track-and-field events to suit the American broadcasters, NBC, having initially proposed schedules wholly inappropriate for a mass American television audience.

Lord Howell died in 1998. The previous year he told us, 'I think that the finance of professional sport has now become obscene and is totally destroying the soul, what I call the soul of the game … people have been trying to buy the soul of the sport, and therefore corrupting it, with disastrous results.' By then his judgement sounded like an anthem for a lost age.

Dassler constructed an international espionage system. He collected files on all of the movers and shakers in world sport. The apparently independent publication *Sport Intern* was in fact his personal propaganda machine. From 1980 until his death seven years later, this publication was an important part of his political armoury.

Dassler was persuasive and, with cash in hand, could overturn cherished beliefs overnight. The Welsh Rugby Union, for example, was furious with him for sponsoring the boots of individual amateur players. Dassler went to Cardiff and, one meeting with the WRU later, he had arranged comprehensive team sponsorship. The administrators, in Lord Howell's words, 'totally embraced Dassler and changed their attitude. He paid the Welsh Union for the right to supply boots and pay the players, and they totally changed the whole of the ethos of their sport.'

Dassler told Howell that he had in his office a tremendous computer and records department, with information tabulated from every periodical and newsletter issued by every sports body round the world. He said it was very natural that if anyone wanted to pursue a career in world sport, they would come to him to get the names and addresses of all the contacts. Rous was above this trade, but Havelange was only too happy to use Dassler's files and networks to get football's top job.

Some sports administrators saw what was happening. Philippe Chartrier of the International Tennis Federation wrote, 'The control of sport could shift from the International Federations due to the pressure of money', and argued that the federations should be properly organised and given the means to do their job. But Dassler's records and little black book of deals and debts were by now the main influence on the big business of world sport. His clinching coup was the formation of the sports marketing company International Sport and Leisure in 1982. It was part-owned by Adidas' Japanese partner, the advertising giant Dentsu. Dassler's Monaco-based advertising company SMPI had combined his capital and contracts with Nally's ideas and marketing nous: ISL became its successor, apparently autonomous but little more than a front for Dassler's operations.

One of Dassler's assistants at Adidas, Klaus Hempel, was the figurehead. By mid-1983, just months after its formation, ISL was handling merchandising and stadium advertising rights for FIFA and the European football federation. Soon after, the International Olympic Committee appointed the company to manage its new fund-raising programme. A few more months and it had gobbled up the merchandising, licensing, sponsorship and supplier rights for the local Olympic organising committee for the Seoul Olympics of 1988.

ISL boasted, in a special supplement to *Time* magazine's European edition at the end of 1983, of its successes in attracting sponsorship for its football marketing programme. Canon, Camel, JVC, Seiko, Fuji, Air France and Cinzano joined Coca-Cola on the list of World Cup sponsors. Sponsors also provided services to the media – a harried press person could borrow photographic equipment from Canon and photocopy on a Canon machine, for example, take a refreshing drink of Coca-Cola for next to nothing, check the scores on television monitors provided by JVC and keep an eye on copy deadlines via the official timekeeper, Seiko. With Dassler's networks in place, ISL rapidly dominated world football marketing in this formative phase of the industry.

Dassler was the mastermind behind the marketing of world sport. Though he and Adidas were not technically a part of ISL, it was indisputably his baby. Blatter was close to the German, and the Adidas chairman, Robert Louis Dreyfus, stated in the mid-1990s that in those early days part of Blatter's FIFA salary was paid by Adidas. Right up to his sudden death in 1987 Dassler was in control of the vast fortunes and those who would generate and dispense them in world sport and football.

Blatter was the head of public relations at the Swiss Association of Sport for two years, before going to Swiss Longines. There, he says, 'I worked in marketing … and it was there that I entered into contact with the big names of the sports world, so the great name Adidas.' Joining FIFA – 'it was an old house, there wasn't yet an office here, I went to Landersheim, to the French section of Adidas, and I worked there during the months of August until December 1975' – he worked in football development and became FIFA's technical director from 1975 to 1981, when he was promoted to general secretary. 'For six years, I was ambassador or itinerant missionary for football. I did the development programme Futuro together with Coca-Cola and Adidas. If we hadn't had Adidas and Coca-Cola, who both supported us during this period, we would have never entered the world of football with such a fantastic programme of development … I will never forget Adidas … without Adidas we wouldn't have had this development programme. Without Adidas I think that FIFA would not be where she is today.'

Horst Dassler is recalled with enthusiasm by Blatter: 'He was an extraordinary man, a man of courage, of initiative, a visionary. He went at the age of 20 years, in '56, with a small suitcase, the first to try to make well-known athletes identify with the brand name Adidas … he was the father of sport sponsoring. One can never repeat this enough. It is he who said that one must associate the product, develop the product. with the sport, and equally to increase sales of sports equipment.'

Dassler was an obsessive workaholic who slept little and showed few signs of tiredness. He was an exceptional motivator, with high expectations of all who worked for him, and did not hesitate to call on personal loyalty. 'Each person was truly persuaded that he was part of the family and not just part of the company, and this was wonderful.' Blatter saw him not only as 'a great salesman, but also a great diplomat', who could have resolved problems in world sport, had he lived: 'He always knew how to fix things when there were differences.'

Dassler and Blatter grasped the vast potential of football in the world's burgeoning global markets, and were effective salesmen pitching their product at the world's top companies. Guinness was one that didn't bite, but that didn't deter them. Blatter knew there were big bucks to be found. Together they approached food companies, bank and insurance companies, to fund FIFA's development programmes and to pay Havelange's debts. But Blatter concedes that it was almost by chance that FIFA fell in with the Coke empire: 'By accident we found that we'd drunk Coca-Cola with a bit of rum in Paris, I remember. I drank Coke, and he (Dassler) said, "One thing you should have is that – everyone drinks Coca-Cola." That day in the same restaurant in a hotel in Paris there was a guy who worked for Coca-Cola in England, and it was like that it began.'

When Blatter talks of Adidas, he uses the word 'we'. Recalling Adidas's dip in fortunes after Horst Dassler's death in 1987, it was because 'we did not pay attention to the market, we didn't see the waves, and we sold this business for a morsel of bread'. In Dreyfus, Adidas' new owner, he sees a strong man in the Dassler mould, a man fit to re-establish and strengthen still further the close ties between FIFA and the company. He sounds angry when fielding questions concerning this close relationship. 'Those who make such reproaches are people who don't know the ethical and moral value of business and of sport.' Blatter's morality means that Adidas gets special treatment, and that if the company is outbid in its sponsorship deal by another sports equipment manufacturer, it is unlikely that the law of the free market prevails. Blatter makes sure that FIFA remembers its debts and honours old loyalties. 'I presented this report to the Finance Commission, to the executive committee, to tell them that the moral value of the Adidas company was worth more than the difference in the financial plan the (American) competitors were offering. If a journalist says that it was biased, it's not true. It is simply that it is necessary to think again that someone has made a particular effort over the years. Since I began they were really committed.' He draws upon tradition to account for the FIFA-Adidas cosy relationship: 'The wider family of football is everyone who is in football, including the economic partners like Adidas, Coca-Cola, also all other manufacturers of sport articles, and the media. The media are just as much our economic partner, and also make up the family of football.'

After Dassler's death, FIFA confirmed that it had assigned to ISL all of the marketing and sponsorship rights for the World Cups up to and including France '98. An option was included in this deal for the 2002 event. ISL even got the merchandising rights for FIFA logos, which had been in the hands of a rival outfit, Sport Billy Productions, whilst John Boulter took over as head of promotions at Adidas and for a while it was business as usual in the global industry of world football. But Horst Dassler's four sisters didn't see things like that. They had been useful to brother Horst, sleeping partners in a quiet boardroom. But by the end of 1990 they'd sold off their 80 per cent share of the empire and the husband of one of them became president of the holding company which was the majority (51 per cent) owner of ISL. Dassler's sisters approved the appointment of Jean Marie Weber as chief executive at ISL.

Within two weeks, two key figures at ISL had had enough. Klaus Hempel and Jürgen Lenz were gone by the autumn of 1991 to set up their own rival operation. Hempel and Lenz set up what became TEAM (Television Event and Media Marketing), just across the road from the ISL HQ in Lucerne. It was all very cosy in Switzerland – FIFA up the road in Zurich, the International Olympic Committee not far away in Lausanne, and the European football federation just a couple of hours down south, on the edge of Lake Geneva. They were sure that there'd be plenty of cash to go round and that the bonanza in sports marketing could fill a few more bulging Swiss bank accounts.

Jürgen Lenz is a star graduate from the Dassler school of sports business. He has a massive presence in the lobbies of the hotels where the football glitterati gather. His grey, silk suit is top of the designer range. He's only – and very comfortably – a little overweight. His eyes are blue and his hair is blond. We don't need to set up a specific appointment. 'Find me in the lobby. I am always in the lobby,' he said, courteously but firmly, caressing his mobile phone discreetly, Swiss politeness blending with German efficiency.

This is a man in charge of his patch. He'd swept us in with him at the VIP entrance to the Champions League Village at the Real Madrid v Juventus game in Amsterdam, little Jim Rosenthal from ITV left behind and looking peeved on the wrong side of the coolly clad bouncers.

Lenz asked us what we thought of the Boyzone performance during the pre-match proceedings. He'd personally selected the Dublin quintet, looking for something entertaining but snappy, fun but without the kind of overkill and razzmatazz you get at the Superbowl, Olympics or World Cup. We told him he'd got it just about right for us, though we weren't too sure what the mass of the Spanish and Italian supporters had made of it.

Lenz's professional pedigree was in marketing, where he ran accounts for an international advertising agency. In 1977 he moved to Adidas to work for Dassler and five years later was one of the first to join ISL, as chief operating officer to Klaus Hempel's chief executive. Dassler gave Lenz the job of developing ISL's marketing concept and business plan. Dassler, not formally in ISL at all, liaised with the International Olympic Committee, 'doing the sports political side', whilst Lenz devised the Olympic Programme sponsorship concept.

Lenz and Hempel proposed a management buyout of ISL after Dassler's death. 'We realised the situation was a little bit like what Princess Diana said – three in a marriage gets a little bit tight,' he told us. 'With the representative from the family, we decided that it gets a little crowded here.' But the sisters never responded to their offer.

The two men didn't hang about. They negotiated a release, including a clause preventing them from working with Olympic clients. But they had a free run at the burgeoning football market: 'We knew where the good business prospects were, and they were certainly more in football.'

Hempel and Lenz didn't rush things. They took a three-month break and then met up again to consider future possibilities. 'To get a sharp mind you've got to get in shape body-wise,' lectured Lenz. So he and Hempel headed south into the hills, spending four weeks at a health farm, exercising for four hours a day and dedicating another four hours to working up 'a blueprint of what a future sports marketing concept in an ideal world would look like'. They then filed away the blueprint, formed TEAM and before they knew where they were they had brushed ISL and IMG aside and won the tender for the television and marketing rights to the relaunched European Cup, the Champions League.

They had been taught well by the German master. They had the three key Dassler insights: make and use the right connections; always have sufficient finance for a fallback position if things don't go according to plan; and use a very short decision-making process. They were able to do what the European Broadcasting Union thought was impossible and got 24 national broadcasters to accept a match schedule on a regular weekday evening slot, broadcast live in prime-time. They were backed by start-up finance of $100 million, provided by a German entrepreneur. Once the television deal was in place, the sponsors were queuing up at their door.

The TEAM work on the Champions League has rebranded European football. The company's aim has been to make the product easy to recognise for the consumer. Music, logos, and regular scheduling achieved this. 'These are simple things,' laughed Lenz. 'You don't have to be a brain surgeon to get these things. The accomplishment is not in thinking them up, the accomplishment is in putting them in place, in actually doing it.'

Doing it is not at all simple. The orchestration of hundreds of outside-broadcast vans, thousands of press and media and thousands of VIP guests is event management of the highest order – and that's before the spectators are even considered. Lenz calls the Champions League 'a product for the people', available on 'free tv'. He believes that it would be a huge mistake to allow it to fall into the hands of media companies which are geared totally towards satellite and digital television. And he calls upon sports bodies to retain their influence and not simply allow the marketeers to take over. (Dr Michel D'Hooghe, chairman of FIFA's sports medical committee, has admitted that sport's priorities can be railroaded by broadcasters' interests. Talking about the midday kick-off time for a game in Orlando during USA '94, he said, 'I deplore that the rights of television are now stronger than the arguments of the doctors.')

ISL, in association with the German firm Kirch, gained the FIFA World Cup marketing and television rights for 2002 and 2006. The price for 2002 was

£600 million, for 2006 £800 million. FIFA retained a power of veto over how these rights might be sold on. Blatter said that this could be used to guarantee that the World Cup remains 'accessible to viewers who do not possess expensive satellite or cable systems'. But £1.4 billion is a lot to recoup. Bids may well come in that reduce the power of veto to a fond memory.

Things did not go perfectly in France '98. Too many companies had got in on the act, conceded ISL's Glen Kirton. For 2002, FIFA and ISL were ready to control the whole marketing programme together. They would find ways of funding the local organising committee, which would no longer be able to fix up its own rights deals. These were the issues preoccupying the football men at France '98 – finance as much as football.

Back at the Adidas Club, like generals following the progress of a major battle, Adidas's senior executives and their FIFA family friends and relations could gaze down from their penthouse vantage-point upon the ant-like, rival armies of football consumers flowing backwards and forwards between the Place de la Concorde and the Arc de Triomphe. Looking south-west they could glimpse the action around their central stronghold, the Adidas Park across the Seine from the Eiffel Tower. If they used their binoculars they could make out the campaign headquarters of their main rivals, Nike, whose own theme park dominated the spacious square beneath the appropriately futuristic Grande Arche de La Défense.

The new FIFA president defended the sponsors against those who accuse companies' guests of taking a disproportionate share of the seats to the detriment of the public and undermining the traditional atmosphere of the match. 'There are not enough directors to fill the stadiums' he insisted, adding that many of the sponsors gave the tickets to children. 'The people with ties bought the tickets', he expanded, 'and distributed them to the young people. So those who say that it was only the people of caviar, well I was there for nearly all the matches and I didn't see a gramme of caviar in the stadiums.'

The sponsor war between Adidas and Nike at France '98 was a close run thing. Nike had its deals with the Brazilian team. Adidas was official World Cup sponsor as well as supplier, the first time one company had ever got this. Adidas came out top in a market research poll of six European countries, with a 35 per cent recognition rating. Nike came a brilliant second (for a company which hadn't sponsored the championship at all) with 32 per cent. Blatter recognises the dangers of sponsors' direct influence on the game, and was worried that Nike, not an official World Cup/FIFA partner but sponsor of the Brazilian team and of Ronaldo himself, had abused its access and position by interfering in team selection minutes before the '98 World Cup final: Nike had 'access to the entire World Cup, access to a player, and this player wasn't planned to be playing in the final. It is like the organiser of a concert if the principal tenor says, "I am a bit off", he says "but come anyway, because during the opera you will manage to sing better". It is this that we thought was done with Ronaldo. Adidas would never have done that, they would never have tried to intervene between a coach and the president of a federation.' Blatter, albeit diplomatically and opaquely, here rounded on Nike as the biggest of those eager to challenge FIFA's exclusive deals with preferred sponsors. The pioneer Coca-Cola was a distant third with 20%.

Dassler would have liked all this. His pupil Blatter certainly did and, as new FIFA president, was working as closely as ever with ISL. After his first World Cup in charge, Blatter, the hand-chosen protégé of Horst Dassler, could reflect upon a job well done: Adidas top of the sponsors and ISL still in place as FIFA's 'second cash box'. Football finances were secure in the hands of the Dassler legacy. The honeymoon period would last a little longer, but ISL's smug overconfidence and collapse into bankruptcy was, three years later, to catapult the protégé into FIFA's biggest-ever crisis.

6

THE BOUNTY HUNTER

The American way

Alan Rothenberg sat in the front row at the French Olympic Committee's majestic headquarters in Paris. He was there to support Sepp Blatter's bid to become FIFA's eighth president. It might have been a long way from his Los Angeles law office, but where there was money to be rustled in sport, you could bet that Rothenberg, the bounty hunter, would be riding into town.

Rothenberg was used to backing winners. He'd got the credit for raising soccer's profile in the USA during the 1984 Los Angeles Olympics, and he'd pulled off a major success as the organiser of USA '94. And here he was chatting to Simonet of the French Football Federation, rubbing shoulders with Chirac's man from the Elysée Palace. As boss of the US soccer federation, he'd nominated Blatter for the FIFA presidency. He looked pensive but confident. João Havelange and Blatter had backed him in the great American adventure of '94. He was here in Paris to pay his debts.

The sight of the pensive but confident Rothenberg took us back to a sweltering night in June '94, as we headed into Manhattan during the first week of the World Cup finals. The train in from Massachusetts was quiet, with not a football fan nor a World Cup poster in sight. We were meeting up with some Irish expatriates at a midtown bar between Lexington and Park. The heat at Grand Central station and in the taxi queue was oppressive and we craved the cool of an air-conditioned bar. How could people play football in this crazy heat? Was the World Cup really happening?

To enter PJ's on any night is to step into a twilight world between the USA and Ireland, but on the night before the Republic of Ireland's game against Italy in the Giants' Stadium, it was more like stepping out of, not arriving in, New York, and being pitched into the heart of Dublin. A lot of locals, though, were hooked on the Houston Rockets *v* New York Knicks shoot-out, live from Madison Square Garden. Suddenly all sport was cut from the bar's TV screens as the channels switched to a bigger story still – a mixture of race, sex, and murder. A white station wagon appeared on the screens, pursued along a Los Angeles highway by a phalanx of black-and-white patrol cars and a swarm of police and media helicopters. One of the US's greatest living sporting legends, OJ Simpson, is in the stationwagon and is holding a gun to his own head. Will OJ shoot himself rather than face a double murder charge for the alleged slaying of his estranged wife and her lover? 'Pull the fucking trigger and get it the fuck over with,' shouts an enraged Knicks fan.

A moderate cheer goes up when NBC switches back to the basketball just in time to see the Knicks wrap up the fourth quarter and go into a 3-2 lead in the best-of-seven series. The local New Yorkers are ecstatic. The Dublin half is happy to join in the celebrations if only as a warm up for their own ceilidh tomorrow night.

USA '94 may be under way, but NBC shifts its focus to Olympic wrestling in the Gay Games, currently taking place in Manhattan. All week in the pages of the *New York Times*, the Gay Games and the World Cup will vie for fourth place behind OJ Simpson, ice-hockey's Stanley Cup and the NBA play-offs. At the same time, there's something utterly logical about the staging of football's quadrennial fest in a country where it's widely regarded as a bit of a joke.

Sepp Blatter delivered an upbeat verdict on the tournament: 'The 1994 World Cup produced a turnover of $4 billion with 32 billion television viewers. I mean no disrespect to other sports by saying that even the Olympic Games cannot compare. The World Cup was a fabulous success.' Success, though, is gauged in economic terms, couched in the statistics so vital to FIFA's commercial and media partners.

Penetrating the generally uninterested US sports market has been one of FIFA's biggest challenges. The USA is part of CONCACAF (the Central, North American and Caribbean confederation) along with Mexico, the traditional power base of football in that region. One of Havelange's long-term allies, the Mexican media magnate Guillermo Cañedo, had been an important figure in FIFA since 1962 and became one of its vice-presidents in 1971, three years before Havelange's accession to presidential power. Cañedo was to become senior vice-president, Havelange's number two, and chairman of FIFA's media committee. His last major task was to chair the organising committee of the USA World Cup finals. Cañedo got into the heart of FIFA at the expense of Curaçao's Mordy Maduro, who complained of 'quite a few irregularities' in the election process.

FIFA could do little about such complaints. Rous and his officials had suspected that results of matches in World Cup qualifying tournaments were manipulated, but the federation's administrators simply ignored the letters referring to a particular country's protest. FIFA's general secretary, Dr Käser, wrote to Rous: 'Quite a number of "incomprehensible decisions" were taken in connection with this tournament but all of them were finally endorsed by their Congress with the exception of the above mentioned Surinam vs. Haiti case which happened after the Congress was over.'

By the early 1970s key positions in confederations and FIFA itself were being pursued by powerful individuals representing interlocking sets of interest within and across confederations. These new power-brokers took little notice of FIFA's protests, snubbing scheduled meetings where Rous raised the usual problems – financial irregularities and inefficiency, dubious refereeing appointments, dodgy delegates and organisational unaccountability.

When Havelange replaced Rous as FIFA president he was helped by his Central American allies, to whom he would grant the 1986 Mexico World Cup finals after Columbia was forced to pull out. The USA was written out of that deal but got its turn eight years later, and with it the chance to exhibit the sport to the biggest consumer market in the world.

The USA team had performed well and reached the semi-finals at the first World Cup in 1930, though with the help of six former British professionals. Its greatest moment was at the 1950 World Cup finals, beating England 1-0. We talked to Sir Walter Winterbottom, England coach/manager, about that historic game in Belo Horizonte, Brazil. 'You cannot make excuses,' he said and proceeded to make several. 'We got beaten, but really it is ridiculous. Now that was a referee who was badly influenced by the crowd. The crowd were all for America simply because they were the underdogs.' So bad refereeing and a partisan crowd were to blame.

'It wasn't a big ground, it didn't hold that many spectators at all,' he continued. 'Why we had to play there God only knows, but the pitch was in dreadful shape. The grass was high and thick, it was Bermuda grass growing in small clusters and it spreads and it sits the ball up.' The ref, the crowd and now the pitch.

Winterbottom relived the agony. 'We hadn't had any practice on it of course. What is happening is the ball is teed up and you are hitting shots over the bar. They were going over the bar. We hit the woodwork eleven times. Eleven times, that's absurd.' Too much paint on the posts cost England the game!

Then, of course there were the perfidious foreign Johnnies whom England were playing against. 'We were shooting in, virtually, and they were doing all kinds of things. They were handling Stanley Mortensen outside the penalty area, you know, tackling, rugby tackling him when he was running through.'

'But here's the real reason,' said Winterbottom, lowering his voice. 'We scored a genuine goal, Mortensen claims and all our players do. What happened was that the ball was going into the net but Mortensen decided he'd head it and he deflected the ball and the goalkeeper fell back into the goal. He was a basketball player, he caught the ball in one hand and threw it out from the back of the goal, and the referee didn't give the goal.' That's it! England didn't really lose the game at all, they were cheated out of it. 'Oh dear,' sighed Sir Walter. Oh dear, indeed.

Whatever, the result entered the record books and the country that gave the people's game to the world was humbled by a makeshift team of immigrants from a country where the game was treated as a cross between a joke and a freak show.

A soccer boom of the late 1970s and the early 1980s was short-lived, and financial backers as well as fans withdrew as the New York Cosmos's all-star, international but ageing side – featuring Pelé, Carlos Alberto Torres, Franz Beckenbauer and Giorgio Chinaglia – was not replaced by players of comparable world stature or high-level 'home-town heroes', as soccer league pressman of the time Jim Trecker explained. Expenses had become so high, he told us, that 'the League just sort of imploded on itself in financial instability'.

Carlos Alberto, captain of Brazil's World Cup-winning team of 1970, declares that very few people know why professional soccer in the United States finished. The problem, he believes, arose when a barely documented Mexican bid succeeded in winning the right to host the 1986 finals and, according to Carlos Alberto, that spelt the end for big-time soccer in the US. 'America was the candidate. Soccer in the US seemed to be booming and was backed by Warner Communication,' he told us. 'The Warner people [couldn't accept] the FIFA decision that Mexico replace Colombia. Mexico was the host as recently as 1970.' Carlos Alberto's voice rose. 'The World Cup the Americans would like to host wasn't 1994, it was 1986. If FIFA had placed the 1986 World Cup in the USA, that was the best market. When FIFA decided on Mexico, Warner Communications said, "We are finished. We don't put any more money in."'

Mexico's triumph over the US says much about FIFA mores and morals and the Havelange style. Henry Kissinger, the former US Secretary of State for Foreign Affairs, made an hour-long presentation to the FIFA committee with a multitude of detail based on commercial analyses. He needn't have bothered. The Mexican delegation was already in the lobby of the Stockholm hotel, following up its eight-minute presentation with preparations for a celebration and victory reception.

The success of the Mexicans suited the interests of Havelange's friends in the Mexican media. Guillermo Cañedo was spotted 'arm in arm' with Rafael del Castillo Ruiz, head of the Mexican delegation, before the Stockholm meeting. Havelange's special commission had recommended Mexico, and he got the executive committee's approval of this at breakfast time on the day of the presentations.

Kissinger considered suing FIFA for breach of its own articles. The FIFA decision, and the manner in which it was reached, were both disappointing and humiliating to the US soccer establishment, as well as Warner, the main financial backers of the North American Soccer League (NASL). With escalating costs and falling revenues at home, and this snub from FIFA and the deal-making networks of world football, it was hardly surprising that Warner withdrew its support.

The false dawn of the NASL meant that soccer would continue to have a low profile in the USA until it was selected by FIFA to stage the finals. Its national side did well enough, in the build up to 1994, to qualify for the World Cup finals in Italy in 1990. (FIFA had banned Mexico from taking part, accusing them of cheating by fielding over-age players in the World Youth Cup. This decision, of course, was viewed with suspicion – Mexico were a strong team and their absence eased the USA's passage to Italia '90. The Mexican ban had come just after the USA had been awarded the 1994 Finals. Costa Rica had topped the qualifying group, so if Mexico had competed it was more than likely that the USA would not have made it to Italy. In the event, the USA lost all three of their games in Italy and finished bottom of their group. But at least they could now claim a recent World Cup pedigree and this would be a boost for business in 1994.)

The choice of the United States as host for the World Cup finals was greeted with derision and scepticism by journalists, commentators and professionals. At the tournament draw in Las Vegas in December 1993, media pundits commented on the tackiness and vulgarity of the event. The draw opened with welcomes from high-profile television, film and sports celebrities. Jessica Lange and Jeff Bridges were there, and Faye Dunaway was one of the co-hosts. 'Hello world, welcome to the USA' was the repeated line as these celebrities performed limited tricks with a football. Bill Clinton came on to state that the country was 'proud and excited' to host the tournament and that 'World Cup fever' had gripped the whole nation right through to the White House.

The three thousand guests at the Las Vegas event welcomed João Havelange for what the host acknowledged as one of the most complicated draws ever conducted, linked as it was to a seeding system and the demographics of ethnic and immigrant communities across the chosen venues. The trophy was passed from Havelange to Alan Rothenberg, linchpin of the organisation World Cup '94. Rothenberg stated that it was with 'pride and humility' that he accepted the trophy for the period of the finals, which he was convinced would 'establish a legacy for USA soccer to flourish at every level of play'.

Soon after awarding the finals to the USA in 1988, FIFA had been active in campaigning against the US soccer federation's incumbent elected president, Werner Fricker. It was directly implicated in the election of Rothenberg as his successor.

When we caught up with him in Paris during World Cup '98, Rothenberg boasted, 'I saved the World Cup. FIFA was gravely concerned that the preparations were not going the way they wanted them to and were seriously thinking about taking the World Cup away from the US. That's when they contacted me and asked me whether I'd be interested in getting involved. I said "yes", they said "You should become president of the United States soccer federation." I said I'm not even a member of that organisation.'

This minor technicality did not worry FIFA and, as Rothenberg tells it, 'Within a few short months we figured out the situation, and so in August 1990 I got elected president of the federation, and shortly thereafter took over organisation of the World Cup.'

At the Las Vegas draw, Roberto Baggio of Italy was presented with not just the Player of the Year award, but also with the Adidas Energizer trophy. Mickey Mouse introduced the viewer to the attractions of Orlando, Florida. Nightlife, cars and people were highlighted as the special qualities of Detroit. Nike, Delta and Opel graphics then led into a sustained Nike advertisement – 'You can't live without … Just do It' – which mixed soccer, sex and youth style.

At the opening ceremony in Chicago on 17 July, Diana Ross tried to take a penalty, striking the ball with a jerky mechanical swing of the leg. The ball rolled painfully and apologetically wide, and in a memorable anti-climax to the razzmatazz of the build-up the goal itself collapsed.

As it turned out, this was no bad omen. Early concerns at the staging of the event in the USA soon disappeared once the tournament started. It had been feared that, in order to create more high-scoring games, the goals would be enlarged; that, to accommodate USA television advertising, single matches would be divided into four time-periods; and that matches would be played upon artificial turf rather than proper grass. But none of this happened. Indeed, scepticism among some was tempered by an eager anticipation of the effect of some brave innovations by FIFA. A subtle amendment to the offside law was intended to favour attacking play. Stricter interpretation of foul and violent play would promote creativity. A new line on how to deal with injured players and the award of three points to teams for first-round wins were further measures planned to boost the image of soccer in the USA. It was plugged as a free-flowing, creative game with little of the overt aggression characteristic of other top-level professional team sports.

The World Cup had a bigger media impact in the USA than many pessimists had anticipated. It was hailed as the surprise sports story of the year, with television ratings 20 per cent to 30 per cent higher than many expected. Live games on the ESPN cable channel attracted viewing figures equal to the rating for prime-time Wednesday Major League Baseball games, and the final attracted nearly nine million viewers on ABC and another 1.5 million on a cable Spanish-language network. Press coverage also exceeded expectation.

Young people were the primary marketing target. Membership of the United States Youth Soccer Association increased by 9 per cent to 2.1 million. The American Youth Soccer Association's membership went up 14 per cent to half a million. The US soccer federation had 16 million registered players, more than any other FIFA member, and most of them were children.

The professional game may have continued to face difficulties in attracting investors, finding adequate stadiums and setting up local franchises immediately after the USA '94 adventure, but where soccer did thrive was where it had thrived before – in the schools, among particular ethnic communities and among women. This is where the sponsorship had already been targeted. The banana company Chiquita Brands International sponsored the Chiquita Cup, Fair Play, Clinics and Soccer Challenges, grass-roots programmes for youth soccer. Chiquita was also an Olympic soccer and US soccer sponsor, and its World Cup marketing drive confirmed soccer's specific market – children aged 15 to 16, women of 25 to 34, and adults of 55 and above. Soccer sponsors associated the game with a healthy, family image. Thriving Mexican leagues already played their matches in southern California, and Hispanic crowds flocked into the Los Angeles stadium to watch El Salvador take on Denmark. Healthy and athletic women, including world champions and potential gold medallists at the inaugural Olympic women's soccer tournament in Atlanta in 1996, embraced the game. More and more children played it. USA '94 reaffirmed the business community's focus upon these segments of the US sports market.

Staging the event well was a matter of civic pride for many and massive personal profit for a few. Direct comparisons with the Olympic Games can be seen here. At the 1984 Los Angeles Summer Olympics, tens of thousands of volunteers were recruited to help at the peak of global cold-war politics. The organisers refused to give the volunteers free lunches; the Los Angeles Organising Committee reported a surplus of $225 million.

At the World Cup Finals ten years on, the same form of exploitation fed in to the event's staggering profitability. No lunches for the idealistic enthusiasts, but the 94,194 spectators at the final in the Rosebowl, Pasadena, paid $43.5 million for their tickets – an average price of nearly $462 per ticket.

The organisers weren't short of a subsidised lunch or two. Scott Parks Le Tellier was featured in the British press in 1993, not just as the managing director and chief operating officer of USA '94, but also as a missionary (with a Mormon background), visionary and evangelist – for football. He became hooked on soccer whilst watching the World Cup in West Germany in 1974. Le Tellier and other key players in USA '94 were eager to make the most out of football's US market.

As an ambitious young attorney Le Tellier moved to LA to meet entrepreneurs on the appropriate sports and professional circuits. He played tennis with Mike O'Hara, head of the sports department in the organising committee of the Games, and soon got on to the committee and into the financial side himself. Speaking to journalist Ken Reich in the post-Olympics euphoria in early 1985, he told how he filled in for the boss, Alan Rothenberg, back at the LA Games. 'Alan was the original commissioner,' said Le Tellier, 'but he was so tied up doing other things and was never there, they figured that the job wasn't going to get done.'

After the successful Games bonuses were paid to employees, in three categories of $2,500, $1,500 and $700. Le Tellier moaned that these were so insulting as to leave a bad taste in the mouth.

A decade on, and working with Alan Rothenberg in a team that seemed to have survived the bitterness and tensions of the Olympic exertions, Le Tellier ensured that things tasted better. For his 50-hour working week in 1991 (for roles of secretary, managing director and chief operating officer), Le Tellier received annual 'compensation' of $174,000, with a further $148,697 for 'other allowances'. In 1992 he got $186,000 and $414,291 allowances, linked to a move to California (where he already was) from an address he'd been using in Virginia.

Three months on from the final game of USA '94, Alan Rothenberg received $7 million in compensation for serving as the World Cup organising committee's chairman and chief executive officer, from the event's preliminary projection of a $60 million surplus. The $7 million comprised a $3 million bonus and a $4 million 'deferred-compensation package for back-pay due', calculated at $800,000 a year, running from August of 1990 through to 1995. Prominent in defence of this decision was board member Peter V. Ueberroth, for whom Rothenberg had worked during the '84 LA Games. One board member was not so supportive, saying, 'I'm against paying a guy for a volunteer job.' Le Tellier, for the chief operating officer role, was voted a $500,000 bonus.

Rothenberg declined the offer of a $350,000 salary, but took the odd $30,000 in 'other allowances'. The state treasury was told that 'the Board of Directors has authorised the payment of salaried compensation to Mr Rothenberg. Mr Rothenberg has elected to defer the compensation pending a determination that a sufficient surplus exists from World Cup USA 1994 Inc. operations to satisfy all other obligations.'

Rothenberg himself has a clean conscience relating to the $7 million lump sum that came his way. 'This sounds terrible,' he said, 'but if you look at the whole eight years that I've been involved, I've been underpaid if you will. I took the job on a non-paying basis, I was offered a very generous salary. I told them that I wouldn't take a salary. When it was over with they could look at the results, and whatever you think is fair … and some very independent high-powered people decided that $7 million dollars was a fair payment.'

A sense of proportion is not one of Rothenberg's qualities. 'The reality is,' he went on, 'my law practice has suffered enormously, so I made a lot less money practising law than I would have otherwise. I'm not asking for people to feel sorry for me, but I saved the World Cup.'

Rothenberg had taken over responsibility for the World Cup organising committee soon after his election as USSF president, and assumed a central position in the tangled networks of the USA's soccer developments, with interests too in the proposed Major League Soccer (MLS) whilst still president of the US soccer federation. What bothers some people is that MLS, which is headed by Rothenberg, received a reported $500,000 from World Cup USA, whose chairman is Rothenberg, to pay for its business plan which it submitted to the USSF, of which Rothenberg is president. No one was very surprised when MLS beat two other bids to set up the national league and then was given $3.5 million by World Cup USA for start-up costs.

No one seemed very surprised either when the Major League Soccer initiative stalled after USA '94. For Rothenberg, it was not so much a football commitment as a coldly logical marketing decision as to how best to exploit the market. He believes that the NASL 'tried to do too much too fast, frankly'. So, with his $7 million cheque in his pocket, he felt little obligation to rush to put in place the new professional format for the game. MLS got up and running eventually, but with few signs that it would ever get close to the market share of other, big-time American sports.

For Rothenberg, soccer in the USA is still 'a sponsor's dream, a marketer's dream'. But launch such a dream, in its MLS version, at the right time for the maximum niche-market impact, when the family audience, solid white-collar, and the female third of all US players are ready. Rothenberg knows the market and told us that players, parents of players and coaches in the USA number more, proportionally, than the equivalent population of the UK. 'But socially, culturally, we have to be sure that our programmes fit within the American way,' he observed, with reference to grass-roots soccer and the cultivation of home-based talent.

For Rothenberg, the World Cup is as much about personal market worth as love of the game. Such financial transactions at the heart of the USA World Cup administration are fundamental to understanding the basis on which the tournament was held. Like the 1984 Olympics before it, the event was staged to celebrate the ways in which the US could meet a challenge and put on an efficient and spectacular global show. But it was also a goldrush for a thrusting and entrepreneurial professional élite. Veteran FIFA insiders have described Rothenberg as a brash LA law man, 'not a football man at all'.

USA '94 generated $4 billion, with a direct profit of over $20 million to the US organisers. But the real legacy of that World Cup was the model of mean, lean and immensely profitable event management. You don't have to like sport to do that. It helps if you do, but the driving force behind USA '94 was a combination of local pride, global posturing and personal and economic ambition.

USA '94 was, in Havelange's words, a source of 'great pride', boosting FIFA's 'reputation as a dynamic and progressive body alert to modern currents of thought and deed'. Havelange beat his chest, boasting of his all-round satisfaction at the event. 'FIFA can reflect upon universal acknowledgement of its exceptional success. It vindicated totally FIFA's decision to award the finals to a country whose tireless efforts to promote our sport have long earned our respect. The short-term objective – to stage a spectacular World Cup with thrilling football, full stadia, fair play and a peaceful atmosphere' – succeeded 'beyond question.'

Chairman of FIFA's organising committee, Guillermo Cañedo, joined the chorus of self-praise, writing in the official report on USA '94 that the event 'was organised to a degree of perfection befitting the prestige of the tournament itself'. This silenced those who had questioned the ability of America to cope with such cultural and logistical problems. Cañedo also praised the high standards of technology and organisation. Nowhere did the Mexican media baron refer to viewing figures or advertising revenues back home in Mexico. There was no mention either in the report of Rothenberg's bonus, described by Hank Hersch of *Sports Illustrated* as an 'unconscionable' level of personal remuneration for an individual purporting to work in a voluntary capacity for a supposedly non-profit organisation.

Three years after the World Cup, Rothenberg's management of World Cup USA 1994 Inc. was in the Californian courts. He was being sued by a former World Cup employee for breach of a contract. Rothenberg's own firm, Latham & Watkins, had handled the World Cup's legal matters, and in December 1996 a column in *Sports Illustrated* described him as 'a self-promoter and … smug', and called this hiring of his own law firm a 'blatant misuse of power'. Rothenberg was called upon to explain his multi-million-dollar compensation package, the use of Latham & Watkins as World Cup's legal counsel, the hiring of his 20-year-old son Bradford who was paid $107,321 for work on the World Cup, and a licensing contract between the organisation and his wife.

Rothenberg had been taken to court by a former employee, Michael Hogue, the director of the US team's World Cup training site in California in the run-up to USA '94, who accused him of a 'blatant misuse of power for personal profit'. Hogue had been brought onto a national committee by Rothenberg in 1990, to develop plans for a national outdoor league. Axed from the World Cup set-up in 1992, he sued for wrongful termination and breach of his employment contract, and, in lawyer-speak, intentional and negligent interference with prospective economic advantage. Hogue, who unsurprisingly had to eat his words, claimed that Rothenberg had prevented him from working in the soccer industry after his contract was terminated.

Hogue was chasing more than $1.5 million, and Rothenberg's side offered, then withdrew, $200,000 in settlement. 'The man has the morals of a bandit', Hogue told the *Los Angeles Times* in 1994, and stuck to his guns. In September 1997 the jury in a Los Angeles superior court deliberated for just one hour after a five-week trial, before 'denying recovery' to claimant Hogue, in a vote of 11 to 1.

Rothenberg was used to winning. He'd campaigned for only 17 days for the USSF presidency in 1990, but romped home with 343.9 votes against incumbent Werner Fricker's 169.66 votes. Stories still circulate of how workers used tweezers to drag back clippings of a newspaper article about Rothenberg that had been pushed under the hotel bedroom doors of hundreds of delegates. His firm, Latham & Watkins, did a great deal of complicated legal work for World Cup USA '94, to the tune of $2.7 million between November 1990 and December 1994. The company was used to such high-profile clients, acting back in 1984 as general counsel for that year's Olympics organised by Peter Ueberroth, who turned up to testify in support of Rothenberg during the trial case.

Rothenberg was a skilful manager of conflicting interests. Ronald Silverman, a former law partner, commented: 'You can't unnerve him, you can't scare him.' He'd controlled the MLS when it had won against two other bidders to the USSF for the commission to establish the national league – as we've said, when he was also boss of the USSF. 'Joining the US soccer federation was like joining the PTA,' he reminisced. The voluntarist spirit was soon quenched: 'Some of these people had to realise,' he explained, that 'there is a big difference between lining the field for a youth league game and running a potentially billion-dollar business.' Not enough of a difference for Rothenberg to change the USSF's status as a charity. USA '94 had more than 400 employees. Many, out of hearing, nicknamed the boss 'Rothenweiler'. The man does little to discourage such stories: 'I don't beat up people because I enjoy beating up people … but if I have to leave some strewn bodies in order to win, within the rules, that's the way you have to do it.'

After USA '94 the court controversies did little to hold Rothenberg back. Just before France '98 he bought his way into one of the three sides owned and operated by MLS. At the time that he became individual owner (though in his own words, 'investor operator') of the San José Clash, he was still president of the USSF. He formed a $20 million investment group to buy the Clash, bringing in the Japanese advertising giant Dentsu. His long pedigree in sports law and administration – in basketball from the 1960s to the 1980s, and owning the Aztecs in the North American Soccer League – served him well in this latest move to own a team in a league he himself had created and headed. Dana Gelin had branded him, in *Sports Illustrated*, a 'shameless self-promoter'. The LA jury recognised his behaviour as perfectly acceptable. 'I put right on the table … exactly what my interests are,' Rothenberg has said. 'I follow the ethical rules that each organisation has.' It helps, of course, if you are in charge of the organisation too.

Football administrators in the USA were still triumphant years after the event about the scale of the success. Sitting at his desk in the USSF's Chicago headquarters, the president Hank Steinbrecher spat bile as he commented on the sceptical climate with which he and others had to contend. 'It was considered a joke, and I heard all the criticisms for so long – the United States could never pull off a successful World Cup, they would never get fans into the stadiums, they never sold sponsorships, they would cut the game into quarters, they have no passion, they have no idea of what it is like to play. Oh, and by the way, their team sucks.' He gave a wry smile, paused and said, 'Well, guess what? All the European press had to eat crow.'

On the field of play, USA '94 was indeed a glorious spectacle. On final day the walk to the ground – the Pasadena Rosebowl – had a dreamlike quality: sunshine and heat, brightly coloured, jovial – not aggressive – crowds wandering by the sprinklers of the suburban neighbourhoods surrounding the stadium. Entrepreneurial adolescents – California's best – plied a lively trade in cold drinks on the sidewalks, a football-pitch length down from the security of their millionaire homesteads. Less-privileged street vendors offered t-shirts hats, flags, soccer balls as well as chilled sodas and beers. Touts looked happy enough, marking up tickets to $800 (£550). It was a far cry from our own memories of youth: the damp and stoic marches through mean streets to Goodison Park and Turf Moor, and the school caps which helped us con our way through the boys' turnstiles for one and sixpence.

The spectacle inside the Rosebowl didn't disappoint. The opening ceremony was lively and entertaining. We wondered what it would be like to be Pelé, who, just because he happened to be a good footballer, can hold hands and skip around the Rosebowl with Whitney Houston. And the Lords of the Rings themselves – Havelange, Samaranch, Nebiolo – were in the best seats in the house to witness this celebration of sport's love affair with consumer culture.

Maybe the match was dull, but who cared? Roberto Baggio ballooned his penalty over goalkeeper Tafarel's bar, giving the game to Brazil. Cue SFX. Francis Ford Coppola could not have created a more evocative scene than the exodus from the Rosebowl. Fireworks, rockets and Roman candles exploded into the afternoon sky. Helicopters buzzed up above, clouded by smoke. As Darryl Hall's World Cup anthem *Gloryland* boomed out, we looked skywards to see a trio of First World War vintage bi-planes fly across. Someone stood on a wing of the lead aircraft and waved to the crowd. 'There goes Baggio, making a break for it,' yelled one wag. 'No it's not – it's OJ,' laughed another.

OJ Simpson had once run fleet-footed around this very stadium, winning the Most Valuable Player award in the American Football Intercollegiate Championship game in 1968. He'd then won the coveted Heisman Trophy, and gone on to become one of the game's greatest stars. How the mighty can fall. It was a sobering counter to the throbbing and vital street culture of the Brazilian and Italian fans in Santa Monica and other LA bases, where carnivalesque rivalry was the order of the evening.

Forgettable game or not, the final was without doubt an *event*. It proved wrong the cynical and world-weary doomsday predictions of soccercentric non-Americans and soccerphobic Americans. And for some professionals it was the crowning glory of their careers. Guido Tognoni discounts the disappointing goalless scoreline of the final. 'It was a wonderful event and a full stadium,' he told us. 'I said to myself, "First of all ... I can never do more for an event than I did for USA '94." And maybe it may not be as beautiful again because we will never have, until we go to the US, ... the big stadium again.'

Hank Steinbrecher, hailing Havelange as 'the father of the rebirth of soccer in the United States', insisted that 'this giant is starting to stir' and made the outrageous boast that 'by the year 2010 the United States will host and win the World Cup.' The USSF/Organising Committee made 60 million dollars, and hundreds of millions for FIFA. 'Surely,' he concluded, 'they'll be back for more sooner rather than later.' FIFA's sorry finances, a decade or so on, might well need more of the same. And a spot in the last eight at Japan-Korea 2002 for the US national side did no harm to the vision underlying Steinbrecher's prophecy.

World Cup '94 reminded sports entrepreneurs of the cultural variety and vitality, global profile and commercial potential of football. Doug Logan, a former promoter of Pink Floyd, the Rolling Stones and Madonna concerts, developed a logo for Major League Soccer which celebrates not just the kick (at the expense of the handling skills so essential to mainstream USA sports), but a 'Pan Americanism not Americanism', with the dominant blue and green of the logo symbolising the sky and the pitch of a global game that, finally, some powerful Americans want a piece of.

As *Gloryland* played over the PA in the Pasadena Rosebowl, it wasn't only football fans who were basking in the sunshine. So too were the Mr Fixits of FIFA and self-confessed 'brash American' soccer entrepreneurs and popular-cultural promoters. They were already counting the benefits of returning to the cradle of consumerism for another World Cup bonanza. Some of the entrepreneurial big boys of the summer of '94 would be prominent in the Machiavellian politics of FIFA throughout the last decade of the century. Rothenberg was one of them. He had come a long way since commissioning Olympic football in '84. It had been one hell of a profitable ride – and the wagon was still rolling.

7

THE BIG BOSS

Eastern horizons

Only the Havelange aura – and that of Saudi's Prince Faisal when he bothered to turn up to a FIFA event – rivalled the presence of the immaculately groomed Dr Mong Joon Chung. Jet-black hair, tall, lean and trim for his early middle age, you knew when Chung was around. His minders surrounded him as he swept through the palm trees of the Sheraton lobby in Abu Dhabi.

You didn't talk to Chung unannounced over a coffee. First, you were grilled over lunch by his factotum, who'd been with him throughout his adult life – even to Johns Hopkins University in Baltimore, where Chung's dissertation in physics won him his doctorate. Patient negotiation was needed to get access to Chung, and even then we were bounced out of his Sheraton suite as soon as the discussion moved from FIFA history to shadier aspects of South Korea's World Cup bid, and to evaluations of Havelange's impact.

One European-based FIFA-watcher close to the strong man of Korean football knew the real stakes. For Chung the Korean FA was an apprenticeship for bigger things. The Big Boss usually had a few matters on his mind – like heading up Hyundai heavy industries, sitting in the national parliament or profiling Korea in Asian and world football politics.

Chung was used to getting what he wanted. One veteran observer of the Asian political scene, Agence-France-Presse man Erskine McCullough, told us that if Korea had lost in the race for the 2002 World Cup Finals, 'the Japanese Embassy would have gone up in flames'. And World Cup Korea-Japan 2002 was a hard fought title. To Korea the most important thing was to have their name before Japan's, 'for historical, mainly political reasons', McCullough mused.

A little over six months before the FIFA executive committee was to make its decision on who would host the 2002 World Cup, the Koreans and Japanese were lobbying for support in South Africa. For years the Japanese had felt that the decision was in the bag. A self-assured confidence brimmed over at their big reception at the Sandton Sun, Johannesburg, on the tail end of the African Cup of Nations in January 1996. Sir Bobby Charlton was on display, plugging the bid. Jim Trecker, PR at USA '94 and US football fixer, lauded the Japanese bid and the qualities of the nation's people. A video relayed football stars saying that if the Japanese did something, they would do it well. The Japanese treated their audience to a hi-tech vision of the virtual football spectacle – it looked as though terraces might be a thing of the past as the country which had done most to accelerate a world media revolution turned its attention to football. How could their bid fail? Hadn't Havelange favoured the Japanese all along? Wasn't the South Korean bid – as we all *really* knew – paper thin? Maybe.

The Japanese were to pay a high price for their smugness when the politically-led bid of the South Koreans got stronger as the race went on. The in-house politics of the FIFA family hierarchy were inscrutable to the Japanese, but not to Chung. He was quick to spot a rare moment of vulnerability in Havelange, in the Big Man's contest with Europe's Lennart Johansson. Using all of the resources at his disposal he struck to catapult Korea into the driving seat.

FIFA vice-president David Will had experienced the race between Morocco and France for the prize of staging the 1998 Finals. 'That was bad enough, the pressures of that were terrible', he told us. But this was nothing next to the run-in to summer 1996, when FIFA was due to select the host for the 2002 Finals. The fight for the privilege of hosting the first World Cup of the new millennium, and the first to be staged outside Europe and the Americas, was still more intense.

As Japan and Korea moved towards the decision date, the competitors followed the French example of a last-ditch assault on the motivations and appetites of key FIFA personnel. 'This was so dramatic, this one. This was just unbelievable,' said Will, flinging his arms into the air. It was ridiculous. I said to Japan and Korea, "I'm not coming to any more receptions, I am not accepting any more gifts." The stuff was arriving at the door, and of course, what do you do? The postman delivers it. It's just ridiculous. The only thing that was missing was the cash in a plain brown envelope. You know, it was unbelievable.' We imagined the postman's daily struggles up the gravel driveway, burdened with TVs, hi-fis, PCs, movie cameras, ornamental vases and decorative kimonos. Enough is too much for the puritan Scot. 'I am not accepting invitations to Japan or Korea,' he said, reclaiming some of the moral high ground. 'This is not out of discourtesy, I am stopping. And I know that most of the Europeans did the same. They just stopped.'

But what had happened before they stopped? And if, by implication, only the Europeans stopped, what did the others continue to accept from the rival bidders? The UEFA president Lennart Johansson was one of those Europeans. He admits that members of FIFA's executive committee were propositioned by nations seeking to host the 2002 World Cup. 'Yes, there were no limits,' he said, 'a bottle of whisky, a camera or a computer, everything was permissible.' Johansson added that he had returned a computer.

Another FIFA executive committee member, Dr Michel D'Hooghe, of Belgium, told us how hotel rooms were garlanded with flowers. More sinister, a lobbyist from one of the bidding countries appeared in the seat next to him on a flight from Brussels to Prague. This fellow passenger didn't stay silent. He talked to D'Hooghe throughout the flight. 'Could this be a coincidence?' the Belgian asked, in a fashion that needed no answer. We responded with a noncommittal shrug. As we left his office we couldn't help noticing the centrepiece of his desk – a magnificent circular green pot, inscribed by Dr Chung, offering his best wishes to D'Hooghe's association.

It's hard to do the arithmetic accurately – we've put the questions to the Koreans and the Japanese, but the face-to-face ones are politely and coldly deflected and the e-mails not answered. Estimates claim that $100 million was spent by Korea and Japan in their campaigns. The escalation and the outcome of the bidding war became enmeshed in internal FIFA politics. They expressed the deep-rooted and simmering tensions between FIFA and the European federation, and the positioning and implicit campaigning of potential successors to Havelange.

In his inimitable style, Havelange had led the Japanese to believe that the World Cup finals were within his individual gift. An Asian venue was very much in his thinking as early as 1986, when he gave an interview to the Swiss magazine *Sport*. There, he spoke in favour of rotation of the finals in Europe and America up until 1994, and 'expressed the wish' that the 2002 event should be given to China. In the autumn of 1987 Havelange travelled to Beijing for further preliminary discussions with China's sports leaders. His encouragement of a Chinese bid was also linked to his IOC manoeuvres. At the time, he believed that a Chinese bid would be awarded the Summer Olympic Games for the year 2000: 'Anyone who can organise Olympic Games is no doubt capable of hosting the Finals of Soccer's World Cup,' he announced disingenuously. World Cups are, as he well knew, more demanding – lasting up to five weeks, 32 teams, requiring nationwide venues.

Meanwhile, as the Chinese dwelt upon Havelange's overtures, Japan and South Korea expressed their interest in developing bids at a meeting of the Asian confederation. FIFA's general secretary Sepp Blatter had visited South Korea's soccer facilities earlier in the year and the aggressive and uncompromising tone of the South Korean campaign was set from the start. A summer Olympics the following year in Seoul was presented by the Koreans as a perfect illustration of the nation's ability to stage such events and the Korean press mobilised against the other potential bidders. China's low standard of living would bar it from meeting FIFA's financial criteria, they argued, and Japan's main sport, baseball, would obstruct any plans to stage a World Cup event there during the baseball season.

The successful Seoul Olympics and a concentration by the Chinese upon their bid for the 2000 Games boosted Korean confidence in the race for the 2002 World Cup. By the summer of 1990 Havelange could tell the Xinhua press agency that as well as Korea, additional candidates for the finals were Japan, Saudi Arabia, China and Malaysia. Asian football standards were improving, he stated, and would be close to those of Europe and South America by 2000. An Asian venue was therefore ideal for 2002. This was the classic Havelange and Samaranch tactic, talking up the candidate to stoke the fires of rivalry.

During the World Under-17 Championships staged in Japan in 1993, Havelange consistently gave the impression to the Japanese that they were the firm favourites, his personal choice. Reservations remained over the lack of English-speaking expertise in Japan and the rising costs of accommodation and transport, but the country was the clear front-runner.

The complacent Japanese trusted that the Big Man could deliver, but cracks were appearing in the walls of his fiefdom. FIFA's own committee practices were being transformed, with more committee members – clustering around Johansson – willing to openly challenge Havelange. The accession of Chung to the Asian confederation's vice-presidential place on FIFA's executive committee added another dissenting voice. Unlike so many other members, the Big Boss was prepared to take on the Big Man.

Chung's route to the vice-presidency was trouble free and he had few rivals. Former businessman Tadao Murata was a more genuine football man, but had far too low a profile to stop the Chung offensive. He had worked in the big conglomerates of Tokyo and London and he knew the score in Asian football politics, being a pioneer in the development of the game in Japan. But he was a generation older and shorter in stature, with a less striking presence than his Korean rival. People liked Dr Murata and he is a nice person; up against Chung, though, he was destined to finish last. Two others contested the election for the seat on the FIFA committee. Kuwait's Sheikh Ahmad Fahad knew a bit about tough battles – his father had been murdered by invading Iraqi troops in the Gulf War. Also in the fray from the Gulf was Mohamed Bin Hammam, of Qatar. Hammam polled a promising vote but Chung pipped the Kuwaiti Sheikh by 11 votes to ten. Murata got just two and was for a time removed from office back in Japan's World Cup bidding organisation. The Japanese were outplayed in this critical contest for the Asian vote and it would cost them dear.

Chung's election on to the FIFA committee raised immeasurably the Korean profile. He had lobbied and campaigned hard, promising much and ensuring the presence of crucial South Asian delegates at the Asian confederation's election. Insiders in the Asian federation relate how he funded voters on epic cross-desert journeys.

So Chung became one of Asia's representatives at the heart of FIFA. He now had the base from which to raise the stakes in the race for 2002. After the 1994 World Cup, Chung announced that he would receive Havelange in Korea to show the facilities and constantly took the opportunity to promote his country's bid. In a statement of exceptional cheek, he even urged FIFA to act 'to prevent an escalation in the "unnecessary war of attrition" between Japan and Korea'.

Chung showed that he meant business. Groomed for power and victory, the Korean heir to the Hyundai giant was not used to losing. In all of FIFA's circles, he carries himself with the *hauteur* of the born élite. He always kept a respectful distance from Havelange, but occupies his own space, exuding confidence and power.

Chung has been born to win, bred for victory. His father, Chung Ju-yung, head of Hyundai, was the real leader of the successful Olympic bid, and five years after the Seoul Olympics he tried to become president of the country. Chung junior was coming into the FIFA boardroom with an agenda of his own which stretched well beyond FIFA's fixture list.

FIFA and its decisions were being swayed by new influences and alliances. In 1994, Asia's confederation secretary Peter Velappan elicited a commitment from Havelange that FIFA would, after its Chicago Congress of the forthcoming summer, give serious consideration to the principle of awarding the finals to two countries. Havelange agreed to form a study commission for this, but proposed no change to the established rules. Velappan saw co-hosting as a solution to the fierceness of the Japan-Korea rivalry, for neither would be prepared to lose. He also believed that co-hosting would boost the Asian presence in the World Cup, with two host-nations automatically qualifying for the finals. As it turned out, Asia was initially given more or less the same allocation for 2002 as for 1998, four places including the two hosts. At France '98 Asia had three places, plus a fourth secured in a play-off with the Oceania champions.

Tunisia, Egypt, Mali and Somalia also presented a motion to the Chicago Congress proposing that the World Cup finals be rotated around the confederations. FIFA general secretary Blatter told the CONCACAF Congress in New York that such a plan would fail, as very few countries in the world possessed the required infrastructure, technology and economic basis to stage a 32-team tournament.

Regardless of the scepticism of the FIFA secretariat, such proposals coming from the confederations (including Europe's discussion documents on the future of FIFA) were opening up debate in committees in a way that the dictatorial presidential style of Havelange could no longer stem. However confident the Japanese were in the bidding process, their reliance upon the patronage of Havelange, and upon their interpretation of and trust in the strength of his word, was to prove misplaced. The Japan bid kept to its strategy, backing activities such as courses in Africa. But the Africans were siding with the Europeans, Chung and Charlie Dempsey of Oceania. With no presence inside the central FIFA committee, the Japanese bid lost ground.

With FIFA committees open to new influences, the outcome of the bidding process for Asia's first Word Cup became unpredictable. By the end of 1994 Havelange sought to stand back, cancelling trips to the Asian Games in Hiroshima and the planned trip to Korea.

Chung, as president of the national football association, organised the Korean bidding committee, of which he was vice-chairman. His emergence as an effective voice within FIFA's major committee gave the Korean bid a priceless boost. He was hardly the faceless bureaucrat, as chief-in-waiting of one of the country's heavy-weight *chaebol*. His bidding committee was full of important figures. In the chair was Lee Hong Koo, then the deputy prime minister and the head of the New Korea Party, who doubled as head of the government's unification committee. Men from the foreign ministry joined the team. Korean embassy staff were brought in. The Koreans placed an agent – called a bidding committee secretary – in their embassy in the country of residence of each member of the FIFA executive committee. Business muscle filled other posts. One of these went on to become chairman of the bidding committee, Koo Pyong-hwoi, chair of the Lucky Goldstar *chaebol*, who was also president of Korea's Board of Trade.

The competition for the 2002 finals turned into a merry-go-round of presentations, press conferences, receptions and hospitality events. Men with votes received mailings, deliveries and invitations. Confederation national championships and congresses were the platform for these, as football administrators and sports media personnel were invited to hear yet again the forceful rhetoric and hyperbole of the contestants.

Everyone wanted to get in on the act. At a meeting of the African Confederation executive during the African Cup of Nations in Johannesburg in 1996, some committee members clearly thought that Japanese *largesse* would get them to another 'Japan-related event coming up in Yaoundé'. A minute dashed such expectations, recording that 'trips there would not be free, and it is clear that the occasion was not linked to Japan's bid for 2002 World Cup'.

Sir Bobby Charlton, with business interests in Africa and franchises such as the World Cup Japan/Bobby Charlton International football shirt, backed the Japanese bid. It was, he sincerely believed, in the best interests of the World Cup. We met up with him in Johannesburg. It had been hot work. We were pleased to get him a cool beer when we talked things over with him afterwards. Charlton was genuinely impressed with what the Japanese had to offer. Their big push in Africa had also been a nice little earner for him and his company. Most importantly, he was learning valuable lessons which he would bring to England's bid to host World Cup 2006. A key lesson which he hadn't learned when we spoke with him (but which he'll have digested by now) is that you should never trust a FIFA president.

The build-up to the May 1996 decision was an intense process of lobbying and promotion. The stakes were higher than any intrinsic to the football world itself. As well as criticising from the start the rival bids, Chung and his compatriots discussed the Korean bid in terms of wider political projects, not just football. When in April 1996 North Korean troops entered the buffer zone separating the two Koreas, so violating the truce that ended the 1950–53 Korean War, General Song Young-Shik, the secretary-general of the South Korean Bidding Committee, argued that such a situation reinforced Korea's case to be given the World Cup finals. 'Hosting the World Cup can play a role in facilitating the reunification process', the General said, proposing football as a means to the peaceful resolution of one of the world's most long-standing conflicts. (Such statements also undercut the Japanese by seeming to remove one of Havelange's objections to the bid. The self-styled ambassador for peace seemed to have erected a huge barrier against the Korean case by saying that the reunification of the two Koreas should be a prerequisite for any successful Korean bid.) With the reunification issue on the agenda, the Korean bid steamrollered ahead. 'I could not find any weak point in this bid,' said Horst Schmidt, secretary-general of the German FA, head of FIFA's delegation to Korea in late

1996. This stunned the Japanese, so confident in their bullet-trains, state-of-the-art stadiums, swish hotels and media know-how.

In his visionary style, General Young-Shik Song emphasised the quality and cheapness of Korea's hotels and transport, praised the country's football heritage, and pledged to gift US$230 million to FIFA's national associations – over a million dollars per country, all the projected World Cup profits. A former British diplomat in Seoul described the Korean bid and claims as 'absolute nonsense – there's nothing there outside Seoul and Pusan'.

Things became rather like a school playground stand-off – my bid's better than yours, my ground's bigger than your ground. Rather late in the day the Japanese realised the weight a politician could add, and hauled in the prime minister to endorse the bid. African aid was still on the Japanese agenda – a youth-coaching course here, a bit from Sir Bobby there, how about a medical seminar or two?

The Koreans, meanwhile, played the peace card to saturation point. They framed the bid as 'a priceless opportunity to again make a major contribution to global peace and harmony, promoting unity among all people, including those of our divided nation'. They claimed they could unite the world through football. The rhetoric rose to a crescendo in projecting the finals as 'a catalyst for peace', and linking 'the beautiful game and reconciliation'. FIFA rhetoric was mixed in with Korean ideology. Friendship and peace through football was a sacred FIFA principle. A united Korea was a South Korean – and US – imperative. This was more than just football: 'If the first World Cup of the twenty-first century could help erase the last vestige of the Cold War of the twentieth century, the tournament would be more than a milestone for football: it would be a milestone for mankind.'

So there we have it – up there with the space race. Chung had bigger goals in mind than World Cup matches. It was even rumoured that Korean industrial heavy-weights had pressurised the European Commission to lean on UEFA to promote the Korean bid. And in early 1999, on CNN, Chung went on record with his ulti-mate goal – the presidency of the reunited Korean peninsula. As a stepping-stone to this, he also announced his willingness to challenge for the FIFA presidency in 2002. 'I have many friends on the FIFA executive committee', said Chung.

The bidding process became caught up in the battles for power within FIFA, especially the emerging challenge of Johansson to Havelange. Tadao Murata, back on board after his sentence of shame, confirmed this, describing bitterly the way in which the Japanese had been caught in the 'crossfire between the FIFA and the UEFA presidents'.

As the day of decision drew closer, it became clear that Korea, with the European members' support, could beat Japan in a head-to-head challenge. The Japanese wouldn't budge right through to the eve of the decisive FIFA meeting – after all, a deal is a deal with the Big Man. In the two days before that meeting, FIFA wrote to the Japanese, asking them to consider the possibility of co-hosting. Former prime ministers of South Korea and Japan, Lee Hong Koo and Miyazawa Kiichi, met as unofficial delegates of their respective governments to seek a diplomatic solution.

The co-hosting option had been strongly promoted by the Europeans on the committee, but Havelange remained totally and utterly opposed to the prospect. 'Forty-eight hours before the vote he was saying "over my dead body"', David Will told us. The Big Man, faced with what would have been a humiliating defeat for himself and for the Japanese bid, was at the last minute persuaded to support the co-hosting option.

Samaranch of the IOC was one source of advice, convincing Havelange to give way and so avoid a divisive vote. With a sigh of relief that echoed around the grand avenues down from their headquarters and around the shores of Lake Zurich, at the end of May 1996 the FIFA committee accepted what now became Havelange's proposal for co-hosting. No vote had been needed. No faction was publicly humiliated. Public self-evisceration would not be required.

Japan and Korea were unlikely bed fellows. Early in the bidding war Chung had argued that Japan's belligerent past rendered it unsuited to the role of World Cup host. For hundreds of years the two countries had been enemies. Japan had ruled the Korean peninsula between 1910 and 1945, subjecting the Korean people to dreadful abuse, including having Korean women enslaved into prostitution for soldiers of Japan's Imperial Army. Chung had called this occupation 'the most barbarous in the history of humanity'. The Japanese embassy in Seoul had even warned its nationals to prepare for the worst should Japan win the hosting honour. Hardly a good foundation for setting up a partnership to run the World Cup.

The decision meant that Chung's political ambitions were enhanced – and his company's prospects were looking good too. Close to US$1.5 billion was lined up to be invested in South Korea, in stadiums, communications, transport and accommodation. It was the country's leading corporations, such as the so-called 'World Cup trio' of Hyundai, Sam Whan Camus and Hotel Shilla, which would benefit from this World Cup windfall. The Big Boss was into big bucks.

Korea would stage the opening ceremony and the opening match, while Japan could have the final. Cunningly, Chung, using the French and Spanish spellings of his country's name, manoeuvred 'Corée' into the first billing in the name, as well as the opening credit of the tournament itself.

In France '98, meanwhile, the receptions and the promos continued. To function-weary FIFA folk, and footsore hacks and researchers, getting to the Korea–Japan reception at Le Meridien Hotel in Montparnasse in that dead time between the semi-finals and the final didn't sound like too much fun. It was a crowded schedule too, with the British Embassy – former palace of Empress Josephine, just down from FIFA's base at Le Bristol – in the diary for later in the day. The embassy was putting on a bit of hospitality for the England 2006 bid.

Dr Chung was waiting to greet us all. His niece, elegantly attired in Western dress, was also there. Talking to her later, we discovered that she lived in London, studied at the Royal College of Art and specialised in gold smelting. What could we say? What prescience, though, for the niece of a *chaebol* top man to be getting this skill on the eve of a meltdown of the Asian economy.

Between the refills and the football gossip, the reluctant partners distributed a
glossy brochure presenting their progress. It's a book that can never be back-to-front
or upside-down, for held one way it's the right way round for Korea, and held the
other way, it's correct for Japan. Equal partnership here means no concession given,
no honour lost on either side.

The brochure presents Korea's ten venues. Outside Seoul, it's a voyage of discov-
ery for the football world. Get on to your local travel agent now to beat the rush.
Get in there with the bigwigs of world football for a match or two at Sogwipo on
the small island of Cheju, off the south-western tip of the Korean peninsula. It's
blessed with the nickname 'sculpture of the gods', and boasts 'fields of blooming
rapee flowers' every spring. But there's no mention of airports or stadiums. Make
sure you check before you set off.

Japan's list of venues didn't include Tokyo or Kyoto or Hiroshima, but the short
commutes from the heart of Tokyo, to Saitama and Yokohama, would nevertheless
be popular spots for the FIFA folk. Oita is another site that would no doubt appeal
to some of the FIFA chaps. It's on the island of Kyushu, between Japan and Korea,
and proudly promotes smiling, naked females occupying the locale's 'famous hot
springs' with their 'highly curative effects'. Site supervisors among the FIFA club
would be rushing for that assignment.

Football has forced through some initiatives that may have taken a lot longer
without the co-hosting. Korea's President Kim Young Sam and Japan's Prime
Minister Hashimoto met within months of the co-hosting decision at so-called
soccer summits. Heads of state normally attend the opening ceremony of the finals,
so negotiations got under way promptly to prepare for the first-ever visit of the
Japanese emperor to South Korea. The simmering hostilities of a recent past could
not disappear overnight. A few games of football would not be enough to make the
Koreans forgive the Japanese for their brutality during the occupation of the peninsula. But the symbolic impact would certainly be great. Neither nation could face
the prospect of losing face in front of the global gaze of the football world.

When the Korean head of state opened the 2002 Finals in Seoul, Chung was in
the picture. As the charmed and charming Korean side raced through to the semi-
finals of the tournament, Chung's power base and personal status looked stronger by
the match. He'd brought in the Dutch coach Gus Hiddink and given him whatever
he wanted, suspended the Korean football season so that the squad could live and
work together, seen through the construction programmes – and taken a Korean
side (that had never won a single match in several previous appearances at the finals)
further than anyone could have dreamed. Chung's own company had been the only
vehicle manufacturer among the 15 World Cup sponsors. It would be churlish to
ask whether the match officials, and one of the assistant officials in particular, in the
Korea-Spain game in which a classy Spanish goal was overruled, drove home in the
comfort of new Hyundais. The Big Boss had done the business.

Chung had not backed winners on every front. He'd not managed to topple
Blatter from the FIFA presidency, but he'd taken Korean national pride and football further than anyone had dared imagine. And next to that the squabbles and

feuds in the FIFA family would be chickenfeed. This could be just a stepping-stone. Getting that one stage further than his father managed, Dr Mong Joon Chung could become the Biggest Boss of them all, helped by his football profile into the presidency of a reunited Korea, in no small part groomed and hardened by his time at the potentially earth-shaking epicentre of global football politics.

8

A RUMBLE IN THE JUNGLE

Johansson and the scramble for Africa

When Nelson Mandela walked out of Cape Town's Pollsmoor Prison in February 1990, his long march to freedom took him to a hero's welcome at Soccer City, a sprawling, modern football stadium on the outskirts of Soweto. Mandela's release heralded seismic changes in South Africa, culminating in the dismemberment of apartheid and the victory, four years later, of the ANC in the country's first democratic elections.

It was apt that Mandela should be fêted in a football ground. Sport was an important weapon in the war against apartheid. Football is the black people's game not just in South Africa but throughout the continent. During times when mass gatherings of non-whites were either banned or heavily policed, South Africa's football grounds were one of the few places where blacks, coloureds and Indians could come together to celebrate common causes.

Six years after his release, in January 1996, Mandela returned to Soccer City, to open the finals of the African Cup of Nations. As a jumbo jet from South African Airways roared low over the open-topped stadium, an adoring crowd gave the new South African president a rapturous welcome. Seated alongside Mandela, surveying the opening ceremonies, were FIFA's President, João Havelange, and the man who wanted his throne, Lennart Johansson, the head of the European football federation, UEFA. The champion and his challenger both knew that with 51 vote-holding member nations, Africa would be the key to winning or losing the 1998 presidential election.

It had taken UEFA a long time to recover from Sir Stanley Rous's demise and Havelange's ascendancy, and the Europeans had been little more than spectators as the Brazilian grew increasingly powerful and dictatorial. They watched as he filled FIFA's most important committees with friends and yes-men. During a period when football in Europe was getting bigger and wealthier, UEFA's top brass were forced to stand aside as more and more of their wealth was siphoned off to the third world, FIFA and who knows where else.

After suffering this for more than 20 years, in 1994 the Europeans finally decided to fight back. In the New York Executive Committee meeting following the USA World Cup, Havelange pushed them into the ring. At the very end of the meeting he handed out photocopies of a document which listed FIFA's restructured committees and their new members. Then he closed the meeting. There was no debate, no discussion, no explanation. For the Europeans, who had again lost out in the reshuffle, this was one decree too many.

Europe's biggest problem was in finding a challenger who was smart and ruthless enough to go head-to-head with the influential and scheming Brazilian. He also had to be trustworthy. Sepp Blatter, FIFA's general secretary, who had offered himself to the Europeans, was not considered. Blatter is clever and ruthless enough, but having worked hand-in-hand with Havelange for so many years, he was not to be chosen for this particular purpose.

UEFA's chosen candidate was their burly Swedish president, Lennart Johansson. Like Havelange, Johansson made his fortune running a transport business. Unlike the Brazilian he comes from humble stock, the son of a carpenter and one of six children. He was president of the Swedish club, AIK Gothenburg before running the national federation and becoming UEFA president. 'I know the smells of the dressing-room,' he says, stressing his grass-roots credentials.

Sweden takes pride in its contribution to world diplomacy and global democracy and Johansson cast himself in this mould. He claimed not to be interested in the power and riches which come with the FIFA presidency. He wanted the job so he could reform FIFA. 'My FIFA would be an international democratic network based on trust, transparency, loyalty and solidarity,' promised Johansson.

Physically, Johansson is a big man, but he lacks the charismatic authority of Havelange. His barrel-chested upper body balances precariously on his spindly legs and, like a bloodhound, his sad face has too much flesh for his skull. When he tells you that he would rather be sitting fishing on a frozen river bank than running for world football's top job, you believe him. However, for the good of the game he stepped into the ring and, like Ali versus Forman 20 years earlier, the main rounds of this heavyweight contest were fought in Africa.

Oroc Oyo compared this situation to the period leading up to the 1974 elections: 'Africa is now like the bride whose hand everyone is seeking.' The former Nigerian FA chief had been at the 1996 African confederation's congress and had watched Havelange and Johansson at the hustings. 'Each of them at every turn of the road was trying to make his case for the presidency. In every speech I was reading campaign strategies.'

Havelange dropped out of the race before the end of 1996, but before he withdrew his candidature, in a repetition of his 1974 campaign, he tirelessly travelled the continent drumming up support for his re-election. His main strength was that he had delivered on his pre-1974 promises to develop the game in Africa. Under his presidency, African representation at the World Cup Finals grew from one in 1974 to five in the event in France in 1998. Many African football leaders saw Havelange as a champion of their cause.

Although by 1996, many Africans believed that he had reached an age when he should retire gracefully, if he had stood, according to Emmanuel Maradas, the voice of African football, they may have voted for him out of a sense of duty or 'out of sentimentality – Africans are sentimental people, loyal to people who are perceived to have helped them'. Unfortunately, this is a trait that Havelange and many other individuals and groups are only too willing to exploit.

Never a man to leave anything to chance, the Brazilian tried to boost his popularity in the continent by suggesting that an African nation should host the World Cup finals in 2006. Once more he played a South African card, but this was different to the ace he held in 1974. Then his platform had been the continued isolation of that country. Now he was welcoming South Africa back into the football family. 'I have no doubt in my mind,' said Havelange in his speech opening the 1996 African Cup of Nations, 'that with her resources, facilities and expertise, South Africa could stage the 2006 World Cup Finals.'

UEFA officials had already declared an intention to support a European bid for the 2006 event. Havelange's intervention on behalf of Africa infuriated them. They viewed his comments in Johannesburg as shameless vote-catching and as part of his attempt to split the growing alliance between UEFA and the Africans.

Havelange's backing for a South African World Cup pleased Nelson Mandela, but the Brazilian's cosying up to Nigeria in the months leading up to the tournament dismayed the South African president and infuriated many others throughout the continent. A love of football is one of the few things which unites Nigerians, and successive governments have shrewdly exploited the people's passion for the game. In 1995 Nigeria had been scheduled to host the Under-20 World Cup finals. This was interpreted as a conciliatory gesture by FIFA to the Africans who were angered by the world body's decision to favour the USA over Morocco as the hosts for the 1994 World Cup finals. It was also planned to ease the re-entry of the Nigerians into world football after the December 1990 ruling which banned them from all competitions for two years after being found guilty of fielding over-age players in international youth competitions. To the bewilderment and anger of the Africans, at the eleventh hour FIFA rescinded Nigeria's status as hosts and switched the Under-20 tournament to Qatar. Officials argued that there were too many health risks in this part of West Africa and that European teams in particular had been unable to obtain health insurance for their travelling teams. Many observers believed that the decision had more to do with world football politics than health. Dr Halim of Sudan called the decision 'one of Havelange's nasty tricks. He had already promised it for Qatar – I don't know why', hinting that Havelange had done a deal with the oil-rich Arabs at Africa's expense. Whatever the truth of the matter, because publicly the campaign to take the competition away from Nigeria had been led by the Europeans, Havelange saw an opportunity to exploit the situation and improve his standing in Africa at Johansson's expense.

In November 1995 he visited Lagos and met with the leader of the military dictatorship, General Abacha, who fêted him like a revered foreign head of state. In return, Havelange apologised for the 1995 withdrawal and pledged to hold the 1997 Under-20s World Cup finals in Nigeria. There were three huge problems associated with this promise. In the first place the 1997 tournament was already scheduled to take place in Malaysia. Havelange's *volte face* infuriated the Malaysians and seriously damaged the ageing president's reputation throughout the Asian confederation. Secondly, decisions of this nature can only be taken by the full executive and Havelange's behaviour was intolerable. It was quickly seen as a potential propaganda coup for Johansson and his supporters, who were already campaigning on the grounds that Havelange was too dictatorial. The affair reached boiling point in Paris on the eve of the 1998 World Cup Draw. What should have been a routine debate took on the dimensions of a crisis, as three and a half hours of acrimonious discussion failed to resolve the issue. For the first time Africans and Asians were forced to greet each other coldly. Europe and South America once more found themselves on opposite sides of the table. The vote, when it was eventually taken, was split along straight regional lines: 11 in favour of Malaysia (eight European plus three Asian) against nine in favour of Nigeria (three each from Africa, North/Central America and the Caribbean, and South America). Havelange's *ex-officio* decision was overturned, but most importantly, for the first time he had lost control of his executive. The battle lines were drawn.

The third and biggest problem for Havelange was the appalling timing of his Nigerian visit. Just as he was busy helping to legitimise the corrupt Abacha régime in Lagos, the writer and poet Ken Saro Wiwa and eight other Ogoni dissidents were hanged at the general's behest. Saro Wiwa's crime was to have led a group of activists who were fighting for the rights of the Ogoni people in the face of what was perceived as the exploitation of their traditional tribal territory by Shell Oil. So long as the money poured in, in Abacha's eyes they could do what they liked with the Ogoni homeland.

Nelson Mandela led the international outrage at these executions. Until the hangings, the South African president played a major diplomatic role in trying to ease Nigeria back to democracy. Now he made an emphatic call for oil sanctions against Nigeria and urged Shell to suspend its $4 billion liquefied natural gas project in Nigeria as a mark of protest, warning, 'We are going to take action against them in this country because we can't allow people to think in terms of their gains when the very lives of human beings are involved.'

Mandela swiftly persuaded the South African Football Federation to withdraw Nigeria's invitation to take part in a four-nation tournament due to be held in South Africa in December 1995 as a prelude to the African Cup of Nations. Both the Netherlands and Israel refused to allow the Nigerian team to set up training camps. Only through Havelange threatening to call it off was France persuaded to allow Nigerian representatives to attend the World Cup draw in Paris on 12 December.

Abacha retaliated against Mandela and ordered Nigeria, the 1994 African champions, to withdraw from South Africa's 1996 African Cup of Nations. As a consequence of Nigeria's withdrawal, the African confederation suspended them for the following two African Cup of Nations and fined the federation a paltry £11,000. Unwittingly, by forbidding Nigeria's Super Eagles, the pre-tournament favourites and the team which would go on to become Olympic champions in 1996, to turn up, Abacha had really done Mandela a favour. In Nigeria's absence, with Cameroon in disarray and Ghana not playing to their usual standard in Johannesburg's high altitude, South Africa was able to win the tournament easily. What was made to appear by the international media as Mandela's and the new South Africa's pre-destination, was in fact determined by political forces off the field of play.

Shell Oil was a sponsor of the African Nations Cup. During the final between South Africa and Tunisia, a man in the crowd below the VIP box and Mandela held aloft a placard with a picture of Ken Saro Wiwa on one side and Abacha on the other under the slogan, 'Abacha and Shell go to Hell!' Meanwhile overhead, and also in full view of Mr Mandela, a light aircraft circled Soccer City in Soweto towing a banner proclaiming, 'Go Well, *Bafana Bafana* [Zulu nickname of the South African team], Go Shell'.

Whatever the impact of Sara Wiwa's execution on Shell Oil, Havelange's proximity to it seriously damaged his kudos throughout Africa. The Nigerian affair was another example of his failing judgement and contributed to his decision the following year not to stand for re-election.

With Havelange reeling, Johansson seemed to have a good chance of gaining support from across the African national associations. The Swede peddled his 'Visions' proposals around the members of the African confederation's executive. Visions suggested reducing the number of confederations from six to four and rotating both the presidency and the World Cup finals around the confederations. Johansson's manifesto stated that he would be happy to see the Africans hosting the World Cup finals in the foreseeable future, with an African at the helm of FIFA.

Johansson made overtures to the president of the African confederation, the Cameroonian Issa Hayatou, a man with a growing reputation as a major player in FIFA politics. If Hayatou were to back the Swede's candidature for 1998 (and so deliver Africa), Johansson would step down in 2002, making way for Hayatou's bid for the presidency.

These initiatives were the sub-text to the Meridian Convention, launched in 1994 to foster greater co-operation among footballers and football administrators in Europe and Africa. A treaty was signed in 1997 whereby 'as equal partners, UEFA and CAF hereby decide to undertake extensive co-operation in areas of football, based on the principles of friendship and mutual respect, and with the aim of promoting the development of football on both continents'. This meant Africa's best players would continue to play in Europe while millions of the Europeans' Champions League-generated dollars would flow back (at least in theory) to Africa and through to member associations.

A key proposal, which was introduced by Johansson and Europe, was to give each African team participating in World Cup qualification one million Swiss francs – potentially, a cool 50 million plus. Visions, rotation, restructuring, development were all vague abstractions, but a million in readies is a concept easily understood in Africa. It's also easily misappropriated. As one African soccer expert said, 'Hopefully, the new money for development promised by UEFA will make the national associations stronger and more autonomous, but there is an equal chance that this initiative will only lead to more corruption.'

Critics of both Johansson and Hayatou have argued that the Meridian deal was nothing short of a bribe. But it was nevertheless too transparent and accountable for the money to end up in the back pockets of those who would actually vote in the Paris elections. The brown-envelope treatment it was not – which is one reason why it did not work for Johansson.

In return for Visions and the cash, Africa pledged to deliver the bloc African vote for Europe's man in the 1998 Congress. This was promised by Hayatou at an executive committee meeting in Ouagadougou on 9 February, before the start of the 1998 African Cup of Nations. 'Africa will not present any candidate for the election of the FIFA presidency,' pronounced confederation general secretary, Mustapha Fahmy. 'It is endorsing UEFA's official candidate, its present president, Lennart Johansson. It is an unequivocal position taken after analysing the situation in the government of planet football.'

With Africa's 51 votes in the bag, the FIFA throne was all but Johansson's. However, he did not fully appreciate that neither Hayatou nor the members of the African executive could guarantee how the votes would be cast in the secret ballot.

Africa's football politics is not monolithic. In the north, the Arabs hardly see themselves as African at all, following their own agenda and resenting being dictated to by a Cameroonian whom they believe to be over-ambitious. Sub-Saharan Africa is rife with differences and disputes between east, west, central and southern countries, and there is also conflict among the linguistic heirs of different colonial masters. It was always highly unlikely that Hayatou could deliver Johansson's much-sought-after bloc African vote.

The Swede's camp was working zealously and drafting the election programme. 'The challenges that lie ahead cannot be tackled by one person alone, in his capacity as FIFA president,' stormed Johansson. 'The world football movement is a community. For this reason, FIFA has to further strengthen its democratic governance, as the United Nations of world football.'

Johansson's manifesto made a full-frontal assault on Havelange and his fortress-FIFA legacy. Pleas for democracy, accountability, openness, transparency and trust were all over this document. But some minnows had grown fat on the back of Havelange's FIFA, particularly in Africa. They wanted secrecy not openness, autocracy not democracy, continuity not change. They wanted to keep their five-star lifestyles, and looked for reasons to rebel against the African confederation's directive.

Just then, in November 1996, with his opponent about to throw in the towel, the shadow-boxing Johansson knocked himself down in an 'off the record' interview with a Swedish journalist – off the record but the hack happened to tape the interview – reported in the Swedish newspaper, *Aftonbladet*. When asked what sets Africans apart as soccer players, Johansson responded, 'They have rhythm, emotions, dance. They move in that way we don't. I do not know what is built into the black race, but I have noticed that they don't seem to like swimming.' Worse was to come: 'When I got to South Africa the whole room was full of blackies and it's fucking dark when they sit down altogether,' chuckled Johansson. 'What's more, it's no fucking fun when they're angry!'

Johansson did not deny these statements. How could he when they had been caught on tape? He claimed that the problem lay in the translation and that he had not used the term 'blackie' in a racist way. Once his comments hit the African press, Johansson was finished. That the UEFA president had made his racist blunder while in Africa to accept an award from the African confederation for his work on development there made him look foolish. To many Africans Johansson revealed himself as just another white, imperious, racist hypocrite.

The damage done by these remarks should not be underestimated. A few weeks later Havelange announced that he would not stand for re-election. Johansson had looked like an outright leader, cruising in a one-horse race. But his 'blackies' comments were enough to cause some African associations to switch their allegiance away from him. They gave many others the pretext to break their promises once Blatter and Havelange got to work on them.

Mystery surrounds Havelange's surprise decision. It was a combination of punches rather than a single knock-out blow which took him out of the fight. The Nigerian affair had him rocking as did the FIFA Executive's decision to reject his proposal of Japan as sole host for the 2002 World Cup. Havelange was in his 80s and the death of FIFA's senior vice-president, his close friend and co-conspirator Guillermo Cañedo, was another setback.

After the publication of his racist comments Johansson struck a melancholy figure on the FIFA circuit. At the Asian Cup in Abu Dhabi in December 1996, he looked uncomfortable in the lobbies of the Sheraton and in the midst of the Arab football schemers who were so smoothly oiling the wheels of the Asian confederation. Little did Johansson know it, but they were also plotting the big Swede's downfall.

For a long time after the 'blackie' affair, Johansson stopped giving private interviews to journalists. We eventually got an interview with him while he was in Cairo for the Under-17s World Championships. The day before we'd had an interview with Havelange, which was more like an audience; we expected something similar with Johansson.

We were wrong. Johansson was staying in a luxurious suite of rooms in the Cairo Marriot, on Gizera Island in the middle of the White Nile, a couple of miles away from Havelange's roost in the Sheraton. From Johansson's room on the 15th floor, if he strained his eyes through the polluted haze shrouding Cairo's suburbs, he could just make out the profile of the great pyramids of Giza.

Johansson's faithful retainer, Rudi Rothenbühler, showed us in. The big Swede rose from a long plush settee and greeted us warmly. He was dressed in an open-neck polo shirt and boxer shorts. His broad, care-worn face told how much the challenge for the presidency was hurting him. Johansson confided, in the spacious and lonely opulence of his suite, that he had considered pulling out of the race in the wake of the racist gaffe. He then turned his attention to Havelange, criticising the Big Man not so much for what he had done, but for the manner in which he had done it: 'It's not acceptable that you get a bunch of papers that you are supposed to take a decision on the same morning as you have a meeting.' Johansson also commented on how the general secretary was given so much power by Havelange: 'He is not the "godfather of football". With all respect to Mr Blatter, who does he think he is?'

Johansson was scathing about the way Havelange had used power and patronage to run FIFA like a personal fiefdom. 'Mr Cañedo for sure was in the media business and he was high up in the FIFA hierarchy. He made a certain kind of business through his position. If someone in the future is in that position, it would be most important that he would not be involved in the decision-making process about media-contracts. This would not be correct.' Johansson was determined to bring order and transparency to world football and to do this he was determined to rid FIFA of Havelange and his cronies. This, and an obligation to his supporters, is what kept him in the ring.

Half an our into our interview Johansson sighed, 'Excuse me gentlemen, I have to get ready to attend a function, but please we will continue to talk while I get changed.' The African confederation had organised a dinner river cruise along the Nile and Johansson was a guest of honour. So as Johansson walked in and out of his bedroom, first in his underwear, next struggling with the gold cuff-links for his dress shirt, we kept our conversation going.

He looked like a man who would rather be on the terrace back home drinking with his wife and his buddies than cruising up the Nile with football's power-brokers. Former FIFA communications boss Guido Tognoni knows Johansson well. 'He is maybe too honest and too naïve for his job,' says Tognoni. He means this as a compliment. Tognoni knows the Byzantine atmosphere of FIFA. Johansson is too nice to survive there. 'He doesn't want power, he doesn't have any personal ambition. But he is not happy with the style in which FIFA is managed,' continues Tognoni. 'He was convinced by his advisers, by UEFA people and others, that he should challenge the president and take over and change the style.'

Two years before Johansson lost the fight for the presidency, Tognoni gave him little hope. 'He is honest, he is not corrupt,' argued Tognoni and this puts him at a crippling disadvantage. 'He doesn't do it for his personal ambition, not at all. I think he would be more comfortable if somebody would take the weight away.'

But nobody did, and Johansson lifted his big frame out of this trough of doubt and got back on the campaign trail, shaking hands with his comrades from Asia, greeting one and all with the candidate's stage smile. He would not let down those who had put their reformist hopes in him. He might have considered dropping out for a quiet life, but he also recalled his own brand of obdurate toughness: 'Havelange did not realise that the new breed inside FIFA are bright and intelligent people, and they cannot be treated with indifference. He thought he could just sweep the new Swede aside, and after a while he found I was just still there.'

Still there, but slumped in the corner on his stool, gasping for air. Havelange had left the ring, but the canvas would not be empty for long. With much fanfare, Havelange's right-hand man was about to step through the ropes. The Havelange legacy was about to become the Havelange–Blatter FIFA Dynasty (HBFD).

9

FROM PROTÉGÉ TO PRESIDENT

Blatter takes the throne

When the counting was over for the 1998 presidential election, Sepp Blatter's 111 votes didn't at first seem to register fully on his visibly shaken opponent. Johansson almost deflated, his massive frame drooping with disappointment. He seemed not to see the implications of this first-round rout, and procedures began to be put in place for a second ballot. Technically, with 80 votes, Johansson had prevented Blatter from securing the two-thirds majority necessary for an outright first-round victory, and was entitled to contest a second ballot, which would be decided by a straight majority.

Then it sank in, or it was made clear to him: his opponent was already home and dry, and he would be crucified in a second ballot. Dignified concession was the only option. Havelange, with heavy irony, praised the European president as 'sportsman, gentleman, leader and friend', whose 'qualities and values' would help the football family enter the next century. The US's Alan Rothenberg just stood by and grinned – to him it represented a job well done. Blatter hailed his defeated rival as 'a great personality, fair and realistic' and pledged 'to unite football' and establish 'continuity in the good sense'. 'I am a servant of football,' beamed Blatter. 'I shall play, live and breathe football,' he said. We expected 'and I will drink Coca-Cola' to be his next utterance. Instead, he announced, 'I am deeply, deeply touched, deeply, and offer a message of friendship, openness, understanding, a message of solidarity.' How this phrasing must have weighed on the shattered senses of the Swedish loser.

It is hard to say exactly when the ambitious Blatter began campaigning for FIFA's top job. Perhaps it was as early as the first day he walked into FIFA HQ. One of Johansson's supporters' biggest complaints in the build-up to the 1998 election was that Blatter used his position as general secretary to campaign for the presidency before he finally declared himself a candidate at the eleventh hour. In the years preceding his election, Blatter was always present at world football's most important events. He had access to every kind of insider-information. From the moment in November 1996 that Havelange declared that he would not stand for re-election, Johansson's camp believed that Blatter was secretly campaigning to succeed his old boss.

Blatter had learned well at the feet of the master and he understood football politics in Africa, especially the politics of the belly, whereby there is little or no accountability, and individuals are ruthlessly self-seeking in a dynamic of survival and corruption. While Johansson busied himself working on the African hierarchy, Blatter, often accompanied by Havelange, criss-crossed Africa in a private jet provided by a Gulf emir, visiting some of the continent's remotest and poorest countries. From the Cape to Cairo and from Dakar to Mombasa, he made whistle-stop calls on the men in the national associations who would be marking the ballot cards in Paris in June. It was a strategy which had worked for Havelange in 1974 and it was about to work for Blatter in 1998.

As the June 1998 presidential election loomed, Johansson became increasingly edgy. Would his most feared opponent be lined up against him? If so, when? Would his manifesto for the reform of world football bring the factions of the football family together? Should no one else stand, would a single-slate succession usher in a period of reform, openness and accountability in FIFA?

As the closing date for nominations drew closer, the Johansson camp appeared more and more nervous, with the smart money on a nomination from inside the FIFA camp. Who was there, able to mobilise the global vote, to offer enough incentives to enough national associations, to outflank a Europe-Africa alliance? The football world knew that there was only one answer to this question – FIFA general secretary Joseph Blatter.

Blatter declared his candidature on 30 March, right on the eve of the deadline, Michel Platini, the French football idol of the 1980s and joint chair of the French World Cup organising committee, as his running mate. The place chosen for the announcement of Blatter's candidature was a masterstroke. He had to be away from his own patch, to stand back from his position inside FIFA, to make the public statement that he was not using it as a campaigning base. So the press corps was invited to the Paris headquarters of the French Olympic Committee.

The imposing building juts out defiantly from Avenue Pierre de Coubertin, like an Atlantic liner. In the entrance hall, a bronze statue of Baron de Coubertin greets us. Climbing the marble steps to the communications amphitheatre, taking in the images of a century of sporting achievement, the world's media were left in little doubt as to the seriousness and significance of the Blatter launch. Down below, a champagne reception awaited the hungry hacks after the formal announcement.

Blatter reminded us of his business and administration experience as an organiser of the 1972 and 1976 Olympic Games. He'd headed public relations for the Swiss tourist board in the 1960s, and been general secretary of the Swiss ice-hockey federation. He'd come to Horst Dassler's notice as 'Director of Sports Timing and Public Relations' at Longines SA, but his relationship with the German didn't feature in the biographical profile distributed at the launch.

Blatter had a campaign slogan – 'FIFA for all, All for football' – and what he called 'a programme, an ideology, a message'. The main emphasis in the message was upon 'the extended football family comprising the crowds in the stadia and the multitude of television viewers', making up 'one fifth of our planet's population – in other words, 1.200 million people', including 200 million players, of whom 40 million were claimed to be female.

Blatter – unlike his mentor Havelange, who is stony-faced in even the most thrilling of moments of the greatest football matches – is an *aficionado* of the game. He claimed that football stands for basic education, shapes character and combative spirit and fosters respect and discipline. It can make a valuable contribution to health, he added. And it's theatre, entertainment, art. 'But, first and foremost,' he told his audience, 'it is an endless source of passion and excitement. It stirs the emotions and can move its enthusiasts to tears of joy or frustration like no other game. And it is for everybody.'

Let football keep its human touch, its spirited play and its constant challenge, pleaded Blatter, 'but above all its universality'. The key word here is 'universality', a veiled reference to the European base of Johansson's campaign. Blatter was nominated by several national associations, initially by Jamaica and the USA. Others supporting and proposing his nomination included countries from the Gulf and South America.

Sitting in the front row in the conference hall of the Olympic headquarters was the big-time fixer, Alan Rothenberg, source of the USA nomination. CONCACAF boss Chuck Blazer told us that he thought his compatriot was 'extraordinarily ambitious … I guess he likes to find a shorter route, maybe an attorney's route, to get there'.

The head of the French national association was also there, suggesting that the pro-Johansson European alliance was far from intact. And the presence of a man from the Elysée Palace showed that there was a French political bandwagon behind the bid of the FIFA insider. This was the dream ticket: glamorous former player, symbolic boss of France '98, hand-in-hand with FIFA's top civil servant, Blatter. Platini's address was a masterpiece of waffle. He didn't want to just 'stand by and watch', he told us, but rather to help 'this game of ours evolve as it passes safely into the third millennium'. With schoolboy enthusiasm he announced his core ideas, 'the joy of the game and the pleasure of winning'.

He appealed to the principle of widening participation in running the game, for players, coaches and referees. Bring in more great players, Platini said, just as Blatter had done in setting up a FIFA taskforce and drawing in Pelé, Beckenbauer, Cruyff and Weah. 'Give back to footballers what is theirs,' pleaded Platini, in 'those places where there is little or no coaching at all'. And help footballers become 'mature adults', giving them a proper education and maybe a career for when their playing days are over.

Platini adapted Blatter's slogan, hailing 'FIFA for all, all for FIFA' – the second FIFA replacing the 'football' in the campaign slogan. Gaffe or strategy? Handily enough, Blatter's ideas coincided, Platini noted, 'exactly with my own'.

Things were getting tough for Johansson. Blatter would hardly be standing on speculation and he had been travelling the world at confederation congresses and national association meetings for the previous 16 months, ever since Havelange announced that he would not be standing for a seventh term. In these travels he was reminding delegates who was really boss and in the know, and proposing the ideal blend of football development and personal aggrandisement that had always appealed to a certain brand of crafty football administrator.

Disquiet in the Johansson camp was tangible. David Will had much to gain as a front-runner for the European presidency should Johansson become FIFA supremo and relinquish the European position. He also had much to lose should Johansson fail. Will's own position begin to look less solid within FIFA's own inner circles.

Speaking to us in March 1998 the Scot put a brave face on how the campaign was shaping up. The African confederation had confirmed its support – 'The executive might not carry 100 per cent with it, but they'll carry a big percentage'. The Johansson team was not worried about rumours that the former eastern-bloc nations would desert and was fully confident that almost the whole of Europe would stay solid. Despite hopes in the Johansson camp that the campaign would make some impact in the Americas, Chuck Blazer confirmed in the run-up that his 30-odd votes could be delivered with confidence. 'In the 1996 Congress in Zurich, North, South and Central America demonstrated they could vote as a perfect bloc. I believe it possible to do again.'

Asia was unpredictable. Havelange had annoyed some in the Far East over the Nigeria affair and had lost friends through his mishandling of the 2002 bidding process. But the Big Man had been good to the influential oil-rich Gulf and most Arab states would be behind whoever Havelange recommended as his successor.

Johansson had not been idle while Blatter was waiting to make public his last-minute entry. In January he was busy handshaking and hugging the top brass of the South American confederation, in Ascunción, Paraguay, celebrating the inauguration of its new headquarters building, the New House of South American Football. Here, for five or six days, doyens of the world football élite gathered for what Havelange called 'the best of South America's football meetings in the last 40 years'.

It was a heavyweight line-up for the ribbon-cutting ceremony in front of three thousand guests. Paraguayan president Eng Wasmosy dubbed the occasion 'a milestone in the heart of South America', and preached that 'the passion awakened by football cannot be unheard by governments. That is the reason why we have given our staunch support to this wonderful work.' The president of Argentina, Dr Carlos Menem, announced that 'this splendid building fills us all, South Americans, with pride'. Havelange was on his right, holding his own bunch of posies.

In this crowded, demanding schedule, Johansson was making his pitch for some or any of the ten available votes on the South American sub-continent. He and confederation president Leoz are pictured – Swedish arm across Paraguayan shoulders – joking together. A gigantic barbecue was laid on at a country estate outside the city. It was fiesta time. A thousand guests attended. The oldest railroad line in South America was fixed to carry guests to the country estate. This was difficult lobbying territory for Johansson. He looked sweatily uncomfortable as he shared a carriage with Leoz and Japanese football boss Ken Naganuma. His inability to speak any language bar his native Swedish or English crippled him at events like this and played into the hands of enemies who saw him as too Eurocentric.

Until he declared himself, wherever Johansson was, FIFA general secretary Blatter could be there too, not an official candidate yet, but always there – shaking hands, suggesting developments, calling for ideas and promising appropriate forms of co-operation and support – in German, French, Spanish, Italian.

In February, the CONCACAF confederation held an executive meeting during its Gold Cup tournament. Johansson's pitch, Chuck Blazer told us, did not convince. 'Interviewed by our exco (executive committee) and other members, he did not demonstrate, by his answers, any greater understanding of our issues,' Blazer said. Neither was the rotund American impressed with Johansson's overtures to Africa, saying the UEFA president was 'if not less Eurocentric, then more Euro-African-centric, a political policy which may be coming undone, at least from the African side'.

The Europeans also asked for, and got, a special session on the programme of Blazer's last confederation congress before the June election, in Antigua. Johansson was wasting his breath. By then Blatter was a confirmed candidate and the Americas had made their choice in his favour.

In Dublin at the end of April, Johansson's team snubbed Blatter, offering the FIFA general secretary no invitation to address the European constituency of the global football family. This looked like sour grapes and, rather than playing up the real strengths of the Johansson candidacy, the Swede's team was being drawn into a slanging match. This had its roots in the concern that Blatter, long before being nominated, was really campaigning behind the scenes. David Will told us, 'It's no secret that he has been widely promoted internationally by the president. The president has openly canvassed for Sepp.'

This enraged the Johansson camp so much that it planned to ask Blatter for clarification of his position at a special meeting called for by a majority of the executive committee not, as Will was at pains to point out, as any 'attack on Sepp', but rather as a matter of procedure. 'I make no bones about my own personal view,' Will said. 'It would be incompetent for him to remain as general secretary. I cannot think that he can act as the employee of the executive committee, whilst at the same time standing to be the president of the executive committee.'

Not everyone in the FIFA family shared this view. We asked another lawyer, Californian Alan Rothenberg, at the Blatter launch whether the will-he–won't-he saga was a conflict of interests. Rothenberg saw no such problem, but the majority on the FIFA executive committee clearly did. The day before the special meeting of the executive committee, a resolution from this majority went to the FIFA president. The signatories to this were made up of the eight European, four African, and one Oceania members of the committee. Dr Chung of South Korea, though widely associated with this grouping, hedged his bets and declined to sign. However, the statement betrayed the divisions within FIFA's central, most powerful committee:

TO THE MEMBERS OF THE FIFA EXECUTIVE COMMITTEE

Resolution proposed by members of the FIFA Executive Committee

Mr President

Dear Members

Prior to the extraordinary meeting of the Executive Committee of FIFA on Friday, 13 March 1998, members of the Confederation Africaine de Football (CAF), the Ocenia Football Confederation (OFC) and the Union des Associations Européennes de Football (UEFA) met for consultations concerning the option that the acting General Secretary of FIFA would present himself as a candidate for the presidency. Based on the statutes of FIFA and considering the political implications which such a candidate would have, the representatives of the respective confederations agreed on the following principles:

1   The duties of the Genera Secretary of FIFA are strictly non-political.
2   The General Secretary of FIFA is bound to a work contract. One of the most important duties of the General Secretary is to organise the FIFA Congress and the FIFA World Cup. Without permission of the Executive Committee a person employed by FIFA cannot, at the same time, be a candidate for presidency.
3   Three months before the World Cup and the Congress in France it is the most important duty of the General Secretary to ensure, by his function, a smooth running of these events and to safeguard the unity of FIFA in this crucial period of world football.
4   According to Art. 43, paragraph (e) of the FIFA Statutes, the General Secretary is responsible for the relations between the Federation on one hand and the national associations on the other. It is hence not acceptable that the highest-ranked employee in the FIFA administration would challenge a candidate who has been presented in due form by members of FIFA.
5   Keeping in mind all these observations, it is evident that the duties of the General Secretary are absolutely not compatible with the ambitions to become president of FIFA. The European members of the FIFA Executive Committee recall the fact that, four years ago, UEFA unanimously declined the offer of the General Secretary to stand as a candidate against the actual FIFA president.
6   Finally it must be stated that nobody should be hindered to be elected in a democratic procedure provided that this initiative is not in conflict with the duties as member of the FIFA administration.

Consequently and considering the developments in the recent months, the undersigned members of the Executive Committee as the supervising body of the FIFA administration take the following resolution and ask the other members of the Committee to give it their support for such decision based on Article 62, para 1 of the FIFA Statutes (Matters not provided for):

Answer	Decision
– Mr Blatter is standing as a candidate	– In which case he has to leave his office immediately
– Mr Blatter is not standing as a candidate	– In which case he has to commit himself in writing to fulfil his contractual obligations
– No decision is expressed by Mr Blatter	– In which case his contract will be suspended with immediate effect until the elections are over

– To be informed about the wording of the contractual relationship, the General Secretary is requested to submit to the Executive Committee a copy of the employment contract with FIFA.

Les membres du Comité exécutif de la FIFA:

Dr João HAVELANGE
Julio H. GRONDONA
David H. WILL *(signed)*
Lennart JOHANSSON *(signed)*
Issa HAYATOU *(signed)*
Dr Antonio MATTARESE *(signed)*
Dr Mong Joon CHUNG
Jack. A. WARNER
Viacheslav KOLOSKOV *(signed)*
Abdullah K. AL-DABAL
Slim ALOULOU *(signed)*
Michel D'HOOGHE *(signed)*
Isaac Davi SASSO SASSO
Ram RUHEE *(signed)*
Gerhard MAYER-VORFELDER *(signed)*
Carlos COELLA MARTINEZ
Ricardo Terra TEIXERA
Per Ravn OMDAL *(signed)*
Mohamed BIN HAMMAM
Senes ERZIK *(signed)*
Mustapha FAHMY *(signed)*
Charles J. DEMPSEY *(signed)*
Chuck BLAZER
Worawi MAKUDI

Lined up alongside the status quo, and the established FIFA hierarchy of Havelange and Blatter, were the South Americans, the Gulf Arabs, at least one further Asian confederation delegate, and all delegates from the Central and North American/ Caribbean confederation.

Within the FIFA executive committee, the anti-Havelange faction looked stronger and more determined than the rest. But the executive didn't elect the president, the national associations did. In any wider vote involving all national associations and where more than a simple majority was required – the basis, in FIFA's statutes, for the election of the president in the first round of voting is a two-thirds majority – much would depend upon the extent to which confederations could deliver bloc votes.

When it came to it, the resolution was simplified to the basic point that Blatter must stand down from his position within FIFA if he declared himself as a candidate for the presidency, but the committee never even got to vote on the issue.

Chuck Blazer, wielding his thirty-odd votes which could have such an important influence on the outcome (remember, the vote of US Virgin Islands has the same weight as that of Argentina or Germany or England) was scathing about the style and impact of the Euro/African pact. It was widely reported that Havelange simply stormed out of the meeting, so making a vote impossible. Blazer denies this, offering an account which highlights the consummate holding powers of Havelange, as well as the ill-preparedness of the Johansson camp.

Blazer told us that the meeting lasted four and a half hours, and Havelange also read to the committee the legal advice of FIFA's lawyers working within the boundaries of Swiss law. This was a strong point, for Italian delegate Antonio Mattarese admitted that the document had been drafted without legal advice or, in Blazer's words, without any adequate consideration of 'the legal issues in Switzerland'. There was, it seems, under Swiss law, no legal obligation to remove Blatter. All agreed on this. In Blazer's words, the resolution was amended, changing the word 'removal' to 'suspension'. Havelange then asked David Will 'three times, in the capacity of chairman of the legal committee', said Blazer, 'to propose the restrictions he deemed appropriate to have a fair election'.

Will refused on the basis that he was too implicated to make a truly neutral judicial-style ruling due to his being a signatory to the original resolution. If legal momentum had to give way to moral appeal then in Havelange's FIFA the pragmatism of the manipulator was always going to retain the upper hand. Havelange concluded that if no-one would take the job on, that was in effect it for the day and he would recall the body – if appropriate – to make a decision on 8 April, the day after the deadline for nominations to the presidency. Then he, along with everyone else, walked out of the meeting.

Blazer portrays Havelange as the voice of reason. 'The president did a good job of trying to gain consensus,' he told us, 'but none are so deaf as those who wouldn't hear. Personally, I believe the president did the right thing and that the Euro/Africans behaved like asses.' And Blazer is right. By failing to take control of the issue, Johansson and his backers made themselves look weak and handed back the initiative to Havelange and the protégé.

Blatter came out of his first skirmish in the election battle looking a lot more dignified than his accusers and smarter and quicker on his political feet than his opponent Johansson. By the time his formal declaration was scheduled he had disarmed his critics by getting Havelange to announce that he was to stand adding that 'the general secretary asked for dispensation from certain duties so as to avoid any possible conflict of interest – a request which complies with a wish expressed by the executive committee.' Problem? What problem?

Until the vote, Blatter chose to conduct all his other duties away from the FIFA offices, which would include continuing to supervise preparations for France '98. Blatter added that this would enable him to comply with the wish of the majority of the executive committee, as expressed at the meeting of 13 March. 'This solution,' he said, 'I'm sure, would also be in the best interests of FIFA and football in this very delicate situation.' The Blatter statement was dated 27 March, as was the Havelange announcement – no danger of getting any wires crossed on this one.

By this one stroke, Havelange and Blatter answered the committee critics. Maybe Havelange would look to move against the committee later. Blazer believed that in the tempestuous meeting of 13 March Havelange wasn't trying 'to break the axis, to split them at all'. But he'd certainly outmanoeuvred his critics again and Blazer recognised that the 'Euro-Africans felt insulted', and a bunch of other terms less appropriate for print.

'But they were so into being dogmatic,' scoffed Blazer, 'that they didn't see conciliation when it was in front of them.' The Johansson camp had been chasing both strategic advantage and the moral high ground. Havelange and Blatter ensured that the Europeans crept away with neither.

As the date of FIFA's first contested presidential election for almost a quarter of a century drew closer, the Euro-African alliance was looking increasingly fragile. One of the most experienced FIFA watchers on the European mainland observed that Blatter would never have declared himself if he wasn't sure he could win: 'Johansson is not as sharp as Blatter, not as clever,' the Dutch journalist remarked. 'Blatter is a good administrator. Johansson's campaign is built around anti-corruption. But he's up against too many faceless people who have been implicated in that corruption, that's why he will lose.'

Johansson had even offered to keep Blatter on as general secretary should he win, but Blatter, Johansson reported, turned him down point blank. Here was serious evidence of the Swiss's confidence. Also, Johansson hadn't managed to prise open the financial issue, to get his hands on FIFA's books. He'd tried at the Cairo executive meeting the previous September. 'He failed and with that went the chance of his presidency,' the Dutchman told us. 'At the bottom of it all are the billion dollar deals with ISL and [the German company] Kirch. It's like Horst Dassler is still running FIFA.'

The European campaign had looked desperate since an aborted campaign launch in Ghent, in January 1998. This was planned alongside the draw for the forthcoming European nations championship. Some 150 reporters turned up for a non-event at which Johansson's campaign team spent as much time bad-mouthing the FIFA hierarchy as talking up its own case.

Because of family commitments, Blatter was not at the draw. He turned European arguments back on his opponents when executive committee member Antonio Mattarese wrote to him requesting that he openly declare his candidature. 'It is mystifying that an organisation that preaches about democracy, unity and fair play could launch such a personal attack, particularly as I was not present because of a family engagement,' said Blatter.

Experienced FIFA and Olympic observers detected panic in the Europeans. Blatter was the one man other than Havelange himself who frightened the Swede – not because of who he was, but because of what he knew. 'Blatter, the man that knows every bit of wheeling and dealing that's going on, because he's the one that has actually had to deliver,' the Dutch journalist told us. 'Johansson had it all tied up and the fact that Blatter was hinting that he would come forward scared the hell out of him, scared the hell out of the Europeans.'

Another veteran FIFA insider put it this way. 'Havelange and Blatter are chained together,' he said, banging his wrists together. It wasn't so much that Blatter wanted to stand, he told us, 'but that he had to stand'.

Once in the open, Blatter's campaign moved up a gear and he hit his strategic targets in Africa hardest. In May he went to Nairobi, Kenya, his first trip to East Africa for twenty years, to talk to the Confederation of East and Central African Football Associations. In his 12-hour visit to Kenya he met officials from Djibouti, Eritrea, Ethiopia, Kenya, Malawi, Rwanda, Somalia, Sudan, Tanzania, Uganda, Zambia, Zanzibar and Zimbabwe, as well as the hosts, Kenya, all keen to listen to his promises. 'After a lengthy meeting with the CECAFA officials, I feel tremendously positive', said Blatter, splitting the Africa-Europe alliance to bits, warning Johansson that 'no candidate had a right to be imposed on the voters'. He also reiterated his pledge to support South Africa's bid to host the 2006 World Cup, and announced a new financial windfall for all the continent's soccer federations – including annual payouts of $250,000 to associations for improving their facilities, and for technical, administrative and marketing expertise.

The previous month he'd targeted Eastern Europe, visiting Zagreb and exposing the fragility of Johansson's European front. He met the Croation president, Franjo Tudjman, took in a Zagreb *v* FC Croatia match, and sat alongside Croatian FA boss Branko Miksa, who said that he was delighted that 'the next FIFA president' had come to the city.

Blatter continued to busy himself confidently, liaising with national associations in the two months of open campaigning. In one of his initiatives, dispatched from his independent address down the road from FIFA House, he offered a reminder of his concern for the poorer members of the FIFA family. 'Dear friends,' he began, *how about a hand-out from your million-dollar allocation from World Cup television and marketing rights? If you lack money, and need facilities for administration, this can help you out* – a 'tailor-made solution,' Blatter called it. The letter was dated 22 May, just days before the Paris election. Platini's Paris address was also at the top of the letter, but

Blatter was the sole signatory – an indication of the division of labour should the dream duo's campaign succeed.

JSB FOR PRESIDENT

To the national associations of FIFA
To the confederations

JSB – MESSAGE no.3

Tailor-made solutions

Dear President
Dear General Secretary
Dear Friends

This information is principally addressed to those national associations which are – as is unfortunately far too often the case – less privileged than others due to a lack of money and the appropriate technical infrastructure and hence the means to run their administration efficiently at national level.

The share of the revenue from the television and marketing rights that the Havelange administration has already apportioned to each national association (one million dollars each payable in four annual instalments of USD 250,000, of which USD 50,000 can already be paid out this autumn) is intended to enable those who need our support to set up a permanent office equipped with indispensable facilities such as a telephone, fax and computers with e-mail. After FIFA technical experts have taken stock of the individual situation for the national associations on the spot, I want to make sure that these associations receive tailor-made assistance in establishing their technical, administrative and marketing programmes. For this purpose, every national association should have suitable possibilities for training and adequate resources for advancement at their disposal. This will in the end also be beneficial to football and instrumental for providing better opportunities.

Thank you for your attention.

Yours sincerely
Joseph S. Blatter
Zollikon, May 22, 1998
Le Football pour tous – tous pour le football

There was nothing technically wrong with such an offer. You couldn't call it a bribe. It was 'officially given by FIFA', said David Will the day after the opening match of France '98, but 'nobody knows by whose decision. Nobody knows who took that decision. The finance committee didn't take that decision, the executive, the emergency committee didn't. This $50,000 has been paid out to a number of countries last week by FIFA, officially.' Will paused for breath. Then, choosing his words carefully, he told us, 'Mr Blatter has apparently said that these are poor countries that needed the money in a hurry. It's bound to be queried, somebody will have to ask "On whose authority was this done?"' But in the end, nobody did.

So it wasn't a bribe. But it was at the least an abuse of bureaucratic power. It seems strange that, having relinquished core duties of his FIFA role for the duration of his campaign, Blatter could still be so closely involved in decisions and initiatives concerning FIFA finances. Tailor-made indeed, with Blatter and Platini cannily at work gathering up the vote for judgement day on 8 June.

At the World Cup draw in Marseilles in December 1997, Havelange had said that his protégé would make an outstanding president. The old partnership played the following fixtures nimbly on a global anti-European card. As early as the beginning of March, a top FIFA insider confirmed, Blatter was assured of at least 15 European votes, not least as 'UEFA doesn't give a shit about world football. UEFA thinks it can go all round the world giving gongs – some Africans will accept anything, any gong – but all they're pouring into Africa is another form of neo-colonialism.'

With Blatter working behind the scenes to fragment the European front and the Johansson energies all but spent in his long-running confrontation with Havelange himself, the scene was now set in the starkest of terms. The elected democrat was up against the hand-picked career administrator – a reformist package or a continuity card?

At the Equinox Conferenec Centre on 8 June, freelance heavies and government agents patrolled the razor-wired fences. A few hours later the FIFA family anointed Blatter as its new president. With public fanfare, England had jumped ship from Europe at the last minute. Alec McGivan, England's 2006 campaign manager looked smug. Graham Kelly of The FA looked as mournful as ever, as if he was yearning for a wet day back in his earlier job at Football League headquarters in Lytham St Anne's, when life must have been so much simpler. Maybe he was just uncomfortable in his seat, or perhaps he saw his future.

As a parting gesture, Havelange the magnanimous eased the passage of several nations to full membership status before the vote. Now Eritrea, American Samoa and Palestine each carried as much electoral weight as Germany, Brazil or England. There were three more votes Johansson could kiss goodbye to.

As it turned out, an African haemorrhage ('I doubt Johansson polled more than ten African votes,' Jimmy Boyce of Northern Ireland speculated to us) and many European defections meant that the three new votes made no difference. Blatter won with a landslide majority of 31, winning 111 votes of the 191 associations polled. In his thank-you speech Blatter pledged to unite football. Why it needed uniting now, after years of his own administration, had obviously not occurred to the majority of voters.

In his last presidential address Havelange said that he took his leave with indelible memories of 'Sepp Blatter at my side for 23 years. I leave, with a clear conscience, the governing body of the world's, the planet's most popular sport.' With his protégé in charge, Havelange would remain close to the action for the foreseeable future.

In the Equinox hall the post-mortem on the result was under way. Questions were swirling. Mihir Bose of the *Daily Telegraph* asked Blatter: 'Was your campaign corrupt? Is FIFA not clean?' Blatter's face tightened, his smile subsided. 'The accounts were cleared in congress,' he snarled, 'no questions were asked then.' Show me my accusers, demanded Blatter. 'It might become uncomfortable for anyone whose name you mention.'

The day after Blatter's victory, Kenya's *Daily Nation* reported how grateful the Kenyan football federation was to Havelange for promising to pay team travel costs to an obscure regional tournament in Rwanda. Chairman of the federation, Peter Kenneth, said in Paris, 'It has been a gruelling battle but in the final analysis we are proud to have been associated with the winning candidate.'

Inside the Paris hotels, as the football started, the FIFA family closed ranks. *Omertà* became once more the order of the day. Copies of documents which we'd been promised disappeared from history, or at least from our grasp. 'It's all gone dead,' conceded one tough veteran at the heart of FIFA's inner circle. 'It's gone absolutely flat. It wouldn't do them any good to try to open things up.'

Everybody knew the game was lost. 'You've got the FIFA you want, you want this FIFA of corruption, that's what you've got. Get on with it,' said one executive committee member to another. The pompous and acidic response said it all. 'Sure it's all about money. Your side didn't spend enough money.'

So the protégé became the president. Blatter is nimble and cunning, but he lacks the Big Man's gravitas. Nobody stands up in FIFA House when Sepp phones. Havelange filled the public spaces he entered. Subjects sought him out and, when allowed, came cap in hand for an audience. Sepp has to work the floor, but he is good at it. What he lacks in awe-inspiring presence, he makes up for with his quick wits, charm and affability. Asked how the new boy was doing in the first weeks of his presidency, Northern Ireland's Jimmy Boyce told us, 'Sepp's PR skills are excellent. He's good at winning friends and influencing people, he seems determined to get what he wants.' The Irishman said that the majority of the FIFA executive were satisfied with his overall approach. We are not surprised.

Once in power President Blatter moved swiftly to neutralise his enemies. In his first ExCo meeting he dropped a controversial proposal to create a special bureau – an inner circle empowered to take decisions outside of the executive committee 'to cope with FIFA's increasing volume of work'. Johansson and his supporters would never have stood for this. Cleverly, Blatter withdrew his proposal at the last minute, proposing instead to double the number of full ExCo meetings. More meetings, more five-star treatment. He went on to form his special bureau anyway, the controversial F-Crew of personal advisors.

In his second meeting he reshuffled the FIFA committees, giving his supporters key positions, but also making sure that potential opponents were kept in the club. David Will was punished for his open commitment to Johansson by being removed from the chairs of the prestigious referees' and legal committees. But he wasn't bounced out of the club altogether. Instead he was handed the grand-sounding but practically irrelevant national associations' committee. For 2002 he was handed the poisoned chalice of the ticketing committee. Ernie Walker of Scotland wasn't so favoured, and was banished from the FIFA family for not smarming up to Blatter after the Equinox vote, unlike many turncoats from the defeated Johansson camp. 'I wouldn't shake the bastard's hand,' he said bitterly.

The Big Man would have been hard pressed to match his protégé's next stroke. Blatter proposed that for the first time ExCo members should be paid, in addition to already generous expenses. He suggested $50,000 a year. Keep your mouths shut for ten years, boys, and you can bank a cool half million. Few dissenting voices could be heard when this motion was tabled. No wonder the trail went so cold on the pre-election accusations. We recalled the words of top football marketing man Jürgen Lenz. Speaking of the FIFA Club, he said, 'It has become so openly corrupt that they do not know that they are being corrupt.'

After his first year at FIFA's helm, Blatter looked to be secure in his tenure. He got more prestige, status and influence a little over a year on from his election, when the International Olympic Committee elected him as its 104th member, at its 109th meeting in Seoul. FIFA's last two presidents were now the longest-serving and the newest members on the IOC, which had announced to the world that it would be cleaning up its act. And Blatter was keeping up Havelange's style in big deals. In May he'd also been in Seoul, signing up the Hyundai Motor Corporation as the official car for the 2002 World Cup. Hyundai beat off competition from Toyota and Opel, France 98's supplier. The chairman of Hyundai is Chung Mon Koo, brother of Dr Mong Joon Chung, FIFA vice-president and son of Hyundai's founder.

Blatter was slipping smoothly into the presidential style. He'd had some awkward moments. Although he'd got an injunction to stop the publication in Switzerland of British author David Yallop's book covering the election of June '98, a Dutch judge concluded that the story of cash inducements for votes 'was sufficiently concrete that Blatter and the FIFA can defend themselves against it.' FIFA's media machine went into overdrive, saying in April 1999 that 'all the payments were entirely above board and there was no question of such payments being "bribes" relating to Joseph Blatter's election to FIFA.'

However, as Ernie Walker reminded us, the world was alerted to the serious scale of corruption at the heart of the Olympic movement by a veteran member of the IOC. 'Too many know too much,' he said, hinting that it was only a matter of time before the truth would out, the full story would be told exposing FIFA's malpractices.

Blatter's honeymoon didn't last long. The simmering dispute between the Asian and the South American confederations over the allocation of places for the 2002 World Cup finals boiled over on the eve of the Women's World Cup in the USA. With Korea's and Japan's co-hosting arrangement guaranteeing each country a berth, the Asians, who had occupied four places in France '98, requested five next time round. Peter Velappan, secretary general of the AFC, said that in January 1999 Blatter was 'sympathetic to our case and assured us of a solution'.

But Blatter dragged his feet, deferring the item at the March 1999 meeting, saying that he would deal with the issue 'personally'. The new president was cornered because he could only give the Asians an extra place at the expense of some other confederation. The Asians targeted South America, saying: 'They have four guaranteed places plus a play-off with the Oceania champion and the possibility of five seats for a confederation of ten members! This is not fair and we cannot accept such a greed.'

Blatter had secured precious votes from Asia and there was a deep sense of betrayal. The seriousness of the Asian concerns was demonstrated when, *en masse*, they walked out of FIFA's extraordinary congress in Los Angeles in July 1999 and declared that 'Asia is compelled to boycott the World Cup 2002'. Further, they ostracised the South Americans, barring them from attending any of their events, and the Qatari, Mohamed bin Hammam Al-Abdulla, resigned from all FIFA standing committees. The other Asian representatives on FIFA's executive committee threatened to follow suit. Suddenly, the FIFA family looked more disunited than at any time since Sir Stanley Rous's difficult relations with members from developing countries three decades before.

Blatter was stung by the Asian boycott and his response was far from conciliatory. 'Naturally, I am personally disillusioned by the way the Asian national associations behaved', he fumed. 'I made a point of stressing the desire to seek an open dialogue … Alas, this appeal for common sense fell on deaf ears.' The Asians, he said, 'misused FIFA's most important body … an affront against our organisation and an insult to the FIFA member national associations'. With only a thinly veiled reference to the largesse enjoyed by the FIFA family, Blatter went on: 'If one is a guest at a sumptuous banquet, it is certainly not good form to get up and leave before the meal is over'.

Appealing to principles of trust, democracy, universality and, of course, solidarity, Blatter worked overtime to hold his 'vision of the house of football together'. 'A boycott', he thundered, 'would shake its foundations and cause its ruin.' These words, if uttered by the Big Man, may have brought the Asians into line at once. But the protégé remained unproven. Unlike Havelange, he had not been able to keep all of his promises and neither did he have his old boss's presidential gravitas. A resolution of sorts was thrashed out between Blatter and the Asian confederation's president HRH Sultan Ahmed Shah of Malaysia in early September 1999. Asia had been offered 'half a slot' for the finals, from the Europeans, the play-off issue to be decided at the end of the year. Asia was to get a deciding game against a country from Oceania, rather than a strong European side. FIFAspeak dominated the reconciled parties, which bore 'no ill-will' and 'underlined their commitment to work together for the good of the game'. The new FIFA president was not having the easiest of rides. The Asian challenge and threats indicated that, under Blatter, FIFA's House of Football could have tumbled like the proverbial house of cards.

10

THE POLITICS OF THE BELLY

Garnering votes and gaining loyalty

Let's suspend disbelief for a few pages and listen to a good story. It is Sunday, 7 July 1998. Tomorrow the election for the most powerful and important job in world sport will take place. The campaign teams for the two runners, Sep Blatter and Lennart Johansson, have had an exhausting day, rallying the faithful and making last-minute pleas and promises to voters who may yet be persuaded to mark X for their man.

It is getting close to midnight. Ensconced in separate wings of Paris's luxurious Hotel Le Bristol, the candidates and their close advisors are making their final calculations. Both men know that the result is going to be close, but Johansson, with the African executive's endorsement in his pocket and written assurances of support from the overwhelming majority of European delegates, feels he has the presidency in the bag 'by about ten votes'.

Let's now nip across town a few miles to the huge Hotel Le Meridien in Montparnasse. This is where most of the national associations are staying. The hotel's extensive lobby and lounge area is packed with the lesser movers and shakers of world football administration. Tomorrow is their big day. Tomorrow they will be king-makers.

Sitting around the lacquered, hard-wood tables, sipping cocktails and coffee, or submerged in over-stuffed easy chairs, the hubbub of the king-makers' excited election-eve gossip all but drowns out the melodies from the grand piano. Who is going to win tomorrow? Some say Johansson and others say Blatter, but almost everybody agrees that it is too close to call.

Tomorrow's congress promises to be a marathon and by one in the morning most of the delegates begin drifting off to bed. Similarly, back at Le Bristol, in the lobby, cocktail lounge and inside the exclusive FIFA Club, things are beginning to wind down as FIFA's glitterati make their way upstairs to their ample suites in preparation for the next day's epic.

It is now 2 a.m. and, as he prepares for bed, Issa Hayatou is a worried man. He has much to gain and even more to lose, depending upon the outcome of tomorrow's poll. He has promised to deliver the African vote for the UEFA president, knowing that, if Johansson wins, he himself will be next in line for the throne when the Swede steps down.

His trademark white suit is hanging in the wardrobe and he has changed into a flowing, ice-blue robe. His deep-brown eyes, set in a broad, handsome face, stare back at him from the bathroom mirror. In a secret ballot, if the incentives are big enough, he fears that the votes which Johansson is counting on will end up on Blatter's pile.

Hayatou has always known it would be difficult to hold Africa together behind Johansson. The Swede's racist gaffe hasn't helped. Issa had been in Dublin for Johansson's final campaign convention – thinly disguised as the UEFA congress. Hayatou had been introduced as the 'man who will deliver Africa' for Europe. But things are coming apart at the seams.

Issa had bumped into Emmanuel Maradas, the editor of *African Soccer* in the gents' toilets at the Dublin congress. It was a strained, chance meeting. Maradas was there to dish out free copies of his magazine to Europe's delegates. His editorial castigated Hayatou and the African executive for backing Johansson. Instead, Africa must vote for Blatter, trumpeted Maradas's piece. Some Johansson supporters believed that Maradas was 'Blatter's agent in Africa'. Was this true? Had Maradas succeeded in splitting the African vote? Hayatou is trying to put such thoughts out of his mind when his phone rings.

Back at Le Meridien, an African delegate who will cast the secret vote on behalf of his national association is also preparing for bed when somebody knocks softly on his door. Dressed only in a starched white jellaba, the delegate dries his hands, leaves the bathroom and opens the door. Two men dressed in expensive pale blue suits stand on the threshold. 'Assalaam alaykom,' says the shorter visitor. 'Alaykom assalaam,' responds the African delegate. 'Please, come in.'

The taller man carries two large briefcases, one of which he places on the table. He clicks it open, revealing rows of neat packages of $50 bills. 'We have come from our country,' says the other, in clipped, Middle East English, 'and we are authorised to offer you, personally, $50,000 if you pledge your vote for Mr Blatter.' Blatter did not authorise this, but there were powerful forces propelling his run-in.

The delegate stares at the money. In his country, $5 per week is a decent wage and most people don't make that in a month. $50,000 would go a long way. All he has to do is switch his vote in the secret ballot. Who is to know? Besides, England has said that it is switching from Johansson to Blatter, and the Swede did make those racist remarks. Anyway, they are both Europeans, so what is the difference? Hands are shaken, the briefcase is clicked shut and the two Gulf Arabs move on to the next customer. The trouble is, the delegate is a man of principle who is fiercely loyal to Issa Hayatou.

Issa reaches slowly for his phone. He is yet to sleep, but already his worst nightmare has arrived. His loyal supporter tells him the bad news. Hayatou slams down the phone and rushes down the corridor where he finds Johansson sharing a nightcap with his right-hand man, Gerhard Aigner, the general secretary of UEFA. Both men are stunned by Issa's report.

Aigner hurriedly gathers a posse of influential Johansson supporters who dash across town in taxis to try to stop the rot. Upright Norwegian Per Ravn Omdal is among them. But it is too late. By the time Aigner reaches Le Meridien the Emir's briefcases are empty. 'Johansson's African vote has haemorrhaged,' is how one delegate put it, 'and Blatter has the election in the bag.'

Fantasy or fact? As of yet nobody who knows has broken the silence to confirm, definitely, the details of this election-eve bribe scandal. But Omdal is adamant that many votes ebbed away from Johansson as a direct result of the Gulf's last-minute intervention. Reading and listening to the carefully chosen words of key insiders leaves us in little doubt that something seriously wrong happened in Le Meridien on the night of 7 June.

Johansson was gracious in defeat, but clearly nonplussed by its scale: 'I do not want to appear a bad loser and I congratulate Mr Blatter on his success. But we were very sure of a certain number of votes and maybe something happened to make them change their minds.'

David Will was angrier and slightly more forthcoming when he told us, 'As far as I'm concerned this is just hearsay, but we heard that a Middle East Country was actually paying out $50,000 for buying votes. I know this because money was offered to countries who remained true to Issa Hayatou really, and would not take the money. I know that many of the people here [Hotel Le Bristol] who were supporters of Lennart Johansson left very quickly from here to get to the Meridien to try to stop this.'

If anybody knows the truth it should be Hayatou. However, in the wake of the election disaster, he was fighting for his political future and choosing his words carefully. Like Johansson and Will, he too hints at shenanigans at Le Meridien: 'We had the majority on the eve of the ballot. It was during the night between 7 to 8 June that things changed. Why? I don't know. There were rumours, but I am in no position to confirm the reason for the reversal of some delegates.' No position to confirm, but in a position to deny, which Hayatou flatly refuses to do. Issa's from Cameroon and he understands how the politics of the belly works in African football. The political scientist Jean-François Bayart's 1996 study, *The State in Africa: The Politics of the Belly* borrows its subtitle from a metaphor in Hayatou's home country of Cameroon. Quasi-feudal traditions of power, patronage and exploitation, he argues, sustain complementary models of corruption: first, *resources of extraversion* are in the hands of minorities with command over or access to scarce resources; second, *positions of predation* allow some to occupy roles providing opportunities for extortion. In such socio-political contexts, people need to live, need to survive, left often with little choice; the politics of the belly is one route to survival. $50,000 for a confidential vote? You can see how understandable, if not routine, the offer of the men from the Gulf might appear to delegates from relatively undeveloped countries in sub-Saharan Africa.

The Confederation of African Football (CAF) was formed in 1956 by Egypt, Ethiopia, Sudan and South Africa – the only independent nations on the continent at that time. The proposal to form an African confederation met stern resistance from the South Americans who, misreading their own history, viewed the African nations as potential dupes of their former colonial masters. However, with strong support from Sir Stanley Rous and Granatkin of the Soviet Union, CAF was formerly inaugurated at its first constitutional assembly in Khartoum in 1957.

In one of the first attempts to use sport as a political tool in the fight against apartheid, the leaders of the new-born confederation expelled South Africa the following year when it insisted on sending either an all-white or an all-black team to the first African Cup of Nations in the Sudanese capital, Khartoum.

With only three members throughout the following years, CAF was a weak political force. By the early 1960s, however, things changed radically as the European powers shed their colonial authority. Newly independent African nations discovered in football a way to advertise their presence on the world stage.

For the post-colonial developing world, however, affiliation to FIFA and participation in international football represented a tacit acceptance of the deep structure left behind by the colonists. Football was a European game and, while some of the names might have changed, the shape of the new nation states which affiliated to FIFA were the same as those imposed by the old colonial powers a century earlier. By playing international football, Sudan, Nigeria, Sierra Leone and South Africa were confirming a social and political map imposed by the First World.

One of Africa's oldest colonial legacies – and one which finds its clearest expression through football – is the division between Arab-Africa and sub-Saharan or black Africa. This is rooted in the slave trafficking which took place from the south to the north of Africa many years before the Europeans and Americans turned African slavery into a global industry. The extent of this antipathy was made brutally manifest during the 1986 African Nations Cup finals in Morocco. The semi-finals saw Cameroon line up against the hosts and Nigeria face neighbouring Algeria. These games were very violent and in both cases the black African players were subjected to extreme forms of racial abuse from predominantly Arab crowds. These events led some senior sports writers to question what lay behind the façade of pan-African unity.

A decade later, in Bloemfontein, South Africa, a group of Egyptian officials and supporters, who had just attended their national team's defeat in the African Cup of Nations quarter-finals by Zambia, were stoned by local black Africans as their coach left the stadium. Later, in the lobby of the hotel where the Egyptian team was staying, it was suggested that FIFA might be considering South Africa as a venue for the World Cup 2006. A disgruntled Egyptian official gave a sarcastic laugh and said, 'They would never trust niggers with the World Cup!'

As Havelange had discovered and exploited earlier, and Rous was to learn to his cost in 1974, there is no love lost between French-speaking and English-speaking

Africa. As the Europeans pulled out of the continent and CAF grew, the balance of power within the African confederation shifted away from the ex-British possessions towards the former French and Belgian colonies. With the Arabs and black Africans at each other's throats, and the Francophone and Anglophile Africans on uneasy terms, the prospect of Hayatou delivering an African bloc vote for Johansson in Paris always looked remote.

When football emerged from colonialism as one of the few institutions which captured the imagination of diverse populations, it became the target for political interference and economic exploitation by powerful political élites. Such is the power of football that, the world over, where the activities of military dictators have stifled open political debate, football has been used to buy time for moribund administrations.

Football administrators are often appointed and fired at the whim of unelected political leaders who want to have control of national teams and their hands on any money which football generates. 'In 1959 we had a junta government,' recalls Dr Halim of Sudan, one of CAF's founder members. Halim gave up his post as president of the Sudanese FA in protest against outside political meddling. 'They wanted to interfere in the work of the FA. They wanted to select the president and all of the committee members.' His old leathery face cracks a wry smile. 'I would not work in this situation. They put in a Minister for Sport who could have been my son! How could I be told what to do by a soldier?'

African heads of state have taken excessive and often manipulative interest in national football affairs. Nkrumah and Rawlings promoted great teams in Ghana. Babingida and Abacha saw the political potential of the game in Nigeria. Doe in Liberia, Nimeiri in Sudan and Mubarak in Egypt are others who have used football politically. Hayatou's Cameroon has been suspended from international football on at least three occasions by FIFA because of the intrusion of the government into football affairs.

Worse than political interference, extreme poverty is the most serious obstacle to the development of football in Africa. Frequently countries are forced to withdraw from international competitions because national federations can't afford to send their teams abroad. In the qualification series of the 1996 African Cup of Nations, a combination of civil war and lack of funds forced 16 countries out. Mali let it be known that, owing to economic problems, they would not be taking part in the World Cup qualifiers for France 1998. Pleading poverty, Gambia withdrew from the qualification stages of the 2000 African Cup of Nations to be held in Zimbabwe, and the government of neighbouring Tanzania announced that in order to finance the country's participation five dollars a week would be deducted from the wages of each policeman!

'With so much poverty, we simply cannot afford to fund football properly,' said Emmanuel Maradas over breakfast in his hotel in Johannesburg. 'The situation is made worse through the stance taken by the World Bank, which has very strict criteria for money lending and equally strict monitoring procedures.' The World Bank's loan conditions forbid spending on sport.

The imposed financial misery of African football is accentuated through the corruption which so often goes hand in hand with the administration of football there. Modern Africa is made up of 'artificial states', many of which are ruled by by jumped-up and corrupt heirs of the colonialists. These artificial states, over which a succession of dictators have ruled, are so rent by tribal factionalisms and ethnic rivalries that it has been all but impossible to construct meaningful and durable civic democracies. Immature democratic experiments have, more often than not, perished, replaced by a range of authoritarian, military régimes and single-party systems with little or no effective civil opposition. In Bayart's formulation, feudal-like traditions of power, patronage and exploitation operate in settings of bureaucratic break-down.

Corruption and the abuse of political power have flourished and become institutionalised. Men in key institutional positions – police, customs officials, immigration officers, military personnel, civil servants – are able to prey upon the civilian population, extracting tribute for services which should be rendered free.

In these countries, where a life of poverty and starvation is the lot of the ordinary people, the most powerful, greediest and corrupt men – the men most on the take – become the fattest. They carry their over-indulged stomachs like status symbols, in stark contrast to the deprived and desperate general population. This is the politics of the belly and it is ruining African football.

Football generates income through grants from sponsorship deals, television contracts, gate receipts and FIFA subsidies. Too often the money which should be spent on football development ends up in the pockets of corrupt administrators and government officials. Maradas referred to this as 'the cancer of African football'. Former FIFA Player of the year, George Weah, sees these corrupt officials as the 'main problem' for African football: 'Our officials are too selfish. Everything is money. They use us, the players, to get money, to steal the money.'

Take Zaire. With its mineral deposits it was once one of the most prosperous countries in Africa, but its post-colonial history tells of a progressive decline into despotic exploitation and economic chaos. Under the rule of the dictator Sesi Seko Mobuto, Zaire's economy has been ruined. In 1994 inflation was running at 6,000 per cent. For decades, commentators have claimed that Zaire's natural wealth has been creamed off by the Mobutu family and there have been no official denials that the deceased President for Life had a numbered account in Switzerland containing more than $4 billion. When they get paid, Zaire's army of civil servants receive as little as $3 per month. It is hardly surprising that corruption is rife. If possible, things have only got worse since Laurent Kabila seized power in 1997.

During the African Cup of Nations in South Africa in 1996 the Zaire national team checked into the Holiday Inn hotel in Sandton City, Johannesburg. Immediately a rumour spread among the hotel staff that $500,000, which was earmarked for the players' and manager's wages and bonuses, had disappeared *en route* from Kinshasa. Back in Zaire people whispered that the Minister had recently purchased an expensive holiday home in South Africa, paying for it in cash. The team's Turkish-born coach,

Muhamed Ertugal, resigned and several of the players refused to play in the next game unless they were paid up front.

The image is conjured of a Zaire official slipping away in the dead of the night carrying two battered suitcases full of used dollar bills. This becomes less of a fantasy when it turns out that most transactions in African football are conducted on a cash-only basis. According to Kalusha Bwalya, the former captain of the Zambian national team, many players do not have bank accounts. 'In Africa nobody trusts cheques anyway,' he said. 'We expect to be paid in cash.' When teams travel they bring along with them sacks full of money. It is little wonder that, with so much poverty in Africa and so much hard cash lying around in football circles, so much of it goes missing.

Manfred Honer has managed the Nigerian national team and worked in 14 different African countries as a football coach and technical advisor. Manfred explained how the rip-off works. 'Someone from the federation or the government minister – sometimes they are one and the same – has all of the money in a safe in this hotel or another hotel and at the end, if everything works quite well, then he is paying some money to the players, but the biggest amount, more than 50 per cent, is staying in his pocket.' He can say that he has paid the team's expenses, even though he's taken the lion's share of the money.

Joseph Antoine Bell, one of Cameroon's best ever goalkeepers, was in the squad for both the 1990 and 1994 World Cup finals. Prior to Italia '90, the squad had gathered at a training camp in the former Yugoslavia. According to Bell, they only had eight battered footballs 'and only one of them was any good'. The team doctor and trainer had no medical gear and the players had to have a collection to buy bandages and other essentials. Yet Bell knew that the federation had already received enough money from FIFA to help the team's preparations. Bell, who in 1990 was a senior professional in France, decided to act to protect the players' interests. He got the team to agree that on the eve of their first game in Italy, the tournament's opener against defending champions Argentina, they would refuse to play unless the federation paid them their wages in advance. He was experienced enough to know that if they were not paid in advance, the money would disappear into the pockets of officials and politicians back in Yaoundé, the capital of Cameroon. In the meantime, he persuaded the players to train and prepare like European professionals, instigating a system of fines to ensure that his teammates turned up on time to practices, meals and team meetings. Bell's strategy worked, at least partially, when at the 11th hour the federation came up with a proportion of the team's wages.

Player power was not enough to prevent the president of Cameroon imposing his personal friend, Roger Milla, on the squad (perhaps just as well as he turned out to be the team's most influential player), nor could it spare Bell from being dropped as first-choice keeper because of his shop-steward's role.

Cameroon went on to make Italia '90 a truly memorable competition, beating Argentina in the curtain-raiser and almost dumping out England in a thrilling quarter-final. They got far enough in the competition for the players to merit bonuses from FIFA. They never received this money, though, because, after the event, the threat to withdraw their labour became meaningless. Instead, the cash ended up in the pockets of greedy administrators and politicians.

Bell explained that Cameroon's USA '94 campaign was just as chaotic and corrupt. In the build-up to the tournament the papers were full of stories of a repetition of the 1990 stand-off over players' wages. Once in the US itself, the situation deteriorated. 'For two days, Henri Michel, our coach, couldn't sleep because he was constantly taking calls from here in America and from Cameroon,' said Bell. 'It is people trying to interfere. Trying to be big men with the team.' Demoralised and in disarray, Cameroon lost their final first-round match of the tournament 6-1 to the Soviet Union – another under-achieving team which likewise was on its way home. After the competition, the bulk of an estimated $4m which should have accrued to the players and been used for football development in Cameroon disappeared.

The Cameroon government disbanded the federation and imposed a new régime which, according to Bell, was likely to be as corrupt as the out-going body. FIFA's response to this political *coup d'état* was to suspend Cameroon until a democratically elected federation resumed control. It was only through the intervention of CAF that Cameroon were allowed, under a special dispensation, to participate in the 1996 African Cup of Nations.

For the 1996 African Cup of Nations, the Cameroon team got their flight tickets to Johannesburg late and lost a night's sleep over a flight delay. They had to play South Africa at altitude in the opening match less than 24 hours after arriving. Not surprisingly, they were hammered 3-0. A further twist to Cameroon's story was added when, much to the dismay of team manager Jules Nyongha, two days after this defeat the former captain of Brazil, Carlos Alberto Torres, arrived at the team's hotel to be introduced as the new 'technical advisor' to Cameroon. Torres had been flown from Brazil by MBM Multimedia Inc., the company which brokered Nike's $7 million sponsorship of Cameroonian football. Torres, who had previously worked as technical advisor for Nigeria for eight months without getting paid, said that this time he wasn't doing anything until he had a big fat contract in his hand.

Nyongha got a stay of execution when his team managed to scrape a 2-1 victory over Egypt, but Yves Yopa, the MBM representative and Torres's chaperon, was confident that after the tournament, Carlos Alberto would be installed as Cameroon's new manager. Nike's directors demanded to see a return on their $7m investment and believed that a world-respected figure such as Carlos Alberto would be good both for Cameroon football and for the profile of their products in Africa. This could have been the first case of an international team manager openly being appointed by the sponsors. As it turned out, unable to get the contract that he wanted, Carlos Alberto rejected the Nike/Cameroon proposal.

People often view big corporations such as Nike as villains in the political economy of world football. However, Yopa explains that in order to receive instalments of the $7m sponsorship, the Cameroon Federation must stick to a budget which ensures that most of the money is spent on football and related projects. Where the politics of the belly rules, financial control by the multinationals may be one of the few ways to stabilise African football.

Two years later at France '98, amid more allegations of fixing and corruption, Cameroon performed wretchedly as a team. The president of Cameroon's football federation, Vincent Onana, languished in gaol awaiting trial over ticket fraud and, once more, there was evidence of high levels of political interference in the national association. Much to the embarrassment of Issa Hayatou, FIFA suspended Cameroon for the second time in three years.

The politics of the belly also severely damaged South Africa's bid to host the World Cup in 2006. Not long after South Africa's victory in the 1996 African Cup of Nations, scandal was engulfing the black people's game. As African football expert Mark Gleeson put it, 'After just four years back on the world stage, revelations of corruption and farcical on-field incidents have threatened to retard this remarkable progress after almost 30 years of apartheid-enforced isolation.'

At the centre of these scandals was Solomon 'Stix' Morewa, the president of South Africa's FA and the man who, next to Mandela, had bathed most in the afterglow of the national team's 1996 triumph. He certainly gained most financially. After serious allegations of corruption and mismanagement, Sports Minister Steve Tshwete appointed a supreme court judge, Benjamin Pickard, to investigate the affairs of the South African FA. Judge Pickard found that Morewa had sold all the marketing and television rights of the South African national team to an Irish-based marketing company called Awesome Sports International. In return for a modest fixed fee, the company made millions of dollars from ticket sales, advertising sponsorships and TV rights. Awesome indeed!

In return for his 'co-operation', Morewa received a $100,000 'loan' from Awesome as well as being given a new Mercedes Benz from a grateful sponsor. Morewa, a trusted member of FIFA's bid inspection team, was found to have paid himself a performance bonus of $10,000. After the African Nations Cup, the SAFA executive voted themselves $3,000 bonuses. However, Morewa's pickings look paltry compared with those of former South African league president, Abdul Bhamjee, who was sent to prison in 1992 for embezzling $1.5 million from South African football.

Ignoring Judge Pickard's warnings about selling out to the multinationals, SAFA has since voted to retain ties with Awesome. It also struck a deal with a US-based marketing company to promote South Africa's bid for the 2006 World Cup. Danny Jordaan, who took over from Morewa, pledged to purge South African football of corruption. If South Africa's World Cup bid had succeeded, he may have had an even harder job on his hands as the big money poured in and the big bellies rumbled.

What marks Africa out is not the fact of corruption but the scale of it. As Bell says, 'In France you might expect that for every $100 coming into football, $10 might disappear, in Africa for every $100 coming into football, $90 disappears!' Africa may, from time to time, yield teams of world-beating potential, such as Cameroon in Italy '90, Nigeria, Olympic champions in 1996, or Senegal, victors over defending champions France in the 2002 curtain-raiser. An African country may one day win the World Cup. But, so long as the politics of the belly dominates African football, its tremendous potential will be stunted.

In revelations about the extent of bribery which has accompanied recent attempts to secure the winter and summer Olympic Games, the finger is pointed in the direction of certain African members of the IOC. Marc Holder, a Swiss lawyer and respected member of the IOC, estimates that between five and seven per cent of the committee were open to bribery and that most of these were Africans. Among them was Congolese wheeler-dealer *par excellence*, Jean-Claude Ganga, the man who mustered Africa for Havelange back in 1974. Ganga bestrode the Equinox in 1998 at the Big Man's last congress. He stood up and recalled Havelange's historic 1974 victory: 'There were no booths in Frankfurt, no cubicles. The vote belongs to the association,' insisted Ganga. 'The associations should be allowed to do as they wish in an absolutely free vote, an absolutely transparent ballot.' Then he addressed not so much the congress floor, as Havelange himself: 'Mr President, you came through the front door in full glory, and I would like you to leave in the same glory through the front door. The vote must be clean, and may the best man win.'

This is the last thing it would be if Ganga had anything to do with it. Famous for years as a hard man of FIFA and IOC politics, he became infamous within months of France '98 as one of the most extensively and consistently corrupt IOC members in the Olympic movement's shakedown on bribery and corruption related to cities bidding to stage the Games. Ganga was exposed within the IOC for, amongst other things, making £30,000 from a land deal set up by those running Salt Lake City's bid for the winter Olympics. When for the first time in its history the IOC expelled members, in March 1999, Ganga got just two votes of support out of 90. Maybe the Big Man stayed faithful to the end. The corrupt Congolese looked in his element at the Equinox in June 1998, toadying to Havelange and electioneering to the end. That Ganga could prosper for so long at the heart of the Olympics and FIFA is testimony to the hold of the culture of corruption in world sports politics.

11

TOUT HEAVEN

Tickets, markets and corruption

The ferry chugged beneath the gaze of Zinedine Zidane, whose brooding image filled the gable end of a building overlooking the entrance to Marseilles harbour. Big Tommy adjusted his ample frame, making himself as comfortable as he could on one of the hard wooden bench seats that covered the small vessel's outer deck. The ferry was bound for Archipel du Frioul, a scattering of fortified rocks that once guarded Marseilles harbour. For centuries the islands were used to isolate victims of the plagues which had ravaged the city. Today it would play host to another pest: Big Tommy and his gang of ticket touts were having a day off.

The gang had been working flat out in the build-up to the high demand Argentina v Holland quarter-final game which had been settled in Holland's favour the day before. There were now three days to go before the semi-finals. Marseilles was to host Brazil v Holland. With Brazil's globetrotting yellow-and-blue fans about to arrive in town, and with the ranks of Holland's Orange Army swelling by the hour, a black market ticket for this game was one of the hottest in the entire tournament. Most of the serious trading would not start to heat up until this evening, so Big Tommy had decreed that the boys would have a well-earned day at the seaside.

Big Tommy's broad Manchester accent pierces the chatter and laughter of French day-trippers as he holds court on the tiny ferry's forward deck. He is a large man, but without much sign of muscle. His flabby pink belly sticks out between his T-shirt and the top of his Bermuda shorts. In his plump hands he grasps a can of lager and a mobile phone – symbols of the ticket tout's trade. Rick, his second in command, is almost as flabby as Tommy. Bob, another member of the gang, is a Londoner with sharp blue eyes set in a tanned, unshaven face. In a former life he might have been a pirate. For the time being, in this life, Bob is working with Big Tommy on a kind of subcontracting arrangement: he uses his contacts and works the streets to get tickets which he sells to Big Tommy, who in turn sells them on at a higher price to 'clients' from England and elsewhere. For Bob, hustling is a way of life. Even on his day off, with a skinny French girl he picked up in a bar the night before, he can't resist sneaking on to the ferry without paying. Chris, the apprentice, is the youngest member of the gang. He is absent without leave from his job in a Manchester warehouse. His young wife's not sure where he is either. For Chris, the excitement of working with Big Tommy during France '98 is irresistible. He's slim and quick on his feet. The gang have nicknamed him The Rat because of the stealthy way he works the streets, scavenging for tickets and setting up punters.

Big Tommy explains that for him and the rest of his gang touting is a logical progression from hooliganism. When he was younger he used to follow Manchester United everywhere and was a key member of their élite hooligan fighting crew. 'But when I got older, had a wife and kids and that, I realised I had to settle down, start making some money. What better than this game?' Big Tommy and the boys do most of the things they used to do *and* make a living out of it – usually without getting arrested or beaten up.

Big Tommy's story is interrupted by the chirping of his mobile. His thick Mancunian accent suddenly becomes respectable middle England. 'Hello? Yes. How many? Six category one, Brazil–Holland. Right, hang on.' He puts the caller on hold. 'Bob, can you do me six bits, cat one, let's say for … carpet chink? Come on, you know you'll get a drink out of that! Yes? Yes. Good!' He goes back to caller. 'Yes we can do that, yes … four hundred dollars a ticket. Okay, good. Flying in from Amsterdam tomorrow. That's no problem, you've got my number. Right. What? You could take up to 30 more. OK, I'll see what we can do and get back to you. Bye.' He switches the phone off. 'Here, lads,' he says, the Manchester back in his voice, 'we can get a proper drink out of this if we can pick up 30 bits by tomorrow.'

The touts have their own coded language – toutspeak – through which most of their transactions are conducted. It's a mix of cockney rhyming slang ('cockel', being a trimmed down version of 'cock and hen', is ten), back slang ('ruof' is four backwards and usually means 400) and 'foreign' words picked up on the road and adapted ('chink', meaning '5', from the Italian *cinque*, a word picked up by the touts at Italia '90, also refers to '500'). A 'carpet' is '300', a 'monkey' is '500' and £25 is a 'pony'.

The more money the touts make the more they spend on drink. 'Getting a drink' means 'making money'. 'Bits' or 'gear' are tickets. Use toutspeak and the punter won't understand the deal taking place. Working the streets, Rat finds a punter with tickets to buy or sell and gets on the mobile to Big Tommy. Rat speaks with the punter in English, but he deals with Big Tommy in toutspeak to get the buying or selling prices, so the punter has no idea of the touts' profit margins.

Tickets turned out to be one of France '98's biggest stories. From the moment that FIFA announced that France was to be the venue the touts knew that Christmas was coming early that year. The first ever 32-nation tournament meant the biggest ever black market.

France is surrounded by countries with football's most populous, prosperous and most easily mobile fan bases. Once Germany, Holland, Belgium, Denmark, Sweden, Spain, Italy and, of course, Scotland and England qualified, the touts knew that business would boom. The well-supported giants of South and Central America – Brazil, Argentina and Mexico – were also coming to France. *Nouveau riche* football nations such as Japan, South Korea and the USA, were through. The surprise qualification of Jamaica, with its large European diaspora, added to the clamour for tickets.

France's stadia were tight. The average capacity of the ten venues was just 46,348. Four grounds held fewer than 40,000 fans. With the exceptions of St Denis and the Olympic Stadium in Marseilles, the French grounds were too small to host a decent English Premier Division match, never mind a World Cup Finals game. Squeezing into the stadiums were press and VIPs and, although the French organisers would not say precisely how many seats were taken out of regular circulation and set aside for special customers, it looked to be as much as 10 per cent per game. Very high, inelastic demand (that is, infinitely gullible fans and relatively small stadiums) meant the touts were laughing.

The French organisers made things worse by rotating national teams around the ten stadiums, ensuring that some of the most high-profile games would be held at the smallest grounds. Two of England's group games, against Romania and Colombia, were played at two of the smallest venues, Toulouse and Lens, two towns close enough to England to be easily accessible by planes, trains and automobiles. This led to a massive demand for tickets. Holding England's hugely attractive last-16 game with Argentina in St-Étienne's Geoffroy Guichard stadium, capacity 42,000, was akin to squeezing a Rolling Stones rock concert into a basement jazz club.

The real bonus for the touts, however, was the way the French organisers and FIFA distributed tickets. For the 64 matches in the France '98 programme a record total of 2,500,000 tickets (an average just short of 40,000 per game) was issued and distributed through a complex formula that was open to abuse. Here are the facts. French residents received 60 per cent or 1,500,00 tickets; FIFA received 20 per cent or 500,000 tickets for distribution around the national associations; sponsors and the grasping 'FIFA family' took a 12 per cent or 300,000 ticket share; and the remaining 8 per cent or 200,000 tickets went to approved tour operators (ATOs) – organisations which came to be known as the licensed touts.

Tickets to French residents went on sale early 1997, months *before* the draw allocating teams to venues was made. So the vast majority of tickets had been sold before anybody knew who was playing against whom and where. The French organisers justified this by claiming that they needed the cash flow to help them to complete their preparations for the tournament. At first glance, this may look like the French government joshing their citizens into taxing themselves to pay for rebuilding and other public projects associated with the World Cup. The opposite is true – the 60% allocation for French residents turned out to be little short of a tax rebate. Until the national side was on the verge of winning the tournament, the World Cup generated little enthusiasm throughout the country. We watched game after game, in bar after bar with only ourselves and the bartender for company.

There was little or no evidence of the French in Nantes or St-Étienne flocking to see Yugoslavia take on Iran or Spain against Nigeria. But there was plenty of evidence that the vast majority of the French who pre-bought tickets sold them on to touts at a considerable profit. If the composition of the crowds at England's games is anything to go on, the black market must have been enormous. The English FA's allocation hovered around 6 per cent, yet stadiums in Marseilles, Lens and St Étienne were up to two-thirds full with English fans.

Article 58 under EC law makes it illegal for any member country to operate a trading system which disadvantages national, racial or ethnic groups from other member nations. The ticket distribution system with its overwhelming bias towards the French clearly violated this principle. A group of individual Euro MPs took the matter to the French courts, but lost their case on a technicality.

Under pressure from all quarters, the French organisers introduced a telephone hotline, ostensibly to give non-French citizens a better chance of getting tickets. However, the French telephone system could not cope with the demand when, on the first day of the hotline, an estimated 20 million calls were made and only 15,000 callers got through. There was also a separate hotline number for French citizens only, and it is estimated that they were almost ten times more likely to get through and obtain even more tickets. Also, if you had a friend working for France Telecom, your chances improved astronomically if you were given the 'secret' number which by-passed the queuing system and gave direct access to the switchboard. A Paris newspaper reported that one caller had been able to buy up to 400 tickets this way.

It is easy to understand why Big Tommy calls France '98 'tout heaven'. He explained how his gang worked the streets in the days leading up to games, buying up as many tickets as they could from the locals and selling them on at huge profits to pre-commissioned clients around the world and, closer to kick-off, to the tens of thousands of fans who came to France in the hope of buying a ticket on the street. The sign 'I buy tickets' in several languages accompanied by an English mobile phone number, was a common sight in the towns and cities of France during the summer of 1998. Nine times out of ten this was held aloft not by ordinary fans, desperate for a single ticket, but by a tout eager to get hold of as many tickets as possible. Hopeful fans usually arrived in Paris, St-Étienne or Bordeaux only to find that the touts had already bought up all available local tickets. And, the more tickets the touts held, the more they were able to control the market price.

The French organisers claimed that this sort of activity would be impossible because tickets were issued with individual names on them, therefore black-market tickets would be worthless. Prior to the tournament, television advertising campaigns in France and across Europe bombarded the public with images of disappointed fans, turned away at the stadium gates because their IDs did not match the name on their black-market tickets. In fact little, if any, checking of tickets took place. 'It was ridiculous of the French to think they could check tickets,' said Ernie Walker, a senior UEFA and FIFA official who was in charge of stadium security in Marseilles and who was also involved in planning Euro 2000 in Holland and Belgium. Any advantages gained in terms of curbing the black market, he claimed, would be far outweighed by the security problems caused by having 'tens of thousands of fans queuing for hours on end as the police tried to check each ticket'.

The names-on-tickets fiasco, according to Big Tommy, also led to another great scam. A group employed by some of the French staff in their central distribution office in Paris used names taken from the telephone directory and issued thousands of tickets to themselves which they then sold on to the black market.

The enterprising French citizenry and incompetent and corrupt French organisers were not the only source of tickets for Big Tommy and his gang. Through its partnership with FIFA, ISL Worldwide acquired 180,000 or 7.2 per cent of the total allocation of tickets, most of which were earmarked for the tournament's 12 top sponsors. The practice of giving large numbers of tickets to sponsors has crept into sport without seriously being questioned. FIFA/ISL tried to justify this practice as part of a larger marketing strategy, but how the acquisition of tickets contributes to sponsors' commercial success is unclear. That FIFA/ISL needed to keep their big sponsors sweet is less of a puzzle.

Sponsors either used their tickets as perks for senior managers and favoured employees or passed them on to the public as prizes. As the tournament approached, we were inundated with inducements to eat, drink, drive and pay by plastic for long-shot chances of winning coveted tickets for the World Cup. Inevitably some of these tickets ended up on the black market, as did some of the 120,000 tickets for FIFA's designated VIPs. The most outrageous case of this, with potentially disastrous security consequences, happened when VIP tickets for the England v Columbia match in Lens were sold onto the black market. Television cameras scanning the VIP box revealed a group of ordinary fans occupying seats a few rows behind Prince Charles and his sons.

The gangs of professional English touts who were roaming around France faced competition, not just from local organised criminals but also from sophisticated teams of North American 'scalpers', many of whom operated from home via the internet. Web pages offering tickets for sale and/or exchange became increasingly common in the build-up to France '98. At the push of a few buttons, corporate executives in Miami or Toronto could off-load their complimentary tickets for huge profits.

Big Tommy recalled a couple of Canadian touts who were working a pitch outside the Sovotel in Marseilles's Old Port prior to the England-Tunisia game. They had 200 'briefs' with a face value of £75 and were knocking them out for £100 a 'bit' for a quick £5,000 profit. Eager English fans gathered around them before Tommy moved in and offered to buy the lot for £20,000. For some reason the Canadians refused, preferring to sell to the fans rather than a competitor. But this refusal spooked the punters who began to wonder if the tickets were fakes, a perception that Tommy did his best to encourage. Things soon turned ugly and the North American scalpers found themselves surrounded by an angry mob demanding their money back. Tommy and his men moved in to rescue the Canadians, escorting them to the edge of the Old Port area and in the process buying up the remaining tickets, which they proceeded to sell on for £150. 'Yeah, we had a good drink out of that one, didn't we Lads' recalled Big Tommy, pausing for breath to take a swig from his can of beer.

It is a difficult balance for touts to find places to cut deals, out of the view of the authorities, but in spaces public enough so that the chances of righteous muggings and heavy losses of blood, tickets, and cash are reduced. That is why more experienced gangs like Tommy's work in teams, with street runners only handling small numbers of tickets and limited amounts of cash at once, using their mobile phones to place orders to get supplies of briefs and off-load accumulated money to a central and secure location under Tommy's watchful eye.

All of FIFA's 200 or so members were entitled to a share of tickets for France '98. Some, like England, attempted to distribute their relatively paltry allocations as fairly as possibly by operating loyalty-based membership schemes. Unfortunately, membership of the England Supporters Club was ten times greater than FIFA's allocation of tickets to The FA. Moreover, not long after France '98 there was uproar among some England supporters when The FA decided to close the existing England members scheme because they had evidence to suggest that it was being used and abused by both touts and hooligans. It has since been revamped and applicants are now carefully screened to ensure that they do not have criminal records for football-related violence or any other public-order offences. However, this still does not stop touts using 'clean' friends and relatives to hold multiple memberships of such a scheme.

Many other national associations, particularly of smaller countries who hadn't qualified, got rid of their tickets in fairly opaque ways – through a friend of friend or on-the-nod. Sometimes corrupt officials simply stole tickets and sold them privately to fatten their own bank accounts. If you got caught you might still catch your biggest match, from a distance. 'They may be in prison, but they are also human beings,' said Pong Moni, the Head Warden of Yaoundé's Central Prison in Cameroon, announcing in June 1998 that eight television sets were to be made available so that inmates could watch the national side's progress during the World Cup. This was good news for the disgraced head of Cameroon's Football Association, Vincent Onana, detained at Yaoundé's international airport and prevented from travelling to France after British TV revealed that he had sold 3,000 tickets, the whole of the Cameroon's allocation, on to the black market. Instead of occupying his VIP seat in Toulouse, Onana would watch Cameroon's debut against Austria from his prison cell.

Approved Tour Operators were allocated the remaining 200,000 tickets. These were companies which, with the blessing of the organisers, put together exclusive packages which included travel, tickets and, sometimes, accommodation and hospitality. Travel companies were invited to submit tenders for Approved Tour Operator status. Seventeen were successful, including five European firms, three of which were British. Massive profits were assured. The standard package for round-one matches consisted of flights, taxis to and from the stadium and a $50 face-value ticket. The actual cost of such a package was $350, but operators were selling them for more than $1,000. They were nothing short of licensed touts.

Companies attempted to justify this high mark-up by claiming that they had to pay the French organisers more than $500,000 for the privilege of ATO status. The

French raked in an additional $12 million from this. The fans would pay for this. Only relatively wealthy people or those ordinary fans who were prepared to go into debt went to the World Cup via FIFA's licensed touts.

If there is anything worse than paying ten times the face value for a ticket, it's paying the money for a ticket which does not exist. Because ATO status was conferred by the French before they distributed any tickets – before operators or anybody else knew the quantity of tickets that they would get – fans had to buy packages on the promise that tickets would eventually materialise. Many of the 17 operators sub-contracted the sales of their World Cup tickets and packages to other, usually smaller, travel agencies. Fans couldn't tell whether they were dealing with officially sanctioned companies (with FIFA-guaranteed tickets) or with one of a plethora of non-accredited companies, like Big Tommy's, which sprang up in the build up to France '98. Many, if not most, of such companies had no guaranteed access to tickets and yet nobody prevented them from advertising in newspapers and on the internet. Tens of thousands of phantom tickets were bought. Countless fans fell victim to these bogus companies, paying hundreds of pounds, pesetas, dollars and yen upfront, only to discover, often on the day of the match itself, that there were no tickets. When they went to get their money back, they discovered that many of these travel companies had been liquidated. In the UK alone at least eight such companies declared themselves bankrupt. There was Great Portland Entertainments, established in 1996 by David Spanton, an undischarged bankrupt with a history of failed ticketing businesses. The Official Receiver estimated that between December 1997 and May 1998 Great Portland 'sold' 40,000 tickets which it did not possess in the first place. After a damning Department of Trade and Industry investigation, the company was wound up with debts of up to £2.5 million, leaving thousands of fans broken-hearted and in debt.

Despite the recession at home, the Japanese turned up in France in force – 35,000 made the trip – and many came hoping to buy tickets on the black market. When it comes to bartering, most ordinary fans are no match for an experienced tout, and the Japanese proved to be particularly vulnerable. Bob boasted of how he had cleaned up in Toulouse for the Japan v Argentina clash: 'Yeah, the Japs were great, you could charge 'em more or less what you liked and they would pay it.'

Along with the British, Brazilians, Germans and Dutch, the Japanese were amongst the biggest losers in operator-related ticket scandals. For their game with Argentina, nearly 15,000 Japanese fans had reserved package tours only to discover that fewer than 3,000 of these delivered on tickets. Consequently, either individual Japanese fans, or representatives of 'dishonoured' travel companies, wandered around the streets looking for tickets. This played right into the hands of the touts, who had already bought up most of the local supply.

According to the touts, one of the hottest tickets during France '98 was for Croatia v Japan. There were two main reasons for this. Firstly, of all the travelling supporters who were hit by the failure of package companies to deliver tickets, the Japanese were hit the worst. Tens of thousands of them paid big money and travelled the thousands of miles East to West only to discover on arrival that there were no tickets. Just like the Dutch, the Japanese were forced onto the black market. But unlike for the Dutch, the English, or the Italians, there is no tradition of barter or haggling in Japanese culture. In Japan the price is the price and that is it. With demand so inelastic and custom so compliant, the touts could name their own price and in the case of this game it was £1,000 a ticket. This is how one of Big Tommy's rivals, Jimbo, got really lucky. He flew into St-Étienne and took a tram to the centre of town. A man dressed in a dark suit and carrying a brief case sat next to him. Jimbo happened to take a brochure out of his bag that had info about the forthcoming match. This caused the stranger to ask Jimbo if he was going to the game. He said he was but was interested in buying tickets, at which point the stranger introduced himself as an embassy official of a certain former Yugoslavian country who might have some tickets for sale. 'How much?', inquired Jimbo.

'They're expensive', replied the diplomat, '£100 pounds each'.
Jimbo had difficulty keeping calm, he sensed a killing. 'How many?' followed up Jimbo.
'One hundred', whispered the Slav.

Jimbo could hardly believe his ears or his luck. The two men got off at the next tram stop and went into the nearest bar where the diplomat opened his brief case revealing the 100 tickets. Jimbo bought the lot for £10,000 and in 24 hours sold them for £100,000, pocketing £90,000.

This was tout heaven, but it could quickly turn to hell. The touts believe that they perform an effective and essential service to football, particularly during large and complex tournaments like the World Cup. Who else, they argue, can redistribute tickets with the necessary speed and efficiency to ensure that stadiums are full and those that want a seat and can pay, get one? They see their roles as indispensable, particularly when a tournament like the World Cup reaches the knockout stages and fans that have been waiting at home make last-minute decisions to travel to quarter and semi-final matches. They have a point, but it is not one that gets much sympathy from the fans, particularly those who cannot afford to pay. Touts are generally despised by fans. 'Treated like scum, worse than drug dealers,' as Big Tommy puts it. Occasionally a naïve tout can get isolated, beaten up, and robbed of tickets and cash by an angry mob, with the police generally turning a blind eye. This is always a dangerous time for the touts. Even though they are providing the desperately needed tickets, because of their profiteering, they are universally despised both by officialdom and by the fans. Things can soon get nasty if the punters feel they are being conned. It is not unusual for a tout to find himself on the end of a good hiding, particularly if he gets isolated from his mates. The police rarely rush to the defence of a tout under pressure from his customers. On the contrary, should they be caught, the police are just as likely to relieve touts of their tickets and ill-gotten cash.

One particularly greedy North American company, Prime Sports International, not satisfied with the obscene profits that it made through the 'legitimate' sale of tickets and related packages, tried to get more of the green stuff through an insurance fraud. The company filed a report of the theft of thousands of tickets and hundreds of thousands of dollars in cash from its Paris office. This was followed by an insurance claim for the value of the tickets and the missing cash. This company, one of the 17 awarded ATO status by FIFA, was already under investigation for not delivering 1,000 tickets which a Madrid travel agency had paid for. French officials and the police became suspicious when they checked the seats corresponding with the missing tickets at the France v South Africa match at the St-Denis. They found them occupied by people who had actually bought their tickets from Prime Sports. When US agents visited the company's Florida headquarters they found the place deserted.

As the World Cup wore on and the ticketing scandals got worse, FIFA officials tried to pass the buck to the French organisers, who in turn claimed the operators were to blame. The aloof, holier-than-thou stances of FIFA and the French organisers became difficult to maintain when the Chief Executive of ISL France, Marc Loison, and Philippe Magraff, a senior consultant working for the French-based subsidiary of FIFA's main global marketing partner, ISL Worldwide, were charged with fraud in connection with ticket sales. According to Glen Kirton, senior vice-president of the parent company, ISL Worldwide had only a minority, non-executive shareholding in ISL France and, anyway, 'ISL France came nowhere near the sponsors' tickets'. From whom, then, did Loison and Magraff get the 2,000-plus tickets which they were peddling using ISL headed paper? Is it possible that the two men used their positions to steal tickets designated for some of the company's biggest customers? Kirton went on the defensive, saying that ISL France had no ties with FIFA and that ISL Worldwide would 'take whatever necessary legal action to protect its good name'. In the end, ISL Worldwide solved the problem of its delinquent relative by buying a majority, executive shareholding in ISL France.

Big Tommy's gang are not the only ones working Marseilles. On the return trip, as the ferry approached the dock, it sailed under the shadow of the Hotel Sofitel, one of the city's grandest and most expensive establishments. Naturally, that's where FIFA's top brass and other VIPs were staying. A gang of touts from London set up shop right in the middle of the lobby. As they checked in, or sat at their tables in the restaurant, well-heeled guests were approached with offers of tickets – all right under the noses of senior FIFA officials.

When criticised for their mishandling of ticketing, the initial response of both the French organisers and FIFA was to point out that no matter how big the stadiums were, demand was always going to exceed supply. 'The only way to do this is the way it has been done,' said Keith Cooper, FIFA's director of communications.

Big Tommy believes that FIFA and the French organisers tolerated the touts because they valued the black market as an efficient distribution system, especially at the knock-out stages of the competition. People with money waited at home from match to match, watching the progress of their teams before committing themselves to travelling, say, for quarter- or semi-final matches. 'Only the touts,' claimed Tommy, with their extensive networks, 'could shift the tickets in the time available.'

With FIFA failing to operate a system that was for the good of the game and its supporters, it was only through the intervention of the touts that large quantities of tickets did get into the hands of ordinary fans, albeit at highly inflated prices. Not that the fans respected the touts for this.

Most touts are sensible enough not to be caught with large amounts of tickets and cash, and usually losses are small, but it is not always so. Big Tommy recalls an incident in Paris when an English mob bought a large quantity of tickets from a French team for $12,000. The following day one of the Frenchmen came to the touts' hotel explaining that when he counted the money he had discovered that the English had paid $2,000 more than they should have. He wanted to return it. Scarcely believing their luck, the English accepted the cash. Several days later the ringleader of the French outfit phoned back offering a second, considerably larger, consignment of tickets for which he needed $25,000 upfront. Remembering the returned $2,000, the English touts believed that the French gang must be trustworthy and went for the deal. On the day of the transaction one of the French team came to the hotel room and told the English that they must come outside, bringing the money, where another gang member was waiting with the tickets in a parked car. Two of the English touts went down with the cash and jumped in the back seat of the car only to find themselves facing a mean-looking Frenchman brandishing an automatic pistol. He promptly relieved them of their cash, dumped them out of the car and sped off into the Paris traffic.

Getting an extra 30 tickets for tomorrow's big game is a tall order, but Big Tommy's confident that with the Rat on the job, the gang will be able to deliver. After a day's rest and relaxation, the lads are ready for the challenge. 'Let's go to work,' barks Big Tommy, sending his men scurrying into the thronging warren of streets and squares surrounding the Old Port.

A few years later one of us [John Sugden] tracked Big Tommy down to his lair in Manchester. He was interested in researching for a book on the football black market, including ticket touting. Tommy was an important gatekeeper into this world. John spent 2000–02 following him, gathering material for a book called *Scum Airways: Inside Football's Underground Economy*. At the time Sugden did not see much of a relationship between this project and our FIFA work, but they would overlap and that overlap would occur in surprising ways during the World Cup finals in Japan in 2002. Tommy had used some of the money he made on tickets during France '98 to set himself up as an independent travel operator. Initially his main customers came from the heavy hooligan gangs that still followed Manchester United and Leeds United on their European adventures. As he built up his company, however, he was seeking to become more and more 'legitimate' and expand into the England travel market.

In February 2002, almost four years after our first encounter in Marseilles, when John met up with him again in the Loaf, a chic new café and wine bar built into a railway arch in Manchester's Deansgate station – Big Tommy was still sitting on the fence, undecided whether or not to make the trip to Japan. With only a month to go before the start of the competition, the ticket market for World Cup 2002 was very uncertain. Japan, where England would play all their games, is not just a long way, it is also notoriously expensive. Stories of having to pay £10 or more for a pint in Tokyo had scared off a lot of England fans. The French and Germans, and the rest of the European qualifiers were even less enthusiastic about converting their precious Euros into Yen. As ever the Irish were exceptional and would travel in their thousands, following their 'boys in green' to the ends of the earth if necessary, even if it meant re-mortgaging their homes. In contrast, the collapse of the Argentine economy and growing impoverishment in Latin and Central American meant that only a few of the most wealthy grandees could follow their teams to Japan and Korea. In the months building up to the start of the tournament the rest of the world seemed decidedly lukewarm about the prospect of spending time and lots of money in the sweltering Orient, perilously close to the monsoon and typhoon seasons.

Unlike the situation for France '98, when many football associations, particularly those from Europe, had lobbied FIFA for additional tickets, for 2002 a lot of federations sent back portions of their allocations. So too did several of the big sponsoring companies, claiming not to be able to afford to put together VIP packages for clients and employees. With so many tickets allegedly available at face value from official sources it was hard to see how the touts could make their usual killing on the World Cup. In addition, because of the scandal that had exploded over the disastrous system of distribution of tickets for France '98, FIFA had vowed to put in place for 2002 a fair, efficient, hooligan-secure, and above all tout-proof system for ticket allocation. As it turned out, FIFA's handling of the ticket distribution for Japan and Korea was worse than that of France and largely because of this the touts would clean up.

Six months previously we had agreed that Sugden would fly out with Big Tommy and a few other spivs to hang around with them in Japan while they worked the tickets. Unless he could be sure that he could make good money, Big Tommy would not travel. Through slurps of cappuccino, he said that he was trying to get together the £35,000 bond that he needed to put up to secure his ATOL license, making him 'fully legit' and able to hire his own planes without having to go through a third party. A few years ago when he was still one of the lads he might have gone just for the hell of it. Now he was a wannabe businessman, and going to the Far East for what might turn out to be little more than a very expensive jolly was off the agenda. 'Anyway,' he went on, 'I've got a big Round Table do the day after the Sweden game and I've got to be here for that, so I'll probably come out on the following Monday.' Thanks to FIFA, Big Tommy had come a long way since Marseilles.

His 'wait and see' approach did not suit Sugden, as he needed to plan ahead. He had come unstuck with Big Tommy's flexible plans in the past and could not be sure whether he would actually go to Japan at all. Committed to write a chapter for *Scum Airways* around World Cup 2002, he decided to gamble and booked with Tommy there and then. Big Tommy lifted his mobile and ten minutes later Sugden had committed himself to a £2,000+ two-week package, that included flights to and from Tokyo, a Japan Railways pass, an internal flight from Tokyo to Sapporo where England would play Argentina, accommodation, and a ticket for England v Sweden. 'What about Argentina?' John asked him. He said that it would be cheaper to get a ticket for this high-demand game out there. Little did John know then how right he would be, but not for any reason that Big Tommy anticipated.

Months before Sugden had mentioned to Big Tommy that rather than just being one of his regular customers, if he did go with Tommy's airline to Japan it would help him if he could be given a few menial tasks to perform. John explained that having a minor operational role and allowing him to be perceived as part of the firm would help him get closer to any action that might take place. Big Tommy said that he would think about it, but nothing more was said until towards the end of May, less than a week before Sugden was scheduled to depart for Japan, when Big Tommy called him at home. 'John, do you still want to do a bit of work for me?' he asked.

'Sure, Tom' Sugden replied 'what is it?'

Tommy asked him to take some tickets over to Japan and give them to some of his customers. Some would come to his home address by registered post, the others he would have to pick up in London on his way to Heathrow Airport the day of his flight to Japan. Big Tommy told John that Emma, his secretary, would fax through the details of the London pick-up over the weekend.

So long as it did not involve him in actually buying and selling tickets Sugden figured that he would be acting within the law so he agreed to be Big Tommy's ticket mule. Two days later the postman called with a registered brown paper envelope from Manchester for which he signed. Inside were nine tickets in total: four for England-Sweden; one for England-Nigeria; two for Ireland-Cameroon; and two for Ireland-Saudi Arabia. The promised fax had not arrived by the time John had left home for London and Heathrow. As his train rattled its way towards Victoria, John called Big Tommy's office and spoke to Emma to find out where he had to go in London to pick up the rest of the tickets. 'You've got to go to a place called Mission Impossible,' she told him, 'there will be a package for you to pick up there.'

Mission Impossible is located near Bond Street underground station behind Debenhams's Oxford Street department store. Sugden dragged himself and his luggage through a thin drizzle down Marylebone Lane until he found the company's discrete, double-fronted, opaque-windowed offices opposite O'Connor's Irish pub and next to a Danish Laundry. He buzzed Mission Impossible and explained his presence to a disembodied intercom before being let in. Inside, at the front desk two pretty young women were working busily at their stations, checking monitors and answering phone calls, while a bespectacled middle-aged man sat at his desk in an open room behind them. Sugden wondered if the man was M, and if so which of the ladies was Miss Moneypenny. One of the women rose from her desk, shuffled through some papers and handed him a white envelope containing his orders. John expected to be told to memorise the contents before eating them. Instead he was politely shown the door and ushered out into the rain.

Sugden caught the Heathrow express from Paddington and during the short journey to the airport examined his latest haul that consisted of four tickets for Ireland's game against Germany, giving him thirteen tickets in all to deliver. The envelope also contained a list of people and places to whom and where he was to deliver the tickets. World Cup tickets had printed on them either individual names or organisations to whom they were first issued. Sugden was intrigued by these sources. Three of the England tickets had individual names on them and had likely been sold on to the touts by members of England's official members' club. The two remaining England tickets were issued to the English FA – that is tickets assigned to FA officials, as distinct from those allocated to the England member' club. Likewise four of the Ireland tickets had come from the Football Association of Ireland and the remaining four from the Czech Republic's FA. FIFA's claim to have a water-tight and tout-proof system for distributing tickets for 2002 was beginning to look a little overstated.

World Cup 2002 was an almost total success, except that is for the fiasco over tickets. To begin with, if you could get one the tickets were too expensive: £75 for the cheapest ticket for the qualifying stages, rising at each stage to as much as £350 face value for the final. This might have been OK for the high-earning Japanese, but it was too much for the relatively poor Koreans and those fans who were flying half way around the world to follow their teams. On top of the thousands of pounds spent on travel and accommodation, English fans, for instance, who wanted to see every stage of the competition, would have to shell out a minimum £1,500 just for tickets. These prices were set by the joint Japanese and Korean WCOC (World Cup Organising Committee) to whom all of the ticket revenues were to accrue. They were way out of the range of the fabled 'ordinary fan' and it reminded us of a comment made by Alan Rothenberg, a US member of the FIFA executive. When challenged in Paris about the excessive price of tickets for Korea and Japan, he shrugged his shoulders and simply said 'watching the World Cup live is not for the ordinary fan. That's why they've got televisions.'

The price of tickets was bad enough and the system for their distribution was worse – unless you were a tout that is. Keeping in mind that the hub of the Spivs' world that John had been investigating is Manchester, it was an astonishing coincidence that the contract for producing and distributing World Cup tickets was awarded to Byrom Consultants, a small British company with its headquarters in Big Tommy's backyard, Cheadle Hulme, south Manchester. Buying, selling and distributing tickets was to be done on line via FIFA's ticket Web site, but by the time the first game kicked off in Seoul some fans who had been allocated and had paid for blocks of tickets, still had not received them. As many as 10,000 tickets allocated to England fans had not arrived before their intended recipients had left for the Far East. It was chaos in Korea and Japan as nervous and angry ticketless fans battled with FIFA's and local bureaucracies to get their hands on the precious tickets. As the early games unfolded it became obvious that large sections of some grounds were not full. This might be expected for some of the low-demand early games, like Saudi Arabia v Cameroon, but not for high-demand matches like Japan's opening game against Belgium or England's first match, against Sweden. The Japanese WCOC was furious as each empty seat meant a loss of revenue as well as some loss of face. In total the shortfall was estimated at two billion yen, which would have to be made up by the ten local prefectures responsible for the stadiums. Likewise the fans were frustrated and furious. Before Japan's opener, at a ticketing centre in Saitama one indignant fan grabbed a hapless ticketing official by the lapels and threw him headlong through a plate-glass window.

Against earlier predictions the confusion and chaos over tickets meant that World Cup 2002 would be a bumper event for the touts after all. As ever there seemed to be no shortage of tickets for them. Big Tommy had said earlier in the year that World Cup tickets would not be a problem. As indicated by the provenance of the ones that John had brought over, tickets were flowing freely to the touts from the usual sources, including many overseas football federations. Big Tommy also claimed to have a high-profile contact who would be able to get tickets out of the back door of Byroms. In fact this did not happen because the person in question (who cannot be identified for legal reasons) came under police investigation for football-related fraud. Certainly the touts were harvesting tickets in bulk. Spivs, mainly from London, Manchester and Liverpool were out in force outside all of England's and Japan's games. An editorial in the Japanese *Daily Yomiuri* suggested that FIFA should cut out the middlemen and give all of the tickets to the touts at the start of the competition. At least they sell the tickets outside the grounds where the games are to be played, the piece went onto argue. The reporter had a point. Like most touts, Big Tommy and his gang are a pretty ugly bunch, but without them there would have been far more empty seats. The real villains of this story are the people who created the conditions that were so favourable for the touts' trade in 1998 and 2002: FIFA, the real Spivs of world football.

12

THE BEST CLUB IN THE WORLD

Cocooning the FIFA family

Perched on the edge of the Avenue Montaigne, Paris's prime designer-store highway, the Hotel Plaza Athénée smacks of conspicuous wealth. The mahogany revolving door is embossed with gold panels depicting prancing ladies, while a traditionally glossy oak reception desk stands opposite vast antique mirrors, whose extravagant gilt frames shine against the deep brothel-red of the decor.

In the marble-tiled hallway, a pianist in a tuxedo feeds the *nouveau-riche* clientele of the bar opposite with clichéd classics. But the Bar Anglais is hardly a bar at all, more a long lounge serving the obligatory Kir Royales at expensive prices. Football folk and their escorts are at home here, oblivious to the prices as FIFA handles the tab. The leather armchairs, and flamboyant historical portraits are all bathed in a yellowy light that flatters the over-made-up customers.

Here, a few months before France '98, top FIFA people arrived for the annual meeting of the International Football Association Board (IFAB). This is the little group that is in charge of the Laws of the Game. It was set up by the British, and has been going since 1886, way before the formation of FIFA in 1904. The British first let FIFA representatives on to the board in 1913. Now it is an equal partner, with four votes alongside those of the English, Welsh, Scottish and Northern Irish. Britain had bankrolled FIFA back in 1947, gifting it the proceeds of the Great Britain v Rest of the World game played at Glasgow's Hampden Park. Now FIFA bankrolls the board. It only meets for an hour or two a year. These meetings used to be in Llandudno, Portpatrick or Torquay. Now board members have to pack their bags for Paris, or further afield.

There's not a lot of arduous work to do at these meetings. As one veteran board member put it, it's a 'rubber stamp'. The 1996 meeting was scheduled for Belfast, but at Havelange's whim the venue was changed. He wanted to welcome old colleagues to his hometown. The board met in Rio. No one objected, exchanging the frosty climes of Ulster for the beaches of Ipanema – a nice little late-winter break for the Brits and the Zurich-based FIFA members and their entourage.

The board meeting in 1997 was switched back to Belfast and the FIFA family turned up for a long weekend at the Culloden Hotel on the shores of Belfast Lough. Once the Saturday-morning meeting was over and the press conference was out of the way, folk could get down to the normal business – catch up with the global gossip, relax at the banquet, look forward to next year's meeting in Paris. There was a lot of talking to be done. Although Scotland had just one member on the board, six members of the Scottish Football Association turned up in Belfast, all accompanied by their wives. The Scottish FA assured us 'that FIFA did not pay the Scottish expenses for the International Football Association Board meeting at the Culloden Hotel in Belfast in 1997.' It can be an expensive business, then, keeping up with the club.

However, the Athénée and the fashion houses of the Avenue Montaigne wouldn't be the FIFA select's base for the World Cup – Havelange ruled out the Athénée because the lobby isn't big enough. And even the Big Man can't block-book the Ritz for six weeks in mid-summer. For France '98 the Family's inner-circle – the FIFA Executive, their partners and respected family elders – decamped *en masse* to Hotel Le Bristol. That's also in the eighth *arrondissement*, one of Paris's most exclusive neighbourhoods. It's on Rue du Faubourg-Saint-Honoré, parallel with the Champs Elysées. Le Bristol is not quite the French capital's most exclusive hotel, but it's better than the local B&B. Established in 1924, it claims to pride itself on discreet class rather than the swanky luxury of its 'palace hotel' rivals. It strives to recapture an historical, regency-style elegance that, nowadays, is distinctly unfashionable. The good-sized lobby, a wash of cream and gold, is an exercise in quiet, if uninspiring elegance – a theme which continues into the spacious, pillared bar, where piped muzac alternates with tinkling of a grand piano and where the powerful scent of stylish lilies is unmissable.

The style here is refined mismatch: well-crafted sofas and ruby-red armchairs; Chinese-style lamps sit on spotless glass tables and Persian rugs are decorated with bold but old-fashioned primary-coloured prints. Cream-coloured walls are finished off with delicate mouldings, though everything, given the hotel's proud boasts of its history, is suspiciously, inauthentically glistening. The raised bar is reminiscent of something you would find in a Merchant-Ivory movie; immaculately dressed waiters flit discreetly among the clusters of tables. At the far end of the lounge, broad windows look on to the stunning walled courtyard, where guests – such as Claudia Schiffer, Naomi Campbell and Stephanie Seymour (who held a private party here) – can catch some Parisian sun while keeping out of the way.

This was the heart of the Havelange empire during France '98. Always in a collar and tie, immaculately attired, the Brazilian held court here, shook hands in the lobby, dispensed patronage, usually looked mean and occasionally smiled. He may have been a regular at Le Bristol when he's in Paris, but the hotel management wasn't ecstatic at the prospect of more than a month of footie types hogging its halls. In the end only 40 rooms were kept for non-FIFA clients, but Havelange had brought in the heavyweights to clinch this. It was rumoured that he had asked the Minister of Culture to get pressure put on the management. 'We were like this,' the hotel manager said, locking his arms together to mime a straitjacket. 'It was difficult,' he added, grimacing at the memory of this far from fantastic experience of dealing with the Big Man.

Le Bristol is not cheap. A night in the cheapest room costs £250. The presidential suite, occupied by Havelange for the duration of the competition, set our weary traveller back £3,500 per night. The remaining suites and apartments range from £760 to £2,800. Typically, the FIFA family took the best rooms. Le Bristol won't reveal exactly how much the Paris sojourn for FIFA's grandees cost, but it is safe to assume that for the same money a mountain of footballs could have been bought, acres of pitches built and thousands of needy children coached and kitted out.

However, Le Bristol is Havelange's favourite Paris hotel. The Big Man can be faulted on many things, but an appreciation of style and the finer things in life cannot be included. From the outside, with its beige-marble façade, sparkling picture windows and understated revolving doorway, Le Bristol oozes class. This is the Big Man's Paris bunker and it's all action when he's in town. On the street an opaque, gilded-glass canopy shelters the busy commissioners in their serge-blue and gold livery. Armed gendarmes patrolling the nearby pavements watch the prim and sprightly bellboys as they fetch and carry the expensive leather suitcases, gifts and shopping bags of FIFA's glitterati from the fleets of limousines in front of the hotel. Silver and gold chandeliers cast a mellow light throughout the foyer, dancing off gold necklaces, inlaid bracelets and diamond-crusted rings from Mauboussin, one of Paris's top jewellers, which are displayed in the lobby in gilt-glass cases – no prices, of course.

One wall of the lobby's inner lounge is dominated by a heavy burgundy-and-gold tapestry depicting a rustic sporting event from the 19th century. A game of *boules* perhaps, or even an historic evocation of French folk football? Wrong. The scene is an early English cricket match, appropriately enough, for the style and atmosphere of Le Bristol is more class-consciously English than classically French – more Pall Mall than Champs Elysée.

Day and night, FIFA's executive members, its elder statesmen, FIFA wannabes and, of course, the FIFA wives and courtesans, (without which no FIFA event would be complete) deport themselves in the lobby of Le Bristol. Most days the imperious Havelange sweeps through, entourage in tow, pausing here and there to kiss the cheeks of a FIFA relative, friend or sycophant.

The busy Blatter, now FIFA's eighth president and fresh from his election victory, darts in and out of the revolving doors on his way to or from some urgent strategy meeting or PR appearance. On the evening of his 1998 election victory we saw him enter the lobby of Le Bristol as we were on our way across town to Le Meridien in Montparnasse – the hotel where the delegations from the national associations were staying. We jumped in a taxi and ten minutes later marched into the Meridien. There he was, President Blatter in the centre of the lobby with his daughter, resplendent in bright-yellow jacket, glad-handing more well-wishers. Had we at last found the secret to his ever-present impact on the election trail? Are there two Sepp Blatters?

The Meridien's where a lot of the business is done and the more public receptions are held. Right in the middle of once-bohemian Montparnasse, its pseudo-1920s style is unintentionally kitsch. The hotel's numerous floors and labyrinthine corridors cater for the mass-market, flashy needs of international (but in no way top-notch) business clientele.

On entering the vast lobby, everything from the burgundy abstract print armchairs to the quasi-abstract art on the walls smacks of bulk purchase excess. It's just the spot for the lesser lights of FIFA and for the congress delegates from the national associations. Some big names gather here too – George Weah, the saint of Liberian football, was mingling here within hours of Blatter's presidential triumph.

Back at Le Bristol, Americans Rothenberg and Blazer, key players and winners in Blatter's election gamble, are frequently found in the lobby. Rothenberg is often accompanied by his smartly dressed wife. Chuck Blazer – the man said by some to have made his first million inventing and marketing the smily face – grins as he barrels his way through the foyer, arm in arm with his attractive companion.

The vanquished have to stay in Le Bristol too, and confront their conquerors on a daily basis. A downcast Lennart Johansson is a familiar sight as he lumbers by, going through the motions of his role as chair of France '98's organising committee. The diminutive Scot, David Will, still a FIFA vice-president but vulnerable and nervous after heavily backing the wrong horse, darts in and out. Head down, pacing the marble floor, a step ahead of his minder, another Johansson backer and now deeply worried man, Mong Joon Chung, of South Korea, slips by.

The president of Oceania passes through the lobby with his spry wife, Annie, and stops for a chat. A New Zealander, Charlie Dempsey is in his late-70s. He is a short, slight man with a well-weathered face, wispy white hair and big, horn-rimmed glasses. He too had backed Johansson all the way, but in defeat Charlie remains unbowed. We had interviewed him first in Cairo on the way to our audience with Havelange. Charlie's a no-nonsense, expatriate Scot in the style of Jock Stein and Bill Shankly. He emigrated to New Zealand when he left the navy shortly after the Second World War. Like many migrant Scots, Charlie took his football everywhere. He played, coached and administered football in New Zealand before climbing the ladder to become confederation president. Oceania is the newest confederation (formed 1966) and one of the smallest. American Samoa and New Caledonia were granted full membership of FIFA at the 1998 congress, bringing the total membership of Oceania up to 12. As a vice-president who sits on a number of influential FIFA committees Charlie's in the know. He tells us how Blatter's people plotted to get rid of him as president of the confederation.

In what promised to be a tightly fought 1998 election, Oceania's votes were highly valued. The problem for Blatter's people was that Charlie was very loyal to Johansson. Dempsey believed that 11 of the 12 Oceania national associations were equally faithful to him. They would vote for the Swede if Charlie advised them to do so. Australia, the strongest football power in the region, was the odd one out.

Usually Australia easily dominates FIFA's World Cup qualification tournaments. Because of the small size and relative weakness of the teams in Oceania, there is no automatic qualification place for the finals of the tournament. Instead, the winner of Oceania has to play off, home and away, against the fourth-placed team in either Asia or South America. The Australians are afraid of the banana-skin potential of such a system. Their worst fears were realised in the qualification stages for France '98. After being 2-0 up at home in the final leg of a play-off game with Iran, Terry Venables's Kangaroos conceded two late goals and were eliminated on the away-goals rule. History virtually repeated itself four years later when in the play-off game for Japan-Korea 2002, Australia took a 1-0 lead to Uruguay only to be hammered 0–3 in Montevideo's Centenario Stadium, the birth-place of the World Cup finals.

Believing that his country would stand a better chance of qualification in a more straightforward league, David Hill, then the president of the Australian FA, threatened to quit Oceania and join the Asian Confederation. Dempsey, from his OFC base, led the resistance to Australia's ambitions to play in Asia. Hill wanted to get rid of Dempsey. He mounted a challenge to Charlie's position as president at the 1998 Oceania Congress. Conveniently for Hill, his ambitions coincided with those of Blatter, who wanted Dempsey's authority removed from the region before the election for the FIFA presidency. According to Dempsey, Hill, backed by FIFA's marketing partner, ISL, flew to the Cook Islands, Fiji and Vanuatu offering officials help if they would back him against Dempsey. None would accept. 'They came to me and explained what had happened and told me that they would vote against Hill,' said Charlie. Staring defeat in the face, Hill withdrew his challenge. Not long after France '98, Hill resigned his position with the Australian FA to pursue a career in Australian parliamentary politics.

Early summer in Paris in 1998: we stood with Charlie in the lobby of Le Bristol chatting about this evening's match between England and Argentina. We had wanted to see this game live, but St-Étienne's hotels were fully booked. Charlie said he could have gone too, but didn't fancy the long journey or the overnight stay in St-Étienne's FIFA hotel, which wasn't up to his standards. Charlie had been FIFA's rep for all of the games in Lens. Again, he didn't like the FIFA hotel so for the few weeks that he was engaged in Lens he chose to make the four-hour, chauffer-driven round trip from his base at Le Bristol. Charlie may be one of the good guys, but he still knows how to get the most out of FIFA's five-star, globetrotting lifestyle.

'Would you like to come and watch the game with me in the FIFA Club?' asked Charlie. When they are not in business meetings, VIP seats or on junkets, the grandees take their ease in the FIFA Club. Unlike the lobby, this club is open only to members of the FIFA Executive and their special guests. It's the place where the family goes to relax and socialise, away from the prying eyes and ears of journalists and related investigators who dog their every move in more public spaces. It is the last place that we would be welcome, but Charlie insists that we join him.

The FIFA Club was housed in a downstairs wing of Le Bristol. The club's French windows open out on to a tranquil garden, set in an elaborate quadrangle rimmed with off-white, mock-Grecian pillars. Neat emerald lawns surround an ornately sculptured fountain. Running water and the tinkling of the fountain's spray blends with the buzz of honey bees as they hover and hop around the garden's fragrant pink and yellow flowers. The drone of the Paris traffic is barely audible. This was a centre of tranquility in the middle of the storm of France '98. In the cool of the evening members of the FIFA family and their guests gather here. They sit under broad, white canvas parasols, in the comfortable basket-weave garden furniture which adorns the patio, relaxing, smoking, sipping cocktails and gossiping.

The game was scheduled for nine o' clock and we returned to meet Charlie in Le Bristol at eight. He was waiting for us in the lobby, with a four-pack of bottled Guinness tucked under his arm. Guinness is Charlie's favourite tipple and, even though the FIFA Club has a well-stocked, and, of course, free bar, it didn't serve Guinness. Charlie brought in his own.

The hairs on the back of our necks bristled as we marched down the long corridor past the security checkpoint and into the main lounge of the FIFA Club. It is a large room, set as if for a night of cabaret, with a scattering of tables, a piano and a small dance floor. In a side room is the bar. On the club's opening night the weekend before the World Cup mezzo-soprano Julia Weill warbled a Parisian welcome to the weary members. As a warm-up to the football final itself, you could look forward to Melbra Rai's 'strong, dark, rich tones and her soft appeal which leave the audience overwhelmed'. Peace missionary Melbra was celebrated by her FIFA hosts as a world figure. She'd marched with Dr Martin Luther King, 'and in 1996 met another Nobel Peace Prize winner, Nelson Mandela'.

But tonight's cabaret is to be provided by England and Argentina, televised on the three large-screen TVs spread around the room. We are presented with the FIFA Club's designer cocktail menu, 'Drinks by Ernst Lechthaler'. It's a lush's wish list. Shall we try a special France '98 creation? What about the 'FIFA Cocktail' (cointreau, lemon, blue cherry, Spumante Rotari Metodo Classico Brut) or the 'Fair Play' (orange juice, maracuja juice, Cognac Remy Martin, Jaya Mango Liqueur, Galliano)? How about a couple of magnums of Piper Heidsiek champagne? In a gesture of solidarity with the fans back home we settle for beer. That it has to be Budweiser or nothing else comes as no surprise. We are the only North Europeans in the place, but a cluster of executives from Coca-Cola, Adidas and ISL are hanging out at the bar. Most of them are American. With them is the tall, bespectacled, white-haired boss of ISL, Jean-Marie Weber. A few feet to our left there is a glass cabinet displaying the World Cup itself, surrounded by sponsors' logos. Nobody else seems to notice it. We are mesmerised, thinking of the passion of millions of people around the world focused on this 18-inch object. In its shadow, the family dispassionately ponders the choice of free cuisine from the FIFA Club's special menu.

What's on offer tonight? Yummy! The 'hen stock' soup with Royans' raviolis looks good. Then we'd be nicely set for the Italian-style veal scallop 'pané' of herbs, mushrooms, cream and carrots, or codfish garnished with red pepper and zucchini olive oil, followed by bitter- and white-chocolate mousse and the cheese board. We settle for peanuts.

Charlie finds a table for us near to one of the screens. As kick-off approaches the lounge fills up, mainly with Latinos, Arabs and Africans. Just before the game gets under way we are asked by an elderly gentleman to move our position a little so he can get a better view. 'Who's that?' we ask Charlie. 'Ach, him?' replies the Scot. 'That's old Lacoste, the guy who organised the World Cup in Argentina in 1978.'

Argentina had been awarded the 1978 World Cup by FIFA in 1973, the year before Havelange took over. It was, after all, South America's turn. But with a failing economy, political upheaval and rampant terrorism, Argentina was still an unusual choice. Few were surprised in 1976 when for the fourth time in two decades the military seized power there. Not long after, the 'dirty war' began. Thousands of civilians, particularly students, intellectuals, journalists and other critics of the junta, were picked up by paramilitary gangs before being tortured and killed. To this day, many bodies have never been recovered. This was hardly an atmosphere conducive for staging the World Cup, but when he became president, Havelange insisted that FIFA stand by Argentina as hosts for the 1978 tournament.

The organising committee was run as a sub-committee of the junta, with the army's General Actis in charge and the navy's Vice-Admiral Lacoste as deputy. Within the junta itself, the greatest rivalry was between President Videlo and Admiral Massera, the latter a close friend and supporter of Lacoste. As 1978 drew closer Videlo and Massera struggled for control over the World Cup organising committee. When General Actis was assassinated, despite terrorists being 'officially' blamed, 'Everybody in Argentina, including the generals, knew that he had been killed by the navy,' said Dr Pablo Alabarces, a professor of philosophy at the University of Buenos Aires, and 'Lacoste took over the World Cup.'

Like the other members of the military, Lacoste realised that a successful World Cup could boost the junta's popularity. It also meant he could become rich. Against all sound economic advice, he spent hundreds of millions of dollars on new infrastructure – stadiums, international airports, communications complexes, television systems – none of which the country could afford and much of which would be useless once the World Cup was over. In Argentina it's an open secret that as the cash was released to fund his programmes, Lacoste made a personal fortune. After the dictatorship years ended, an investigation was held, but nothing could be proven. Pablo Alabarces speaks for many Argentineans when he says that 'the level of corruption during the preparation for the World Cup in 1978 was the biggest fraud in Argentinian history'.

Famously, Argentina had to beat by Peru by at least four clear goals if they, rather than their greatest rivals Brazil, were to progress to the knockout phase. The Peruvians collapsed to a 6–0 defeat and Argentina went on to win the competition. It was Havelange's first World Cup and he basked in the inglorious victory of the host nation.

In 1986, though, on the day of the Argentina v England match that was to become infamous for Maradona's 'Hand of God' goal, *The Sunday Times* ran its lead front-page story on the 1978 match. The Peruvians were reported to have received their bribe in two ways: 35,000 tons of grain shipped to a Peruvian port over the following two months and the unfreezing by the Argentine central bank of a $50 million credit account. Citing two football officials and one senior civil servant who worked for the Argentinean junta, the journalist Maria-Laura Avignolo alleged that the match was fixed through direct negotiations between the two governments.

'An extraordinary game,' recalled Sir Walter Winterbottom, the former England coach in an interview he gave us before his death in 2002. For the first quarter of an hour he remembers that the Peruvian side 'overran the Argentineans. They played marvellously. Now they wouldn't have done that if there was a fix-up.' But then something happened which changed Sir Walter's view. A Peruvian missed what he called 'the best chance of goal-scoring I had ever seen in my life. The bloke mis-kicked it and he was only about four yards out of goal and he had an open goal ... it looked as though it had been specially cooked, this thing, this match.'

An Argentinian journalist, Carlos Ares, expressed his suspicions to Lacoste. He said that the FIFA vice-president 'threatened me. I had to take exile in Spain.'

Of course, the people of Argentina took to the streets after their team's victory. It was the first chance that they had to gather in large numbers in public since the 1973 military takeover. The glow of winning the World Cup would not last long, though, and the generals knew that even if Argentina went on to retain the trophy in Spain in 1982, the junta, faced with continuing political chaos and economic collapse, was running out of time. If success in football could generate, albeit fleetingly, popular support for the government, they thought, what more could be achieved through fighting a war?

When Argentina surrendered to the British after the Falklands/Malvinas conflict, junta leader General Galtieri resigned in disgrace (he became a janitor in a Buenos Aires apartment complex), and Lacoste, who had been promoted to admiral, took over as head of the junta for a week while Galtieri's successor was decided. Once democracy returned to Argentina, Lacoste found himself out of a job but, while he undoubtedly had blood on his hands, unlike many of the other junta leaders he escaped prison, instead exiling himself across the River Plate in Uruguay. He continues to live there in some luxury unless he is travelling as a privileged emissary of the FIFA Family. Havelange is ruthless with enemies, but he takes care of old friends.

We looked around the room, wondering how many more crooks, torturers and murderers surrounded us. Then the emotional roller coaster which the game became kicked off. Argentina's early penalty, Owen's wonder goal, Beckham's sending off, England's heroic ten-man resistance and, ultimately, Batty's dreadful spot-kick miss. We were up and down in our seats as the FIFA Club, for the briefest of moments, became like a real football bar. When it was all over, we accepted Lacoste's condolences. Charlie finished his last Guinness and shuffled off miserably to his room as we made for the bar and FIFA's free beer.

The family saves the best cuts for its own, but other branches of the wider football family are well fed, too – such as the 12,500 accredited journalists who had converged on Paris for the opening stages of the competition before dispersing around the country, following the fortunes of their respective teams and their supporters. Many went home once their national team had been eliminated, but many others stayed on, returning to Paris for the closing stages of the competition. With no matches to cover, this was party time, as most of the sponsors threw celebrations for the media and other VIPs. The media had been pretty kind to France '98. The French organisers repaid the friendly reporting by throwing the biggest party of all for accredited media in the Equinox Centre, the same venue that had staged Blatter's spurious election to the FIFA presidency. It was some bash, held in three linked halls, each the size of an aircraft hangar. It started at eight and finished at six the following morning. Everything was free, with endless supplies of every drink imaginable, including hundreds of gallons of Bolly to wash down a dazzling array of food. All night long, in one hall, a succession of live entertainers kept the dance floor heaving with sweaty bodies. Top of the bill were France's equivalent of the Spice Girls and a leggy Brazilian Tropicana dance troupe. Another hall had been turned into a casino. Journalists and photographers crowded the tables, playing blackjack, poker and roulette with free chips. In the third hall a booming disco attracted most of the younger crowd.

Status meant little here as the press-agency men, the paparazzi, writers for the heavies and the glamour boys and girls from television and radio let down their hair and partied till dawn. It must have cost the French organisers a fortune, but for them and FIFA, if it kept the media happy, it was money well spent.

There are some journalists and lazy academics who toady to the organisations like FIFA and the International Olympic Committee because they get too fond of the junketing good life which so often accompanies the administration of international sport. 'We may be mere nibblers at the droppings of the cornucopia,' concedes veteran sports writer Peter Corrigan, 'but largesse does come our way.' He claims that the 'media, however are not very sophisticated in their anticipation and are so overcome by gifts, little pens, T-shirts, baseball hats and the like, that we would have sold Manhattan for even fewer beads than did the Red Indians'.

It was easy to see what he meant when you saw the thousands of journalists marching around France with their France '98 blue rucksacks, stuffed with gifts that would thrill the kids back home and provide fond reminders of the big event. The England 2006 bidding team understood the message, too, issuing invites to the bash on the British Embassy lawns and coming up with a few spare tickets for the Three Tenors concert for chaps from the international news agency, Reuters.

Some become part of the organisations which they started out by reporting on. Some even collaborate in producing edifying 'official' histories and heroic hagiographies of past and present leaders – all done, of course, on five-star expenses.

During the World Cup, what Ronaldo ate for breakfast was more important to most Brazilian journalists than discovering the connections between Havelange and Nike – just as finding out Glen Hoddle's team selection was given a higher priority by the English media than the underhand tactics of England's 2006 campaign. This, of course, is what the public wants. It fuels the gossip of the fans. But maybe fans want more than just the ebb and flow of World Cup trivia, which is carefully controlled by FIFA in its press conferences and releases.

The FIFA Club has both a real and a metaphorical meaning. We'd been inside the real one, but were more familiar with the other one – the one that includes the media, the sponsors, the secretariat, the retired officials and the rest of those keeping their noses in FIFA's trough. The FIFA family is not cheap to run. It has almost charity status in Switzerland, so doesn't make profits. It spends all its money on football and itself. For between 1998 and 2001 the FIFA accounts projected income of a little over 691 million Swiss Francs, around £288 million. Virtually all this gets spent, or redistributed, with total expenditure pitched at around 658 million Swiss Francs. A lot goes back – unmonitored – to member associations, but plenty's kept in hand to get on with the business.

Expenses for 'presidential activities/executive committee' were budgeted at a cool 20 million or so Swiss Francs (£5.9 million), including the ExCo's expenses of £1.25 million per year. From 1998 'presidential offices' got by on around £638,000 per year. 'International relations/presents' weren't forgotten, claiming about £19,000 for 1999. But the real gift was membership. And FIFA accountants know how to keep members comfortable.

Outside of the FIFA club and the close family, ordinary fans are kept in the cold with their noses pressed up against the windows, watching the feasting while Big Tommy and the rest of the touts pick their pockets.

'This [FIFA] is the best club in the world,' is how one truly canny, veteran UK survivor of global football politics described it. 'Come on lads, do you know a better one? World travel, cars at the airport, five-star hotels, lavish lunches and a daily allowance to boot?' He couldn't give it up. Could we? Could you?

There is a price, though, said the same insider. 'They give you this and they give you that and then they come back and call in your debt. You, over there, go and kill.' Family rivals were united on this front at least. Democracy and transparency in the FIFA accounts weren't worth dying for. What price transparency if it meant losing your membership card to the best club in the world?

13

BIDDING WARS

Winners and losers in the World Cup hosting game

'We will provide full backing to the bid to host the 2006 football World Cup in England,' proclaimed the Labour Party's manifesto of 1997, on the eve of its historic landslide victory. A few months later cameras flashed as British prime minister Tony Blair clasped hands on the doorstep of 10 Downing Street with Dr João Havelange, president of world football's governing body, FIFA. Alongside the prime minister and the president were members of the FA top brass, Keith Wiseman and Graham Kelly.

Kelly started in football politics as a pen pusher in the salty breezes of the old Football League's headquarters up on England's Irish Sea coast, at Lytham St Anne's. He moved to The FA's headquarters at Lancaster Gate as secretary. When football became sexy in the 1990s, Kelly's fly-away hair, crumpled suits and face to match hardly fitted the game's slick media image. Off-the-peg trousers were replaced with designer Italian suits. Out went the barber's shop and in came the hair salon. With a new diet and regular exercise, Kelly shed a few pounds and the chief executive's new look was complete.

The FIFA president emerged from a half-hour meeting with Blair fluent in the rhetoric of the English bid – you are the cradle of the game; you have a great pedigree, hosting (and winning) the 1966 World Cup and staging an exemplary Euro '96; and, by 2006, you will have the ultimate stage for the game, a rebuilt Wembley Stadium. 'It's the personal wish of President Havelange,' FIFA's interpreter, communications boss Keith Cooper, recited, 'that the FIFA executive committee will decide, in two years' time, that the World Cup of 2006 will indeed take place here.'

For Havelange, the handshakes at Downing Street offered a chance to show that, despite his imminent retirement from the job that he'd monopolised for the last quarter of the twentieth century, he was still the Big Man. He may have been stepping down, but he still had an agenda – not least to secure the presidency of FIFA for Sepp Blatter, his long-term right-hand man. England still had some influence in the world. If by dangling the prospect of hosting the World Cup Havelange could persuade the English to ditch Johansson and declare instead for Blatter, it would be a good day's business.

For Blair, it was an opportunity show off his French. What a change for Havelange to deal with an English official who actually spoke more than one language! Alluding to the sports minister Tony Banks's lack of foreign-language skills, Graham Kelly joked that Havelange's visit was the first occasion he'd known Banks to be lost for words.

This was not Havelange's only visit of this kind. Four months before his visit to Blair, at the draw for the France '98 World Cup in December 1997 in Marseilles, Havelange had also backed the South African bid. Earlier still, back in 1993, a German delegation visiting FIFA House in Zurich had received the Big Man's endorsement for *their* campaign. Talk up all the bids and rule out nobody – until the votes were counted for the presidential election at the Paris Congress.

Havelange's encouragement was enough for Blair. Together, the National Lottery, The FA and the Premier League had assembled a bid development fund of £9 million, and the prime minister reiterated his wholehearted support for a process which involved showering information and favours on FIFA's executive committee at the tax-payers' expense. At one time the race to host the World Cup was settled by voting in the FIFA congress, but a few years before Havelange's accession to the presidency, his predecessor Rous had shifted the responsibility for this decision to the ExCo: now, nobble them and you got the big prize. In May 1999 football's 24 most pampered men and their womenfolk were to be flown to and from London and put up in the best hotels for their hectic, publicly funded holiday. Shopping at Harrods, circle seats at *Phantom of the Opera*, and a royal party with Prince Charles at Highgrove. For dessert there would be VIP tickets at the FA Cup final.

When England hosted and won the World Cup in 1966, things were different. The world came to England then. Sir Stanley Rous was the key figure. He was FA secretary when the 1966 tournament was awarded to England, and FIFA president soon thereafter. African and Asian nations withdrew at the qualifying phase, and in the finals England played all of its games at home, at the national stadium. It was a cosy, domestic scene when Sir Stanley handed the World Cup trophy to compatriot Bobby Moore in London.

Even Jacques Chirac, on France's World Cup victory in July 1998, could not claim this degree of stitch-up. As Sir Walter Winterbottom, the England team manager from the post-war period until the early 1960s, told us, 'Stanley could use his influence. Personality goes a long way.'

Huddersfield Town fan Sir Harold Wilson, the prime minister of the time, milked the glory of the summer of '66 for all it was worth, squeezing into the post-victory photos with Moore, Stiles and the Charlton brothers. Rous, ever the defender of the boundary between sport and politics, sardonically commented that it was the players, not the prime minister, who had won the trophy.

A few months after Havelange's visit, Alec McGivan, leader of the England 2006 bid, sat nervously among the media folk and interested parties at the back of

FIFA's congress hall as the vote for FIFA's new president took place. The solemn-faced Graham Kelly was there, and did not seem happy in the exalted company in the Paris Equinox Centre. Glum at the most relaxed of times, he looked fidgety, shunned by European colleagues who were offended by the bellicose arrogance of the England 2006 bid and the clumsy attempts of England to gatecrash the corridors of European football power.

The stakes were indeed high. Kelly's man, FA chairman Keith Wiseman, had polled a measly 12 votes out of 51, trying to get on to the European federation's executive in Dublin back in April. Since Bert Millichip had retired from The FA, England did not have a single representative in any of the big committees of UEFA or FIFA. Without a presence in the corridors of power, England's 2006 bid looked lost. Kelly was only too aware of this: 'We're seeking to strengthen our international position,' he told us. 'We see ourselves as one of the major nations, and not to have a seat on the UEFA executive committee is unfortunate to say the least, but we are doing everything possible to rectify that. We are hoping to secure representation in the near future.' Speaking to us before the UEFA vote, he boasted, 'We have a very broad strategy to get people out and about, within UEFA and FIFA.'

Jürgen Lenz of TEAM told us that the aggressive England 2006 campaign had 'alienated England and was the cause of such a low vote for Wiseman at the UEFA Dublin congress'. Jimmy Boyce, the ebullient, curly- haired president of Northern Ireland's FA agrees: 'Let me tell you,' he said, 'I think that in terms of grounds and facilities England are the ideal hosts. Personally I want them to get it, but I don't think they will.' The clumsy and arrogant way England handled its 2006 bid ensured that few voted for Wiseman, explained Boyce. He raised his voice, 'The trouble with the English is they think they are superior to everyone – and they are not!'

According to Boyce, there are three reasons why England would never come close to winning enough support for their 2006 bid. First, there is The FA's betrayal of Bert Millichip's unwritten agreement with the Germans. When we caught up with him in his Birmingham law offices, the former FA chairman said he had made no formal deal, but he did hint that some kind of accommodation had been made. Millichip was close friends with German and French colleagues. In the late 1980s, when hooligans had English football's reputation in tatters, Millichip had managed to persuade them to back England's unfashionable bid for Euro '96. Without that support, Sir Bert told us, England would never have landed the tournament. He didn't bid for the 1998 World Cup, because he knew that France had the edge. At that time, 'Germany said that it would like to announce its interest to run at 2006,' he told us. 'All I have to say is that I may well have indicated we will support you, at that time, but there was no agreement.' No agreement, no contract, but maybe a promise and a handshake.

The leadership of the European federation supported the German bid for 2006. It claims 'to have taken a decision in favour of Germany' in 1993, though there was no formal record or communication of the decision. When the UEFA secretary faxed the English FA, confirming UEFA support for a German bid, David Davies of The FA reported he had Blair's full support for England's counter bid.

The Conservative government's sports minister, Ian Sproat, said that the 'undemocratic hole-in-the-corner way UEFA has acted' had caused him extreme concern. Tony Blair called it 'a cosy stitch-up,' and Davies claimed that the politicians and the sports administrators were 'deeply shocked by actions which run counter to all democratic instincts that we believe world football should stand for. Informal, unannounced pacts behind closed doors are no substitute for democracy and fairness.'

How inconvenient for Blair and his chums that somebody had stayed awake at a meeting of the FA's International Committee in August 1991. It was minuted that, 'it had been decided, further to a conversation between Sir Bert Millichip and Lennart Johansson, and discussion with the French Football Association, to withdraw the English application to stage the World Cup. In return, the French had agreed to support the English application to stage the European Championship in 1996.' This may explain why no English bid for 2006 surfaced until after Millichip's retirement as FA chairman and the euphoria of Euro '96.

Within mainland Europe it was widely understood that the 1991 agreement carried through after Euro '96. 'Kaiser' Franz Beckenbauer, figurehead of Germany's 2006 bid, says England would never have been given the chance to host Euro '96 without German backing. 'But Germany supported England and, in return for that, Millichip assured Egidius Braun [president of the German federation] that England would back Germany's bid for the World Cup.' The FA's denials rankle with Beckenbauer: 'We were very disappointed by the behaviour of the English FA. We still are.'

Lennart Johansson was equally adamant on this issue. 'We had a gentleman's agreement,' he told us. 'All the big nations were present and they know we said "Let's go to England for Euro '96 and to Germany for World Cup 2006"'. The honourable Swede felt that he had no choice but to back the German bid, a stance which would cost him votes in Paris.

It was obvious to the FA's men that the England bid wouldn't stand any realistic chance if Lennart Johansson became FIFA president. Just days before the presidential election, Kelly and Wiseman pledged The FA's vote to Blatter. This, according to Boyce, was their second big mistake. The English FA had already joined with more than 40 other European national associations and signed a letter promising that they would vote for Johansson. When, at the last minute, they switched to Blatter's side, they earned the enduring contempt of most of Europe's biggest football nations, many of which were represented on the FIFA executive and would still be there when the 2006 decision was made.

The third and most damning error of judgement by Wiseman and Kelly was their bungled attempt to get rid of David Will as the four UK associations' representative on the FIFA executive. Thwarted at Dublin's UEFA Congress, Kelly and Wiseman thought they could muscle their way into the FIFA Club by ousting the Scot and replacing him with Wiseman. To do this they would have to gain the support of at least one, and probably two, other home associations. It was unlikely that the Scots would turn against their own man, so Kelly and Wiseman shifted their attention to the Welsh and the Irish. Kelly claims that turning on Will was suggested by Havelange and Blatter in March 1998; and also advised by 'our own government'.

When we met up with Jimmy Boyce at Paris's festival of football in the Place de la Concorde on the eve of Brazil's opening game with Scotland, he was furious with the treachery of the English FA. 'It happened just a few days after the Dublin Congress,' he told us. 'I was walking around the boundary at Clontarf cricket ground, watching Glamorgan play Northern Ireland, when I got a call on my mobile.' Boyce raised his hand to his ear mimicking the call. It was the secretary of the Welsh FA. 'Hello, this is David, David Collins,' said Jimmy, rehearsing the other end of the line. 'Has Keith [Wiseman] or Graham [Kelly] called you yet?' Boyce told Collins they had not. 'Listen, they will. They want to get Will out of the FIFA exec. They need our support and are offering big development money to persuade us. I think, if the money's big enough, my board will vote for it.'

For a moment Boyce, who was due to succeed Will when the Scot's tenure was up in two years' time, thought the English were trying to bounce him back in the queue. 'No,' said Collins, 'they want rid of Will now, and for Wiseman to take over immediately. All we have to do is sign a letter telling FIFA that we no longer support Will as our rep.'

Boyce told Collins that he thought Will was doing 'a superb job', and that he would see him removed 'over my dead body' and hung up.

Not long afterwards, Kelly contacted Boyce and invited him and the secretary of the Irish Football Association, David Bowen, to London for the FA Cup final. The night before the game the two Irishmen were wined and dined by Kelly and Wiseman at the Royal Garden Hotel. After the meal Boyce and Bowen listened to the proposition. An unspecified amount of money, at least as much as had been promised to the Welsh FA, would be granted to Northern Ireland for football development. For a small and relatively poor football country, the offer must have been tempting. To their credit, though, Boyce and Bowen stayed loyal to Will and rejected the English offer totally. Back at Lancaster Gate, Alec McGivan complained to his staff that 'we can't budge the Irish'.

The Welsh FA weren't so high-minded and soon £3.2 million was on its way from Lancaster Gate to Cardiff at a rate of £400,000 a year over the next eight years. Not long after, Michel Zen-Ruffinen, then the acting general secretary of FIFA, received a letter from the English and Welsh FAs suggesting that because David Will no longer had majority support from the UK associations he should be removed from the FIFA executive. Right on the eve of the World Cup, Graham Kelly was still trying to oust Will. He pledged the English vote to Blatter, and immediately spoke with the Swiss, asking him to 'remind Havelange to speak to Jim Boyce about the FIFA British vice-presidency'.

But no FA committee had been consulted on the deal with the Welsh. Millichip and the old guard had bided their time, watching as the men in suits, led by Kelly and Wiseman, turned their beloved FA into a laughing stock. They saw their chance and struck, accusing the two men of operating independently of the FA's constitution. With realism and dignity, Kelly resigned on the spot, 'because at the end of a lot of discussions we were unable to convince the executive committee of the appropriateness of what we did'. Principles at last, but too little and too late to save Kelly or his former chairman who, with less honour, was forced to resign a few weeks later.

So in the political context of the world game, the England bid for the 2006 World Cup looked cocky and the FA leadership appeared sadly out of its depth as it dived into the murky waters of European and FIFA politics. Graham Kelly's efforts 'to strengthen our international position', as he put it, by 'being on the inside track, knowing what's going on', will look like one of the most embarrassing own-goals in the history of football politics.

England's bungled coup achieved the opposite of what its protagonists had hoped for. Long before the story broke, David Will knew of the FA's underhand attempts to unseat him. In the early days of France '98 he told us that FA vice-chairman Geoff Thompson was opposed to a strategy that had not been placed before the FA's own committee. Will told us that the plotters 'have not thought the consequences through, they've isolated themselves in Europe'.

When the story came out it looked like the English would be reprimanded. But in true FIFA style – no agenda, no paperwork – Blatter called the English in to a meeting at Zurich in early 1999. By now The FA had publicly backed David Will as FIFA executive member through his full tenure, way beyond decision time for 2006. The old guard at Lancaster Gate had gone. All could be swept under the thick carpets in the meeting rooms and halls of FIFA House. FIFA never mounted any serious investigation into the affair. Boyce confirms this: 'No, nothing. Not even a phone call. I was really surprised when Northern Ireland wasn't contacted. Of course they [FIFA] were up to their necks in it anyway. Once it came out and England went cap in hand, they could hardly discipline them. FIFA wanted David Will out. I don't think they knew the details of the deal with the Welsh, but I don't think they cared so long as they got rid of Will.'

Boyce agrees that the incident damaged the case for the UK association's special vice-presidential position in FIFA. Some committee members – Chuck Blazer and Jack Warner of CONCACAF prominent among them – went on to oppose the position, but in Los Angeles at FIFA's 1999 Congress the decision over the position was taken away from the executive committee. 'David is a popular guy,' sighed Boyce, 'but England's actions have severely weakened our position.'

The FA could now wash its hands in public. Geoff Thompson announced that The FA had 'had a lot of problems to deal with', and now it must get the 'ship back on the proper path, bring integrity back to The FA, build bridges with the UK associations, and FIFA and UEFA'.

As the bid was self-destructing at home, the 2006 team made its presence known abroad. Sir Bobby Charlton found himself on the manicured lawns of the British Embassy in Paris a couple of days before the World Cup final, in a gathering of diplomats and politicians, FIFA Club members and hangers-on, football wheeler-dealers and media folk. He spoke fluently and wistfully of memorable World Cup moments and was ushered back on stage after omitting to mention the 2006 campaign. And a few months later one of the newest elected members of the FIFA executive, Dr Joseph Mifsud, was welcoming Sir Bobby and other campaign team members to Malta. Charlton, Sir Geoff Hurst and Tony Banks were the high-profile members of the delegation.

Sir Bobby was a practised globetrotter. His company, Bobby Charlton Enterprises Ltd, had changed its name in September 1993 to Bobby Charlton International Ltd, and was looking to expand its worldwide markets. It was famous for its football schools but the company's annual report also pointed to 'promotional and consulting services based mainly in the field of football' as its principal activity. In 1992 the company reported pre-tax turnover as £902,008 on the sports school and related activities, and £132,130 on corporate hospitality. This report identified the UK as the biggest market – £782,143 against just £34,979 from the Far East. The 1993 turnover saw the Far East figure almost halved, and the UK figure reduced dramatically to £217,564. The company's fortunes and the balance of the finances were to change for the better during the following years, as Sir Bobby lent his support to Japan's World Cup 2002 bid. The 1994 report showed a revival of turnover in the UK, up to £664,957, and a dramatic rise in Far East business, £221,569. Corporate hospitality now accounted for £242,990, almost 30 per cent of total turnover. The company's two major markets in the 1995 report were again the UK (£571,023) and the Far East (£515,549), the chairman's salary now hitting £133,501, plus a few emoluments including one of between £50,001 and £55,000. By the mid-1990s the soccer schools were seen as less important: 'The company's principal activity' was now 'the running of an international soccer consultancy service based around soccer coaching schools and a hospitality business'. The 1996 figures were still high, the UK generating £434,533, the Far East £375,583, but the directors described the year's trading as 'disappointing'. The 1997 report, after the decision on the hosting of the 2002 World Cup, showed a loss of over £200,000. Soon Sir Bobby had resigned, on 2 October 1997, and the company moved on to a 'principal activity' of 'the receipt of royalties for the use of its name and the management of sports images'.

Maltese member Mifsud was new to the FIFA committee and, despite welcoming the England delegation believed strongly that bidders should not impose themselves upon individual committee members. 'A presentation should be made,' he said. 'There should be a code of ethics for ExCo members. Giving the World Cup should be a decision which is for the real good of football, it should be outside our scope to gain personally from our position.' Said with sincerity, but Dr Mifsud was one of those invited to speak with Tony Banks in London later in the year. Of course he came.

Doomed as it clearly was, the England 2006 bid and the beanos at the heart of it rolled on. For you have to do this to get the World Cup, as the ExCo members (and Sepp Blatter) have independent, purportedly secret, votes. And the serious players in the race to win the 2006 Finals continued to be equally praised by members of FIFA's technical committees when they visited the bidding countries.

One veteran member of such visiting delegations confirms that you have to accept the promises of the bidding teams. Faced with pretty pictures of designs of future facilities, you can't call them con-men or liars. The facilities looked thin in Korea when its bid was rated of equal merit to Japan's, but you couldn't tell the top *chaebol* in South Korea and their chums in the government that you thought that their bid had about as much substance as Brazil's warm-up for the France '98 final. You have to believe them, and trust that in this case, Korean national pride would deliver the state-of-the-art, soon-to-be-superfluous stadiums.

On top of the £9 million kitty, the England bid had lots of help in kind. Whitehall seconded personnel on to the bidding team. Partners came on board as the race heated up – British Airways, Marks & Spencer, Nationwide and Umbro initially, with the *Daily Telegraph* and Deloitte & Touche joining these 'official supporters' of England's bid.

In Japan and Korea, where they know a lot about alliances between the institutions of state, finance and civil society, experienced football bureaucrats commented on the political credibility of the England bid. They were impressed when a starry-eyed Blair beamed bonhomie from the glossy campaigning literature. And Sir Bobby is immensely liked and respected throughout world football. His column in *Target 2006*, the bid's official newsletter, was restrained, a touch lighter than some of the earlier more bellicose outpourings from the bidding team: 'Our bid combines professionalism with passion and our visits have provided an opportunity for us to present our case to stage sport's greatest occasion. We have set out England's strengths clearly and succinctly rather than drawing comparisons with other bids.'

Do the English people want the World Cup Finals? Who knows? Nobody asked us. The success of Euro '96 excited The FA so much that they broke promises left, right and centre to grasp for the World Cup. This coincided very nicely with the Labour Party's development of its manifesto and its aim to stage mega-sports events.

Imagine what might have happened. Three years into its first administration, the Labour initiative would have landed the finals and boosted its chances for a second term in office. On the run-in to the election campaign for not-so-New Labour's third administration, England is about to host and win the World Cup. Well, who knows what a devolution re-shaped United Kingdom would have made of that? It would be a dream ticket for targeting the central floating vote of middle England, if that came to pass; but the 2006 bid still looks like the closest alliance of interests, around English sport, of the state, finance and civil institutions. It was never enough to win FIFA's big prize though. Labour's people found it tough going dealing with the politics of world football. It seemed to be tiring sports minister Tony Banks. But when in November 1998 the *Financial Times* reported that Banks was withdrawing active support for England's bid, he countered this with a reassertion of the prime minister's 110 per cent support for the bid.

'The bid is a national one based on an alliance between the whole of English football, the government and business', proclaimed The FA in a minute to the Culture, Media and Sport Committee of the House of Commons. Tony Banks was only the most visible element in a huge government operation to secure World Cup 2006 for England. Behind him were amassed the faceless legions of Whitehall. The Foreign and Commonwealth Office (FCO) and related government 'intelligence' brokers were central to England's 2006 bid. The FCO made no secret of its role in the bidding wars. It listed as its major functions: gaining access to key decision-makers; providing assessments of the attitudes of international sporting bodies and key decision-makers; offering ministerial and other high-level official hospitality in the UK to key-decision makers and opinion-formers; offering sponsored visits to the UK to specially targeted decision-makers, opinion-formers and others likely to be able to influence the bidding process; facilitating the visa applications of visiting personnel connected with the bid; helping with the production and dissemination of publicity/propaganda; identifying and briefing UK-friendly journalists to be used in the promotion of positive image; organising special events and other functions at overseas missions and residences for the promotion of the bid; and arranging formal and informal approaches to influential decision-makers by the head of mission and senior diplomatic staff.

This is nothing short of a spook's charter. The 2006 team was not just backed by one of the world's oldest and most extensive intelligence-gathering networks, it was part of it. A former ambassador served as international advisor to the bid. Together with two other staff, also on The FA's payroll, a junior FCO officer, and a member of the support staff, they all had offices in the FCO 'enabling them to liaise between the FA, the Department of Culture, Media and Sport and other government departments and diplomatic posts.' This unit of specialist fixers all but ran, from behind the scenes, England's 2006 bid.

As the summer 1999 deadline for the submission of bids approached, The FA's 2006 campaign went into overdrive. All members of the FIFA executive, with wives and partners in tow of course, were invited to London for the Cup final in May. Wining, dining, theatre-going and an audience and dinner at No.10 with Prime Minister Blair were added attractions. The main lobbying event was lunch, hosted by Prince Charles. Wembley, Downing Street, Harrods, Covent Garden and now the Royal residence at Highgrove. This was the hardest of hard sells.

Only days before the deadline, The FA played its trump card and launched England's Welcome to the World. 'An invitation to the whole FIFA family,' read the glossy promotional magazine, 'to all 203 footballing nations.' They were invited to send a group of 12 children with up to four adults to spend two weeks in England during the World Cup Finals – should England be awarded those finals. This is the catch: you only get this if your country votes to have the party in England.

Anyone who has been involved in sport will know that there is a gift culture. Teams exchange pennants, players swap shirts, town councils host civic dinners and visiting athletes and administrators give each other mementos to remind them of their stay in 'our town'. We should not be surprised to see this gift culture in operation at the upper reaches of world football. Reflecting on his inspection trips to the Far East, Scotland's Ernie Walker recognized this as part of international sport's rituals. 'What do you do when the Mayor of Nagasaki offers you a present?,' he asked us. 'Stick it up his arse?'

However, the gift culture should not be boundless and it must be distinguishable from the graft culture which has grown up around the bidding for sports events like the Olympic Games and the World Cup. 'England's Welcome to the World' was couched in the language of sports gift culture. 'We want our World Cup to be for young people everywhere,' beamed Sir Bobby. 'England 2006 will offer everyone a World Cup that young people will remember for the rest of their lives.' Had this offer been made *after* England's bid had been successful we could have applauded it as a wonderful gesture. That it was made *in advance* of any decision showed it to be nothing short of a very expensive inducement. Consider the costs for the 812 accompanying adults (who are these 'youth leaders' anyway?). Even using restrained costings it could hardly have cost anything less than £2,000 per head, which adds up to £1,624,000. Now let's add in the 2,436 children. Even if they were to be hosted free by English families (and that was by no means certain), they would have cost at least £1,200 per head, adding up to a cool £2,923,200. This puts the total estimated costs of the junket at over £4.5 million, one of the biggest such financial inducements in the history of football or any sport, including the Olympics.

The financial detail of the English bid made interesting reading, with little real accountability to the English Sports Council/UK Sport for the money from the National Lottery. Whatever the costs though, the team certainly moved quickly, getting Sir Bobby Charlton on board, as well as Sir Geoff Hurst (the hat-trick scoring hero of England's 1966 victory, Sir Geoff had a forthcoming biography to profile, and had been opportunistically knighted by New Labour). And these top names weren't in it just for fun. Sir Bobby was accounting for his time, invoicing the bid as he went. Gary Lineker was rewarded with a hefty annual retainer for his name and profile. Some members of the team were apprehensive that Sir Bobby might get to know just how much Lineker was getting. Also, some of the committee felt that it was a pity that Lineker didn't see his role as a more active one, and as a way of putting something back into the game. Most in McGivan's creative advisory team – one of whom moved on to become a spin doctor for Prince Charles – were not paid. But the consultancy provided by Matrix Communications was paid, though never tended for: (Lord) Dick Newby's conversations with McGivan didn't always seem to find their way into wider strategic discussions about the bid.

Meanwhile, in the wake of confirmation of Olympic scandals around bribes for votes in bidding processes, FIFA issued its guidelines for the World Cup: no excessive hospitality, no personal gifts worth more than £70. Ho hum. What's the cost of a suite for a heavyweight FIFA ExCo member and his lover, garlanded with flowers, at Claridges?

The English FA and other bidders just continue to pay lip-service to FIFA's guidelines and provide room service to the men with the votes. Come to England. Look, in our video promo, at Stonehenge, at mock-ups of the new Wembley, backed by The Lighthouse Family crooning the campaign hope, 'We can be lifted, lifted from the shadow'. Then we'll take you wherever you want to go.

In seeking to light this particular New Labour beacon, however, some tricky questions arise. Not least, who is wooing whom? Asked whether it was Blair or Havelange who suggested the Downing Street visit, press spokesman Alistair Campbell, uncharacteristically vaguely, replied, 'To be honest, I can't exactly remember. We certainly anticipated that he (Havelange) would get involved in the bid.' Cancel your appointments, Prime Minister, the Big Man's in town.

FIFA guidelines notwithstanding, the bidding war didn't stop at theatre tickets, maybe not even at £9 million or £10 million. How do you cost, in any realistic way, all that government support? It makes you wonder if Downing Street ever quite figured out the nature of the global game it so cheerfully joined. But the England team continued to dream the impossible dream. Its thinking was hopelessly optimistic and naïve: a bit of spin about the dangerous streets of Johannesburg and the untrustworthiness of the typical African football administrator and, hey presto, the ExCo member, urged on by his wife or partner perhaps, may well vote for five weeks in Knightsbridge and comfortable seats at the new Wembley next to the Blairs.

With the exception of the high-profile interventions of Banks, the government was at pains to conceal from the general public its heavy involvement in the bid. Manchester United's decision to withdraw from the 1999–2000 English FA Cup forced the government to reveal its hand. Against the wishes of most of the strong football nations in Europe and contrary to the views of Lennart Johansson and other senior officials at UEFA, one of the first things Sepp Blatter did when he graduated to the FIFA Presidency was to launch the first World Club championship. Scheduled to be held in Brazil in January 2000 and organised along the lines of the World Cup, the new competition proposed to bring together the world's regional club champions to compete for global supremacy.

Like Havelange before him, after his successful election Blatter had promises to keep. The inauguration of this 'World League' would give the minnows of world football an opportunity to display themselves on the world stage. Teams from the Gulf, Central and North America and the Caribbean, Australasia, Asia and Africa – regions where Blatter garnered many votes in his election – would be given the chance to measure themselves against the might of South America and Europe. The new championship would also facilitate further money-making opportunities for FIFA's precious commercial and media partners and provide yet another regular, five-star party for FIFA's extended family.

Western Europe is where the world's best players perform in the game's strongest and best-supported domestic leagues and cups. They do this in the context of an already congested pan-European competitive calendar and international schedule. There is not the need, the room or the appetite for another global football competition. Manchester United, one of the biggest names in the game, won Europe's Champions League in 1999. In the same year they won The FA Premier Division and, in front of specially invited FIFA guests, they also won the world's oldest football competition, The FA Challenge Cup. The introduction of the World League notwithstanding, with domestic titles to defend and involvement in the expanded format of the European Champions League, the 1999–2000 season already promised to be the busiest in the club's illustrious history. The World League was a competition too far, particularly as it was scheduled to be played at the height of the English domestic season. Something had to give. It should have been the World League. Instead, prompted by The FA, newly knighted manager Sir

Alex Ferguson announced that Manchester United would not be participating in the FA Cup. Ferguson made it clear that the decision was taken under considerable pressure from The FA, the 2006 team, and the British government.

As veteran journalist Peter Corrigan pointed out, Manchester United becoming European champions at this juncture provided an opportunity for pandering to Blatter and his cronies that The FA could not miss. By delivering the European Champions to the boys in Brazil in January 2000 McGivan and his team believed England's bid in the minds of Blatter and his executives would be hugely enhanced when they made their selection for 2006 later in the year, due in March. McGivan was a veteran of the political scene in Britain, and had worked for the Gang of Four breakaway Labour politicians, as the first ever full-time member of staff of the Social Democratic Party, before boosting his profile as events manager for Euro '96. But he was outfoxed when FIFA ExCo member Chuck Blazer had the decision date put back to the original schedule of July 2000. New sports minister Kate Hoey passed the buck to her predecessor, Tony Banks, stating: 'I think it absolutely imperative that Manchester United play in the FA Cup. I would not have felt it was the role of the Minister of Sport to be asking Manchester United to go to Brazil. A number of errors were made.' This upset United's chief executive, Martin Edwards, who claimed that it wasn't the club's decision to withdraw, that it was a decision made 'with the full backing of the government and The FA … a joint decision. Now, for the new sports minister suddenly to enter the arena … I suggest she does her homework properly and I suggest the government gets its act together because we did this in support of the last sports minister.'

Keith Cooper, FIFA's media spokesman, denied that Manchester United's participation in the World League would have any bearing upon the 2006 decision. However, FIFA ExCo members Jack Warner and Chuck Blazer praised the sagacity of England's position and hinted that it would stand them in good stead. Cooper's view was then confirmed by Blatter himself, who in October had urged Manchester United to play in the FA Cup, but suggested that The FA make the club participate in the new FIFA initiative.

Government-driven, the England 2006 bid was presented in Zurich on 9 August 1999. The English flew in, bidding team and press pack together, and irritated FIFA by arriving late. Tony Banks, by now moved aside as minister of sport, had been handed the role of special envoy for the bid. This was a canny piece of positioning by Blair – *all credit for me if the bid comes off, not my fault if the envoy loses it.* To FIFA, this sub-ministerial presence was downgrading the bid, an insult to them. The English stagemanaged the bid submission for the press, then left. They saw no other bid, spoke to nobody else, saw nothing of the informal lobbying.

Meanwhile, after all the bids were presented, a Bavarian oompah-pah band played on the terrace of FIFA House with its spell-binding view over Lake Zurich, and wild mountain flowers framed the flow of wine and beer as President Blatter entertained FIFA insiders, hangers-on and self-selecting press. In dark shades and casual shirt, and cracking jokes revolving around double-beds in Africa, Blatter rubbed shoulders with the favoured of the FIFA family. This included outsiders in the bidding war, Brazil, and carefully calculating serious bidder Germany. The Brazilians and the

Germans – let alone the emotional favourites, South Africa – showed real savvy in the bidding process. For Brazil, and particularly for Ricardo Teixera, boss of Brazilian football, former son-in-law of Havelange, the stakes were high. Under pressure and under legal investigation for his activities in Brazil, his slate would be wiped clean if he were to land the 2006 finals – Teixera could do without a bad result in the bidding contest. Within weeks, Havelange would be announcing that Brazil was considering withdrawing its bid – 'I'd prefer to lose a finger than lose a hand; in order to win you also have to know how to lose,' he said. 'If Brazil are not to be hosts of the 2006 World Cup, I can guarantee they will be in 2010.' If Havelange himself was unlikely to be sitting in the stands of a rebuilt Maracaná in his mid-90s, the mid-term strategy would certainly suit his surviving nearest and dearest. It would suit Teixera too, to have his slate wiped clean by Brazil's fifth World Cup triumph in 2002, followed by the aspiration to bring the finals back to Brazil eight years later. Havelange knew a thing or two about such cover-ups, cleared as he was of charges for financial irregularities, and spared investigation by the junta, when he'd slipped into the FIFA presidential seat back in 1974. And by now, the Brazilian television and marketing agency Traffic – broker of Nike's deal with the Brazil national side and with individual stars such as Ronaldo – had clinched the TV contract for the FIFA World Club Championship. In talking of knowing 'how to lose', Havelange could lull any future opposition into a false sense of strength. Blatter had promised, after all, continuity in the FIFA family.

Back in Lancaster Gate, at last the cat was out of the bag. Forget the separation of sport from politics, forget tradition, forget the fans: anything, including The FA Cup, was expendable in the pursuit of 2006. Soon after this debacle The FA was to move, apropriately enough, from the calm avenues and pastures of Hyde Park to the sleazier streets of Soho. Meanwhile, a House of Commons Culture, Media and Sport Committee commended the English bid, saying, in prominent bold type in its summary volume: 'So far, The Football Association's bid to stage the 2006 World Cup appears to be well-conceived, well-managed and well-executed. The support offered by the government, most notably the Minister for Sport and the staff of the British Embassies and High Commissions, appears to have been exemplary.' This might just be the most integrated and fully developed case of the political exploitation of sport in the history of the country. Towards the end of her first administration Prime Minister Margaret Thatcher needed the Falklands War to help secure a second term in office. You could see Blair's populist thinking in backing the 2006 bid. Never mind broken promises, underhand deals or England's reputation for honesty in the gutter, just listen to the people sing. But England was never at the races for this one. A bungled bid was to get worse and worse in the run-in, as the campaign team looked for excuse after excuse as the fragile promises of votes frittered down to a paltry two – four and a half million pounds each, at the most modest of costings. Germany and South Africa slugged it out to the end. The Labour government and The FA had been listening to the wrong focus groups.

The outcome of the 2006 bidding wars made world headlines. Less than a month before the 2006 vote, the technical inspection team's report was published and

England was ranked third behind Germany and South Africa. Sir Bobby Charlton declared the findings 'an insult'. Tony Banks called them, 'ludicrous, laughable'. For once Banks was correct. It is widely accepted in football circles that the Premiership's network of modern stadiums is among the best in the world and, with a redeveloped Wembley, in terms of playing facilities, media technologies, tourist capacity and related communications, England's case, in terms of existing infrastructure, was undoubtedly the strongest.

Germany's was a virtual bid, in as much as the country's existing football infrastructure is dated and in much need of significant upgrading which the German bid promised to do only if Germany was awarded the tournament. With the exception of Soweto's FNB Stadium (Soccer City) South Africa's bid was based almost entirely on apartheid-era rugby facilities, with huge problems associated with communications and accommodation yet to be resolved.

Banks and McGivan finally got the message and went on an aggressive offensive, accusing both UEFA and FIFA of conspiring against England. They were of course right, but refused to accept that the whole England 2006 strategy had encouraged such conspiring. Whatever the truth, insulting the voters moments before the election eradicated even the slenderest of chances that England would prevail.

The predictable 'hooligans abroad' Charleroi episode during Euro 2000 did, however, provide the England 2006 team with a convenient smokescreen under which to creep away, blaming unruly fans for the bid's failure. But even before the first plastic chair was thrown, the England bid was long dead in the water. Even with the might of foreign office support, England 2006 was a lost cause. Lacking absentee frontman Gary Lineker – on a hefty retainer, but usually too media-busy to turn up for international duty – the bidding team of seconded foreign office veterans, promotional and political operators such as McGivan, faithful figureheads such as Sir Bobby Charlton, and parvenu dignitaries such as New Labour-ennobled Sir Geoff Hurst, dashed around the world smiling at Fifafolk, all to no avail. England's bid showed all the symptoms of an empire on the wane. Like Keegan's team at Euro 2000, it was all puff and bluster up front, clumsy and self-deluding at its core, aging and not up to it at the back.

Throughout, the tone of England's campaign won few friends. It was seen to be arrogant, imperious and negative. The blend of neo-imperial and New Labour arrogance in the bid irritated and sometimes infuriated key players in the power games of FIFA's ExCo, such as Chuck Blazer of CONCACAF. Champions League mastermind, Jürgen Lenz, of crack Swiss agency TEAM, considered the bid to be aggressive and alienating. There was widespread indifference and sometimes hostility towards the bid, particularly in the way that it dismissed South Africa's prospects and amplified a moral panic about crime and political instability in the former colony. Most outside of the rival binding camps agreed that while South Africa would have to overcome a number of infrastructural and social problems, it was the most deserving. At a certain point, once it became obvious that England stood no chance, The FA's bid should have been withdrawn, and it should have pledged economic and political support for South Africa's bid. This might have tipped the scales in South Africa's favour, and given England and perhaps even the UK the moral high ground from which to make an earnest and honest bid to host the event in 2010. Instead, the champagne flowed and the band played on as the English marched head on into the final humiliation in Zurich.

The international media like to deny or at least marginalize the skulduggery and realpolitik of the international power struggles around world sports and the most sought-after sport mega-events. Thus the world media, rather than probe the politics of international diplomacy and deal-making in the world economy, found it easier to point to individuals. In this the media come close to portraying the world of sport politics as a series of interpersonal battles. Thus one man, the then 78-year-old New Zealander, Charlie Dempsey, was vilified in the world press when Germany won the FIFA ExCo decision for 2006 by a single vote. Dempsey had voted for England but not registered a vote for anyone in the next round after England's elimination. He had left to fly back to his Oceania base, claiming, in his own words, that he was confident that the FIFA committee's vote would secure the decision for South Africa. However, South Africa was a vote short of gaining a 12–12 outcome in the vote, a tied outcome that would have to have been broken by the casting vote of the committee chair, the president, Blatter. Blatter fumed, across the world media, that he would have cast this for South Africa. If Dempsey had recast his vote in support of South Africa, Blatter would have been able to gift the tournament to the African confederation, thus paying off some of the debts that he'd accumulated on the way to his electoral victory in 1998. Dempsey became FIFA's, the world media's, and especially the South Africans' whipping boy and scapegoat in the media backlash to the German victory. Nobody talked about the two Middle East votes that were lost by the South African bid. It was easier to door-step Dempsey and chase rent-a-quote politicians in New Zealand and Australia, than ask how other forces beyond the savvy of Kaiser Franz Beckenbauer and the glamour of model Claudia Schiffer could clear the path for a German triumph.

Wherever you were in the world for the few days after the 2006 decision, you could see the haunted and hunted face of Dempsey dominating news items in the print and broadcast media. 'A right Charlie!' bawled *The Sun*, screaming in its caption to a flustered looking Dempsey: 'This old git made a fool out of football'. Dempsey was hounded throughout the weekend. 'A donkey's vote – South Africans livid at Dempsey's faux pas', reported the Saturday edition of the *Newcastle Herald* in New South Wales. It was still the main sport story on the Monday: 'Fall on the sword – Dempsey told to avoid the sack by resigning'. Vivek Chaudhary in *The Guardian* labelled Dempsey as 'the man who killed an African dream.' Dempsey was widely reported to have reneged on an OFC decision to back South Africa should the federation's preferred candidate, England, be eliminated. Dempsey has denied such allegations, reiterating his claim that Oceania never passed any resolution of commitment to South Africa after the elimination of England. Some members of the Oceania confederation requested that he back South Africa after the elimination of England, but there was no vote taken or mandate confirmed. Oceania's general secretary, Dempsey's younger daughter Josephine King, confirms that six national associations – a majority of the confederation's members – confirmed to her by telephone that their president could 'use his own discretion' if or more likely when it came to a second round.

In September 2000 in Brisbane and Sydney, just weeks after the vote, Dempsey was cocooned in the bosom of the FIFA family gathered to enjoy the Olympic football tournament. On one sunny Sunday morning, leaving the Novotel in Brisbane in his FIFA car, to fit in a spot of golf with his wife Annie, he bumped into Issa Hayatou, president of the African federation. Befitting the FIFA rhetoric of family, loyalty and interdependence, the two men embraced. Hayatou, stylish as ever in light but immaculate lounge suit; Dempsey, in baggy khaki neo-imperialist shorts and casual shirt – 'Ah, Charlie,' spluttered the man whose continent was said to have lost World Cup 2006 at the hands of Dempsey, 'your Guinness, where's your Guinness?' As ever, FIFA knew that continuing to look after your own was the surest way of continuing to keep the skeletons securely locked in your own cupboard.

There was, however, another story. Deutschland AG is the nickname for the whole of Germany conceived as one large company, with all Germans as shareholders. As the day of the vote was approaching several new business deals with Asian countries were announced, worth several billion marks or new-fangled Euros. The Federal Security Council of Germany gave permission, on the 28 June just a few days before the 2006 vote, to deliver 1,200 bazookas to Saudi Arabia. Deals were put in place to aid troubled Korean car manufacture Hyundai, family business of FIFA executive committee member Chung. South Korean plastic manufacturers Sewon Enterprises was bought by the sponsor of the German FA, Bayer. Chemical giant BASF announced investments worth 800 million marks in South Korea up to the year 2003. Bayer also announced huge investments in Thailand, home of FIFA ExCo member Worawi Makudi, known for his sideline in Daimler dealerships in the expanding Asian market: the polycarbonate production in the Map Ta Phut plant would be tripled on the basis of this investment. Not all of these connections could guarantee votes for Germany. But on the inside, it was known that key votes coming Germany's way did come from the delegates from Saudi Arabia and Qatar, if not Korea. Charlie Dempsey whispered darkly, in a corner of FIFA's hotel in Brisbane, that there was much to tell on this story, but that FIFA politics were now more dangerous than ever, and it might be too risky to tell it. And Charlie would still want the privileges of ambassadorial status or family retainer at FIFA events.

There remains much ferreting and investigative work to be done to account for the outcome of the bidding wars. However, such work must recognize that this story is not one of individual personalities – in the 2006 case, Beckenbauer versus Charlton, Tony Banks versus Claudia Schiffer. Or even of the big players, like South Korean Chung in getting Korea so successfully into the picture for the 2002 bid. That's surface stuff. The votes of the 24 individuals on FIFA's executive committee are cast not according to any logic of rational organizational life, or in starstruck spontaneity, but within a framing context of a complex international politics and a persistingly influential geo-political historical legacy. These international power struggles can be adequately understood only if the historical, the political and the sociological contexts are recognised as one and the same thing, in a post-colonial global network of business, politics and sport, and the struggles for power that are at the heart of world sport's governance. These contexts, though, also include the propensity to personal gain and sometimes corruption among those who participate in these struggles for power.

There is a school of thought that believes Charlie's absence and abstention could have let Blatter off the hook. 'When in doubt follow the money' is a good guiding principle to use when trying to get to the bottom of complex and shrouded power games. Find out who benefits most and you usually have your prime suspect. While Blatter might have supported South Africa in public, privately and certainly from a FIFA-business point of view Blatter may have favoured Germany. The German-Swiss knew that a World Cup in Germany was more secure, more media-friendly, and that greater profits would be guaranteed for FIFA and its partners if the competition were to be held there rather than in Africa. Particularly since some of them had sizeable vested interests in Germany.

And the preferences of the partner sponsors are far from marginal influences on FIFA's decisions. The 2002 World Cup had more official sponsors than ever before, three more than in France '98. The fifteen companies paid a total of 290 million pounds – somewhere between around 10 and a little over 20 million pounds each. They were Adidas (sports kit), Avaya (communications), Budweiser (beer), Coca-Cola (soft drinks), Fuji Xerox (copiers/copying), Fuji Film, Gillette (razors), Hyundai (cars/transport), JVC (video), KT-Korea/NTT-Japan (telecommunications), MasterCard (credit services), McDonald's (fast-food), Philips (electronics), Toshiba (computer hardware), and Yahoo (internet/cyberspace). These companies or equivalent blue-chip sponsors would much prefer a 2006 World Cup at the heart of the second-biggest consumer market in the world, rather than somewhere with great promise but even more volatility, on the African continent.

In this scenario a disgraced Dempsey became a convenient scapegoat for Blatter, who could hold his hands up to the Africans, telling them that if it wasn't for Charlie he would have kept his promise and delivered the World Cup finals to Africa for the first time. Now he had the 2006 World Cup in his own back yard and he could keep African favour (and precious votes) by campaigning strongly for World Cup 2010 to be in Africa, full in the knowledge that by then he would be well into his 70s and possibly fading out of the picture.

The world's media had hounded Charlie. In true paparazzi fashion they also got to his wife and his daughter Josephine: 'To be honest with you, it didn't really bother me' Charlie explained, 'but when they started to get at my family I said to myself, that's it and decided to quit.' Deciding to jump before he was pushed, in resigning the presidency of Oceania Charlie also gave up his FIFA status, became exiled from his beloved FIFA family, and temporarily lost his membership of the best club in the world. There are always losers in the bidding wars and for a while it looked like Charlie was one of them. But he didn't look like a loser when accepting his honorary membership for life at the FIFA Seoul congress at Korea/Japan 2002.

Sitting in his hotel bedroom on the eve of the vote for the country that would host the 2006 World Cup Finals, Dempsey was hemmed in by external pressures. South Africa courted him to the last – Nelson Mandela rang him in the middle of the night, offering inviting trips to South Africa's glitziest golf courses and holiday haunts. The Germans adopted more underhand tactics; an anonymous letter – was it a hoax, or an attempt to set up and frame the wily New Zealander? – was slipped under his bedroom door, saying it would be more than worth Charlie's while to ring a certain telephone number in Berlin. For all his street-fighting survival skills, Charlie was feeling the pressure. He sought advice from the Oceania general secretary, his daughter Josephine King. Rattled and fatigued already, Charlie teetered on the edge of exhaustion as he fought off sleep waiting for her faxed advice. When it came, it was clear as a New Zealand Summer sky:

STRICTLY CONFIDENTIAL: By Fax

6 July 2000
Mr Charles J Dempsey CBE
President OFC

Dear Mr Dempsey

Your two senior lawyers have considered your position – the allegations of bribery which are already circulating concerning you, which have even reached New Zealand, and the latest letter you have received under your door, offering you a bribe (which could possibly be a set-up).

In the light of the importance of this matter, the enormous pressure which has been placed on you, and with the spotlight on you these lawyers' considered and strong advice is that you cast a vote only for the first ballot.

However, when the second ballot comes, you should not cast a vote, nor under any circumstances should you enter the ballot box nor should you mark a ballot paper, even with an abstention.

Their view is that your life's reputation has not been tarnished to date and it is not in your best interests, nor that of your family, nor your Confederation, to put that at risk. Once lost it is never regained. Even though you may be the innocent party.

Yours sincerely
Josephine King
General Secretary

From that point, Charlie played it by this particular legal book. Josephine had also taken a telephone poll of selected Oceania national associations, and when she got to six members supporting the legally recommended position, she stopped counting. She knew which national associations to leave off her calling list, and some, like Dr Muhammad S. Sahu Khan, president of the Fiji Football Association, would accuse Dempsey of defying the Confederation's position and mandate. However, Charlie was consistent and insistent on this. Oceania had never voted to give Charlie an instruction to back the South African bid. A recommendation had been made by Dr Khan, Charlie recalled. But it had never been formalised, never established as the Confederation's position, policy or majority view.

As we've related, Charlie Dempsey survived the assault from the world's media. Two years later, on a crisp winter's day at one of his favourite Auckland golf clubs, he could reiterate that he had no regrets over his actions, that he had nothing to be ashamed of. And the Oceania office, and his home address, had received many letters of support over his stance. Some of these were from the football networks of his adopted country, displaying the anger of the Australasian underdog:

> July.19: Dear Chas
> At this time when you are being vilified around the world for sticking to your principles, we'd like you to know that we admire you for not succumbing to bullying and coercion.

And, 'God bless your honesty and integrity,' from James at the Church of St Joseph, Orakei.

One of Charlie's former players, from his coaching days at the Eastern Suburbs club, wrote:

> That is the most important aspiration in life – to have credibility, honesty and integrity in your sporting and business career. You achieved all of these … You can hold your head high, Charlie: New Zealand soccer has benefited enormously with your stewardship and the game is the loser with your decision to leave the front line.

The note was signed 'David and Kathleen, 15 July'.

Some sympathisers showed a more astute grasp of FIFA politics than did most of the world press:

> Dear Charlie
> We find it ironic that the prime minister and the minister of sport are quick to criticise circumstances they have no knowledge of and a sport they have shown little support for in the past – such government politics have no place in sport anyway!
> We also find it ironic that people have failed to appreciate the fact that the Asian Confederation crossed the floor with its four votes to support Germany instead of South Africa as promised.
> We hope you enjoy a well-deserved retirement playing bridge and golf and again thank you for what you have done for New Zealand soccer and the Oceania Confederation over the past 30 years.
> We would also like to thank you belatedly for your assistance in enabling us to purchase tickets for the France '98 World Cup – a dream come true and an experience never to be forgotten!
> Kind regards, Tim and Helen [son-in-law and daughter of one of Charlie's old chums]

The Colonial Carriage Company/Mercedes Limousines wrote Charlie a retirement card, saying 'Have every happiness, we enjoyed driving for you and appreciate the business you gave us.' A golfing chum slammed the New Zealand prime minister and 'an ungrateful society', and urged Charlie to get to his Middlemore golf club more often. More and more letters and cards flooded in, all with the message that Charlie's honesty, integrity and intelligence were beyond reproach. 'Best wishes and don't let them wear you down,' faxed a Rotarian acquaintance on 10 July, from the Englefield Bathroomware company.

Ordinary football people recalled Charlie as their Man of the People, one offering to head up a 'Charlie must stay' campaign: 'By the way, not only do I treasure what you have done for football, I remember the time you gave me in your own home many years ago when I was seeking support for a soccer project' (David, 10 July 2000).

And the regional business elite wasn't slow to offer Dempsey moral and potential legal support. Simpson Grierson law firm, through Rabin S. Rabindran, remembered a Singapore Airline Priority Passenger dinner four years ago, sharing a table with Charlie and his wife. When the 2006 decision and its aftermath came out, Rabindran told Charlie on 13 July that

> it is very evident that you had the support of the majority of the Oceania Football Confederation for you to exercise your vote as you deemed fit … If some of the issues you are having to deal with become an issue with FIFA, I am sure that the Hon. Michael J. Beloff QC, who is the leading sports lawyer in Europe and a good friend of mine, will be happy to be of assistance. Michael, who is also president of Trinity College, Oxford, is a member of the Court of Arbitration of Sport and one of the leading legal brains in England. I enclose some material about him which makes interesting reading. One of the newspaper clippings asks 'Is this the most influential man in Britain?' I will be very happy to speak to Michael if the need arises. I however do hope that the matter will just fade away.
>
> I take the opportunity to let you know that like me there are numerous people in this country who know that you have always been a man of great integrity and honesty. I am sure that your great service to football in New Zealand and the countries in this region will never be forgotten. We wish you and Annie all the best. With kind regards.

Networks across Australia and the Pacific Islands were also mobilised. Charlie and Annie loved their time at their holiday home on Queensland's Gold Coast. On 11 July, general manager of Soccer Australia, Ian Holmes, wrote in his personal capacity to say how sorry he was 'for the treatment you are receiving at the hands of the media, politicians and soccer community … Your decision is one of courage. You should be applauded not condemned. Do not take notice of the uneducated and uniformed views of your detractors.' On 18 July, Gold Coast Soccer Inc.'s Keith Young wrote saying 'you'll always be welcome, and let's share the odd glass of Guinness'.

On 12 July, the Samoa Football Federation weighed in with its support:

> Talofa lava from Samoa! Against all the odds, here's one Oceania member right besides you! You have done a lot for the Oceania countries … to ensure we are supported morally and physically at all times. For this we have always pledged our trust and appreciation of your exemplary leadership. May it strengthen you and your family to know that we are with you in thoughts and understanding at this very controversial period. Please accept our deepest and sincere feelings of compassion and encouragement to you and your family. We pray also that our God Almighty will give you strength and courage to move on and continue through a related and happy life.
>
> Cheers and God Bless, Soifua, President.

George Cowie, national coach of the Solomons, wrote thanking him for all the developments, his integrity and honesty, on 12 July.

From the UK, Sir Bobby Charlton wrote:

> Dear Charlie
>
> Sorry for the late reply to your letter, but we have had the most wonderful week in Scotland and since have been to China and Singapore on Manchester United business. The work for the club has been very refreshing after the stress of the bid but it doesn't compare at all to the stress you have been under. I hope you are enjoying your break from all things football and spending some time with Annie for a change.
>
> What happened in Samoa and Mr Blatter's behaviour made me understand your decision clearly and if each member were as independently minded as yourself, I think the game would be much more fairly run. You can rely on me to let all know of the respect you are still held in by myself and many here in the UK.
>
> You are always welcome at Old Trafford whenever you visit England and golf is always available if that's what you would like.
>
> Norma sends her love and best wishes to your family and rest assured we will be in touch if ever we are near New Zealand.
>
> Congratulations on your decision, Charlie, and your career in Oceania has been nothing short of miraculous. You can now leave it to others while you can now smell the roses for a change.
>
> Take care, Charlie,
>
> Bobby and Norma with love.

Geoff Thompson, FA Chairman, got back from a holiday after the wearying summer of the 2006 vote and the Euro 2000 tournament, and wrote on 17 August of his

sincere disappointment at the way in which you were treated by the media and others on your very courageous actions with regard to the vote for the

2006 World Cup … You have been a good friend and I know you will continue to be a good friend to English football and to my wife and I personally. Please give our love to Annie and keep some for yourself,

With all good wishes, Geoff.

Allen Wade, legendary author of The FA book of coaching, poured out all the English bitterness of the post-Rous years in a typewritten letter that in its very form was like a dirge for a dead dynasty:

Dear Charles,

I have followed with dismay the trials and tribulations to which you have been (are) subjected over the voting procedure for a future World Cup. Who do these people think they are? It was entirely foreseeable that when the TV revenues began to flow the number of sticky fingers exploring the pudding would increase pro rata and that the hitherto unsuspected interest of politicians in the world game would blossom as never before. Football will pay a dear price for encouraging the involvement of that lot.

Sir Stanley must be turning over in his grave at the antics of our bid team, especially those of the wizard of Westminster.

New Zealand should remember that your leadership installed your country as a leading country not only in Oceania but much further afield. Don't let the bastards grind you down, Charles – as if that were likely.

God bless, Allen.

Charlie's sympathisers included not just the old-world UK football elite, the ordinary football folk of New Zealand, and the business and football networks of his country and his region, but also key personnel in FIFA itself, as well as in UEFA. Gerhard Aigner, UEFA general secretary, wrote on 11 July of his disappointment at the views expressed by Bill MacGowan, secretary of the New Zealand Football Association, after all of UEFA's continued support for Oceania:

It is also very unfortunate the way your attempt to be neutral has been misrepresented by your New Zealand colleagues. We condemn in particular the statements from the governmental sources of New Zealand that are entirely in contradiction with the spirit of the statutes of FIFA which do not permit political interference in the sporting context … rest assured FIFA holds you in high esteem … With best wishes in this difficult time.

UEFA president Lennart Johansson wrote from his home address in Solna, on 17 August:

Dear Charlie

What happened before, during and after the election for 2006 is nothing but a disaster. However you must know that more and more people – when they get the facts – honour you for what you did. I sincerely hope that one day the true story will be officially known, so that you can get the redress you deserve. All of us in UEFA will always honour you and remain your true friends.

I thank you again for your long lasting friendship and I will one way or another see to it that we will meet again.

Greetings also to your daughter Josephine King. She is really an intelligent, loyal and brave lady. Warmest regards also to you and your lovely wife.

Keith Cooper, FIFA's director of communications, apologised in a letter (written in a personal capacity) for getting a point wrong on what had taken place in a FIFA executive committee meeting, in an appearance in a BBC live interview on Friday 7 July, talking about threats to Charlie and the family: 'This error … occurred solely in the attempt to deflect criticism from you and to explain to the public the courage and transparency of your actions.' He explained that people were 'starting to realise that you acted honourably'. Cooper added that he hoped that his own interview might have been a positive influence on or towards this softening of opinion among the wider public.

'You go with honour and distinction,' wrote Cooper, 'towards golf course and family. Oceania owes you a great deal. … The important thing is that you can live with your conscience, as I know you can, for you have done nothing wrong: on the contrary.'

Dempsey's own favourite letter among this extraordinary outpouring of support was the pithiest and most mysterious: 'Dear Sir, Thank you very much for your vote. You save many lives. Leave it for 2012. A.J. Meys.'

2004 would be FIFA's next World Cup D-day, for the 2010 World Cup. The Dempsey story indicates how high the stakes remain in such bidding wars. Despite Blatter's sympathetic statements on Africa's moral rights to have the 2010 World Cup, the background politics of such bidding processes continue unabated.

FIFA's continuing fiscal crises mean that it needs two reliable, financially lucrative World Cups to follow the 2002 Asian extravaganza. Germany in 2006 will deliver one of these. Blatter's own success always rested on the destabilization of the African continent/confederation as a whole, dividing to rule. After Issa Hayatou was defeated so heavily in his challenge for the FIFA presidency in 2002, the African confederation looked more split than ever. Blatter-backers had included football superstars Abidele, Pelé and George Weah. These Africans were soon turfed off Hayatou's CAF committee, and declared an interest in running against Hayatou for the presidency of the confederation. The overall situation looked good for Blatter, and not so good after all for Africa. A defeated African candidate in the 2002 presidential election, a continually divided African confederation, a persistent belief that South Africa could not handle the logistics of a World Cup tournament, and Africa would soon appear as the least convincing candidate to meet the economic criteria so central to the concerns of FIFA and its commercial partners. The majority of

FIFA's economic partners are US-based global corporations. It would be no surprise, particularly after the strong on-field run of the US team to the last eight in Japan/Korea 2002, if a late US bid for the 2010 World Cup were to accumulate mounting credibility. The bounty hunters would be back in town, with smiles on their faces and dollars in their bank accounts.

14

THE TERMINATOR

Blatter cleans out FIFA House

As noted in the Preface to the 2003 edition of this book, on our FIFA quest we often divide up research responsibilities so that we can cover more ground on our slender budgets. During the 2002 World Cup Alan Tomlinson concentrated on the Seoul Congress and followed up some research trails in the South Pacific and Oceania region. John Sugden was in Japan, to pick up the FIFA scent and also to gather material for his book on football's black market, *Scum Airways*. John's two projects overlapped around the question of tickets.

The distribution of tickets for France '98 had been bad, but as considered in Chapter 11, contrary to FIFA's predictions Japan/Korea 2002 was even worse. Sugden's own ticket situation was precarious. He had one for England v Sweden and a spare ticket for England v Nigeria that he would not be using. This belonged to Big Tommy, a tout, who had decided not to come to Japan after all. Eventually John sold it at face value to Huw, an English businessman who worked in Tokyo. During the transaction Huw showed him a ticket for the England-Argentina game that he had bought from a tout for £500. It was issued to FIFA, and this came as no surprise. Tickets for the England-Argentina encounter with a face value of £100 each were available on the black market at £700 apiece. According to the *Daily Mail* and London's *Evening Standard*, some bore the name of Mohamed Bin Hammam of Qatar, whose reputation was already badly tarnished. It was Bin Hammam who was accused by Farah Addo of being the man who offered him the $100,000 bribe to vote for Blatter in 1998.

Sugden did not have a ticket for the coveted England-Argentina game and could not afford the touts' prices. Then he reacquainted himself with Charlie Dempsey and his luck changed. The New Zealander was tracked down at FIFA's Tokyo headquarters in the Westin Hotel in the city's Ebisu district. Built on the site of the old Sapporo brewery, the Westin is typical FIFA five-star stuff: black marble floors; towering Doric columns; sweeping ballroom staircases; gold and mahogany trim; and overstuffed couches for overstuffed FIFA officials to sit on in a cavernous lobby. FIFA delegates, administrators and officials from the company's new marketing wing, seemed to have occupied at least half of the 700 rooms. The cheapest standard room in the Westin cost US$250 per night. At the other end of the scale the Imperial Suite was on offer for a staggering US$3,000, but this was not good enough for the FIFA executive and their hangers-on, who could not be seen consorting with the hired help. Thanks to the magic word, 'resecuritization', it would be more largesse for them in Tokyo's most exclusive hotel, the 77-room Seiyo Hotel in the city's exclusive and famously expensive Ginza district. The Seiyo Ginza made the Westin look positively shabby. There are now six-star hotels, suggest this should be altered to recognise this. Prices there ranged from US$300 to $2,000 per night. You can bet your life that Blatter and the family elders bedded down in the best and most expensive rooms, 'designed to reflect the convenience of a private residence.' If the costs for the FIFA fat cats' sojourn in Paris in 1998 had been astronomical and obscene, the bills for luxury in Seoul and Tokyo must have been on a scale not seen since Caligula ruled the roost in Imperial Rome.

There is something obscene in the chief executives and major shareholders of an organisation that is for all intents and purposes bankrupt living in the lap of luxury, spending money raised through mortgaging the football future of the next generation. It is worse than the ageing couple who selfishly decide to re-mortgage the family home – bequeathed to them by their parents and grand parents – and sail around the world on a first-class champagne cruise instead of leaving a nest-egg for their children. In FIFA's case Blatter and his crew are making the cruise on the basis of what their antecedents might themselves earn in the future.

Given the huge losses that FIFA had incurred under Blatter's stewardship, it would have been more appropriate for them to lodge in one of Tokyo's infamous capsule hotels. For less than US$25 Blatter and his cronies could have had a coffin-sized chamber among a stacked honeycomb of others. The experience of a capsule hotel for a month might have stood a few of them in good stead should, sometime in the future, a Swiss prosecutor find them guilty of fraud and demand custodial sentences.

When he arrived at the Westin, Sugden put a call through to Charlie's room on the off-chance that he was in. He was, and invited John up to talk with him. Charlie had an executive suite of rooms to himself, on the tenth floor, costing $US1,000 a night. The 81-year-old looked diminutive and slightly frail as he sat in the middle of a large, overstuffed Chesterfield couch watching Mexico-Croatia on TV. 'Do you want to watch the game?' he asked. 'Not if you don't', John replied. Charlie turned it off.

The former president of the OFC had been on a bit of a roller-coaster ride since he was forced to resign over the 2006 World Cup hosting scandal. This had boiled down to a three-way race between England, South Africa, and Germany. The ex-pat Scot had been a staunch supporter of England's bid, but should England be eliminated in the first round of voting, he had been requested by some members of the Oceania executive to cast his vote for South Africa in the second and deciding ballot. We tell the full story earlier in the preceding chapter, 'Bidding Wars'. There's no doubt that Blatter used Dempsey as a convenient scapegoat to take the flak over Germany's victory over South Africa.

After a few months in the wilderness Charlie was made an honorary president for life of the OFC and invited by Blatter to serve as a member of FIFA's disciplinary committee. Dempsey's rehabilitation was complete at the 2002 FIFA congress in Seoul. Charlie recounted how, as everybody was getting ready to leave the congress hall, a beaming Blatter, still flushed with his landslide victory over Issa Hayatou in the presidential election, strode to the podium and announced one more item of business. He proposed that Charles Dempsey be elevated to join a small and distinguished group of surviving honorary life members of FIFA. Only 25 such honorary memberships had been bestowed in FIFA's 100-year history, and sixteen or so of them were still living the good life. 'Usually something like this would be put to the floor for a vote,' explained Charlie. 'Instead Blatter just stood there and said "And I don't think we need to vote on this do we?" and began clapping his hands.' Soon, like sheep, the whole hall was clapping and Charlie was an honorary life member. This means that he can attend any or all FIFA events, all first-class expenses paid, without having to do anything.

Charlie's honorary life membership was another Blatter masterstroke. The best possible way of keeping him on side, particularly if he had sensitive information about the 1998 or 2002 presidential elections and the 2006 vote, was to keep him inside. Asked his opinion about the Blatter presidency, Charlie simply said 'I can't really say anything bad about Blatter now that he's honoured me.' No need to show the dirt in public; FIFA's laundry is a family business.

There is a downside to this pampered life of luxury. 'I'm not really interested in any other teams in this competition except England and Ireland,' confessed the New Zealander. 'When they've finished playing I'm going home, and to be honest with you I can't wait.' This was the first FIFA event that Charlie had been at for more than three decades where he had no official functions or duties to carry out. The FIFAcrats keep themselves busy. Breakfast meetings about this, that, or the other piece of World Cup trivia, stadiums to oversee, disciplinary committees to convene, referees to appoint and a seemingly endless series of official functions to attend. Without portfolio, Charlie seemed weary of it all. 'Most of the FIFA officials here technically know little or nothing about football,' he asserted. 'I only came really to pick up my award, and I'll go home as soon as I can. Sometimes I think that the fans are not right in the head. Coming all this way and paying all that money, spending thousands while we live in luxury for nothing,' he sighed.

Through Charlie's eyes, the FIFA Club appears a bit like royalty, paid for and pampered, but cut off from the real world. Charlie didn't know a yen from a yam, as he didn't have to spend any local money. He had no idea of how to use Tokyo's marvellous transport system as, like the rest of them, he travelled in special FIFA VIP cars and luxury coaches. In short, Charlie was socially isolated and lonely. He told of the many occasions, in places like Japan, Thailand and Taiwan, when he had been presented with female escorts that were available for him to spend the night with should he care to. Of course, he turned them down. Charlie might have five-star amenities at his service, but he had no idea of what fun it could be to join the spontaneous global party taking place amongst a multinational cast of supporters nightly in downtown Tokyo's Roppongi. As far as the members of the FIFA Club were concerned, Tokyo might just as well be Seoul (or Paris, New York or Buenos Aires) as, apart from specially laid on and interminably tedious cultural presentations, they had little or no informal contact with the outside world. Charlie was bored and wanted to go home. A lyric from the Eagle's classic anthem *Hotel California* springs to mind: 'You can check out any time you like, but you can never leave.' Such a lovely place, such a lovely place.

Towards the end of their conversation John and Charlie talked about football and England's relatively poor performance in its 1-1 draw with Sweden. Before John left Charlie asked him if he was going to watch England play Argentina. John told him that he hoped to as he had booked a flight to Sapporo and had a hotel reservation there, but added that he was not yet sure if he could get a ticket. 'Would you like me to put your name down for a complimentary one?' Charlie asked. 'Well, if it's not too much trouble,' John replied, trying to conceal the excitement in his voice, 'that would be great.' He gave Charlie his passport number and the telephone number of his hotel and Charlie promised to call him the next day to let him know if he had been able to secure him a ticket.

As good as his word, the following morning Charlie telephoned Sugden at his hotel and said the magic words, 'That's OK, John, I've put in for a ticket for you for the Argentina game and it should be alright.' John could not thank him enough, but before he put the phone down Charlie asked if he was going to the game that day, Japan's long-awaited opening fixture with Belgium in Saitama. John told Charlie that he would like to go but didn't have a ticket. The New Zealander offered to take him as his FIFA VIP guest, an offer gratefully accepted. In order to get the ticket, Charlie explained that he would have to travel with him on the FIFA coach and come with him into the FIFA VIP lounge. This was more than John could have hoped or asked for. Not only would he now get to see the co-host's opening match, but with luck and a little help from Charlie, he would also have the opportunity to mingle with many of the top brass and let them know that *Badfellas* was in the making.

Later that afternoon Sugden made his way across Tokyo once more and met Charlie in the lobby of the Westin. Charlie needed to make a call of nature and the delay meant that they were the last ones to board the FIFA VIP coach for the hour-long journey to Saitima. There were only two empty seats left and they were on the back row. John felt very conspicuous as he walked down the aisle past the in-crowd: dark-blue FIFA blazers with wives and consorts in their day-at-the races finery. It had felt uncomfortable enough the last time the authors were amongst this lot in the FIFA Club in Paris in 1998, and that was before *Great Balls of Fire* had been published – not one for the Christmas stocking of your average FIFA blazer.

So he was glad when he made it to his seat next to Charlie and the president of the Dutch football federation, Mathieu Sprengers, and his wife.

The coach edged its way through Tokyo's bumper-to-bumper rush-hour traffic and up onto the network of elevated toll-roads that bring commuter traffic in and out from the suburbs and outlying cities and towns. Tokyo dwarfs most other cities, including New York. It sprawls around Tokyo Bay, a mass of corporate skyscrapers and high-rise apartment blocs interconnected through a concrete and steel network of flyovers and bridges. It is orderly, spotlessly clean and serviced by a transport system that makes its UK equivalent look mediaeval. If a train is more than a minute late it is considered to be a national disaster.

While England struggles to build a single national stadium, the magnificent stadium at Saitama is one of 16 that Japan and Korea constructed for the 2002 World Cup. (What will happen to them after the competition, and who will foot the bill for their construction and maintenance, are interesting questions that are beyond the scope of this particular book.) The stadium looms out of a bucolic landscape of rivers and paddy fields like a giant luminous spacecraft. Less than a week ago, before the England-Sweden game, John had made his way there with the masses via a train from Tokyo Station and then one of the hundreds of buses specially laid on by the local prefecture. It had been a smooth trip, as had the return journey for the majority of the 50,000 ordinary fans making their way back to the big city. But the FIFA VIP treatment was hard to beat. While the fans filed past, the FIFA coach swept up to the main entrance, cleared by outrider bikes. Charlie and John disembarked onto a red carpet that led past lines of bowing Japanese attendants in traditional Japanese costumes into a spacious reception area, where they were given their tickets and passes to the FIFA VIP lounge just behind the Tribune d'Honneur.

Inside was a who's who of international football power brokers. With a little help from Charlie, John was able to make contact after contact, securing quotes and future appointments with key figures as they sipped fine wine and nibbled at delicate parcels of sushi. Before the game Charlie introduced him to Franz Beckenbauer and Michel Platini, two former football legends widely tipped as future big players in FIFA's power game. Platini had already made his first moves by being elected to the French FA and serving as a special adviser to Blatter for his presidential election campaign in 1998, and sticking around for the first four years of Blatter's rule. Then in 2002 he was elected onto both the FIFA and UEFA executives. Rumour had it that Platini was manoeuvring himself – or was being manoeuvred – to challenge for the UEFA presidency next time around. Having a member of FIFA's inner-circle, one close to the sinister-sounding *Führungsgruppe* – F-Group, the leadership group, known colloquially as the F-Crew – at the heart of the powerful European federation was already a major coup for Blatter, especially since the Frenchman was elected to the UEFA executive at the expense of the Norwegian Per Ravn Omdal, a longstanding supporter of Blatter's leading adversary, Lennart Johansson. But, according to another FIFA insider, the rehabilitated Guido Tognoni, 'Platini is Blatter's friend and adviser, but he has his own agenda. He wants to be president of UEFA, but I do not think that he is clever enough.'

His first few rounds in the FIFA power game looked to have taken their toll on Michel. Under a tousled mop of dark curly hair, the crumpled blue-suited French icon looked like a tired and overweight actor in an advertisement for French cigarettes. By contrast the slim, fit-looking Beckenbauer ('the Kaiser'), sharply dressed in an expensively tailored light-brown jacket and beige slacks, looked like he was about to get changed to play in the forthcoming match. As ever Beckenbauer was keeping. his cards close to his chest. The cognoscenti, however, believed that he was being lined up as a possible successor for Blatter. 'As usual, Beckanbauer says that he is not interested in holding any office within FIFA,' commented Tognoni, 'but he is famous for changing his mind at the last minute. He might have ambitions to succeed Blatter.'

The Swiss president had vowed to step down, if he were given the choice that is, after a second four-year term. Either through Blatter's patronage or through a head-to-head challenge with Blatter himself, Beckenbauer would make a formidable candidate for the FIFA presidency in 2006. The suave and multilingual Kaiser, the man who won the World Cup as captain and manager and who brought the finals to Germany, looked unstoppable. But, as Graham Kelly, the former Chief Executive of the English Football Association said, 'Could Blatter afford to step down?' Would he not be tempted to stand again, if only to keep prying eyes away from FIFA's books? Havelange had only walked away when he was sure his man would continue to hold the reins of power.

If either, or both, Platini and Beckenbauer succeed in becoming presidents of UEFA and FIFA they will be the first ex-professional footballers to occupy the commanding heights of the game they had both played so elegantly. Whether they could do so without carrying other people's baggage would determine whether or not this would be a good thing for football.

New Yorker, Chuck Blazer, the general secretary of CONCACAF, the North and Central American and Caribbean federation, barrels his way into the VIP lounge – the first time we'd seen Blazer at a big tournament without a new 'companion' hanging off his arm. 'Trade 'em in for a new one every World Cup,' he once told us when we asked about the girl he had in tow the last time we met. Now he looked fatter than ever and grey had long outnumbered black in his ever-unruly mop of curly hair. The man who is said by some to have invented and patented the smiley face – an unevidenced myth he's done little to discourage – had a scowl on his own flabby, jowly and ashen-grey face. Being Jack Warner's number two and helping Guido Tognoni and Urs Linsi find ways of balancing FIFA's books was obviously taking its toll on the overweight American.

Blazer was one of those handing Blatter his get-out-of jail free card when the American concept of 'resecuritization' was introduced into FIFA's accounting procedures. This is another word for 'factoring' – a process whereby you place in the debit side of the balance sheet earnings that you anticipate from future deals. FIFA had balanced its books by including revenue raised through a bond secured through Crédit Suisse First Boston Bank. Linsi, the man who would later replace Zen-Ruffinen, helped to broker this deal. Cosily, and far from coincidentally, in a former life Linsi had worked in senior management positions for Crédit Suisse for more than 20 years. The monies raised though the bond amounted to $420 million, and were based on revenue projections for the 2002 and the 2006 World Cups. This was not the first time such a bond had been raised to bail out a global sports organisation. In 1999, the despot of Formula One motor racing, Bernie Ecclestone, raised £950 million on a bond backed by TV and advertising revenues. Without doing the same, FIFA would have been heavily in the red, even bankrupt.

Jim ('I'm not telling you my real name'), a compatriot of Blazer's, is a sports photographer and long-time FIFA and CONCACAF watcher and snapper. He's been watching Blazer's act for years and is suspicious of his motivations, eschewing the niceties of FIFA etiquette and branding Blazer a 'big, fat sleaze bag'. He was critical of the fact that CONCACAF held so many meetings and events in Las Vegas, linking this to Blazer's gambling fixation, and suggesting that the venue was used so much in order to cater for Blazer's wider connections in the entertainment and sports-gambling world. 'Why,' asked the photographer, 'should the USA national team have to play so many of its games in a rinky-dink college stadium in Vegas (Sam Boyd Stadium) when there are so many other better grounds scattered around the country?

Blazer's interest in linking Vegas with soccer is a matter of record. In 1999 Blazer was instrumental in bringing CONCACAF's Champions Cup tournament to the Nevada gambling resort, declaring that it had been his 'vision' to help make Las Vegas a premier soccer destination.

Neither can Blazer's commercial interests in betting be doubted. He is the owner of MultiSports Game Development, a company that, among other things, specialises in on-line betting. In 2001 MultiSports got together with Prisma iVentures – the media arm of the Kirch group (the TV rights holders for World Cups 2002 and 2006) – to form Global Interactive Gaming Ltd. As a spin-off from this deal Blazer and Kirch wanted to set up an on-line gambling company for this World Cup. 'Can you believe that' said the photographer. 'A senior member of the FIFA ExCo wanting to organise a global betting operation around the results! Anyway Blatter got wind of it and took Chuck into the woodshed and told him he was out of order.' Blazer was forced to abandon the scheme.

The photographer went over the old story of how CONCACAF president Jack Warner campaigned hard to make sure that Blazer and not Alan Rothenberg got the extra CONCACAF place on the FIFA executive committee, saying: 'Alan (Rothenberg) might be a little greedy, but he's basically a nice guy, an honest guy.' Jim added that Warner didn't trust Rothenberg to go along with some of his business dealings and schemes. The photographer labelled Blazer and Warner as 'crooks'; alone with Warner in an elevator in the Honduras a little after Blazer had secured the CONCACAF place on FIFA's ExCo, Jim observed, 'Hey Jack, sure was a good job you did on Rothenberg'. The CONCACAF president 'just smiled, and said, "Yeah I fucked him good didn't I?"'

While you might take the hearsay and the testimonies of a photographer with a pinch of salt, when Michel Zen-Ruffinen, then still FIFA general secretary, threatened to take legal action against both Blazer and Warner, it was time to take notice. Zen-Ruffinen raised questions about the decision taken by Warner and defended by Blazer, not to allow Mexican, Dr Edgardo Codesal to stand against Warner in the CONCACAF presidential elections held in Miami in April because, they argued, 'he was a paid CONCACAF employee'. Following such a precedent it could be argued that Blatter, himself a paid employee of FIFA, had been elected under false pretences. Zen-Ruffinen suggested that FIFA's Bureau of Legal Matters should look into this decision. This led to a strongly worded letter of protest to Blatter from Blazer and a torrent of abuse aimed at Zen-Ruffinen from Warner. 'FIFA must never again give a man's job to a boy,' raged the man from Trinidad.

This was by no means the first time that Warner had been accused of election fraud and sharp practice. Zen-Ruffinen believed that similar blocking tactics had been used to secure Warner's earlier 'unopposed' re-elections to the CONCACAF presidency. When, for instance, the FIFA general secretary went to the FIFA archives to recover the correspondence relating to Warner's 1989 electoral triumph he discovered that all of the documents written about this affair had disappeared. We remember being in Marseilles in 1998. Warner was staying with his wife in the Sofatel at the entrance to the city's Old Port harbour. He reported that his room had been burgled and £60,000 of his wife's jewellery had been stolen. Luckily, he could claim recompense through FIFA's insurance.

It is Warner's wheeling and dealing in television rights that has done most to tarnish his reputation, and by proxy that of his ally Sepp Blatter. Zen-Ruffinen claims that Blatter and his mentor Havelange are deeply implicated in a series of decisions to sell television rights for World Cups Italia '90, USA '94 and France '98 to Warner's company for US$1. Warner had to work harder to get his hands on the rights for Japan-Korea '02 and Germany '06 because, before they went under, ISL put the TV rights for the Caribbean region out to tender. Warner's rival, CSTN (Caribbean Sports Television Network), won this. When ISL folded the German media giant, Kirch, became the overall owner of the rights for 2002 and 2006. They withdrew CSTN's subcontract claiming that the company was not technologically sophisticated enough to deliver Kirch products. Warner leaned on Blatter – threatening to withdraw his backing for the World Under-17 youth championships that were scheduled to be played in Trinidad and Tobago – to get his own company back into the frame. When this became public and questions were raised over the potential conflict of interest if the FIFA ExCo was to award TV rights for FIFA competitions to one of its own members, Blatter came up with another of his famous body swerves. Instead of awarding the rights directly to Warner's company, they were given to the CFU (Caribbean Football Union) for a peppercorn fee with the proviso that any profits were to be ploughed back into football in the region. Who runs the CFU? Jack Warner, of course.

Warner's sullied reputation was further tarnished when *Daily Mail* correspondent Andrew Jennings alleged that he was behind a conspiracy to falsely represent Haiti at the 1998 presidential election in Paris. The legitimate representative of the

Haitian FA, Dr. Jean-Marie Kyss, was stopped at the airport by immigration officials and prevented from leaving the island. In his seat and voting on behalf of Haiti at the Equinox Centre in the French capital was Anglo-Trinidadian, Neville Ferguson, who is a 'special assistant' to – you've guessed it – Jack Warner.

Graham Kelly remembers his own distasteful encounters with the man from Trinidad. 'As a member of the FIFA ExCo Warner had one of the precious 24 votes that would decide who would get the World Cup in 2006. I didn't go on many 2006 campaigning trips but I went on the fateful one when we went to see Jack Warner,' he told us.

'Bobby [Charlton] and Alec [McGivan] and Tony Banks had gone to see Chuck Blazer in New York and I caught up with them in Trinidad to see Jack Warner. Interesting trip. That was my first exposure at the period to that current climate when Blatter was considering standing. We were being cultivated, being warmed up to the idea of voting for Blatter and getting World Cup bid votes in return.' But there was no such thing as a free lunch with Jack, recalls Kelly. 'Warner could be quite demanding. He would want work permits, he would want every consideration being given to work permit applications for players from that region and he wouldn't hesitate to ask. It is a pain. You are going out there to meet them and he wants special favours. It's very difficult. You've got to go through certain procedures. I found it very difficult. I suppose he comes on to our campaign office and they come on to me and say "We've had Jack Warner on ..." Well, it can be quite difficult because there are rules.'

There are Kelly's rules and there are Warner's rules. Warner wasn't exactly subtle with the English delegation. First he lectured them on the evils of post-colonialism and then he hit them for favours.

'On the first morning of our visit in Trinidad Warner gave us a dressing down saying things like, "You are widely perceived as imperialistic, you British lot. You've got a very bad attitude towards us downtrodden colonials; you're stuck up, imperialistic. You've got to alter all that and become more in tune with the modern world. You have got to be friendlier towards us. All that's outdated. Treat us in a better manner. You've got to be more forthcoming towards us."' Kelly gave an ironic chuckle. 'After his lecture he asked us for work permits and asked if the Jamaican national team could play at Wembley!'

With friends like Blazer and Warner does Blatter need enemies?

After the game Charlie introduced John to Guido Tognoni. Like Blatter, Tognoni is Swiss. A trim 5ft 10in., with wavy, light-brown hair, he is a sprightly early-middle-aged survivor of Swiss sports politics. Guido's the spy who came in from the cold. He was sacked as FIFA's media man by Havelange after he had been implicated in a potential challenge to the Brazilian's presidency, a 1994 plot to get rid of the Big Man and seize the throne for Blatter. Tognoni reckons he was made a scapegoat, sacrificed by Blatter to save himself. After a while spent working as an ice-hockey administrator he went to work with UEFA. By then, with the collapse of ISL and a series of financial scandals, Blatter's presidency was rocking and he brought Tognoni back on board (as 'special adviser to the president') to help steady the ship, perhaps also bringing with him UEFA's secrets. His main brief was to help to set up FIFA's own marketing wing to replace the bankrupt ISL. Tognoni made a good apologist for Blatter and claims to harbour no resentment over his earlier shock sacking, which is not what he was saying a few years earlier, just after having got the chop. No wonder he was brought back in. Asked, a little after his axing back in the mid-90s, whether there was anyone else who would speak, and whether he'd been privy to all the deals in his decade with Havelange and Blatter, the answer was crisp, precise and telling: 'No – nobody knows more than I do, and there are not many people who would talk … Yes, I was, I was in all those meetings.'

Lyndon Johnson famously said of FBI director J. Edgar Hoover: 'It's probably better to have him inside the tent pissing out than outside the tent pissing in.' Blatter was not slow to take this line, knowing that it's better to have your potential critics or informers sharing your urinal. Bringing Tognoni back in is yet another Blatter masterstroke. He was there for over ten years, running things with Blatter at the heart of the 80s and 90s boom, and has more tales to tell than any one else from that time – apart from Blatter and Havelange themselves.

After the Japan–Belgium game, on the way back into town Charlie offered to take John as his guest to the Ireland–Germany game the following day. Ibraki is a good two-hour drive from downtown Tokyo. The following evening Sugden sat at the back of the comfortable, air-conditioned FIFA VIP bus around a large card table, laughing and joking with Charlie and several other FIFA blazers from the Cook Islands and countries in Oceania and the Asian confederation. As they got closer to Ibaraki's Kashima stadium – which looked like a *Star Wars* movie set – out of the window could be seen thousands of green, white and gold-bedecked Irish trudging through the evening heat towards the stadium. John began to feel guilty about the position of privilege that he now found himself in; he justified this on the grounds of access for research, but still felt a mite over-privileged as he watched the masses straggling by. Not that this seemed to be bothering anybody else on the bus, not least the representative from Singapore, who had his wife and four children with him: twin daughters of about 12 or 13, and a couple of toddlers of about 4 and 2 years old respectively. The whole family had complimentary tickets for the best seats in the house.

Most of the time in the VIP lounge was spent helping Charlie track down Beckenbauer, Platini and the former Brazilian star, Zico. He wanted them to auto-graph the new Adidas football he had with him in a plastic carrier bag, which he was going to donate to a charity auction to be held at his golf club in Auckland when he got home. During the game John sat just to the right of Gerhard Mayer-Vorfelder, the new Blatterite president of the German football federation, and two other senior German football officials. It was worth the trip just to see the smug-ness vanish from their faces when Robbie Keane smashed in Ireland's last-gasp equaliser.

On the way back to Tokyo, Charlie told John that he would no longer be going to the England–Argentina game. He was returning to New Zealand because his wife was alone and one of his grandchildren was unwell. This made John slightly anxious, since the VIP match tickets were given out inside the VIP lounge, and without a VIP accreditation pass he doubted that he would get in to pick up his ticket. Charlie reassured him, saying that he would make arrangements for the ticket to be picked up from FIFA's headquarters in Sapporo.

Sapporo is about 500 miles north of Tokyo and after an uneventful flight John arrived mid-afternoon on 6 June, the day before the Argentina game. After breakfast the next day he made his way to the Sapporo Park Hotel to pick up his ticket. When he presented himself at the FIFA desk a pretty Japanese receptionist in a smart, pale-blue suit escorted him up to the sixth floor and the FIFA offices, where he met Malaysian Alex Soosay, who Charlie had said would have everything ready for him. Soosay was seated behind a small desk with a stack of multi-coloured match tickets in front of him. Checking his list, he saw John's name next to the allocation of Mr Dempsey. Some of the FIFA VIP tickets, including Dempsey's allocation, were in an envelope downstairs at the FIFA reception desk and Alex instructed the receptionist to take John back down and give him his ticket. The envelope, with 'Mr Dempsey' scrawled on it in black felt-tip, was at the bottom of the pile. As she flicked through the stack of envelopes John saw one with 'Col Gaddafi' printed on it. The Libyan leader had been a key supporter of Blatter's during his recent election. His son, Al Saadi Muammar Gaddafi, vice-president of the Libyan Arab Football Federation, had hosted a pro-Blatter campaign meeting in Tripoli in April 2002. In the closing address the Libyan leader encouraged the delegates to 'make the right choice for African football to move forward' and vote for Blatter. He then led them on a tour of the ruins of the presidential mansion, bombed by the Americans during the Reagan era. 'Better not give me Gaddafi's by mistake' John thought to himself.

John returned to the Sapporo Park just before 2pm to talk with Islington/London-based Emmanuel Maradas, the editor of *African Soccer*. Maradas is a journalist, but he's also one of approximately 450 'FIFA Committee and Panel Members' who join the FIFA Club in its most coveted outings, and a member of Chuck Blazer's Media Committee, apparently in his capacity as a representative of Chad. Before Maradas turned up John spotted David Will and his wife Margaret lunching together in the hotel's restaurant. David had a hunted and haunted look about him, more pronounced than it had been three weeks earlier in the Glasgow Hilton, at the Champions League final: 'My lips are sealed', he'd smiled then. Now it looked like they were bolted together forever. It was hardly surprising, since he had been one of Blatter's leading accusers in the run up to the election. Will chaired the committee that had been set up to scrutinise FIFA's and Blatter's finances. In addition he had been given overall stewardship of FIFA's ticketing plans which, as we have seen, were in a state of chaos. Will was exposed on this and if Blatter was out to get him – which he surely would be – the emerging ticket scandal would give him a perfect excuse. David had had his fingers burnt talking to us before, when he allowed a Dutch journalist to sit in on an interview in Paris in 1998. The Dutchman's story for a football magazine in Holland had been reworked in a German newspaper that exaggerated the claims made by Will about corruption behind Blatter's rise to power. Will had been carpeted by Blatter for that and had lost positions on some of

FIFA's highest-status committees. With his membership of the Club at stake he was unlikely to be willing to talk now.

John strolled up and said hello. Margaret beamed, but David could only manage a weak smile. John went through the formality of asking for an interview and predictably David refused. Apologising, he explained that he was under a lot of pressure and said this was neither the time nor the place for him to break his silence. 'Anyway, I am still involved in an investigation of FIFA's finances and, like with any auditing process, I am bound by rules of confidentiality'. 'But there's lots that I could tell you!' blurted out his wife. She wasn't seriously offering an interview, but Sugden told her that he would bear it in mind.

Will did give a quick response with regard to the reputed 'withdrawal' of the legal case against Blatter lodged in the Swiss courts by eleven members of FIFA's ExCo. The so-called withdrawal was supposed to have taken place in a meeting held shortly after Blatter's election triumph at which Will was not present. David said: 'It (the case) cannot be withdrawn. They are not charges and as such cannot be withdrawn. It is a requirement of Swiss Law that once financial matters of the kind raised by us emerge that there must be a legal response and an investigation by the Swiss courts. As far as I am aware, once in the system such issues cannot be withdrawn. As far as I'm concerned the case is still with the Swiss prosecutor.'

Will's interpretation was confirmed by Urs Hubmann, the Zurich prosecutor responsible for Blatter's case: 'It still has to be established whether there was substance in the allegations of financial irregularities brought against Blatter,' he said. 'Any decision to drop the proceedings was irrelevant, because what was under investigation was a so-called "official offence" which Swiss law required to be further investigated.' In the long run then, Blatter's precious Swiss law, which he has used so deftly to protect himself in the past, could have proved his downfall.

Later we sent Will (along with all the other members of the FIFA ExCo) a fax, asking for information and views about FIFA's recent troubles. At least he had the decency to reply (unlike the rest). if only to confirm his vow of silence. 'As you will appreciate, my position is (to say the least of it) very sensitive at present, and I am afraid that my feeling is that I should make no comment at all on the subjects referred to in your letter.' It's official: *omertà*.

John left David and Margaret to finish their lunch and joined Maradas in the lounge, sitting back in one of the comfortable white-leather sofas. We first interviewed Emmanuel in Johannesburg in 1996, long before Blatter entered the lists for FIFA president. Since then, through his influential African magazine, he had become more and more vociferous in support of the Swiss, and in equal measure more and more condemning of UEFA boss Lennart Johansson and his allies. 'I see you have been talking to your friend,' he said, pointing his large thumb back over his shoulder to where David and Margaret were still lunching, and proceeded to implicate Will and Johansson in his conspiracy theories tying global football politics to ethnocentric and post-colonial European interests.

He talked about the support that Europe had given to Africa through the Meridian agreement, whereby UEFA channels money and technical support to

African football through CAF's Cairo office. He reiterated the line spelled out in his editorial in the May 2002 edition of *African Soccer*: '*African Soccer* continues to regard Meridian as a neo-colonial construct. Africa has lined up blindly behind European positions in FIFA to the point where many wonder whether UEFA's Swiss head-quarters has not also become CAF's base'. Maradas goes on to describe the Meridian as 'useless, designed to bend the minds of naïve Africans without education'.

As Paul Darby has pointed out in his book, *Africa, Football and FIFA*, and we have argued at length elsewhere, in our study *FIFA and the Contest for World Football – Who Rules the Peoples' Game?*, Maradas's general line of argument – particularly about the Europeans and neo-colonialism – can be convincing. But it begins to fall apart around the sharper focus of support for Blatter. Asked 'Is it not possible that Blatter is exploiting this neo-colonial rhetoric for his own purposes, using *you* to strengthen his own power base?', Maradas concedes that this might be the case, but thinks that 'Blatter is sincere – certainly a better option than Johansson who, like Stanley Rous before him, is a colonial racist, a prototype of a racist.' This was strong stuff and certainly did not match our own experience of the genial Swede, but Maradas insisted on the point and said he was happy to be quoted.

After discussions about Meridian, the conversation turned naturally to the question of Blatter's *Goal* project. Blatter launched *Goal* in 1999 as a develop-ment programme for individual national associations whose needs are judged on a case-by-case basis. With a budget of 100 million Swiss Francs, 80 million US dollars, it is an apparatus through which cash can flow directly from Zurich into needy associations without being laundered through the confederations. Ostensibly the money is used to develop infrastructures like the construction of headquarters, technical centres and football grounds. We thought that it would be worth taking a closer look at how the tailor-made solutions were put in place, and so Alan Tomlinson took up the trail in the South Pacific.

Vanuatu is one of the beneficiaries of the *Goal* programme. Tomlinson was in Port Vila, talking to people about football, looking for Johnny Tinnsley-Lulu, presi-dent of the national football federation, and vice-president of the Oceania confed-eration. He walked along the seafront to the edge of town, as far as a dilapidated storehouse, Trader Rick's. Rick was looking down on his luck. The store was closed and the paintwork was tired. The yellow was grey and the red was a dirty pink. Alan walked on and took a sharp right into the hills. Thousands of people were streaming towards him. Some said good morning, hailed him in the local pidgin Baslama with a passing 'halo'. Some little girls just looked and then turned away and giggled. It was a colourful crowd. He got to the Ministre de Jeunesse et Sports, in the middle of a run-down complex where you could also find the football federation. The fence was barbed wire and the gates were locked. The football federation had decamped to New Zealand for the confederation's Nations Cup. Maybe Alan would catch up with them there in a couple of days.

The thousands steamed on, in brightly coloured clothes, contented-looking, more procession than mob. It was worship-day at Port Vila's big outdoor cultural centre. Tomlinson was greeted with more warm smiles, not as the only white man in town, but more as a returning sinner, a lost brother. This was the passion of the local poor. Not football, but God.

It was hot and getting hotter. Alan spotted a corner Yumi store across from the cemetery, stocked up with water and headed for the city's main stadium. This was off the tarmac track, along brown and dusty stone trails. The neighbourhood was busy, with naked little kids astride battered plastic bikes, women chasing chickens under the weekend laundry, a family group engrossed in *boules*, a battered red pick-up van spilling over with youths looking for something to look at.

Port Vila stadium had none of this hustle and bustle. Something had stirred here once, but now nobody was reading the signs, and the signs had given up. They hung around the sides of the stadium like homeless hoboes: 'Winfield 25s, Unbeatable …' then nothing. 'Origin energy', directed nowhere, dead if not buried. Australia's 'Victoria Bitter', ousted now by the local brew. 'Telecom Vanuatu Ltd, *parrain officiel*' for a Port Vila mini-games of long ago: '*votre liaison avec le monde*', the sponsor still boasted to a long-gone audience. 'Mitsubishi Motors' was a taunt to the former crowd, who'd be lucky to get a grown-up bike. The Health Ministry also called for 'tobacco-free sport', a reminder that 'smoking reduces fitness'. Like everything in this smiling but nervy town, this was half a statement, a door opened but still chained, like in the threatening inner-city block. Smoking kills, even in Melanesia.

Was this a football-mad country? Although Trader Rick's was closed, there was a football on the roof, above the doorway of the house behind the faded façade. Port Vila Stadium was open but empty – no sign of any football fever here. Outside the stadium three kids were bouncing footballs in the shade of a concrete booth by a mini-basketball court. The hoops were rusted and nets ragged. Even the metal backboards were ripped and jagged, graffiti framing the promo: 'Asco Motors – Oh what a feeling' had a mocking timbre. Feeling the inside of a Toyota would be a dream too far for the kids on this court. FIFA's millions certainly weren't doing much for the city's old main stadium and its environs.

Tomlinson had been looking for Johnny Lulu, but the faxes and phone calls remained unanswered. The Blatter legacy in such corners of the worldwide FIFA family was clear to see though. The Vanuatu Football Federation's development strategy for the country, with over 80 islands comprising the idyllic South Pacific archipelago, looked galvanised, though, by Blatter's own *Goal* initiative. Port Vila's main stadium could lie there blighted and rotting, a testimony to earlier neglect, as the US$424,827 poured into four pitches and a technical centre elsewhere in the city, due to be opened in August 2002.

Seven OFC members, all small island nations in the South Pacific, were, by the time of the election for the FIFA presidency, benefiting from *Goal*, to the tune of US$4,200,106. FIFA has committed itself to 80 million US dollars' worth of development, with *GOAL* offices in all six federational locations. Asia has three: Kuala Lumpur in Malaysia, Dubai in the United Arab Emirates, Colombo in Sri Lanka. There are four in Africa: Cairo in Egypt, Abidjan in Cote d'Ivoire, Gaboraone in Botswana, and Yaoundé in Cameroon; Central and North America and the Caribbean have two, in Port of Spain in Trinidad and Tobago, and Guatemala City in Guatemala. South America has just one, in Ascunción in Paraguay, and Oceania's is in Auckland, New Zealand. A central development office is based at FIFA itself, in Zurich. Mapped onto the planet, this is a serious level of development for the southern hemisphere. It has also provided perfect campaigning opportunities and a handy schedule for Blatter during the months preceding the election for the presidency.

Tonga football boss and FIFA Congress delegate Ahongalu Fusimalohi certainly didn't dissuade the FIFA president from dropping in to 'shovel the first mound of soil to officially launch the Goal project for Tonga', at Oceania's ordinary congress the week before the World Cup kick-off. In lounge suit and grey silk tie, garlanded by a necklace of orange blooms, a half-smiling Blatter brandishes a grave-digger's shovel. Maybe, as the Tonga football association's general secretary was saying his 'few inspiring words', Sepp wondered what kind of hole he was digging himself into. He needn't have worried too much. He was part of the conference programme, guest of honour for the groundbreaking ceremony, and joining in a traditional tree-planting ceremony too. The football association secured its 26-acre site from 'its patron and avid supporter, His Majesty the King of Tonga, Tafa'ahau Tupou IV', and the project comprises four natural-turf playing pitches and a residential national training centre/academy doubling up as the association's headquarters. Issa Hayatou was at the congress too, but his address was second-order stuff alongside the president's role in the proceedings.

Vanuatu's groundbreaking (or foundation-stone laying) ceremony was done in traditional style, Johnny Lulu presiding over the pig-killing part. Sir Bobby Charlton had gone to the Solomon Islands for the opening of the renovated Lawson Toma stadium. Blatter had become quite familiar with this part of the world. He'd been to Samoa, where $927,914 had been poured into the J.S.Blatter Playing Fields Complex, two international standard pitches on a 15-acre site gifted by the government. Blatter was there for the turf-turning ceremony in October 2000. He couldn't make it for the inauguration the following summer, but the head of the *Goal* office, Mohamed Bin Hammam of Qatar, could. He was responsible for selection and approval of projects, and could always be relied upon to step in for Sepp. Adrian Wickham of the Solomon Islands reports FIFA as being 'very happy with the progress of the project', and praises FIFA for its complementary forms of development funding, and associated forms of technical assistance: 'Taking all these into consideration, one can fully appreciate FIFA's broad and innovative approach towards improving football worldwide.'

Blatter had been talking 'tailor-made solutions' since his campaigning days of 1998. This had now become a mantra of loyalty, established as part of the FIFA family's lexicon. Josephine King, general secretary of the Oceania confederation, describes FIFA's *Goal* officer for the area as: '… responsible for overseeing the implementation of the tailor-made *Goal* projects targeted for our region. The aptly named *Goal* project is an initiative started by FIFA President Sepp Blatter, aimed at supporting the less developed national associations.'

Goal was a Blatter masterstroke. As the FIFA finances were collapsing, the *Goal* initiatives continued to get off the ground. As long as *Goal* monies arrived, the men with the votes in the congress weren't going to bother themselves about the financial shenanigans back at FIFA House. And the calendar of approvals, inaugurations and completions gave Blatter a worldwide stage on which to promote a positive, developmental dimension to his presidency, whilst his enemies plotted in out-of-touch committee rooms.

In his revelatory presentation to the executive committee, Zen-Ruffinen commented on Blatter's 'abuse of the projects *Goal'* in his African travels: 'Visiting ... was abused for campaigning for the re-election. The prioritisation of the need analysis of countries was changed by the President in the presence of witnesses according to his travel schedules so that he could inform each visited country that it had been selected for the programme. For example, in the priority orders Cameroon was replaced by Burkina Faso, Congo DR by Cape Verde, Angola by Botswana.' The financial aid programme (FAP) of Somalia was questioned after its football association chairman Farah Adda 'did not support the picture of the "FIFA family"', making his 'accusations in connection with the 1998 elections.' In 'the CONCACAF region' in particular, 'many associations are still persuaded that they will lose any financial support if they do not support the current regime'.

Blatter had got *Goal* approved within a year of assuming the presidency. The 12 development offices – at least in the bigger confederations – have a responsibility for between 15 and 20 projects for national associations. If the full programme survives, that's at least 140 to 150 projects, comfortably over two-thirds of the member nations of FIFA. You need a two-thirds majority to win the presidency. If *Goal* materializes fully, any big football powers of the world seeking to change the power base of FIFA would have little chance of success. As Charlie Dempsey comments: 'There are more Have-Nots than Haves in FIFA. If the Have-Nots get anything, they'll stay faithful. Blatter's been very clever. *Goal* isn't delegated to the confederations, it's run from FIFA. We know he's done wrong, but he's got us this.'

Blatter stoutly defends the *Goal* programme. Talking to BBC *Newsnight*, he said: 'This is so lovely, I have to tell you. In 1998, the one item of which I was proud, accepted by the congress, I said I am launching the GOAL project. I do it and now it is said it is for my promotion. No'. But sometimes 'No' does mean 'Yes'.

Blatter's enemies have accused him of using Goal as a vote-catching instrument.

'Isn't *Goal*, like Meridian, also a neo-colonial instrument?' John asked Emmanuel Maradas.

'No, it is not' replied Maradas. 'This goes directly to the individual federations – not into CAF's coffers like the money from Meridian – and is used for developing grass-roots infrastructure.'

'Still,' John pressed him 'even in this World Cup there have been many stories about problems and corruption surrounding some of the African teams. How can you be so sure that the money from Blatter's *Goal* project does not end up in some corrupt official's back pocket?' John reminds Maradas that he was our initial source on the extent of corruption in African football. Maradas had explained how most corruption took place at the level of the national associations. 'But now things are changing,' he insists. 'We now have a new class of younger and better-educated administrators and all over Africa you can see that the money that comes through *Goal* is being spent wisely, mainly on offices and communications equipment so that each country can have a permanent football administration and infrastructure. Without that there can be no development.'

Despite Maradas's earnest arguments, as we've shown earlier, while abject poverty and 'the politics of the belly' still rule in parts of Africa and other parts of the underprivileged world, the *Goal* project will be wide open to abuse.

Hayatou's challenge to Blatter was a topic that animated the man from Chad. As with the last two FIFA presidential elections, for 2002 Africa with its 50-plus votes would be a key battleground. It had a particular edge this time because Issa Hayatou from Cameroon, the president of the African federation, had thrown his hat in the ring. In doing so he had picked up the baton of Blatter's last challenger, Lennart Johansson, and was launching a campaign based on the key principles of transparency, accountability and democracy. Maradas believed that Haytou's decision to stand had been a foolish one. In his editorial in the March edition of *African Soccer*, Maradas had published a thinly veiled warning to Hayatou not to get involved in FIFA's family fall out:

> Above all, though, our football leadership must be aware of the siren voices of Africa's supposed – but sadly fickle – friends. The current manoeuvres have every appearance of a power struggle in which the challenger is potentially doomed to failure and Africa, if it is not very careful, will be cast in the role of cannon fodder. Continental unity is fragile enough without African blood being spilt fighting other people's battles.

That afternoon in the Sapporo Park, Maradas was more damning about the CAF leader's ill-advised joust with the incumbent FIFA president. 'Hayatou is finished. He has nothing more to offer. I campaigned for him in 1988 because there was nobody better than Issa around at the time. But he should not have stood against Blatter.' Maradas's main criticism is that Hayatou is a stooge of the UEFA hierarchy. 'He was a fool, a puppet of the Europeans with no vision of his own. Who designed and made the trophy for the African Cup of Nations? The Europeans of course'. This might strike some neutrals as a trivial point to make, but on such issues and sometimes trifles are many FIFA feuds fuelled. Maradas went on: 'Hayatou thinks that people from his own continent are incapable of such craftsmanship. What has he done for African football? Nothing. He just watches while our best young talent haemorrhages to the European leagues. This is a new kind of slavery. He has done nothing for his own country Cameroon – where corruption is still rife – and little or nothing for Africa. Now he wants to run and clean up world football, ha!'

Maradas believes that Hayatou was a pawn of the Europeans, and was deliberately sacrificed in a conspiracy to replace Blatter with a UEFA man in 2006. 'Hayatou ran a bad campaign. He was duped by the Europeans, who launched vicious personal attacks against Blatter – not just against his policies, but questioning the integrity of the man himself. If you are going to do this you have to be sure that everything in your own back garden is clean.' Maradas went on to tell how he tried to talk Hayatou out of standing. '"Issa you are a stupid man," I told him. "UEFA have set you up. They don't want you around in 2006 by which time they will have their own candidate". I warned him that if he lost the election – which was always certain – because of it he would be burned in the 2004 CAF elections. With Issa Hayatou out of the picture the way would be clear for UEFA's man – probably Beckenbauer – to walk in.'

There is some logic in this argument as in return for Hayatou's continuing support for Johansson and his policies, UEFA would be obliged to back his candidacy, but after the electoral rout could argue that a stronger challenger should be found next time around. UEFA's biggest problem in their struggles against both Havelange and Blatter has been coming up with a credible challenger. Even Johansson himself was a very reluctant and decidedly unexciting campaigner in 1998 – he only stood because there was nobody else. Similarly for 2002, while UEFA had plenty of back-stage, committee-room stalwarts, none of them was capable of standing up to and defeating Blatter. But by 2006 all of this may have changed, particularly with men like Beckenbauer or even Platini waiting in the wings. By then Hayatou may well have become an unnecessary obstacle. In this scenario, if Blatter's landslide victory over the Cameroonian leads to his demise at CAF, it is no bad thing for any prospective UEFA challenger for the FIFA presidency in 2006

'But surely,' John asked Maradas, 'as a fellow African you should be supporting him and encouraging your readers likewise?'

'In its own way that is a racist assumption too,' replied Maradas. 'Just because he is a black man, an African, that we as black Africans must support him rather than Blatter who is obviously a better man for the job.

"But what about the accusations of bribery made by Farah Addo, a fellow African and Somalian vice-president of CAF?' John asked in reference to the story broken by Andrew Jennings in the *Daily Mail* where Addo claims that he was offered US$100,000 to vote for Sepp Blatter in the 1998 presidential election. The Somalian claims that Mohamed Bin Hammam of Qatar, a member of the FIFA executive committee, offered the unsolicited bribe.

'Addo is a stupid man,' retorts Maradas, adding his suspicion that some Europeans, even from within the UEFA administration, were supporting Addo in his claims.

Addo has been threatened with legal action by Mohamed Bin Hammam over these allegations and, in an astonishing letter to Issa Hayatou, reproduced in full at the beginning of the book (in Chapter 1, 'Blattergate'), the man from Qatar claims that the Somalian was involved in some deranged plot to mastermind the takeover of world football by Moslems. Bin Hammam asserts that Addo wanted to discredit Blatter, get Hayatou elected as FIFA president and install himself as the next president of CAF. In another strange twist to this story, according to Martin Lipton, writing in ESPN's soccernet column in April 2002, Bin Hammam had also approached Saleh Abdullah Kemal, head of Saudi-based Dallah Avco corporation – believed by the FBI to have helped to fund Al Qaeda – to help to pay for the hire of the Gulfstream 111 jet that Blatter was using to hop around Africa and the Gulf during his 2002 election campaign. As Lipton put it, 'even if he didn't know it, consorting with people who may bear some responsibility for the most heinous act of terrorism the world has known is hardly "For the Good of the Game".'

Maradas would not countenance any of this, instead trying to turn the tables. 'The truth is' he continued, 'it was the Europeans that were offering the bribes in Paris. In a room on the fifth floor of the hotel. There were 43 delegates packed inside. They were offered $10,000 if Johansson beat Blatter and $5,000 if he lost. I can prove it.' But he doesn't. 'Then, the night before the vote itself at 3 a.m. Hayatou dashed over to the delegates' hotel and with Fahmy offered inducements for Africans to vote for Johansson. I was there. I saw it.' Maradas opens his large hands, palms out appealingly. 'Why is it that just because we Africans are poor, after every election we are accused of being corrupt and accepting bribes?' The big issue here is who is the most corrupt – the prostitute, the client, or the pimp? Those who accept bribes, those that offer them or those who benefit from the transaction without getting their hands dirty? Nobody has claimed that Blatter was directly involved in the so-called bribes, but if Addo is telling the truth, there can be no doubt who benefited most: Joseph 'Sepp' Blatter.

Maradas then began to undermine much of his case by trying to defend his own integrity, even though it had not directly been questioned. He and his wife and son were staying in the same top Japanese hotels as FIFA's top brass and it was highly likely that FIFA was footing the bill as a reward for Maradas's work for Blatter in Africa. Unsolicited, Maradas began to bemoan the fact that the UEFA camp had attacked him, accusing him of being on Blatter's payroll, claiming that *African Soccer* was a FIFA (i.e. Blatter) funded magazine. 'My magazine is not funded by FIFA,' he said, 'but I do get $4,000 sponsorship from them for each edition. In exchange for this the magazine carries some advertisements for FIFA Marketing and their sponsors. Then I am attacked for taking money off Havelange! I was searching Africa looking for a once famous player in Zaire, Mdage Mulamba, whom I had heard was dying of Aids. We wanted to see if there was anything that we could do to help. Havelange heard about this and wanted to help – that is the kind of man he is – so he authorised FIFA to pay my expenses which came to £5,200. At the time Zen-Ruffinen authorised the cheque. Then, later, he went to the press claiming that I was on the FIFA payroll! How can this be called bribery?'

This is a moot point. It can be called bribery if this influences what you write in your journal. In articles and editorials in the three editions of *African Soccer* published before the Seoul election, Blatter's virtues are celebrated and the activities and policies of Hayatou and his supporters rubbished. Of course, these views may be valid, even based on solid evidence and sound argument. But because they coincide with the interests of the people who help to pay the bills, they must be considered tarnished. On the basis of his post-colonial arguments, perhaps he had been right to use his magazine to campaign against Johansson in 1998 and Hayatou in 2002. This does not mean however that he was right to campaign for Blatter and paint him as a latter day 'Africa's Robin Hood' as Maradas put it. If, as has been admitted by Maradas himself, Blatter and his supporters were helping to finance him and his magazine, then his credibility as an objective journalist is shot to pieces; but his validity as a witness to Havelange and Blatter's FIFA powerbroking is stronger than ever.

At what point does a person become co-opted, step over the line, become one of the Badfellas? This is a question that we asked Graham Kelly. 'Its unreal, once you get inside it it's unreal, it's the same at The FA. If you asked them where they go over the line they wouldn't know they'd gone over the line. This is the point. They come into it for the right reasons. I haven't rehearsed this and I haven't thought about it before, but I would say certainly over 50 per cent of the people that I have worked with in football have gone over the line and are now in it for the wrong reasons, but they would have no idea when they crossed that line ... They look at you as if you're crazy if you leave the stuff behind or instruct the girl at the desk not to take the parcel.' If Maradas had not already stepped over the line, then he was pretty adept at redrawing it to suit his personal, political and professional purposes.

Before the England–Argentina game the VIP lounge was crowded with many of the usual suspects. Fashionably late, Blatter, looking more and more each day like Rod Steiger's Napoleon in the film *Waterloo*, swept imperiously into the long room having just arrived in Japan after his triumph in Korea. Blatter knows the authors of this book because of their critical work on FIFA. That is why he does not care for either of the 'English Professors' as he once called us, spotting us lurking outside a FIFA committee meeting in Cairo. 'Evening, Mr President,' John said as he marched past Blatter several years later on his way to the gents at Japan/Korea 2002. Blatter gave him a sideways glance, smiled crookedly and kept walking, no doubt making a note to himself to have the head of the person who had let one of these English professors in.

We were helped in some of our early work by FIFA's media boss, director of communications Keith Cooper, who had assisted us with access to useful respondents and historical documents, and helped us get media accreditation for France '98. A few weeks after the World Cup finals in Asia the long knives were wielded and Blatter sacked Cooper along with six other administrators. Both the fact of Cooper's dismissal and the brutal way that it was done revealed a new and worryingly ruthless streak in the re-elected president. We have first-hand experience not only of Cooper's integrity with regard to his civil service-like neutrality in relation to the FIFA family's political in-fighting, but also of his doggedness when defending FIFA as an administrative body. But in Blatter's brave new world you are either with him or against him. 'I was called in by the acting general secretary,' recounted a stunned Cooper, 'not the president whom I have known for almost 30 years, but who was unable to tell me himself – and told I was being dismissed as from today. It really was quite brutal.'

He should have known the style. Back in 1995, Tognoni had been shown the door. But not by Havelange or Blatter. It was the head of finance who told Guido goodbye to 'one of the greatest jobs in the world you can have', as the axed man mournfully recalled: 'He was delegated. I was disappointed at Blatter. He didn't even have the courage to tell me what was really going on. He didn't have the courage to tell me this,' he echoed.

The press release announcing the start of Blatter's purge was chillingly terse:

> Zurich 10 July 2002 – FIFA has yesterday and today parted company with seven employees. The decision to terminate or not extend these employees' contracts comes as part of FIFA's restructuring process. President Joseph S. Blatter will present a proposal concerning the future structure of world football's governing body to the Executive Committee at its next meeting on 23/24 September 2002.

Clearly, Blatter had no intention of being bullied or, in his eyes, betrayed, by either his executive or his administration ever again. According to Tognoni, Blatter's problems with the executive were already well on the way to being solved. 'Blatter's stubborn at times,' explained Tognioni. In the past he couldn't control his executive like Havelange could. But at the last ExCo elections he tipped the balance in his favour by getting rid of Omdal and Matarrese and getting Platini, Vorfelder, and Spain's Angel Llona on board – all his supporters'. Now it was time for him to turn his attention to his administration.

The first head on the chopping block was that of Michel Zen-Ruffinen. 'If you have in your own house a traitor, this is bad,' Blatter blurted to Jennie James of *Time* magazine, in the Glasgow Hilton on Champions League night: 'Have you ever heard of Brutus?' he continued, comparing Zen-Ruffinen to Shakespeare's backstabbing assassin. This time it was Caesar who would wield the knife. 'Zen-Ruffinen is bad, not naïve and he's just not very smart,' was the way Tognoni summed up the outgoing general secretary. 'Grondona got it right when he said, "I wouldn't put him in charge of a troop of boy scouts let alone FIFA." Now I feel I must apologise to the scouts!'

Zen-Ruffinen had been the rising star in FIFA House when Tognoni was being shown the door and he still harbours resentment that the young Swiss lawyer and former referee had occupied the seat that he coveted for himself. 'I left FIFA seven-and-a-half years ago because of Zen-Ruffinen's gross incompetence. No matter what he tells you, Zen-Ruffinen's charges against Blatter are a pack of lies and that is why they have been withdrawn from the Swiss courts.'

Zen-Ruffinen had been allowed to hold onto his job until immediately after the World Cup then he was out. 'I can say nothing until after 29 May,' he told us in the lobby of the Glasgow Hilton in mid-May. He wasn't saying much when the inevitable axe came. Several big job offers immediately came his way, and a FIFA severance package that could help him bide his time in deciding on his future. Here he was in Japan, in the VIP lounge, looking relaxed and chatting to David Davies of the English FA. Infamously, on the eve of the 1998 election, England had abandoned Johansson and publicly declared that they would vote for Blatter. This time they had done the same but in reverse, by dumping Blatter on the strength of Zen-Ruffinen's allegations and vowing support for Hayatou.

In the weeks after his re-election Blatter moved swiftly to consolidate his power base. Loyal F-Crew members and other cronies were quickly moved into key positions. Fellow German-Swiss Urs Linsi replaced Zen-Ruffinen as boss of the administration, and Blatter's former personal communications advisor, the German, Markus Siegler, made himself comfortable in Cooper's old office. With a tame executive and a loyal, Germanic praetorian-guard around him Blatter would be more despotic and more difficult to shift than ever. With the Kaiser waiting in the wings, there would be smiles on the faces of officials of the Deutscher Fussball-Bund in Frankfurt, but one can only wonder at what, back in Brazil, the Godfather must have thought of the Swiss-German cabal at the heart of his beloved FIFA.

As he took his seat near to the half-way line for the England-Argentina showdown, Sugden noticed that sitting right behind him, coincidentally next to Lennart Johansson's secretary, was an American tout or 'scalper' who less than an hour before had been hawking tickets for outrageous prices outside of the stadium. More evidence, if it were needed, of FIFA's inability to police itself. He turned away from the tout and looked around the ground. The scale of support for England was mightily impressive. Tens of thousands of English fans had made the journey to Sapporo and their numbers were swelled by thousands of Japanese who had adopted England as their number two team. The stadium was awash with St George's flags, from Portsmouth to Carlisle and most places in between. While national flags were allowed, outrageously FIFA, worried by the prospect of 'ambush marketing', had outlawed the wearing of any product bearing the logo of any company other than that of one of the official sponsors inside the stadium. The centre pages of the official *2002 World Cup Spectator Guide* contained the following statement and warning:

> Through their financial and product support the Official Commercial Affiliates of the 2002 World Cup contribute greatly to the success of the event. However, other companies try to take advantage of the worldwide stage provided by the FIFA World Cup to promote their products and to gain a false association, but the fact is these 'ambushing' companies don't invest one penny to support the event – they simply rip it off!
>
> Do not bring commercially branded material (company names, logos, etc.) into the stadium such as flags, banners, hats, balloons, scarves. Please be aware that stadium Security will be removing all such items at the stadium entrances.

Sugden wondered if anybody would spot his Nike trainers. It would have been embarrassing to have to stand in his stocking feet in the FIFA VIP lounge at half-time. By now John had managed to convince himself that England were sure to spoil an otherwise excellent day by losing to Argentina. Famously, of course, they didn't. Owen fell, Beckham stepped up and nightmare memories of St-Étienne 1998 ended as his penalty went straight past the spot on which the keeper had been standing and struck the back of the Argentine net like a thunderbolt. Led by the colossal Rio Ferdinand, the English defence played faultlessly and when the final whistle went, Adam Crozier and David Davies of the English FA danced and hugged each other like long-lost lovers.

After the game, surveying the VIP lounge and watching the FIFA blazers polish off what was left of the wine and sushi, and knowing what we did about the treachery endemic within their Machiavellian world, John wondered to himself who, if any of them, could be trusted. He recalled something that the canny FIFA photographer had told him. 'With FIFA it's not a question of who's wearing the black hats and who's wearing the white hats. It's more a question of black and dark grey hats.' Waiting to catch the VIP bus back to town John bumped into Zen-Ruffinen and chatted briefly to him. He would not say too much, perhaps because of 29 May, but what he did say was 'all of the things that I have said about him, all of the charges that I have made against Blatter are 100 percent true'. And looking into his eyes, it was difficult not to believe him.

It remains hard to see how FIFA could ever reform itself from within. There is too much at stake – everyone's an insider, a beneficiary, a club member. It has worked too well for too many for too long. Machiavelli wrote that 'men should either be treated generously or destroyed'. Tognoni learnt what he meant in 1995, forced out by the Havelange clean-up after Blatter's foiled coup. The then general secretary had, as Tognoni recalled, sought to usurp Havelange, 'tried to challenge him, tried to put a knife in his back'. Tognoni and Michel Galan, not Blatter, bore the brunt of the Big Man's revenge. Keith Cooper and six other FIFA loyalists would also do well to take solace in Machiavelli's musings in July 2002, when Blatter was obliterating the legacy of Zen-Ruffinen's administration and they all had to go. Blatter's inside group, the special bureau he'd had on his agenda since winning the presidency, could now be neatly put in place. Blatter had learned well from Havelange. He knew that 'it is much safer for a prince to be feared than loved'.

15

FIFALAND

Imagining world football's future

We look skywards and gasp as a laser-guided fireball lights up the Nevada night. 'Ladies and Gentlemen,' a disembodied voice booms around the packed auditorium, 'welcome to Fifaland Las Vegas where Players Win and Winners Play!' More fanfare. 'Welcome to the Championship Game of the 2024 World Soccer Series!' We had made our pilgrimage to Montevideo to visit the site of global football's beginning. Now, in our dotage, we were in the pleasure capital of the world to witness its end. FIFA Incorporated had grown out of the rubble of its crumbling, amateur parent. This tainted body had finally collapsed after shenanigans and controversies that surrounded the awarding of the World Cup to Germany in 2006 and Saudi Arabia in 2010 were made public. Then, when two German journalists finally proved that presidential elections had been rigged, its very latest president was forced to step down. An American lawyer was installed as caretaker president. He at once abandoned FIFA's charitable façade and floated the organisation as a limited company on the world's stock markets. He raised billions of dollars, mostly from the media and marketing industries which already had a huge stake in making sure international football, in one form or another, survived. One by one the confederations, which were by now totally dominated by business interests, followed suit and were themselves gobbled up by FIFA Incorporated.

No longer concerned with massaging their over-inflated egos or buying their votes, one of the first acts of FIFA's new board was to get rid of the hangers-on, the sycophantic relics of the *ancien régime* who themselves had grown fat as modern football flourished. FIFA also gave up the unpredictable and damaging practice of auctioning the World Cup to the highest bidder and instead searched for a permanent site.

Las Vegas was the obvious choice. FIFA bought the Tropicana Hotel on a prime site on the Strip and razed it to the ground. In its place they built Fifaland, a 20,000-room hotel complex, with ten acres of casinos, bookies and slot machines, 200 bars and restaurants, an underground shopping mall, 20 swimming pools and a state-of-the-art media centre equipped for 10,000 journalists.

Fifaland dwarfed the MGM Grand and New York New York across the street and towered above Mandalay, Luxor, Excalibur, Bellagio, Paris and the other theme palaces which had turned Vegas into the dream capital of the world. Its centrepiece was a 100,000 all-seater auditorium with retractable roof. With the roof closed a range of artificial weather conditions could be created, to make the game more like the real thing. The spectators, of course, were protected from these fake elements. The arena also had a playing surface which, like pulling open a drawer, could be manoeuvred out of the complex and into the open air. Once outside it was watered and manicured by an army of groundsmen. Inside, the auditorium floor could now be used for concerts, business conventions, political rallies and a host of other money-making ventures.

As Fifaland took shape, FIFA's enforcers set about restructuring world football so that it would feed into the yearly World Soccer Series. On its centenary in 2004 FIFA bosses had already rewritten the statutes to make the organisation constitutionally sound as a dictatorship, run by the president and his own inner circle, and the pseudo-democratic congress of cronies and dependants. Domestic and continental franchises still played their annnual competitions but there were no longer senior national teams. Those larger clubs that had survived the financial madness of the 1990s and the first decade of the twenty-first century were mostly owned by the same interests which now ran FIFA. They were allowed to keep their players until they peaked, which FIFA set at 26 years of age. Up until that age they could also represent their countries and play in the biennial Olympic-FIFA Junior World Cup in Disney's Olympus complex in Florida.

Each year, as the best players reached their prime, they become FIFA's property and were placed in an American-style draft system. The 24 commercial franchises who participated in the World Soccer Series (Team Nike, Team Adidas, Team Budweiser, Team McDonald's, Team Ford, Team Hyundai, Team Microsoft and the rest) have players allocated to them according to how they and the players are rated from the previous season. The most highly rated players go to the teams that achieved least and vice versa. This way FIFA keeps its competition competitively balanced. Some thought that this system resembled a rigged slave auction. But Fifaland is the only show in town, and few turn down the opportunity to play there.

In return for putting their names on the backs of the greatest players in the world, FIFA demands and receives generous payments from the blue-chip companies that own the precious franchise teams. An unintended welcome by-product of replacing national teams with company ones is the end of football hooliganism. Years ago, fuelled by misplaced national pride, thuggish fans might have fought one another on the beaches of Marseilles, but no-one rampages in Vegas for the sake of a company logo. Back in 2002, the Koreans and the Japanese had piloted a well-orchestrated and unthreatening football passion ripe for further exploitation in Fifaland's tourist packages.

Back in Vegas, seamlessly, the announcer's voice faded and Wagner's 'Ride of the Valkyries', FIFA's newly adopted anthem, assaulted the eardrums. Team Nike, captained by the balding 40-odd-year-old Ronaldo, and Team Adidas, led out by his slightly younger rival, Michael Owen, jogged into the arena. Tackling of any sort had been outlawed by FIFA after the 2006 World Cup and certain forms of steroids were now legal. This enabled many of the best players to continue their careers well into their forties.

The game itself was entertaining enough. The goals were bigger: ten metres long by four metres high. A new scoring system had been invented by FIFA, one that awarded one point for a penalty, two points for a goal scored from inside the area and three points for one from outside the box. Off-side disappeared ten years ago. There was plenty of action at either end. The arbitrator in his instant-replay, virtual-reality helmet, ensured that there was absolutely no room for physical contact. With weary grace and circus trickery, the ball was lobbed, dribbled and pinged around the field.

It was a bit like watching one of those old PlayStation video games. In the last minute of the final quarter, Ronaldo's 30 metre pile-driver almost broke the net. Team Nike won 27-25 and succeeded Team Budweiser as World Champions. Like the rest of the audience, we applauded politely as the octogenarian president handed over the World Series trophy, the Golden Goose Egg, to Ronaldo.

We filed out of Fifaland heading for the Strip with time and money to spend. Having been bombarded with special effects for three hours, it was hard to tell whether it was night or day, whether we were inside or out. The casinos would be open all night and we could take in the Professional Bull Riders' competition over at the MGM. We might even catch the together-again Spice Girls' late show at Caesars Palace.

Dream? Nightmare? Or vision of the future? Shortly after we first penned this chapter, back in 1999, this dark fantasy came a small step closer to reality, thanks to Chuck Blazer when he sat next to Kirk Hendrix, president of Las Vegas events, who announced that the Central, North American and Caribbean soccer club championships would be held in the casino capital of the world. 'Our intent is to make this a success and bring it back on an annual basis,' Hendrix said. 'We would like to develop Las Vegas as a soccer destination. We think Las Vegas and the soccer community can be great partners,' he told the *Las Vegas Review Journal* in July 1999.

While the vision of Fifaland as described above may never happen, the wholesale transformation of football is more likely to come to pass. It is inevitable if the people – that is, all of us – passively accept that there is no choice but to allow the game to be driven with the bullish and ultimately self-destructive logic of big business. We cannot turn back the clock but we can still have a say in the shape of things to come.

Either through incompetence, greed or vainglorious notions of pre-destiny, the league of gentlemen, the blazer-and-slacks brigade, forfeited their right to rule world football a long time ago. As Graham Kelly put it, 'The FIFA executive committee know they are part of a massively discredited regime, which, had it been in charge of a local Sunday league, would long ago have been subjected to the most rigorous inquiry and its officials banned from holding office indefinitely'. Should this come to pass, there is however a danger that their places will be filled by slick-suited chief executives or high- flying commissioners, with scant regard for football's traditional culture, yet another breed of bounty hunter muscling in on the action. What football needs at every level is representative and responsible government. For this to happen the administration of football has to be rooted in accountable institutions and subject to the law.

After reviewing the state of the global governance of sport in general, Sunder Katwala concludes, in his book *Democratising Global Sport* (2000), that 'it is difficult to find anything in the world quite so badly governed as international sport'. He goes on to say that: 'Reform of international sporting governance is not inevitable but it is possible. Sporting governance is in a state of extreme disequilibrium – the tensions between the global revolution and unmodernised governance must eventually bring change of one sort of another. But change is likely to come from an uncertain combination of different forces – change from within, pressure from outside and change through collapse and crisis.'

In 1998 and 2002 FIFA had a clear opportunity to 'change from within' and recover its position as the guardian of the world game. But, as both the 1998 and 2002 FIFA presidential elections illustrated, turkeys do not routinely vote for Christmas. However, the democratising of FIFA may yet come about 'through collapse and crisis'. The bankruptcy of ISL in 2001 and the implication of senior FIFA officials, including the president himself, in this debacle, shook the organisation's foundations and renewed calls for democratic reform. Of potentially more significance than the alleged corrupt practices of individuals within or close to FIFA is the organisation's financial crisis. There is clear evidence that media and marketing interest in football, at least at the world level, has peaked or even gone into decline. Without the huge financial surplus that accrues to FIFA from such arrangements it is unlikely to be able operate on the same lavish scale in the future. Without the 'cash box' brim full and overflowing, the 'black-boxes' of extra cash in secret accounts, the deals and alliances that have maintained FIFA as a fiefdom and kept the likes of Havelange and his protégé, Blatter, in power for nearly three decades, it will no longer be able to hold. If this comes to pass then calls for democratic reform, both from within and without, may become irresistible. As Jim Boyce (the president of Northern Ireland's football governing body) asked us in the lobby of the Glasgow Hilton, the night that Real Madrid triumphed over Bayer Leverkusen, 'Who will clean up FIFA?' So far, because of sport's protected status as a politics-free zone, FIFA (like the IOC) has been relatively impervious to outside pressure for reform.

One of the defining features of the twentieth century was the acceleration in the range and extent of international government organisations (IGOs) and their non-governmental equivalents (INGOs). In 1909 there were only 37 IGOs and 176 INGOs (including FIFA), while in 1996 there were 260 IGOs and a staggering 5,472 INGOs. In part the growth in the number and reach of IGOs has been a response to the dramatic expansion of INGO activity. Whether they be charitable organisations such as OXFAM, political lobbyists such as CND, or global organisations of criminals and terrorists, national governments have collaborated, through bodies such as the United Nations and its satellites, or the European Union, to monitor and exert a degree of influence over INGO's activities. Hitherto, sport in general and football in particular, have been exceptions to the rule, though as the European football federation UEFA has learned with respect to a number of issues, the European Union can affect both its practices and the basic finances of the European game.

Up until now, the formal political presence of government in world football has been limited, usually, to token and largely ceremonial functions. Attending opening ceremonies of World Cup matches or hosting lavish dinners for Fifacrats and their retinues are among the roles routinely adopted by government representatives within the network. Interaction between national governments and FIFA tends to become more pronounced only when world football is perceived to have a bearing on the national interest, or where autocratic states such as Gulf nations merge the functions of state and civil institutions, effectively annihilating any autonomous sphere of civil society. Interaction between FIFA and government typically occurs around bidding for and hosting major international tournaments, particularly the World Cup finals. Mega-events in sports are staged for corporate profit, personal aggrandisement, and for state-driven national pride.

Otherwise, FIFA's engagement with state politicians usually only happens when it seeks to help one or more of its member associations prevent political interference into its affairs by its national government. Herein lies a clue that helps us to understand why up until now FIFA has operated largely beyond the reach of any international and democratically accountable legal framework. FIFA, like the IOC, was established by a class of people who thought themselves to be selfless, well-meaning, and right-thinking gentlemen, who believed in the separation of sport from politics as a sacred principle. According to this view, politics and politicians could only violate sports integrity. People like Jules Rimet, Arthur Drewry, and Sir Stanley Rous felt duty bound to protect football from the overt interference of politicians, and the organisation that they helped to mould has continued to operate according to the same principles. This is a position that has, for the most part, been respected by mature democratic governments that rarely, if ever, meddle in the affairs of sports' governing bodies.

Of course, such a stance was naïvely self-serving from the outset, and is even more so now. It is a confidence trick that has been made easier to carry off because of the façade of democracy under which FIFA operates. As we have seen, when it comes to making major decisions, such as electing a new president, every member association has one equal vote. Thus, when it comes to the equity of representation, FIFA seems to occupy the moral high ground. However, often those who cast votes are not themselves elected and neither are they accountable to any broader constituency. Furthermore, because FIFA elections operate a secret ballot, they can and have been rigged to ensure that those who are best suited to serve the interests of big business are elected and re-elected. In this way, without any genuine democratic accountability, self-styled sporting aristocrats and autocrats have manipulated and exploited global sport for their own financial and vainglorious purposes. Millions of dollars, in the form of over 500 so-called development programmes, have poured into projects and budgets of smaller national association FIFA members over the years, with scarcely any accountability. As Guido Tognoni starkly put it, asked whether you could monitor the national associations' use of funds: 'No you cannot. You have to trust the president of an African national association that he will only represent his national association. If he comes and says "I want the money now", what can you do? You cannot say "Please show me where you go with it." You have to trust them.' But the issue of accountability didn't seem to worry the man now back at the centre of FIFA administration. As he also observed of FIFA's way of working: 'You had the African, as long as you give.'

We would not want national governments to run football. But at a domestic level democratically elected governments should, through a legally constituted and independent agency, exercise a guiding, and if necessary, a restraining influence over the game. If other important and formerly nationalised utilities such as gas, water, electricity and the rail network have to be accountable to government watchdogs, then the same should apply to something as important to the national psyche as football.

At a regional level a similar arrangement could be worked out between, for instance, UEFA and the European Commission/Parliament, itself (in part at least) a democratically elected and representative body. At the very least, such an arrangement would force these two bodies to come together and work out a sensible legal framework for the development and continued vitality of football in Europe, one through which the EC protected football from the business predators rather than inviting them in to feast at the top table. Similar arrangements could be worked out between football federations and regional IGOs in other parts of the world.

FIFA itself must be brought within the embrace of an accountable international organisation such as the United Nations, perhaps under the wing of this organisation's cultural framework, UNESCO. Under such an arrangement, FIFA's off-shore financial status would have to end. All of its important decisions would be scrutinised by officials, themselves accountable to a broader electorate and within a wider legal framework.

Obviously, these are ideal solutions with huge practical problems. When it comes to corruption, the UN and the EC have their own problems. A restructured and more accountable FIFA would continue to exercise authority over all member associations. This is not to suggest that politicians should run world football and here it is important to distinguish between political control and political accountability. Control suggests uncontested domination, whereas accountability rests upon representation rooted in transparency and the capacity for reform. In this regard, while FIFA is right to continue to protect its member associations from the political interference of those who would seek to control football, it is wrong to continue to protect itself from outside scrutiny and accountability.

Finally, it is necessary to address the 'should' question and respond to criticisms of the above arguments that have been raised. 'Why', it has been regularly asked, 'should we make a special case for football? After all, isn't it just like any other object of production/consumption and shouldn't it too be subject to the forces of a global economy?' Leaving aside the issue of whether or not any sphere of industry and/or culture should be exposed to unbridled global commercialisation, football is a special case in as much as it is one of a number of realms of cultural production that have considerable meaning beyond straightforward consumption. Theatre, opera, ballet and other dimensions of 'high' culture would have died out long ago had it not been for high levels of state and private protection and patronage. The French have long battled to preserve distinctiveness for French cinema in the face of Hollywood's relentless quest for global dominance. Early in 2000 the impresario, Andrew Lloyd Webber, bought a number of prominent theatres in London's West End which had been threatened with closure. In announcing his take-over, Lloyd Webber stated his belief, in an interview with *The Independent*, that it was important that these theatres did not fall into the hands of 'pen-pushers and number-crunchers' who had less regard for the their artistic value than they did for real-estate and profit. The rationale for such protectionism is that certain aspects of culture are so deeply connected to community and national identity, and of such critical importance to local and/or world heritage, that to allow them to be radically altered, or even destroyed, by market forces would be seriously damaging to the quality of life for people today, and for unborn generations. There is no reason why such arguments cannot be extended to cover other aspects of popular culture, including football.

In Europe, South America and Africa, football, perhaps more than any other area of popular culture, captures the collective imagination and animates the discourse of citizenship. Yes, football matches are widely consumed by live audiences, increasingly through television, and large quantities of football-related apparel and memorabilia are bought worldwide. However, football clubs and national teams carry meanings beyond the moment of consumption. They stand for things such as community, tradition, social solidarity, local and national distinctiveness: they provide sources of identity formation and expression at local, national and cosmopolitan levels. Such attributes may not be easy to package and sell, and may even stand in the way of profit-driven 'progress', but they are deeply significant in the non-utilitarian enrichment of existence for uncountable millions of people. While accepting that these 'attributes' can also, under certain circumstances, lead to less socially constructive manifestations such as nationalism, racism, sexism and hooliganism, football still needs to be protected from the more avaricious and predatory trends and practices of an unregulated global capitalism. FIFA, as currently constituted, is patently, obviously incapable of providing this protection. For this reason, it and comparable sports organisations should not escape the attention of those commentators and activists who are dedicated to the democratic reform of the global political economy.

FIFA could seek to gain some credibility in the eyes of a sceptical public by opening its financial books, coming out from behind the veil of Swiss secrecy and banking laws that have protected world sports organisations, as well as hoarders of Nazi gold for half a century and more. It could ask those national football federations that have accepted huge and regular handouts to say precisely where the money has gone. It could look to use the profits from bonanzas such as World

Cup finals to develop the game at the grass-roots. It could make moral interventions in the richest pastures of the world game, the European leagues. It could review the membership and composition of key committees, so that henchmen of the president cannot sell on media rights for FIFA events to their own cronies or even their own companies. It could give the executive committee proper and useful functions, such as setting the budget and advising and consulting on major contracts and genuine tenders. It could begin to act with integrity for the good of the game, rather than for the ego and self-aggrandizement of the badfellas and their cronies.

But this would not be Havelange and Blatter's FIFA. Their FIFA, the HBFD, has listed ten rules to follow 'for the good of the game': 'Play to win; play fair; observe the laws of the game; respect opponents, teammates, referees, officials and spectators; accept defeat with dignity; promote the interests of football; reject corruption, drugs, racism, violence and other dangers to our sport; help others to resist corrupting pressures; denounce those who attempt to discredit our sport; honour those who defend football's good reputation'.

It's a worthy list, adorning the 2000 launch booklet for the *Goal* project. Yet viewed next to the list of allegations (albeit dismissed, or sidelined for the moment) in the criminal complaint submitted to the Swiss Public Prosecutor, rather than alongside the images of the black kids and toddlers with their rush-games and makeshift balls, it looks like worthless, hypocritical humbug.

Football, rightly so, will always have an important commercial dimension. However, we need to return to the guiding principle which allowed the game to flourish so magnificently in its golden years: football first, business second. To achieve this, 'for the good of the game', supporters, current and former players, politicians and honest sports administrators need to collaborate in the fight for the soul of the people's game. But as the recurrent narratives of the FIFA story show, the current beneficiaries of FIFA's flawed system of governing and regulating the game won't give up their privileges without a struggle. See you in the trenches and on the terraces – or in Vegas.

SEQUEL

Badfellas on the run

After his 2002 re-election for his second presidential term, Sepp Blatter, as we saw at the end of *Badfellas*, needed to ensure that FIFA could recover from the financial crisis of the ISL bankruptcy, whilst also keeping faith with the supporters who had kept him in power, and this meant more favours and continued handouts. In short, FIFA and Blatter needed money, and lots of it, and for FIFA this meant success-ful men's World Cup events, competing sponsors willing to outbid each other to have the men's World Cup profile (and all FIFA's other events), and broadcasters ready – whatever the scandal and the crisis – to keep contributing the lion's share of the increasing revenues as FIFA's finances were rebalanced and began to grow dramatically.

We provide here a selective update of the thirteen years of Blatter's regime of dictatorial control, corruption and maladministration, since surviving the ExCo challenge of 2002 and the criminal complaint lodged in the Zurich court by the eleven members of the ExCo.[1] To contextualize the period, this update is preceded by a timeline of crises and events over those years, up to the Extraordinary FIFA Congress in Zurich in February 2016. The update is our selective look at particu-lar moments and issues characteristic of the Havelange-Blatter FIFA Dynasty, the HBFD as it moved into its fifth decade since Havelange won the presidency in 1974 and brought Blatter into FIFA the following year. It is a selective chronology but concentrates on the long-game, as intensifying scrutiny and investigative revelations on the excesses and corruptions of the HBFD brought more forces into play – from academics like ourselves, to leading investigative reporters such as Andrew Jennings; from legal systems in Switzerland and the US, to agencies such as Transparency International. Numerous notorious and infamous – and also many anonymous – badfellas have run amok in the Blatter years, even as the net was tightening on their grip on power and as the Swiss and US authorities closed in on FIFA and its associated confederations and their culture of complicity, collusion and corruption.

Timeline, 2002–16

2002 Blatter (we employ here his own favoured rhetorical form of the meteorological metaphor) rides the storm of internal dissension, external critique and financial meltdown.

2003, August: Blatter and FIFA's law firm seek to restrict distribution of *Badfellas: FIFA family at war.*

2004 FIFA introduces ethics process.

2005 FIFA ExCo reaffirms commitment to MasterCard as partner/sponsor.

2006, May: Home of FIFA opens in Zurich, at a cost of £166 million.

2006, 15 September: Lord Sebastian Coe accepts chairmanship of FIFA's revised Ethics Committee, its first independent chair.

2006–07 FIFA drops MasterCard and opts for Visa as partner/sponsor.

2006 World Cup in Germany.

2006 Blatter and FIFA's law firm fails to curtail publication of Andrew Jennings' book *Foul.*

2006, 7 December: Chief Judge of the US District Court, Loretta Preska, condemns "FIFA's conduct" in negotiating its sponsor contract as "anything but 'fair play'", condemning marketing/TV chief Jérôme Valcke for lying to both MasterCard and Visa during the negotiations. Valcke resigns his position.

2007 Coe withdraws from his position as chair of FIFA's Ethics Committee.

2007, 27 June: Valcke returns to FIFA, and is appointed to the top job in the administration – general secretary.

2007 After an unopposed election, Blatter secures a third tem as president by acclamation in Congress.

2008, 16 June: Blatter celebrates ten years as FIFA president.

2010 World Cup in South Africa.

2010, 2 December: FIFA ExCo votes to award World Cup Finals in 2018 and 2022 to Russia and Qatar respectively.

2011, 10–11 May: Mohamed Bin Hammam organizes the distribution of payouts to Caribbean football officials, for pledges and promises of votes in the upcoming FIFA presidential election, with Jack Warner his go-between.

2011, 29 May: FIFA Ethics Committee suspends Bin Hammam and Jack Warner and launches an investigation into the bribes in the Caribbean.

2011, 1 June: Blatter secures fourth term as president, with 172 votes (17 against and 17 abstentions).

2011, 23–24 July: Mohamed Bin Hammam banned from football-related activities for life by FIFA Ethics Committee.

2011, December: Transparency International walks away from its advisory role on reform at FIFA.

2011, 4 December: Havelange resigns life-membership of the IOC days before release of its report on amoral – if not then illegal – financial ISL practices.

2012, July: New ethics process introduced with Investigative and Adjudicatory Chambers and independent chairs.

2012 Chuck Blazer wired by the FBI for conversations with associates at the London 2012 Olympics.

2013, April: Eckert report on ISL/FIFA dealings and financial transactions including 'commissions' paid to former president, Havelange. Blatter's handling of the case, while general secretary, is described as 'clumsy', but not leading to 'any criminal or ethical misconduct'.

2013, April: Simmons Report, for CONCACAF, confirming long-established corrupt practices of Jack Warner and Chuck Blazer.

2013 Blatter berated, booed and hissed in Brazil at Confederations Cup as Brazilian social discontent targets FIFA.

2013, 25 November: Chuck Blazer confession at United States District Court, Eastern District of New York, Brooklyn.

2014 Blatter in Brazil for the World Cup, keeping a low profile in a luxury penthouse on Ipanema seafront.

2014, 13 November: Eckert Report 'redacts' (more accurately, cuts and censors) Garcia Report on the 2018/2022 World Cup decisions.

2015, 27 May: US Department of Justice serves indictments on fourteen FIFA-associated personnel, and the Swiss authorities and the FBI swoop during a dawn raid on the Baur au Lac luxury hotel in Zurich.

2015, 30 May: Blatter wins fifth presidential term, defeating the stalking horse Prince Ali bin/Al Hussein of Jordan by 133 votes to seventy-three.

2015, 2 June: Blatter announces his intention to stand down, citing his lack of a convincing mandate, though choosing to stay until an Extraordinary Congress – later set for February 2016 – at which FIFA reforms would be presented and FIFA's ninth president elected.

2015, September: Blatter and Michel Platini suspended for ninety days in relation to 'disloyal payments', a long-delayed and non-contracted payment of two million Swiss francs from FIFA to Platini.

2015, 2–3 December: FIFA ExCo accepts FIFA 2016 Reform Committee proposals.

2015, 3 December: Swiss authorities swoop, in liaison with the FBI, on the Baur au Lac, Zurich.

2015, 21 December: Blatter and Platini suspended by FIFA Ethics Committee from all football-related activity for eight years.

2016, 26 February: Congress accepts the reforms; UEFA general secretary Gianni Infantino becomes FIFA's ninth president, the second youngest since the inaugural president, Robert Guérin.

FIFA seeks to silence the critics[2]

We knew we had them on the run when, in August 2003, the county court bailiff of Brighton County Court (England, UK) called at our personal residences to deliver some court papers. These were from Nobel & Hug solicitors, Zurich, on behalf of two plaintiffs – FIFA (Plaintiff 1) and Joseph S. Blatter (Plaintiff 2) – and constituted an application for an injunction against *Badfellas*. The request was to forbid the four named defendants – the two of us, the publisher, and Amazon Germany – from distributing the book for as long as seven specific passages, and the photograph of Sepp Blatter on the front cover, were included in the book; the application was framed as a "petition" in regard to "injury to personal status", FIFA itself being viewed for legal purposes as a person, as well as Blatter. The injunction was refused. The papers issued a request for "a so-called super-provisional injunction, e.g. order precautionary arrangements to be made immediately for the time being without hearing the opponents. This will be subject to *high urgency*. High urgency results in this case from the immediately pending the [sic] launch of the book … in Switzerland" (pp. 8–9) by the publisher and Amazon. The high urgency case was based on the perceived threat that publication and distribution, in Switzerland, would make "another circle of persons … aware of the accusations", and that the launch of the book would cause "injuries to someone's personality … as with each additional delivery of a copy, more and more persons would be made aware of the false and slanderous allegations of corruption" (p. 9). Distribution of the book "threatens to cause a serious and irreversible injury to the personalities of the Plaintiffs. Any distribution of the book will daily increase this injury to their personalities due to more and more new purchasers being able to read the statements of Defendants 1–2" (p. 8), these latter being the two of us. What were Sepp Blatter, and his legal representative Professor Dr Peter Nobel, so concerned about? What, more precisely, were the statements that prompted FIFA as an institution, and the FIFA president, to invest this level of time and resources in seeking to silence a couple of academic researchers?

There is an air of indiscriminating panic about these legal papers. The claims move quickly from talk of a perceived threat to the personalities (image, or reputation, presumably) of FIFA and Blatter, to a harder and more certain assertion that publication "would" (not "might" or "may") have deleterious effects on the public personality of the organization and its president. In order to make the legal case Professor Nobel and his team had to both contextualize the work, and engage in their own interpretive exercise:

> The material environment of the book may be assumed to be of judicial notice: In the summer of 1998, Plaintiff 2 was elected President of FIFA, the World Football Association, succeeding Havelange, his long-term predecessor. In June 2002 his appointment was approved by an overwhelming majority. Overall, the book "Badfellas – Fifa Family at War" is a "broadside" against FIFA, the World Football Association and its President Joseph S. Blatter. To the average reader, the title of the book "Badfellas – Fifa Family at War" creates a clear association to the mafia and implies behaviour of a contemptible character of Plaintiff 2 and other functionaries of Plaintiff 1. In summary one may state that FIFA is portrayed as a corrupt organization, the exponents of which, under the cover of sports, allegedly have nothing else in mind than

to enrich themselves and play power games. (See "Badfellas – FIFA at war", page 7, 33–35, 38, title and back pages).

(p. 12)

Not for the only time in these papers, in the final reference to the book in the above quote, its full title is incorrectly listed, or abbreviated, with the omission of "family". And the papers use the word "corrupt", even though we were more cautious than our accusers by mainly providing the evidence to allow the neutral reader to reach their own conclusions. The two reviews excerpted on the front and back covers of the book – from the *Independent* newspaper, and *Total Football* magazine – did use the noun "corruption", and were selected by our publisher as an acceptable interpretation of the story. Professor Nobel alleged: "Portrayal of situations and persons in the book 'Badfellas – Fifa at war' [sic] is neither globally true nor accurate in the detail" (p. 12). FIFA's lawyers picked up on five other passages relating to: the book title; former general secretary Michel Zen-Ruffinen's documentation of FIFA's organizational practices, in the wake of the ISL financial collapse of 2001 and in the build-up to the 2002 FIFA presidential election – as catalogued in the criminal complaint emanating from eleven members of the FIFA ExCo; a comparison with business practices in the corporate world; a comment on the leadership style of the FIFA president; and accusations of bribery in return for support that would have worked in Blatter's favour at the FIFA presidential election that took him from the general secretary's office to the president's suite in Paris in 1998. The five charges are in turn rebuffed in the fuller published account,[3] and here we consider just two of these: the question of the book title, and Blatter's leadership style.

The book title is subjected to some sophisticated semantic deconstruction: "The meaning of the word 'Badfellas' is a colloquialism for 'bad boys' on the one hand and to the average reader, to [sic] combination of 'Bad' and 'Fellas' will clearly generate associations with the famous Mafia film 'GoodFellas' by Martin Scorsese" (p. 13) As members of the "Fifa family", the Plaintiffs' behaviour is therefore "put on an equal footing" with members of the Cosa Nostra, "given a Mafia-type aura" (p. 13) Evidence offered for this case (Exhibit 8 in the petition) is an extract of the film from www.filmsite.org. No more detail is given, on, say, which members of the "FIFA family" might best be compared to Robert de Niro or Joe Pesci! One wonders how business is really conducted at FIFA House or the Home of FIFA when its highly paid legal specialists are musing through Scorsese's back catalogue. But more seriously, this interpretation by the top legal minds of Switzerland, and the most powerful man at the time in world football, was spot-on – as the FBI and the US attorney general would confirm twelve years later by bringing to bear the RICO legislation on the corrupt practices of selected FIFA-connected and other related football officials and businessmen.

The legal papers disputed the credibility of the sources cited with regard to Blatter's and FIFA's shortcomings. But Michel Zen-Ruffinen's internal ExCo document (cited in Chapter 1 of *Badfellas* above) was pithy and powerful: "FIFA is flawed by general mismanagement, disfunctions in the structures and financial irregularities", he concluded, and eleven members of FIFA's ExCo, listed in the "Blattergate" chapter above, concurred. Only two of these, medical man Dr Michel D'Hooghe and Senes Erzik of Turkey, were still on Blatter's ExCo a decade on. Zen-Ruffinen was to depart the scene soon after Blatter's re-election, succeeded by Urs Linsi, and then by Jérôme Valcke. Zen-Ruffinen had played for high stakes; to reiterate the allegations, the criminal complaint was challenging Blatter's "persistent, systematic *secrecy* tactics" and "equally persistent *stalling* tactics", claiming that according to FIFA statutes "there … is no room for authoritarian, autocratic powers of leadership on the part of the FIFA President". In other words, Blatter acts against the statutes, without transparency, as an autocratic, essentially unaccountable, dictator. The legal papers of Professor Nobel claimed that the complaints documentation/process had been "abated", although they offered no evidence that the charges/offences were without foundation, and ignored much of the case that the submission made about the modus operandi of the FIFA president.

On the question of leadership style, and in reference to the concluding paragraph of the "Blattergate" chapter – by all means re-read this in the context of the overall text – Professor Nobel's papers objected to the statement that Blatter is

> consolidated in power by a group of henchmen and sycophants; the family values and the dynasty, for the moment, are intact. FIFA House is like a court of the *ancien-régime*. Running FIFA is a matter of mastering not the football rulebook, more Machiavelli's *The Prince*.

No objection was made regarding the authoritarian and autocratic style of the FIFA president, as described explicitly in the complaints document, but here the "accusation" is seen as "serious" in that it implies that Blatter "put his personal interests above those of FIFA" (p. 16). But the reference in *Badfellas* to Niccoló Machiavelli's classic manual on the art of political survival promoted an extraordinary response from FIFA's legal team. This requires close consideration and so we quote it directly and in full:

> In addition, in a direct comparison with Machiavelli, the symbol for reckless and unlimited power politics that stop at nothing, Plaintiff 2 [Blatter] is portrayed as morally deficient and inferior. This comparison is even intensified by the malicious statement that the rules of football (and therefore the *central principle of fair play*) would not be applied. For the President of the most important sports association of football and the sports association as such this means derision and derogation. Calling the organization a court of the *ancien régime*, makes one imagine the picture of a Byzantine system, in which the ruler is above the law and any means of the system are fully available to him, associated with corruption, patronage and reckless power politics. This passage is solely directed at bringing FIFA and Joseph Blatter into disrepute.
>
> *(p. 16)*

On the contrary: the passage in question was directed at summarizing how FIFA's president gained power, held on to power, and adopted a particular leadership style by which so to do. Close colleagues and rivals of Joseph Blatter have provided testimony after testimony, cited not just in works by investigative researchers and investigative journalists, but increasingly across the world media – confirming the accuracy of this portrayal.

Overall, the legal petition claimed, indeed asserted, that none of the passages selected, and pored over in such forensic legalistic detail, "are true and appropriate":

> On the contrary, this is an actual defamatory construct, grouped – quasi in crescendo from passage to passage – around terms like "corruption", "Cosa Nostra", favouritism and mismanagement" [sic.] and "vote-buying". These accusations are massive, both individually and globally.
>
> *(p. 17)*

Indeed they were, as agencies encountering FIFA close-up for the first time – such as Transparency International, which at the end of 2011 withdrew from its advisory role on the FIFA reform trail after FIFA appointed a specialist to chair the reform committee[4] – were to increasingly discover. We did not get called into court to defend our work – the dissenting ExCo members had retreated inwards for a year by the time of the injunction – but the threatening legal papers now read like a confessional tract rather than a contestation of the validity of our research and the revelations contained within the book. The bullying tactics worked to some degree though, in that the print-run of *Badfellas* seemed to swiftly expire. We have always said that investigative work on a body such as FIFA is a long-haul commitment; this re-issue of the book is in part our riposte to the legal shenanigans of FIFA, but also an opportunity to show that Blatter at the time knew just how authentic an account the book is of the HBFD, and so feared, quite rightly, that as the evidence stacked up, the "injuries to personality" would soon reach an inoperable level. In September 2015 in Las Vegas, the The Mob Museum (the National Museum of Organized Crime and Law Enforcement) opened an exhibit, "The 'Beautiful Game' turns Ugly", offering "a breakdown of the kickbacks, secrecy and match-fixing associated with the scandal" at FIFA, and the "rampant corruption that plagues the Federation". By then, FIFA's lawyers knew that any attempts to silence the critics were doomed.[5]

Liars[6]

MasterCard had been a long-term sponsor of UEFA's Champions League, the annual European club competition, and of the UEFA European Championship, the four-yearly competition between Europe's national teams. It had also been a FIFA World Cup sponsor for sixteen years up to and including the 2006 World Cup. The story of how MasterCard lost this partnership to Visa is a telling one, and is revealing of the dubious practices of central FIFA employees and officials. FIFA, at its board/ExCo meeting of 26 October 2005, had confirmed its commitment to keep working with MasterCard as its selected partner/sponsor for the forthcoming cycle, 2007–14, and "at that point, FIFA never communicated or intimated that MasterCard was anything other than a respected and valued business partner. MasterCard, throughout the negotiations, remained positive towards concluding a deal and never displayed antagonistic actions, but instead simply acted in accordance with the Agreement and trademark statutes to enforce its invaluable intellectual property rights", as was stated in the report of the United States District Court, Southern District of New York, the following year. But things were to turn sour.[7]

Mastercard International Incorporated was the plaintiff in a legal action against FIFA. On 7 December 2006, Loretta Preska signed off a 125-page document that comprised a wholesale condemnation of senior figures in the FIFA administration, both employees and officials/committee members – most prominently, Jérôme Valcke, then marketing head, and Chuck Blazer, member/chair of powerful committees such as media/marketing. Judge Preska's report concluded that MasterCard could proceed with an injunction against FIFA, preventing the implementation of any FIFA/Visa deal, and asserting its own rights to the sponsorship contract from 2007 on. The report also said that all of MasterCard's costs could be awarded to the company. What was the evidence that led to such a conclusive report; and what led to a compromise-cum-resolution whereby MasterCard did not pursue this further in the courts, or push for its legal rights?

First, the evidence: here, the figures of Valcke and Blazer are the most prominent ones. Judge Preska pulled no punches in her introduction:

> Section 9.2 of MasterCard's most recent sponsorship contract with FIFA gave MasterCard the first right to acquire the FIFA World Cup sponsorship for the next cycle. As is set out in detail below, FIFA breached its obligation under Swiss contract law to give MasterCard the first right to acquire the next round of sponsorship. In addition, FIFA's conduct in performing its obligation and in negotiating for the next sponsorship cycle was anything but "fair play" and violated the heightened obligation of good faith imposed by the applicable Swiss law (as well as FIFA's own notion of fair play as explained by its president).[8]

The report tells (p. 3) how FIFA's negotiators "lied repeatedly to MasterCard", assuring its long-term partner that, consistent with the company's "first right to acquire", FIFA would sign no deal for post-2006 sponsorship rights with anyone else – unless it did not reach an agreement with MasterCard: "FIFA's negotiators lied to VISA when they repeatedly responded to the direct question of whether MasterCard had any incumbency rights by assuring VISA that MasterCard did not." FIFA's negotiators kept VISA up-to-date with detailed descriptions of where things were in the FIFA-MasterCard negotiations, "while concealing from its long-time partner MasterCard both the fact of the FIFA-VISA negotiations as well as the status of those negotiations – an action FIFA's president admitted would not be 'fair play'".

Valcke is personally condemned at the beginning of the report: FIFA's marketing director lied to both MasterCard, FIFA's long-time partner, and to VISA, its negotiating counterparty, to both of which FIFA, under Swiss law, owed a duty of good faith. Who, then, didn't FIFA's negotiators lie to? CONCACAF general secretary Chuck Blazer was also picked out by the judge (paras 213 and 214, pp. 73–5):

> 213. Chuck Blazer, a member of the FIFA Executive Committee and the FIFA Marketing & TV AG Board (Trial Tr. p. 230, l. 20–22), testified as to the March 14, 2006 FIFA Marketing & TV AG Board meeting. Mr. Blazer's testimony was generally without credibility based on his attitude and demeanor and on his evasive answers on cross-examination. 9 … (para 214) based on his evasive answers and his attitude and demeanor, Mr. Blazer's testimony as to the March 14, 2006 Marketing & TV AG Board meeting is rejected as fabricated.

The report conceded that some "portions of the FIFA witnesses' testimony were credible", but overall

> their testimony was generally not credible, based on their attitude and demeanor and the varying degrees of impeachment they suffered. In contrast, the MasterCard witnesses were credible, based on their attitude and demeanor and all the other evidence in the case.
>
> *(p. 23, fn 3, para. 56)*

Judge Preska highlighted the duplicity of the FIFA negotiators. Valcke was encouraging Visa to find an extra US$30 million to equal the MasterCard bid whilst simultaneously reporting back to FIFA committees which believed that they were, in effect, ratifying the MasterCard partnership:

> While the FIFA witnesses at trial boldly characterized their breaches as "white lies," "commercial lies," "bluffs," and, ironically, "the game," their internal emails discuss the "different excuses to give to MasterCard as to why the deal wasn't done with them," "how we (as FIFA) can still be seen as having at least some business ethics" and how to "make the whole f***-up look better for FIFA." They ultimately confessed, however, that "[I]t's clear somebody has it in for MC."
>
> *(p. 4)*

MasterCard, recoiling from FIFA's shabby business dealings, accepted $90 million in compensation and went away leaving the World Cup to others more willing to negotiate with the mavericks from FIFA's administration and key committees. Temporarily shamed, Valcke left his post as head of marketing, re-emerging just a few months later as general secretary – now number two to the FIFA president, in the latter's old job. Blatter seemed to be holding things together within his inner circle and especially the triumvirate of president, general secretary and finance director; but as FIFA became regular news for the wrong reasons, and as Andrew Jennings[9] continued his dogged and relentless pursuit of evidence concerning FIFA's routine organizational practices and its "financial machinations" – as Zen-Ruffinen described them from the inside – Blatter was becoming increasingly exposed and unable to extricate himself from crisis after crisis simply by hackneyed appeals to the "universality" of the game, and to the "immense social and cultural power of our game" rooted in "partnerships always based on respect, efficiency and solidarity".[10] "For the Game. For the World", the FIFA president reaffirmed in the footer to his foreword address to the 2010 financial report delivered in Zurich in May 2011. Fewer and fewer people were being seduced by this idealistic rhetoric and humanistic hyperbole, and the power balance looked to be shifting, with a pledge by Blatter to strengthen the procedures whereby further malpractice might be bled from the infected arteries of the FIFA body.[11] But the FIFA president had won his fourth term, and although he could no longer solve crisis after crisis through inducements and rewards, he based his survival strategy on remodelling his image and rebranding himself and claiming a legacy as a reforming leader.[12]

Traitors

On 16 June 2008, Blatter wrote gushingly to the Qatari, Mohamed Bin Hammam, thanking him for his contribution to the campaign that, a decade earlier in June 1998, had gained the Swiss the presidency of FIFA. "Without you, dear Mohamed, none of this would ever have been possible." Blatter called on the rhetoric of the team: "Everyone knows that in football, very few matches are ever won by one player alone. Therefore I would like to thank you for your support and above all for your tireless work back then." What was this "work" without which Blatter couldn't have become FIFA president, and without which he could never have consolidated his dictatorial hold on power throughout the first decade of his presidency and beyond? What kind of "player" was Bin Hammam in the campaign team that garnered the votes of FIFA Congress delegates who elevated Blatter from chief executive/general secretary to president back in 1998? The book *Badfellas* shows just how dependent Blatter had been on Bin Hammam's personal wealth and close contacts with the Qatari elite and ruling family in his first run for president.

The grateful tributes from Blatter to Bin Hammam were to be shattered in the following years; a successful Qatari bid in December 2010 to host the men's World Cup in 2022 was followed by a falling out between Bin Hammam – by then president of the Asian Football Confederation (AFC) – and Blatter, stimulating a challenge from Bin Hammam the following year for the presidency itself. This challenge was scuppered by the revelations that Bin Hammam had passed hundreds of thousands of US dollars to notorious Trinidad and Tobago politician and CONCACAF president Jack Warner, for dispersal to FIFA Congress delegates from the Caribbean. The precise circumstances of the fallout between Blatter and Bin Hammam remain unclear, although without doubt Bin Hammam believed that the biggest payback by Blatter for his support over the years would be to honour an understanding that the Swiss would step down from the presidency with the Qatari emerging as the president-in-waiting. But Blatter had reneged more than once on this commitment, and won his third term in 2007. Bin Hammam hung on, but when it was clear that Blatter aimed to stand for a fourth term in 2011, Bin Hammam resolved, from his high-profile base as AFC president, to challenge for the presidency.

It was now inevitable that the alliance that had once shaped influential FIFA powerplays in the decade after the Brazilian Havelange passed on the reins of power, was not just in disarray, but had utterly disintegrated. In the mid-1990s it was becoming clear that sport was becoming increasingly important in the tiny oil-rich dictatorship of Qatar. Sport held the power to raise the international profile of the country, whilst simultaneously professing the collective and meritocratic values of team play. It could create new global markets via the staging of sports events and so provide an economic alternative for when oil might begin to run dry. Members of the Qatari elite could operate effectively in positions that combined lobbying and diplomacy, speaking for the less-well-off neighbours of the Asian Confederation as well as the developing football culture of the small state itself. When one looks closely at what was going on within the FIFA corridors of power, one name emerged – albeit alongside some influential figures from Thailand, Malaysia and Saudi Arabia. Mohamed Bin Hammam was working hard from the mid-1990s for acceptability at the highest levels of the AFC, and in the informal corridors of power of FIFA. If Michel Platini – of course, later to become UEFA president and one of those on the FIFA Executive Committee to vote for Qatar as 2022 host – was the public face of Blatter's bid for the 1998 presidency, Bin Hammam was the behind-the-scenes patron providing private flights and unlimited funds for Blatter (the latter temporarily leaving his post as chief executive in order to campaign for the presidency) to jet around the world telling Congress delegates what he could do for their football associations and their national football development. And it is always worth reiterating that this was in a power context in which – as remains the case in the post-Blatter period – a single vote from Vanuatu or American Samoa was equal to a single vote from Brazil or Germany. Bin Hammam and his sources in Qatar provided and funded the "tireless work", as Blatter put it to his "dear Brother", signing off "en profound amitié", that secured Blatter the FIFA presidency. It all seemed plain sailing to Blatter, reminding Bin Hammam that in 1998 he'd "vowed to look to the future with determination and energy to realize the necessary reforms and objectives".[13]

Blatter has been a genius of Machiavellian scheming and organizational survival, not least because when challenged he dropped people ruthlessly. Bin Hammam, fêted by FIFA in those formative years in the 1990s, architect of Qatar's classic lobbying strategy to win the vote for the 2022 World Cup, and rising star as president of the Asian Confederation, learned what it means to take on Blatter and the FIFAcrats. He was dropped by his Qatari patrons when the 2022 Finals were awarded, was outmanoeuvred by Blatter in his bid for the top FIFA position, and found himself isolated and alone when the dirty washing emerged in the FIFA laundry basket.

Ethical storms

As FIFA has got richer since it bordered on bankruptcy in 2002, it has generated and experienced escalating crises of credibility and ethics. More than $3.8 billion was generated by FIFA for the World Cup cycle 2014–18; in World Cup year 2014, participant member associations and clubs received $476 million, a 13.3 per cent increase; $900 million was put by for Football Assistance Schemes and related initiatives for 2015–18. Despite the crises, the scandals and the corruption, it was business as usual for the financial forecasters within FIFA.[14] This financial robustness has allowed FIFA to continue its core business despite the expanding work of its Ethics Committee in responding to escalating levels of alleged corruption and breaches of the ethical code. Here we focus on ethical issues stemming from the award of the 2018 and 2022 World Cup Finals to Russia and Qatar, looking in particular at FIFA's internal investigation into the December 2010 vote that decided on these. There are many issues that could be considered here, including the question of the role of the Russian Federation's representative on the FIFA ExCo, Vitaly Mutko, in that bidding and voting process, and his undeclared conflict of interest when casting an ExCo vote as Vladimir Putin's minister of sport – a position that, in effect, made him Putin's place-man on the world sport-political stage.[15] However, in the last five years of Blatter's regime, Qatar dominated the headlines in the corruption debate. Human rights issues, labour exploitation, the absurdity of the careless consideration of the bids, in terms of infrastructure and climate; all these made Qatar an easy target. Blatter defended the decision but, reportedly, inwardly fumed as the USA lost out to Qatar. The full story of this outcome is told in the *Sunday Times* investigative reporters Heidi Blake and Jonathan Calvert's *The Ugly Game*,[16] based on what they labelled the "FIFA Files", which were in fact files from the server of the AFC, copied to/by FIFA on the basis of a request for access to background material for an ongoing investigation. It is not reported what the source was for those files received by the *Sunday Times*, or where that source has since worked, or moved for work. In that Byzantine world of betrayal and treachery sifting truth from spin remains tantalizingly and frustratingly difficult. And in *The Ugly Game* we are told that the young whistleblower of 2002, Michel Zen-Ruffinen, had by 2010 become one of the informers (if not one of the badfellas) himself, advising lobbyists for the USA bid for 2022 on how the bidding processes worked. He was promised a £230,000 consultancy fee, and, presumably swallowing his whistle as he took on the task, the former referee and erstwhile FIFA general secretary was now peddling his insights to the highest bidder.[17]

As the Qatar controversy raged, Russia remained relatively untainted in the fallout from the 2010 decision. Blatter, in his public utterances, could justify the two decisions. A first World Cup Finals tournament in the world's largest country, and its ninth most populous, for the first generation of its post-communist transformation, fits the FIFA globalizing mission of spreading the infrastructure of the game, confirming its reach across the globe; "We go to new lands" as Blatter put it: "Never has the World Cup been in Russia and Eastern Europe, and the Middle East and Arabic world has been waiting a long time. So I'm a happy president when we talk about the development of football." Blatter was talking to Reuters immediately following the announcement of the decision in Zurich on 2 December. The Qatar decision soon dominated the headlines, but there was an air of inevitability about the Russian success, and the country's president, Vladimir Putin, was speedily en route to Switzerland to laud the outcome. During the celebratory party he would be reunited with Mutko, his minister of sport, tourism and youth policy since 2008; and Roman Abramovich, owner of Chelsea Football Club in London. They looked like they were certain winners from early on in the process, and winning the 2018 event was a form of coronation, an affirmation of all the background work undertaken over the previous few years. But we skip forward almost four years on from that decision day in 2010, to 13 November 2014 for the – and no prizes here for pithiness – presentation of Hans Joachim Eckert, of FIFA's Adjudicatory Chamber: the *Statement of the Chairman of the Adjudicatory Chamber of the FIFA Ethics Committee* on the *Report on the Inquiry into the 2018/2022 FIFA World Cup™ Bidding Process Prepared by the Investigatory Chamber of the FIFA Ethics Committee.*

Before going any further, it is worth clarifying the context here. Since 2004, FIFA had inaugurated, reviewed and revised its ethical procedures. In September 2006 the English former Olympic champion, Lord Sebastian Coe, became FIFA's first chair of its new independent Ethics Committee: "FIFA is delighted to have Sebastian Coe as chairman of this committee. His personality and integrity, which is renowned the world over, will ensure that he is the best possible person for this role," Blatter announced.[18] Coe reciprocated:

> I am delighted to have been selected for this important role. Inspiring young people into sport is a personal passion of mine. To do this, we must protect and promote the ethics and morals of sport for future generations. My role as the chairman of London 2012, as an IAAF council member, as a member of the UK Athletics Council and as the chair of FIFA's Ethics Committee will involve me in this area at the very highest level of sport.

Fine words, but perhaps Coe hadn't read the small print describing how these new processes worked. Or maybe FIFA hadn't specified the level of remuneration for the role. Or perhaps Coe saw a batch of cases and papers and simply thought "what I am doing here?" He was soon gone, stonewalling a door-stepping Andrew Jennings as the dogged reporter asked him to tell the world at least something about his experience in such an important FIFA position.[19] The new ethics process outlasted Lord Coe's tenure, but by 2012 a new and more elaborate model was in place.

As part of this new process the Investigatory Chamber would investigate and report; its Adjudicatory Chamber would then make judgements about what to do in response to the findings of the investigation. The new independent chairs, who were soon dealing with the inquiry into the 2010 World Cup Finals allocations, were Michael J. Garcia, a former US attorney, chairman of the Investigatory Chamber; and Hans Joachim Eckert, a German lawyer, chairman of the Adjudicatory

Chamber. The process sprang into life just as Chuck Blazer was off to the London Summer Olympics wired-up with his FBI keychain around his neck, talkative as ever, gathering invaluable testimony for the agents back in New York. Back at the Home of FIFA, the Garcia investigation took more than eighteen months, cost an estimated US$7 million, and, under lock and key and confidential to all but a very few FIFA insiders, it amounted to around 350 pages; the Eckert statement on the Garcia report runs to a little under forty-two pages. Eckert concluded, in section 8.4 on "Findings", that the evaluation of the bidding process "is closed for the FIFA Ethics Committee"; that the investigation into the bidding process was fully in line with the FIFA Code of Ethics; that he himself, Eckert, supported recommendations "made by the Chairman of the Investigatory Chamber"; and that his Adjudicatory Chamber could examine "specific cases if the Investigatory Chamber opens Ethics proceedings against officials based on information obtained during the FIFA World Cup™ investigation". Verbiage? Cover-up? Legalese? Take your pick. Garcia responded with a strong condemnation of Eckert's version of events, referring to "numerous materially incomplete and erroneous representations of the facts and conclusions detailed in the investigatory chamber's report"; Eckert excluded, for instance, criticisms of the practices and culture of many of the members of the FIFA ExCo.

Eckert claims to have focused upon not the high-profile individuals central to the process, but rather the activities and conduct of the bid teams looking to host the 2018 and 2022 Finals tournaments. The short Eckert summary began to be referred to as a classic case of cover-up under the veil of the editorial process; in French *redacteur* means "editor", and redaction has become a euphemism for the process of cutting or censoring a source or text. Eckert's forty-two-page summary – based on selections, cuts and interpretations as he saw fit – sought to defuse the controversy surrounding the December 2010 situation. Garcia resigned his position as chair of the Investigatory Chamber within weeks, in December 2014, lambasting FIFA's "lack of leadership" and calling Eckert's judgements into question: "No principled approach", Garcia wrote, could justify Eckert's "edits, omissions and additions".

The structure and language of the Eckert statement requires close scrutiny. Almost half of the report is devoted to a summary of FIFA decision-making processes, ethics procedures and a history and description of bidding processes. In his "main findings", Eckert presents comments bidder by bidder: Australia, Belgium/Holland, England, Japan, Korea, Qatar, Russia, the USA. The most controversial cases, Qatar and Russia, were buried in the body of the report – a convenient perk of the alphabet one might think – as Australia (a little over two pages) and England (a little over three pages) were reprimanded; Australia for inappropriate use of consultants and payments to Jack Warner, the then CONCACAF president, as well as distributing monies ostensibly for "football development" in the countries of some ExCo members; and England for looking to garner the support of a FIFA vice president, Jack Warner again, and proffering "football development funds" to Oceania's then-president, Reynald Temarii (the latter soon to be suspended after a *Sunday Times* investigation revealed his openness to bribery in the World Cup bidding process). Eckert added that "England 2018 accommodated, or at least attempted to satisfy, the improper requests" of ExCo members, "thereby jeopardizing the integrity of the bidding process" (Section 6.3.5, p. 24), albeit "to a rather limited extent". Eckert devotes a little over four pages to the Qatar case, confirming massive financial machinations between Qatari Mohamed Bin Hammam and two named figures: Jack Warner and Reynald Temarii. But it is noted by Eckert that Bin Hammam "did not have a formal role with any bid" (Section 6.6.6, p. 28), however much he might have paid to ensure that, for instance, Temarii remained ineligible to cast his ExCo vote having been already suspended for a year by the FIFA Ethics Committee. Eckert adds that even if Temarii had been able to cast his Oceania Confederation's vote for England (2018) and Australia (2022) this would have made little difference, so "the occurrences presently relevant did not affect the outcome of the FIFA World Cup™ 2018/2022 bidding process as a whole". (Section 6.6.6, p. 29). Meanwhile, Bin Hammam, widely recognized for twenty years as one of the most effective deal-makers in world football – as the *Badfellas* text made clear – was fading from the picture, an invisible presence in the Qatari bidding story, at least in the Eckert take on the process. Bin Hammam is now damned as the man who led "the most corrupt World Cup bidding contest in history" and brought the world's biggest single-sport event to his desert nation as he moved "through the corridors of world football greasing palms and striking deals; revealing the ugly venality of the men who control the beautiful game".[20] Sworn to silence by his superiors in the ruling political class within Qatar, Bin Hammam's isolated existence in Doha – evocatively portrayed in Blake and Calvert's *The Ugly Game* – is a silently echoing testimony to the corruption and betrayals of trust that Eckert's evasive and timid report seeks to deflect.

In a summarizing comment in an earlier report on FIFA culpability in relation to financial scandals concerning ISL and unofficial payments to then-president Havelange, Judge Eckert concluded that "President Blatter's conduct could not be classified in any way as misconduct with regard to any ethics rules", though the "conduct of President Blatter may have been clumsy because there could be an internal need for clarification, but this does not lead to any criminal or ethical misconduct" (statement dated 29 April 2013, section II, p.5).[21] Say it again Judge. "Clumsy" Blatter then, but not culpable; nor, one might add, particularly capable. Eighteen months later in his statement on Garcia's report on the Qatar/Russia World Cup decisions, Judge Eckert himself was looking clumsy in defence of the indefensible. Actions can be seen in numerous cases, he reported – with the innocent exception of the Belgium/Netherlands bid – to have jeopardized, damaged or undermined the credibility and integrity of the bidding process; but only to some or a limited extent, and none serious enough that they could be seen as "suited to compromise the integrity of the FIFA World Cup™ 2018/2022 bidding process as a whole" (Section 6.8.5, p. 34) – Eckert's mantra for letting any suspected nation off the hook, letting all of the bidding nations off with a slap on the wrist. But there was not even a slap on the wrist for Russia in response to its prompt efficiency in disposing of paperwork and leased computers that were said to have been destroyed by their owners, and its apparently unsuccessful approaches to Google for access to email accounts. Eckert would comment in his overall assessment of the findings contained in the Garcia Report that:

> As regards the procedural framework for conducting bidding procedures related to awarding the hosts of the final competitions of FIFA World Cups™, the Investigatory Chamber of the FIFA Ethics Committee did not find any violations or breaches of the relevant rules and regulations. The Chairman of the Adjudicatory Chamber of the FIFA Ethics Committee fully concurs with this finding.
>
> *(Section 8.2, p. 40, of Eckert's statement, 13 November 2014)*

This notion was not shared by a furious and soon-to-resign Garcia. And it is widely believed in the networks of the football business that a dedicated team within the Home of FIFA has, for a sustained period, been hard at work redacting the Garcia report in minute detail, in readiness for its "full" publication. The internal FIFA processes that generated the Garcia Report and the Eckert whitewash are yet another example of the toothlessness or inherent collusiveness of FIFA's ethical processes during the Blatter reign. Eckert even credited (p. 34) Blatter with enabling the Ethics Committee's Investigatory Chamber, as part of the 2012 reforms, to conduct the inquiry; and Blatter is praised for ensuring FIFA's cooperation throughout the investigation. Eckert concludes that "it must be made clear that President Blatter did not violate the FCE [FIFA Code of Ethics]" (p. 34). The bidding processes should be improved, he added, guaranteeing more transparency based in term limits for ExCo members, recusal of ExCo members in votes concerning their own nations, a rotation system, independent expert bid evaluation, and enhanced reporting requirements. This is quite a list for reform of the process; Blatter was, as "the leader of FIFA", called upon to address these recommendations. But although Eckert implied that the chair of the ExCo should have made ExCo members' obligations "more explicit", Blatter was presented as essentially blameless for any flaws and failings in the process.

The cases continued to pile up for the Ethics Committee and Chambers, as did the monies for a series of World Cup tournaments that refilled the FIFA coffers. Andrew Zimbalist has noted that for the South Africa 2010 and Brazil 2014 tournaments, FIFA, having approved a host country's proposed operating budget, then covered the bulk of these operating costs itself but then retained all of the revenue stream from the World Cup cycle. So even when committing to a "legacy fund" after-the-event payment – in the case of South Africa, US$42 million – FIFA, with no responsibility of course for the host country's provision of infrastructural needs such as stadia, transportation and communication, could at the end of 2010 report "an accumulated surplus of $1.3 billion".[22] Blatter could smile and claim financial acumen and widespread credit as the billions rolled in from the sponsors and broadcasters. But behind the glossy surface of the spectacle and genuine thrill of the sporting contests, FIFA folk were lining their pockets or doing the kind of deals that were making fraud, embezzlement and corruption an almost routinized opportunity for confederation and/or FIFA officials. The voting controversy over Germany 2006, portrayed in "The Terminator" chapter in the *Badfellas* text, was always going to linger, and it came as no surprise when the irregular payments of millions of dollars relating to World Cup bidding, were exposed. In early March 2016 the Freshfields 380-page report commissioned by the German Football Federation presented its conclusions concerning the bidding process for the Germany 2006 World Cup.[23] These were far from conclusive, neither proving nor ruling out vote-buying in the 2000 decision. The report did, however, highlight suspicious payments made by Franz Beckenbauer to Mohamed Bin Hammam in 2002; £7.1 million was passed from the German, via a Swiss law firm, to the account of Bin Hammam's company, Kemco. Beckenbauer was already implicated in a £5 million payment paid as a bribe for the votes of four Asian members of the FIFA ExCo. The millions of revellers with such great memories of their carnivalesque pleasures at the Brandenberg Gate and other big-screen venues in 2006 will remember the event less fondly as the German hero's reputation continues to dissolve, symbolizing the stench of corruption behind the joyous spectacle. Germany 2006 continues to generate allegations concerning that vote. Charlie Dempsey's decision not to vote in the second round was recounted by Andrew Jennings in *The Dirty Game*, in which there is reported a "rumour" spread by well-known Mr Fixit figure, Fedor Radmann: "the arrangement was that Charlie would leave the vote, go back to the Dolder Grand Hotel and collect a briefcase left for him in the cloakroom. It contained $250,000".[24]

In relation to South Africa 2010, we note here one particularly revealing case related to the country's successful bid for the 2010 World Cup, as recounted in the US Department of Justice's FIFA indictment of 20 May 2015.[25] "In or about 2004," the indictment document states (p. 80), FIFA ExCo members were considering the bids from Morocco, South Africa and Egypt to host the 2010 World Cup. Jack Warner mobilized the "cultivated ties with South African soccer officials" that he and members of his family had worked on over the years, including South Africa's failed bid to host the 2006 World Cup. In one instance, Warner got a member of his family to fly to Paris "and accept a briefcase containing bundles of U.S. currency in $10,000 stacks in a hotel room from Co-conspirator #15, a high-ranking South African bid committee official". This money was transported to Warner, in Trinidad. Warner, with Chuck Blazer, visited Morocco in 2004 where a Moroccan bid official offered Warner US$1 million for his vote. Warner worked the South African connection though, getting FIFA, the South African government and the South African bid committee to "arrange for the government of South Africa to pay $10 million to CFU [Caribbean Football Union] to 'support the African diaspora'" (p. 82). These monies were understood by Chuck Blazer to be "in exchange" for his own, Warner's and a third FIFA ExCo member's vote. Blazer – Mr 10 per cent to the end – claimed that Warner offered him "a $1 million portion of the $10 million" payment. South Africa got the 2010 World Cup after an ExCo vote on 15 May 2004. There were six years to go until the event itself. And when the South Africans were unable to move the US$1 million directly from government funds, a scheme

was hatched whereby FIFA officials siphoned monies from funds supposedly destined to support the World Cup, and sent the US$1 million to Warner's CFU. In
three wired payments from a Swiss FIFA account, between January and March
2008, the US$1 million arrived in a Bank of America "correspondent account in
New York, New York", to be credited to CFU and CONCACAF accounts controlled by Warner at the Republic Bank in Trinidad and Tobago (p. 83). Warner then
diverted sums – one of US$200,000 – to personal accounts in his own name, and
also laundered sums through intermediaries; between January and March 2008, for
example, he had US$1.4 million transferred to the account of a business associate's
supermarket chain, and within weeks these monies were moved on to a personal
account in the name of Warner and a family member. The US$10 million wired
to the CFU had been administered by Jérôme Valcke, FIFA's general secretary, the
man branded a liar in the New York's Southern District Court just two years earlier. Warner passed on most of Blazer's share of the bribe by wire and cheques, and
messengers and couriers in Blazer's Manhattan CONCACAF office, fattening the
American's accounts in the Cayman Islands and the Bahamas. But the Warner payments fell short by US$246,500; little wonder that three years on, Blazer, fuelled by
revenge as well as greed, was to turn on Warner.

The FIFA house of cards begins to shake

A year before Eckert presented his 2014 statement to a disbelieving world, and
no doubt some audible sighs of relief in Russia and Qatar, CONCACAF's former
general secretary Chuck Blazer was confessing his guilt to a "sealed proceeding" in
a New York courtroom. He'd had a busy year, informing for the FBI and trying to
deflect the investigators from his old confederation who were looking into his and
Warner's misdeeds. In April 2013 the Simmons Report into the financial dealings
and administrative practices of Blazer and Warner had concluded that:

> Jack Warner and Chuck Blazer each violated the CONCACAF Statutes by
> presenting financial statements to the Executive Committee and the Congress
> that contained false representations and material omissions and that did not
> fairly and accurately represent the financial condition of CONCACAF and
> the disposition of its assets.[26]

Simmons had chased both Blazer and Warner for evidence, documents and meetings. Warner replied that on 11 June 2011, when leaving his CONCACAF position,
he had relinquished "all ties with football-related activities", and had no records
or documents pertaining to the committee's lines of enquiry; Blazer's New York
lawyers, writing in February and March 2013, said that Blazer was in dispute with
CONCACAF over "funds due", and could not respond to the request in such a
one-way process: "The amount owed to Mr Blazer is very substantial." He was still
chasing the deal and the monies, even as he was preparing to plead guilty to all that
his country's justice system was now bringing to bear on him. His and Warner's

downfall and departure, though, hardly led to a reformed CONCACAF. Attorney General Lynch, speaking in December 2015, sounded flabbergasted at the gall of those who took over the confederation. In her remarks announcing the superseding announcement to the May indictments, she sounded incredulous that Alfredo Hawit, who had "ascended to the position of CONCACAF president" when it was vacated in May, "then, as alleged, assumed the mantle of those same corrupt practices".[27]

On 25 November 2013, Blazer appeared before Judge Raymond J. Dearie in the United States District Court (Eastern District of New York).[28] There for the government were three assistant US attorneys, on behalf of Attorney General Loretta E. Lynch, who a year-and-a-half later would be catapulting FIFA into world headlines on an unprecedented scale following the first FBI/Swiss police swoop in Zurich. It was a "sealed court" to safeguard the "integrity of the investigation" – in Dearie's words – thus guaranteeing the exclusion of any members of the public. A farcical preamble saw Dearie ask the court clerk, Ellie, not just to "seal the courtroom" but to then "do me a favour and just open the door, and see if there is anybody lusting about in the hallway yearning to get in here". Perhaps the judge was missing his public and in the absence of any gallery to play to was constructing his own piece of theatre. He didn't seem too knowledgeable about this FIFA thing either: "There are ten charges, if I am not mistaken, ten charges in total ... Involving these organizations. I don't know how you pronounce it, FIFA." His puzzlement solved by his clerk, he moved on the proceedings in dialogue with the wheelchair-bound Blazer.

Blazer had been cooperating with the US authorities since 2011.[29] There was much to cover, and Dearie heard his guilty pleas to ten counts, covering:

- conspiracy to commit acts of racketeering activity, one of these "with other persons in or around 1992 to facilitate acceptance of a bribe in conjunction with the selection of a host nation for the 1998 World Cup"; also, beginning "in or around 2004 and continuing through 2011, I and others on the FIFA Executive Committee agreed to accept bribes in conjunction with the selection of South Africa as the host nation for the 2010 World Cup".
- the defrauding of FIFA and CONCACAF, by "taking undisclosed bribes", transferring monies by email, phone or wire in and out of the USA, to the Caribbean for instance, including "funds procured through these improper payments" that "passed through JFK Airport in the form of a check".
- the defrauding of the IRS, returning no tax returns and paying no tax from 2005–10.
- violation of federal tax law in not declaring to the Department of the Treasury, whilst a resident of New York, a Bahamas bank account.

The charges added up to a thieves' charter for the expansionist years of FIFA and CONCACAF growth. In Judge Dearie's words, the charges "identify FIFA and its attendant or related constituent organizations as what we call an enterprise, a RICO enterprise. RICO is an acronym for … Racketeering Influenced Corrupt Organization". Blazer's serial criminality added up, in the charges, to "conspiracy to corrupt this enterprise through the anticipated payment of funds pursuant to various criminal schemes".

Blazer was far from a lone crook, of course, in the FIFA hierarchy. And Jack Warner's schemes reached still further than just the Caribbean or the Americas. The CONCACF president, from Trinidad, cooperated with Mohammed Bin Hammam in what the US Department of Justice called the "2011 FIFA Presidential Election Scheme".[30] Bin Hammam asked Warner, on 1 April 2011, to convene an extraordinary congress of the confederation, though Warner offered just his pet Caribbean Federation (CFU). Here the cockiness of the enterprise built by the HBFD played into investigators' hands: Bin Hammam (Co-conspirator #7, as the indictment labels him) arranged for US$363,537.98 to be wired to Warner, in Trinidad & Tobago, via Bank of America in New York. Delegates from national associations, including two from US territories, gathered in Port of Spain on May 10–11, and were, during the course of the event – on condition of entering a hotel room alone – offered US$40,000 in an envelope, and asked, or instructed, to tell no-one. Not all of those approached wanted to pocket the money, and one contacted Chuck Blazer at the CONCACAF offices in New York, informing him of the scheme. Warner responded with brutal cynicism: "There are some people here who think they are more pious than thou. If you're pious, open a church, friends. Our business is our business." Not if you trespassed on US legal space, Warner was to learn, as the indictment also documented his receipt from Bin Hammam of US$1,211,980, some of which he sought to launder through the bank accounts of family members. By now the partnership between Warner and Blazer had wholly disintegrated.

The conspiracy, money laundering, fraud and finance-law violations confessed to by Blazer meant that in due course many other guilty parties would be brought into the frame as the US investigations progressed. We also showed in *Badfellas* how the dubious business dealings of the company Traffic were part of the corrupt wider networks of FIFA and the confederations. In 2011, one of Warner's successors as president, Jeffrey Webb, was to negotiate a US$1.5 million bribe from Traffic, relating to the rights for World Cup qualifying matches. With Blazer heading into the hands of the FBI, and the following year gathering evidence for them, the foundations were being laid for the indictments of 27 May 2015.

Wakey wakey! Baur au Lac and the FBI/Swiss authorities raid

Havelange and his successor – the Swiss, Joseph 'Sepp' Blatter – had between them secured the presidency for 11 spells since 1974, Blatter having won his fifth term in the presidential election vote conducted on the last Friday in May at FIFA's 2015 Congress in Zurich. This electoral process had been marred two days earlier by the sensational indictment, early on Wednesday morning at an elite Zurich hotel, of fourteen people related to the football business of FIFA-affiliated confederations.

Four of these had held positions as president of a confederation: Jeffrey Webb from the Cayman Islands was the incumbent president of CONCACAF – the Central and North Americas and Caribbean Confederation – and Trinidad & Tobago's Jack Warner had held that position before him; Uruguayan Eugenio Figueredo and Paraguay's Nicolás Leoz had been presidents of the South American Confederation, CONMEBOL. These positions had carried with them a vice-presidential position on FIFA's Executive Committee (ExCo). A further ten individuals were arrested, four of them with strong FIFA connections: Costa Rica's Eduardo Li had been about to join the ExCo as a CONCACAF delegate; Julio Rocha of Nicaragua had held a position as a FIFA development officer, with a brief to introduce football projects around the world; and Rafael Esquivel and Jose Maria Marin were past presidents of, respectively, the Venezuelan and Brazilian Football Federations. The other six indicted individuals comprised British citizen Costa Takkas, personal attaché to Jeffrey Webb and a former general secretary of the Cayman Islands' Football Federation; and five media/sport marketing executives (three Argentineans [one with dual Italian citizenship], one Brazilian and one US citizen).

FIFA employs around 400 people; and FIFA committees, commissions and bureaux were peopled by, at one 2011 count,[31] 387 different individuals. FIFA supports an increasingly successful Women's World Cup, age-banded tournaments around the world, and innumerable development schemes for the majority of its member (national) associations/federations. But the indictment of the FIFA Fourteen brought into unprecedentedly sharp relief, for a global audience, the malpractices and endemic corruption of highly-placed FIFA-related and connected personnel; the voices of those who could claim to be untainted were drowned out in a tsunami of negative coverage and general condemnation of the overall organization. Some such individuals may believe, genuinely, that their endeavours are idealistically channelled "for the game, for the world", as the FIFA slogan trills – but few were willing to listen to arguments about the injustice of condemning the many for the crimes of the few. In a blitz of global media coverage following the indictment of the FIFA Fourteen, the world heard within three days from the victorious Blatter that he would not serve out his fifth term; he would resign to allow a successor to be elected at a forthcoming Extraordinary Congress, fixed later for February 2016.

Blatter talked of his recognition that his victory did not represent a mandate to speak for the whole of the football world, although he pledged to stimulate the necessary reforms that might regain FIFA some credibility in the wake of the dramatic dawn raid of 27 May carried out by the Swiss authorities on behalf of the US attorney general, the FBI and the US revenue services. FIFA was redefined as a RICO ("Racketeering Influenced Corrupt Organisation"), operated by some of its members as an "enterprise" to serve its own and its co-conspirators' interests rather than the stated goals of the organization itself.[32] In paragraph 265 of the indictment presented to the world, the suspects were charged with, over a period from 1991 to the present, "knowingly and intentionally" conspiring "to violate Title 18, United States Code, Section 1962(c), that is: 'To conduct and participate, directly and indirectly, in the conduct of the affairs of such enterprise through a pattern of racketeering activity, as defined in Title 18, United States Code, Sections 1961 (1) and 1961 (5)'". We can see now why the "integrity of the investigation" was being so closely safeguarded during that Brooklyn court hearing at which Chuck Blazer made his guilty pleas; the FBI, the Inland Revenue Service, and the United States Department of Justice had been biding their time. Their investigation, stimulated by the brilliant work and reporting of Andrew Jennings,[33] was the ticking time-bomb that at any point could shatter the foundations of the HBFD. The key point, the ideal targeted venue, it turned out, was Blatter's last election pitch on home territory; the audaciousness of the raid was electrifying. Loretta Lynch held nothing back in her scathing comments as she announced the indictment of "nine FIFA officials and five corporate executives" for racketeering conspiracy and corruption.[34] She announced "the unsealing of charges and the arrests of individuals" in the "long-running investigation into bribery and corruption in the world of organized soccer" by the powerful triad of the US Department of Justice, the FBI and the IRS. The forty-seven-count indictment against the FIFA Fourteen – seven of whom were arrested in Zurich on that May morning – included "charges of racketeering, wire fraud and money-laundering conspiracies spanning two decades". Football events served as vehicles in broader "schemes" to line executives' pockets with bribes. Defendants and co-conspirators were identified as having used US-based banking and wire facilities, and US venues, in their scheme-plotting meetings.

Just six months later Lynch would once again be addressing the world as Swiss police, in cooperation with the FBI, pounced again at Baur au Lac, this time arresting two "new defendants" – Alfredo Hawit and Juan Angel Napout – as part of a dawn raid on the morning of Thursday 3 December. These were just two of sixteen "current or former soccer officials" facing charges from the US Department of Justice.[35]

Crooked man or rotten system?

The RICO scenario was not predictable in any precise way, but it was unfolding with the dramatic inexorability of a theatrical tragedy. The previous year Blatter had spent the carnivalesque World Cup in Brazil virtually in hiding, cocooned in his luxury penthouse suite at the far end of the Ipanema waterfront in Rio de Janeiro. The year before that, at the Confederations Cup in the same city, he'd been booed and derided at any public appearance he made. "FIFA Go Home" slogans littered the graffiti sites and public squares of Rio: "Fuck FIFA" posters plastered the bus shelters and adorned the makeshift placards of young people across Brazil's World Cup venues, from cosmopolitan Rio to the Amazonian outpost of Manaus. Blatter and his World Cup cash cow were emerging as a toxic brand, the alliterative acronym FIFA transformed into a guttural explosion of widespread contempt and simmering dissidence.

Blatter, nevertheless, had entered 2015 with a determination to take up the FIFA presidential reins for a fifth term. There were howls of opposition, but after a presidential election that threw up an inexperienced Jordanian royal against him, he mobilized his electoral base, the FIFA Congress, and polled 133 votes to Prince Ali bin Hussein's seventy-three. Not quite the two-thirds necessary for a straight win, but enough to convince Prince Ali's advisers that he should not push for a second round of voting. Blatter supporters, particularly across Asia and Africa, expressed gratitude and loyalty, saying how much Blatter's FIFA had done for them and their countries' football development. Some alleged that opponents and critics of Blatter were little more than residual imperialists and/or racists.

But within three days Blatter had announced that his mandate was insufficient for him to hold the presidency for a full term, and proposed plans to withdraw when the process of electing a new president could be completed. Four months later he found himself suspended from world football activities, for an initial ninety days, by his own Ethics Committee; along with FIFA general secretary Jérôme Valcke, and long-term protégé Michel Platini, president of the European Football Confederation, UEFA. The net was closing in on an extended network of FIFA personnel whose activities could be said to be sustaining football's governing body as a form of corrupt "enterprise". US and Swiss legal proceedings implicated increasing numbers of FIFA-linked personnel, and in mid-October FIFA itself showed an unprecedented capacity to mobilize its internal ethical processes against its own two top employees, as well as UEFA's Platini.

The Racketeer Influenced and Corrupt Organization Act (RICO) was passed in the USA in 1970, a complex legislation designed, in the words of US law professor Pamela Pierson, "to penetrate organizations and impose liability on those who orchestrate criminal acts but insulate themselves with layers of underlings and bureaucracy".[36] Attorney General Lynch had warned in mid-September that further arrests were more than likely, and that these could include "entities", or football bodies, not just individuals or commercial companies.[37] She was adamant that the investigation was not going to fade away: To "anyone who seeks to live in the past and to return soccer to the days of corruption and bribery, cronyism and patronage: You are on the wrong side of progress". She wouldn't be drawn, though, on whether targets might include Blatter himself.

Within weeks, however, Blatter and Platini had been questioned by Swiss authorities, Blatter as a "suspect" regarding his relationship to dubious media contracts awarded to Trinidad's Jack Warner; and, explosively, both Blatter and Platini (the latter as "somewhere between a witness and a suspect") on an orally agreed £1.3million payment to Platini in 2011. This outstanding sum was paid to Platini just prior to the FIFA presidential election that clinched Blatter his fourth term, allegedly for work done a decade or so earlier but unpaid because of FIFA's fragile finances at the time. Within a few days FIFA's Ethics Committee had imposed a ninety-day suspension on the two presidents, who had been hand-in-glove since Platini had been Blatter's face-of-football running mate during the latter's successful campaign for the presidency in 1998.

So by early October, just three weeks before the deadline for nominations for the presidency, FIFA itself took Blatter out of his presidential chair, and undermined the credibility of Platini as a candidate to succeed him as president. An Ethics Committee founded only in 2004 suddenly looked like it could take the initiative on internal matters. Blatter still aspired to be cleared and back in the chair for the forthcoming February Congress that would elect his successor and provide him with a platform to depart on his own terms by claiming the glory as the Great Reformer. But he was looking increasingly desperate and diminished, the comic turns outweighing the gravitas in a narrative beyond his control like never before.

So how did it come to this for the man who joined FIFA in 1975, and learned the marketing and governing games from his mentor Horst Dassler of Adidas, and the previous FIFA president Brazilian João Havelange; and who was seen by many as a Machiavellian master of organizational manipulation? Following Machiavelli's *Prince* the slippery and ruthless Blatter adopted the modus operandi for a leader that it is "better to be feared than loved", as we demonstrated in the *Badfellas* study. Blatter became synonymous with the slide at FIFA from collusion to corruption. He deflected criminal complaints begun in the Swiss legal system by his own Executive Committee in 2002, as well as accusations of power-hungry manipulation of FIFA processes, maladministration for personal gain, financial malpractice, and abuse of FIFA's organizational statutes. He and Valcke were roundly condemned as unreliable witnesses in a New York court in 2006, where they were exposed for unethical and corrupt conduct relating to their ditching of MasterCard as a major World Cup sponsor in favour of Visa. But the FIFA crisis is not solely, or primarily, a story of flawed management and opportunistic profiteering by self-serving individuals. The system itself, as FIFA has grown and the global commodity of the World Cup has grown with it, has been vulnerable to the ambitions and manipulations of individuals, but the high-profile names netted in the scandal should not obscure the key question of how the conditions of corruption could be allowed to thrive so widely in the first place.

In 1931 C.W. Hirschman, FIFA's Dutch general secretary, embezzled and lost the bulk of FIFA's funds, but was permitted to return to his native Netherlands on a FIFA pension for life.[38] FIFA then moved from Paris to Zurich, and reconstituted itself within a generous and opaque system of organizational autonomy and financial unaccountability. FIFA has been allowed to grow within the terms of a non-profit organization, an association constituted – in the terms of the Swiss Civil Code – for "non-commercial purpose" and dedicated to the needs of its members, answerable only to its annual gathering of members: in FIFA's case its Congress. You could change the names of the culpable and the corrupt, but the problem is institutionally embedded and systematically reproduced. As FIFA grew, and the continental confederations with it, a tentacle-like network of football officials could seize the opportunity to prosper from, and widely exploit, the football business. It became, in the words of the US Office of Public Affairs and its federal racketeering laws, an "enterprise", a set of interconnected organizations exploited by individuals for personal gain. The Ethics Committee will have its work cut out to investigate all of those, including Franz Beckenbauer, who have gained immorally from access to and involvement in the FIFA enterprise. Blatter may have been an architect of this enterprise for forty years, but lax Swiss regulation, the commercial interests of partners such as Adidas, and rapacious careerists from all six continental confederations have been the making of the FIFA scandal. Removing Blatter from the front of the stage may not change the trajectory of the narrative unless the 2016 reforms are implemented with the utmost seriousness and commitment. A new president with the purest motives and the cleanest of CVs may find at FIFA an organizational structure that is hugely demanding, if not impossible, to reform from within – rooted as it is in the decision-making power of the Congress. Blatter is a symptom – albeit a very significant one – but not the single cause, of a rottenness at the heart of the Swiss associational model, and of its vulnerability to misappropriation and global greed.

Blatter's last stand

He'd been courted by prime ministers and presidents and flattered worldwide as the FIFA Men's World Cup escalated in value; but Blatter looked to have the knack of surviving successive crises whilst Executive Committee members around him, past and present, were receiving suspensions from FIFA and/or coming to face legal charges in their own countries or indictments by the US authorities. He looked to have manufactured a way out of FIFA on his own terms, ushering in a presidential contest scheduled for February 2016 in which his protégé Michel Platini could become the football governing body's first ever player-celebrity president. But when in early October 2015 FIFA's own Ethics Committee suspended Blatter and Platini for ninety days – as part of an investigation into a case of "disloyal payments" – Blatter's image and credibility plummeted to an all-time low. Blatter became a byword for corruption, a focus for ridicule and abuse. He'd hidden himself away in Ipanema in bodyguarded luxury at the Brazil World Cup in 2014, as the streets and bus-shelters – from the centre of Rio to the favelas – screeched "FIFA Go Home" and "Fuck FIFA". Following his suspension, Blatter the Bogeyman was even burned in effigy (one of them labelled "THIEFA") at English Bonfire Night celebrations in November, and provided the source of a pub-quiz team name ("Splatter Blatter"). Meanwhile, Blatter told the world that in a near-death moment the angels had won a battle with the devil, securing his survival. A few days before FIFA's scheduled announcement of the eight-year bans for both Blatter and Platini, Vladimir Putin stated that Blatter ought to be proposed for the Nobel Peace Prize rather than investigated for breaches of ethics.

At the beginning of Christmas week 2015, following the formal announcement of the bans, Blatter addressed the world looking battered and bruised, his upper right cheek plastered over, his baggy eyes shrieking weariness. Yet he summoned up some of his old defiance, attacking those whom he claimed had betrayed his work, including Europeans and "British nations" that had treated him like a "punching bag".

Blatter and Platini were investigated by FIFA's Ethics Committee in relation to a payment of £1.3million (CHF2 million) made by FIFA to Platini in February 2011 for work done nine years earlier. This work was claimed to be based on an oral contract or verbal agreement, although one "with no legal basis in the written agreement signed between both officials on 25 August 1999", as the Ethics Committee ruled. Soon after the payment had been made, Platini, in his position as UEFA president, had announced the European Confederation's support for Blatter in the forthcoming election for the FIFA presidency in May 2011. Both Blatter and Platini were said to have failed to "show commitment to an ethical attitude". Blatter also "violated his fiduciary duty" and demonstrated "an abusive execution of his position as President of FIFA". Neither was said to have engaged in "bribery and corruption" (which would have brought a life ban); but both broke FIFA's ethics code by "offering and accepting gifts and other benefits", and failing to declare conflicts of interest.

Blatter and Platini go back a long way, as the *Badfellas* story told, to the platform they shared at Blatter's launch event for the FIFA presidency in Spring 1998 at the HQ of the French Olympic Association in Paris. Watching and listening to them provide a mixture of enthusiastic vision and rhetorical promise for the future, with Blatter exploiting the youthful Platini as his face of football, was revealing. And following a hugely successful France 1998 tournament that enhanced Platini's non-playing profile, Blatter made the contract with him, shoehorning him into committee positions at UEFA, and from there on to the FIFA Executive Committee. Platini's ascendancy to the UEFA presidency in 2007 was assured; a very senior former UEFA figure said: "There were FIFA administration people travelling around Europe making the campaign for Platini."[39] It is astonishing to think that the two individuals at the head of the two most prominent and wealthy football federations could conduct business like a couple of barrow-boys at the local market, and that the chair of a finance committee of an organization of FIFA's scale and profile could permit a £1 million-plus payment to an individual on the basis of a nod and a wink. But that chair back in 2011 was Argentinean Julio Grondona, who died in July 2014 but had been pivotal to financial dealings ranging from the approval of Blatter's undeclared salary to the misuse of World Cup funding in the build-up to South Africa 2010. Doing deals the Blatter-Platini way had become routine, and the downfall of the two presidents has confirmed a rottenness at the heart of football leadership and governance that is all the more worrying because of how long it has taken figures in positions of responsibility to act in response to the excesses, abuses and corrupt practices of a FIFA which now demands, if it is to survive at all, a root and branch review and a radical overhaul.

If an emboldened generation of FIFA careerists and employees can ride the storm of US indictments and the actions of the Swiss authorities – establishing an open and meaningful working dynamic with representatives of the six continental federations, and ensuring that a new president is not permitted to adopt Blatter's (and his predecessor's) dictatorial model – there is some hope that the unity of world football can be preserved. If not, splits and breakaways could see a fragmentation of the world game in ways that it would take generations to overcome. This crisis of credibility, not a Nobel nomination, is Blatter's legacy; and Platini's tragedy is that he allowed himself to be mired in the "enterprise" dealings of a FIFA that the FBI and its US partners has now shown to be one of its primary targets. In the final chapter we follow the FIFA story through to the *dénouement* of the Extraordinary Congress, consider Blatter's flaws in the leadership/presidential role, and reflect on the opportunities for change and reform that this moment of potential renewal and redemption offers.

Notes

1 This chapter draws upon material previously published by Alan Tomlinson as follows: *FIFA: The Men, the Myths and the Money* (London and New York: Routledge, 2014); "Joseph Blatter is nur das Symptom", *Der Tagesspiegel (Sport)*, 2 December 2015, www.tagesspiegel.de/sport/fifa-skandal-joseph-blatter-ist-nur-das-symptom/12665172. html, accessed 2 December 2015; "Ethics man", *When Saturday Comes*, Vol. 348 (February 2016): 11.

2 This section is an abbreviated adaptation of the account of the injunction in Tomlinson, *FIFA*: 137–42.

3 Ibid.

4 See www.bbc.co.uk/news/world-europe-15996806, accessed 2 December 2011.

5 See www.themobmuseum.org/press_releases/the-beautiful-game-turns-ugly-new-mob-museum- display-explores-corruption-of-fifa/, accessed 31 March 2016.

6 This section is an adaptation of the account of the MasterCard-Visa case in Tomlinson, *FIFA*: 142–4.

7 "United States District Court Southern District of New York, MasterCard International Incorporated, Plaintiff, v. Fédération Internationale de Football Association, Defendant, 06 Civ. 3036 (LAP)", New York, 7 December 2006, So Ordered: Loretta A. Preska USDJ., para. 263: 91.

8 Ibid.: 2–3.

9 Andrew Jennings has researched and presented several brilliantly illuminating BBC *Panorama* documentaries on what he called FIFA's dirty secrets, beautiful bungs, and the organization's collusion with individuals in some of the continental confederations. In "FIFA & Coe" (a BBC *Panorama* broadcast) there are some reconstructions of the New York court case.

10 The previous two phrases are the words selected by Blatter in his foreword to the FIFA financial report presented to the FIFA Congress in May/June 2011, when referring to the South Africa World Cup of 2010. He also added: "Thanks to the conservative and careful financial policies that we followed in the 2007–2010 period, we have been able to considerably increase our investment in football development programmes, and in 2010, we were able to give each member association a total extraordinary FAP payment of USD 550,000 and each confederation USD 5 million" (p. 7). Such a strategy, amounting to a handout totalling around US$144.4 million, should not be underestimated in any assessment of the allegedly wavering but recurrently sustained power and influence of the FIFA president.

11 Tomlinson, *FIFA*: 144–5.

12 "Sepp Blatter wins FIFA president election", *Independent*, 1 June 2011, see www .independent.co.uk/sport/football/news-and-comment/sepp-blatter-wins-fifa-president-election-2291733.html, accessed 3 July 2013.

13 The letter, headed "10 years of presidency", and dispatched on the headed paper of "Le Président", is in the possession of the authors.

14 *FIFA Financial Report 2014*, presented to 65th Congress, 28–29 May 2015.

15 See Alan Tomlinson, "FIFA: 'For the game: For the world'? The world governing body's escalating crisis of credibility" in Alan Bairner, John Kelly and Jung Woo Lee, eds, *Routledge Handbook of Sport and Politics* (London and New York: Routledge, forthcoming 2017).

16 Heidi Blake and Jonathan Calvert, *The Ugly Game: The Qatari Plot to Buy the World Cup* (London: Simon & Schuster, 2015). See also the detailed story pieced together and told by Philippe Auclair and Éric Champel, *FIFAGATE, Comment le Qata a fait exploser le système Blatter* (Neuilly-sur-Seine: Éditions Michel Lafon, 2015), which has a particularly useful timeline for the explosive months of May–July 2015.

17 Blake and Calvert, *The Ugly Game*: 222–3, 235–9.

18 "Code of ethics approved – Lord Sebastian Coe to be chairman of Ethics Committee", FIFA Media Release, 15 September 2006.

19 The memorable encounter is shown in the BBC *Panorama* broadcast "FIFA & Coe", broadcast on 29 October 2007.

20 Blake and Calvert, *The Ugly Game*: 3.

21 "Statement of the chairman of the FIFA adjudicatory chamber, Hans-Joachim Eckert, on the examination of the ISL case", 29 April 2013 (pdf in possession of authors).

22 Andrew Zimbalist, *Circus Maximus: The Economic Gamble behind Hosting the Olympics and the World Cup* (Washington, DC: Brookings Institution Press, 2015): 31.

23 Freshfields Bruckhaus Deringer, "Deutscher Fussball-Bund e.V., Interne Untersuchung – Untersuchungsbericht", 4 March 2016.

24 Andrew Jennings, *The Dirty Game: Uncovering the Scandal at FIFA* (London: Century/ Penguin Random House, 2015): 84.

25 "United States of America against Jeffrey Webb, Eduardo Li, Julio Rocha, Costas Takkas, Jack Warner, Eugenio Figueredo, Rafael Esquivel, José Mario Marin, Nicolás Leoz, Alejandro Burzaco, Aaron Davidson, Hugo Jinkis, Mariano Jinkis, and José Margulies, also known as José Lagaro", Indictment 15 CR 0252 (RJD)(RML), United States District Court, Eastern District of New York. Filed in Clerk's Office US District Court EDNY, 20 May 2015, Brooklyn Office (164 pages). The page references given in these accounts of World Cup scandal and corruption refer to this document.

26 *CONCACAF Integrity Committee Report of Investigation*, presented to CONCACAF Executive Committee, 18 April 2013, Section 3 (7.64): 112. The chair of the committee which produced this 144-page report was Sir David A Simmons.

27 See Note 32 below.

28 "United States of America Against Charles Gordon Blazer, Defendant (Case 1:13-cr-00602-RJD, Document 19, Filed 06/03/15)", Sealed Proceedings, 25 November 2013 (40 pages), United States District Court, Eastern District of New York, US Courthouse, Brooklyn, New York.

29 See Mary Papenfuss, Christian Red, Teri Thompson and Nathaniel Vinton, "Soccer rat! The inside story of how Chuck Blazer, ex-US soccer executive and FIFA bigwig, became a confidential informant of the FBI", *New York Daily News*, 1 November 2014, www.nydailynews.com/sports/soccer/soccer-rat-ex-u-s-soccer-exec-chuck-blazer-fbi-informant-article-1.1995761, accessed 1 October 2015. For a racy, informative and illuminating account of Blazer's racketeering career, see Mary Papenfuss and Teri Thompson, *American Huckster: How Chuck Blazer Got Rich From – And Sold Out – The Most Powerful Cabal in World Sports* (New York: Harper, 2016). Papenfuss had been approached at a book launch by Blazer's long-term partner Mary Lynn Blanks – they had been "young moms" together in earlier lives. Blanks blurted out: "I've found myself in the soccer mafia, but if I tell you about it, they'll have to kill me" (p. 227). Blanks became a key source for Papenfuss and Thompson's evocative account of Blazer's spell as an FBI plant, his overall abuse of his CONCACAF position, his absurdly indulgent lifestyle based on fraud, corruption and celebrity.

30 See Section I on "Criminal Schemes", pp. 89–94, from the May indictment (see Note 25 above).

31 Tomlinson, *FIFA*: 39.

32 See Note 25 above, for full detail of the May indictment document.
33 Andrew Jennings has made invaluable contributions to the study of financial and institutional corruption at the heart of FIFA's global networks, in his rigorous and revelatory journalistic work and books. For the latter, see *Foul! The Secret World of FIFA: Bribes, Vote Rigging and Ticket Scandals* (London: Harper Sport, 2006); and *The Dirty Game*, see Note 24 above.
34 "Attorney General Loretta E. Lynch Delivers Remarks at Press Conference Announcing Charges Against Nine FIFA Officials and Five Corporate Executives", *Justice News*, Brooklyn, New York, United States, Wednesday 27 May 2015, www.justice.gov/opa/speech/attorney-general-loretta-e-lynch-delivers-remarks-press-conference-announcing-charges, accessed 27 May 2015.
35 The quotes by Lynch from December 2015 are from her statement on the day of the indictments, in "Attorney General Loretta E. Lynch Delivers Remarks at Press Conference Announcing Law Enforcement Action Related to FIFA", *Justice News*, Washington DC, United States, Thursday 3 December 2015, www.justice.gov/opa/speech/attorney-general-loretta-e-lynch-delivers-remarks-press-conference-announcing-law, accessed 5 December 2015.
36 See, for historical, political and legal context, Pamela Bucy Pierson, "RICO, corruption and white-collar crime", *Temple Law Review*, vol. 85, 2013: 523–74; and for the US Department of Justice's interpretation of FIFA as a RICO enterprise, Note 25 above.
37 Lynch was speaking in Switzerland, alongside the Swiss Attorney General Michael Lauber. See www.nytimes.com/2015/09/15/sports/soccer/us-attorney-general-predicts-more-charges-in-fifa-case.html?_r=0, accessed 16 September 2015.
38 Pierre Lanfranchi, Christiane Eisenberg, Tony Mason and Alfred Wahl, *100 Years of Football: The FIFA Centennial Book* (London: Weidenfeld & Nicolson, 2004): 74.
39 Tomlinson, *FIFA*: 81.

CODA

The end of a dynasty – Badfellas re-formed?[1]

FIFA's time to choose: "Historic" moment or more of the same?

In the end, no third early-morning swoop decimated the ranks of confederation or national association delegates arriving on that cold, icy and drizzly late February morning in Zurich in the days preceding FIFA's Extraordinary Congress at which its new president would be voted in – although armed police hovered around the gated entrance to the Baur au Lac, scrutinizing a pressman's credentials; and the hotel's security guard shooed us away, saying that photographing the private spaces of the hotel was a breach of Swiss law. His tone became more assertive as we queried his status: "Who are you and what is your authority," we asked; "I don't know about the law in your country," he responded, "but in Switzerland we are allowed to stop you taking photos from the sidewalk outside the hotel." So we walked around to the other side of the hotel, for longshots of the front entrance lobby, where fleets of jet-black limousines continued to arrive, dropping off conference delegates who scurried into the lobby fleeing the wet sleet blowing down from the Swiss Alps and in from the uninviting waters of Lake Zurich. The hotel is but a stone's throw away from Lake Zurich's picturesque pleasures, and around the corner from Bahnhofstrasse, one of the world's most expensive shopping streets and a favourite destination for FIFA wives accompanying their men on international football business. Watches at Rolex a couple of blocks down included a chunky hi-tech number with a pricetag of CHF 21,000, if you'd nothing better to do with your ExCo expenses. But the shops seemed eerily quiet the day before the FIFA Congress up at the Hallenstadion.

The presidential candidates were doing the rounds of the confederations, and UEFA's Gianni Infantino was sounding increasingly upbeat about his prospects. He'd not looked out of place or off-the-pace in a generally mediocre field; and after all, this was – as any long-term and disinterested FIFA observer could see – the most open presidential election in the organization's history. Infantino's main opponent was the debonair Sheikh Salman Bin Ebrahim Al-Khalifa, president of the AFC, from the dynastic royal family of democracy-lite super-rich Bahrain, a man with a degree in English Literature and History. Little was known of his past curricular specialisms or of current reading habits – there was too much ruling to be done as a family duty. Although a form of support had been pledged to Sheikh Salman from Issa Hatyatou's CAF, Infantino was confident of widespread support from within Africa. The only other candidate likely to poll more than a very few votes was Prince Ali bin Al-Hussein, a younger scion of the royal ruling family of Jordan, and a graduate of Britain's military academy, Sandhurst, and the USA's Princeton University. Prince Ali had been the stalking horse, garnering an honourable seventy-three votes against Blatter's 133, in May 2015; but without a constituency to call upon apart from a cluster of support in the west of Asia, there was little reason to see him as a threat to the frontrunners. Ali had even lost his nomination from the AFC to the FIFA ExCo a few months earlier, and was more likely to be brushing up his military skills than heading up FIFA after the February vote. He polled twenty-seven votes in round one. The fourth candidate was former FIFA insider Jérôme Champagne, who must have had a loser's consolation bottle of Bolinger ready-corked; a heavyweight on paper, he came over as a flyweight in person. His career in the French diplomatic service, following an elite education in politics and languages at some of the world's top institutions, had taken him to postings in Oman, Cuba, the US (Los Angeles), and Brazil. But one of us asked him, at a meeting at the European Parliament in Brussels in January 2015 hosted by the NewFIFANow lobbying group, how he could reconcile his reform manifesto with his eleven years at the heart of FIFA – particularly his membership of Blatter's notorious "Führengruppe" which essentially usurped power and authority from the ExCo and its administration during Blatter's early years, as documented above in the first chapter of *Badfellas*.[2] He shrugged his shoulders and with a Gallic hangdog expression said; "I tried but I failed." In round one he polled seven votes, a pitiful but predictable return for the candidate most associated with the old regime, the HBFD. The fifth contender, South African businessman Tokyo Sexwale, had pulled out as expected. His CV included sharing time on Robben Island with Nelson Mandela, and fronting South Africa's version of the British television show *The Apprentice*; he'd made encouraging noises to and for Infantino in the campaign, urging other African countries beyond South Africa to support the Swiss/Italian. Sheikh Salman and Infantino were head-to-head, as the first-round vote confirmed, Infantino claiming a slender three-vote lead, eighty-eight to the Bahraini's eighty-five. Many in the Hallenstadion gasped with surprise; they'd trusted the reports that solid voting blocs would be coming in from the confederations. It was now looking like a "keep-Sheikh-Salman-out" voting pattern.

In the morning session at the Congress, 179 of the 207 national association votes backed the reform committee's proposals (these are considered and evaluated in more detail at the end of this chapter), which included fixed terms for the president and officials; transparency on salaries/compensation; a slashing of the bloated committee structure (from twenty-six to nine, with independent chairs of key committees such as finance); abolition of the discredited Executive Committee, to be replaced by a new FIFA Council, including at least six women nominated from the confederations; strategy-setting by the Council, in liaison with the Congress; and a lessening of the power of the president by separating the "political" and "management" functions of the role. Additionally, eight more places were to be added to the Men's World Cup finals, and core human rights were to be adopted into the statutes.

A few years earlier a UEFA source had said to "keep a lookout" for Gianni Infantino; the Swiss/Italian, new to UEFA, was seen as the most ambitious and capable figure in the European Confederation, even eyeing FIFA's top position, via, perhaps, a stint as general secretary/chief executive alongside Blatter's preferred presidential successor. All looked to be going to plan until autumn 2015, with UEFA president, Michel Platini, favourite in the race to succeed Blatter. Then came the bombshell of the Blatter and Platini suspensions, and Infantino had a swift decision to make. Stick around to support a disgraced mentor, or leap over his shamed and crumpled body in a bid for the top job itself. Cannily he managed both; initially looking like a faithful UEFA man in getting enough nominations to keep the European Confederation's hat in the ring should Platini not be cleared, but ready to make the leap. When in December the FIFA Ethics Committee banned both Blatter and his former protégé Platini for eight years, the Infantino campaign roared into life, fuelled by €500,000 in financial backing from UEFA (approved by that confederation's executive committee). One wondered what the terms of such an arrangement were, and just what favours might be called in should the UEFA general secretary win the race.

Infantino's journey has been a classic Swiss trick, the famed neutrality of his home country translating into a "universal" claim that trumps the Eurocentrism of his UEFA position. He promised more money and resources for the needy and less well-off national associations, whatever the current hole in FIFA's projected income over the next two controversial World Cup cycles in Russia and Qatar. In his few minutes addressing the Congress he wowed the hall, asking why it was not possible to reinvest 25 per cent of FIFA's revenues in football development, since FIFA's money "is your money". Applause and swelling support catapulted him into his first round lead over pre-Congress favourite Sheikh Salman; twenty-seven further second round votes got him comfortably over the line. Bloc-based votes, and an alleged pact between Africa and Asia, looked what they now were – fictions, demolished in a more open and transparent field that Infantino played to perfection.

At FIFA's new football museum – reported to have cost £100 million, though for the two floors of the museum itself a more modest £22 million was quoted by the curator/director Guy Oliver – for his first official appearance as president, Infantino echoed Pope Francis's putdown of Donald Trump, saying that bridges not walls should be built as part of FIFA's reuniting process. The bridge-builders will need time, beyond just the 60-day deadline for the implementation of the accepted reforms. But the FBI may call again and FIFA cannot be rebuilt in a day. US Attorney General Loretta E. Lynch was unequivocal on this point in Washington DC on

3 December 2015, which synchronized with the round-up of further suspects in Zurich and elsewhere. Reviewing the charges to hand, she said of the outrageous betrayal of trust and unconscionable scale of corruption embedded in FIFA: "And the message from this announcement should be clear to every culpable individual who remains in the shadows, hoping to evade our investigations: You will not wait us out. You will not escape our focus."[3]

Yet for those without reason to hide or remain in the shadows, FIFA can be pruned, cleansed and reconstructed in its processes and its culture; and Gianni Infantino, a member of FIFA's 2016 Reform Committee, has up to twelve years in which to make good on his promises. He will be less well paid in the presidential role than he would have been in the secretary general position, but has insisted that he is not there for the money. If he lasts the pace, makes the serious and radical reforms work, cultivates a culture of participation and contribution at FIFA, keeps the World Cup parties going with sufficient revenue and turnover whilst opening the doors and safes of the Home of FIFA to scrutiny, he may go down in history as the saviour of the disgraced body. As the youngest FIFA president since the first incumbent, France's Robert Guérin in 1904, he may have time on his side. However, if he fails, he will be consigned to history as a Blatter clone and Platini *apparatchik* whose reformist vision was just another smokescreen. As he opens the books and the doors of FIFA, and talks to the relieved and liberated employees and the delegates from the confederations, he may ponder some of the excesses of his countryman Blatter's seventeen-year rule and career-long contribution to the malpractices and rackets of the HBFD.

What can Infantino learn from Blatter?

At the beginning of June 2015 Blatter had fallen on his sword four days after securing a fifth term as president of FIFA. The sword was a blunt one; he did not resign, but reaffirmed his position as caretaker president, looking to usher in a successor as president at a special Congress, later confirmed for February 2016. In September, however, he was hauled from his presidential suite at the Home of FIFA in Zurich when FIFA's own Ethics Committee suspended him for ninety days to enable the investigation of dubious financial arrangements between him and the European Football Federation's president, French footballing legend Michel Platini. An early Christmas present arrived for Blatter on 21 December with FIFA's announcement that both he and Platini would be banned for eight years from all football-related activity. Although many inside FIFA considered that the self-serving and corrupt financial dealings between the two warranted a life ban, an appeal to the Ethics Committee resulted in a lowering of the ban to six years a few days before the February 2016 Extraordinary Congress. The pair had appeals rejected by the Court of Arbitration for Sport (CAS) but continued to plead the victim's case of persecution as much as any credible or objective plea of innocence. But they cut a sad sight whenever and wherever they appeared in that epoch-changing late February, shorn of their status and unsupported by the apparatus of power to which they had both become so accustomed.

For seventeen years as president, Blatter consolidated a fiefdom framed according to the Swiss Civil Code's not-for-profit model of an association, calling for a minimal organizational structure comprising only a president, secretary, treasurer and a membership assembly working to agreed statutes, all lightly monitored by Swiss regulators. Blatter, a careerist Swiss marketing man, knew this system well – as we showed so vividly in *Badfellas* – having joined FIFA in 1975. Initially his survival skills looked to be unmatched. But eventually, and as successive crises and revelations sparked moral and ethical challenges of increasing volume, intensity and geographical and political reach, the voices of criticism and opposition became deafening. We watched him smooth and manipulate his way to power in Paris's Equinox Hall in 1998, and we have monitored his various strategies and machinations during a dictatorial rule that has sought to deflect and deny the various accusations and allegations that have been the watermark of his regime. True to form, he has called in the lawyers to look for every possible loophole that might allow him to crush dissent and eliminate opposition, and enable him to leave FIFA on his own terms as the self-appointed reformer of a system that he did to much to soil and tarnish.

So, in the end then, what went wrong for Blatter? A good counsel might have alerted him to rising tides of opposition, but – again as we showed so graphically in *Badfellas* – just as in Machiavelli's *Prince* his power was long based upon the cultivation of fear rather than love. Fear, of course, curbs the voices of criticism; and while he held on to power, Blatter considered it a relatively simple task to tame the dissenting voices. Gianni Infantino, the new FIFA president, would do well to take heed of Blatter's leadership follies and overall abuse of the presidential position. Here we consider just four such abuses.

First, Blatter *mixed and confused presidential responsibilities with the executive role.* This may be a common confusion in business, but Blatter took it to its extremes. In seeking to micro-manage a growing portfolio and expanding workforce, he never enabled employees within the organization to reach their full potential; nor did he delegate responsibility in any meaningful way. His was a regime of claustrophobic mismanagement, premised on a sense of his own omnipotence. Blatter cultivated cabals, hugely effective for periods, but with a built-in fragility and a tendency to implode.

The F-Crew (or "Führensgruppe" as FIFA insiders named Blatter's informal advisory group of the early 2000s) comprised aides, consultants and advisers to the FIFA president, most of them with no formal position in the organization. We showed in *Badfellas* how much resentment this fostered: bypassing official bodies and formal channels, and marginalizing the Executive Committee (ExCo) created deep dissatisfaction within FIFA; as did legitimating the "take-it-as-it-comes" responses of delegates who took the money and ran, or spotted opportunities for self-aggrandizement in their own part of the world in some wing or branch of FIFA's extended worldwide "enterprise", to use the RICO term. Blatter's controlling style might have worked successfully for him, and could be sustained over a long period as long as it was small-scale; but, as became clear, such a style could not control the larger scale of a continually evolving worldwide operation.

Second, it is the case that in most organizations at crisis point a whistleblower eventually emerges, one sufficiently disillusioned to speak out. Blatter, accustomed to unchecked and unadulterated power, began to *assume that fear lasts forever.* He mentored ineffectively, creating a culture of resentful acquiescence; but in recent years more and more former FIFA insiders have appeared willing to overcome their fear and talk openly about how the organization has conducted its business. Blatter for years induced the silence of such figures, one former member of the "Führensgruppe" departing with a reputed CHF8 million in return for keeping quiet. But when the disillusion spread, a silence that was based upon fear, threats and payoffs became harder to enforce.

Third, Blatter believed that *as leader he could pick and choose areas of moral responsibility.* He claimed that he could not monitor everybody all of the time, that corrupt practices across the other side of the world were not his responsibility. He consistently stated that it was not his job to keep continental confederations such as CONCACAF "under control". It took until 2004 for FIFA to institute an ethics process/committee, and this vacuum encouraged and sustained ethical contradictions and malpractices that, alongside the leader's lack of moral responsibility, set the tone for a culture routinely lacking in transparency and accountability. FIFA representatives and committee members could exploit opportunities for personal gain unhindered by internal monitoring or institutional accountability. But for the FBI, and the US tax and legal authorities, FIFA is not defined merely by the tenets of the Swiss Civil Code. It is, as we saw in detail in the preceding chapter, an "enterprise", a RICO, a corrupted and corrupting racket. The US indictments served upon the FIFA Fourteen on 27 May 2015 ignored the Swiss model of FIFA as a not-for-profit association and imposed another definition of FIFA, one that viewed it as an endemically corrupt organization and network. Blatter's deflection of responsibility for the acts of others looked absurd, and his leadership was exposed as morally bankrupt.

And, fourth, Blatter began to believe in his own infallibility and *took FIFA's partners for granted.* As the cash cow that is FIFA's Men's World Cup gained dramatically in value (72 per cent of FIFA's revenue of more than US$5.7 billion for the cycle 2011–14 was from marketing and television partners, almost wholly generated by that single event), the product looked lucrative and assured: higher global audiences, contented broadcasters and sponsors.[4] It seemed there was little to do to sustain this beyond feeding and milking the cash cow. But "Fuck FIFA" and "FIFA Go Home" slogans and posters at the Brazil World Cup in 2014 began to supplant FIFA's idealistic slogan "For the Game. For the World". Greed, exploitation, arrogance and corruption were the rebranding themes. Routinely timid corporate sponsors began to make stronger-sounding statements, tokenistic statements from inside Blatter's FIFA no longer reassuring them – although the broadcaster organizations remained revealingly mute. Despite a lifetime's experience of working with partners, Blatter showed neglect bordering on contempt for such key relationships.

What can Infantino and other leaders in the rudderless organizations of a widely discredited world of international sporting governance, learn from Blatter's fall? First, rather than blurring presidential and executive roles, he could have sought to share power, to work with an active and engaged ExCo. Second, he could have built an organizational culture of encouragement and aspiration, fuelling collective and collaborative debate, stimulating innovative thinking on important issues suited to FIFA's new riches, global reach and a humanitarian redistributive potential. Third, he could have – way before the introduction in 2004 of an ethics process that began to operate as a combination of show-trial and cover-up – displayed a genuine commitment to moral responsibilities and ethical principles. Fourth, Blatter's FIFA could have worked *with* its partners, particularly the sponsors but also the broadcasters, to realize an organizational and shared vision; to look, for instance, to translating CSR-speak into an innovative message of positive collaboration in a troubled world.

But Blatter, for so long criticized by few and checked by no-one, did none of these; the consequence was a dictatorial regime, increasingly crisis-ridden but sustained over five presidential terms by a lax Swiss polity and a fearful, silent chorus of sycophants. Blatter's predecessor as president, Brazilian João Havelange, held the presidency for six terms from 1974, his five re-elections being uncontested. Blatter had inherited and consolidated a dictatorial model of the presidency, based on silence and collusion and embedded corruption. Now that the HBFD has fallen, FIFA's ninth president would do well to learn from the mistakes, excesses and follies of the disgraced Swiss and his equally disgraced Brazilian mentor.

FIFA's 2016 Reform Committee led its recommendations, in its final report published in December 2015, with a statement concerning the "Principles of Leadership" that should guide the organization into the future. "FIFA is currently going through the worst crisis of its history. The current crisis should also be considered as a unique opportunity for FIFA to renew itself," was the opening gambit, followed by the aspirational principles: responsibility, humility, tone at the top, respect, and candour. This reads like a checklist of everything that the outgoing and shamed HBFD had lacked in its forty-one-and-a-half years "at the top".[5]

Redemption time

There are several responses to the downfall of Blatter. "Jail the lot!" says Andrew Jennings, the strap line of *The Dirty Game* acclaiming him as "the investigative reporter who brought down Sepp Blatter". Get the Swiss authorities to close down FIFA, suggests "ethical business" campaigner Jaimie Fuller, a voice of the NewFIFANow alliance, and arch-critic of FIFA and those businesses that remain partners of the soiled brand. But who are "the lot"? FIFA has 400 or so paid employees, and the number of committee members from all over the world has in recent years reached a similar level. Are they all corrupt? Complicit and colluding some may be, walking a tightrope of moral and ethical ambiguity. And, to counter Fuller, why would the Swiss want to dismantle FIFA rather than assist in its reformation?

Where would such closures end in the land of secret bank accounts and the harbouring of Nazi gold?

We need to recognize what FIFA accomplishes as well as the often dubious ways in which these accomplishments are achieved; the real question now is not whether there is corruption within FIFA's bureaucratic and organizational layers, or embedded malpractice within its corridors and cabals of higher power; it is, rather, to ask, as we have done recurrently throughout this book, *how* such practices have been sustained over this remarkable dynastic period of the Havelange/Blatter presidencies. And to add a further and critical question, how action can be added to revelation? Now that the HBFD is at its likely end, how can such criminal and corrupt modus operandi be prevented in the future? We have seen how FIFA's corrupt practices were in place long before the US legal and tax-checking authorities, and the FBI, emerged on the scene to confirm the embeddedness of corruption within the operations of some of the most privileged networks of the FIFA-related hierarchy. Yet FIFA now claims to be capable of internal reform; to repeat, President Infantino was a member of the 2016 Reform Committee, and the Congress that elected him to the presidency earlier that day gave a resounding acceptance of the Reform Committee's proposals. We conclude the chapter, and indeed this book, with a review of the proposed, internally generated reforms for a cleaner, leaner, more credible post-Blatter FIFA.

The "2016 FIFA Reform Committee" proposals accepted by the FIFA ExCo in December 2015, ratified and accepted as statutory changes at the Extraordinary Congress in February 2016, were said to offer, in Acting President Issa Hayatou's words, "improved governance, greater transparency and more accountability". Hayatou, some might say, is a high-profile survivor of the HBFD as the senior vice-president still standing, in no position to take on the role of acting president. Equally, from his mauling in the Seoul Congress vote where Blatter secured his second term as president, one could see Hayatou as a victim of the machinations and manipulations of the HBFD. But there he was, outlasting the lot, statesmanlike in his declaration after Infantino's victory: this historic conference, he announced, will help FIFA "win back the trust of the world", and we must "implement all these reforms; joint action is essential if we are going to protect the future – a brighter future – of FIFA" and "emerge from this dark period".[6] A move out of such a dark period will not, however, be achieved unless new ways of working with and across stakeholders and constituencies are established, both within FIFA and throughout its relationships with the confederations and national associations. With this in mind, we review the main proposals in the package of reforms.

Term limits (of a maximum three four-year terms) for the president and forty FIFA Council members (the replacement for the ExCo) certainly has the potential to counter corruptible ossification, and *diversity* is a principle that will not be contested; indeed for many in FIFA diversity is a top priority as the Women's World Cup matures and cements football's hold on the global fan base. There is to be an addition to the statutes, too, on *human rights*, which links of course to issues and controversies concerning, for instance, exploitation of labour on World Cup projects such as Qatar 2022. This should also be enshrined in the checks on potential participants – figures such as Sheikh Salman of Bahrain, whose candidacy for the FIFA presidency was greeted by Americans for Democracy & Human Rights in Bahrain (ADHRB) as a breach, by FIFA, of human rights. The Bahraini was essentially accused of negligence, if not direct culpability, relating to his government's "crackdown, retaliating against players and clubs alike for their peaceful activities during the protest movement", and in supporting his candidacy the ADHRB claimed FIFA had "violated human rights provisions of the OECD's Guidelines for Multinational Enterprises".[7] FIFA's Ethics Committee had confirmed Sheikh Salman's candidacy in mid-November 2015, even after the ADHRB had written to Acting President Issa Hayatou informing him "that it had informed Blatter in 2013 of its 'deep concern' over allegations of human rights violations involving Sheikh Salman in the Arab Spring of 2011".[8] The question of how individuals gain positions in the autonomous continental confederations is another critical matter, a huge question that can only be answered as part of a collective examination of the issue, perhaps a case of the "joint action" that Hayatou may have been referring to in closing the Extraordinary Congress. The human rights question was also reaffirmed as a major challenge for FIFA in April 2016 when Harvard professor John Ruggi wrote, in a report commissioned by FIFA itself, that "the responsibility of those organizations [such as FIFA] to address human rights risks with which they are involved [,] exists independently of any government's abilities or willingness to act on its obligations".[9] The ethos of the post-HBFD FIFA will be tested robustly in the sphere of human rights, and Ruggie joined the growing ranks of specialists and commentators in condemning FIFA's rotten and corrupt culture:

> What is required is a cultural shift that must affect everything FIFA does and how it does it. The result must be 'good governance,' not merely 'good-looking governance'. To put it in the simplest terms, FIFA, the global football enterprise, must transform itself into a modern organization.[10]

That is easier said than done by an organization claiming to represent the interests of a complex and heterogeneous political and cultural world, and there are many flaws – economic and ethical – in the modus operandi of innumerable "modern organizations"; but as our *Badfellas* study shows, the roots of corruption were embedded decades ago, and in his testimony at sealed proceedings of the US Eastern District Court on 23 November 2015, disgraced former CONCACAF chief Jeffrey Webb confirmed the taken-for-granted nature of the scams, schemes and frauds within the FIFA and confederational networks: "I understood at the time that it was unlawful to accept bribes and embezzle funds in connection with my duties as a high level official of FIFA, CONCACAF or CFU. I deeply regret my participation in this illegal conduct."[11] Regrets he may now have, but as he took the kickbacks and bribes ("side payments") when awarding commercial rights to World Cup qualifying matches for CFU nations "in or around 2012" no doubts, ethical concerns or morals held him back: "At the time I understood this to be a bribe offer, and I believed that such offers were common in this business."[12] How right he was, in this matter-of-fact and illuminating confession. Ruggie is right to emphasize the imperative of deep and genuine cultural change within FIFA and its networks.

The appointment of *independent committee members* to be involved in key decisions by finance, development and governance committees should feed into increased transparency of financial processes, and *auditing the activities* of these independents will be useful as a form of monitoring. It is also proposed to *reduce the number of standing committees* from twenty-six to nine. Blatter, following Havelange, used committee positions and privileges as forms of patronage. However, nine committees, if they are given tangible tasks, will be less open to patronage and could – if genuinely briefed, supported and monitored – work much more effectively. The nine, as accepted at the Extraordinary Congress cover: governance, finance, development, organization of FIFA competitions, football stakeholders, member associations, players' status, referees' business, and medical matters.[13] Within hours of Congress's acceptance of this culling of committees, interested parties were bemoaning the loss of voice on, for instance, women's football (absorbed into the business of the competitions committee) and seeking reassurances that they would not be unrepresented in the new structure. In guaranteeing fair and equitable representation, FIFA will have to beware that it does not reproduce its flawed and bloated model by introducing subcommittees, working parties, and the like, that have little function beyond perpetuating a culture of favours and expenses.

So if *integrity checks* are completed in a meaningful way on potential Council and committee members, and if a proposed football stakeholders' committee represents wider interests (clubs, players, leagues) with a manageable brief, there could be a genuinely radical overhaul, steered by the FIFA administration itself but in informed and open debate.

The most jargonistic phrase of all in the Reform Committee's proposals is the most important: *"Separation of political and management functions"*; "political" here means not so much vested interests as policy principles and directions. Here, the FIFA Council would set overall strategic directions, and the general secretariat's business would be to operationalize/implement the strategy. Blatter could not separate these functions and sought to micro-manage and control; and some believe that Platini has done at UEFA what Blatter did at FIFA. In the words of Lars-Christer Olsson, the Swedish CEO of UEFA from 2004–07, Platini's presidency was "moving the organization [UEFA] back to what it was in the early 1990s ... an executive president mixing the political set-up, committees and administration ... creating the first foundation for what you've had in FIFA all the time."[14] We can see here how the HBFD was so close to being sustained, and extended, in the process whereby Platini was the clear favourite to succeed Blatter – up until the revelations of the duplicitous duo's dubious and absurdly self-serving financial arrangements.

However, in Hayatou's "historic" Congress, FIFA chose Gianni Infantino and he was quick to prioritize the seriousness of and the need for implementation plans for the proposed reforms. And they are truly radical reforms, with major structural and cultural implications and consequences: formulate policy as part of open debate and reflection, identify and accomplish work-tasks in the standing committees, get individuals to do more work for less glory (and fewer and lower payouts). Putting these changes in place would be a new restorative model for FIFA. Crucially, the president would have to work within these processes, and not just over and above them in the style of the Havelange/Blatter dynasty.

There is also the question of Congress, with its 209 members, which needs to consistently respond positively to the new structures and processes. It remains, in the FIFA statutes, the supreme body of FIFA, and yet the Reform Committee report made no explicit mention of the relation of Congress to the evolution of strategy undertaken by the Council (albeit recommending an extra annual Congress at which such matters might be raised). The 209 national associations are not likely to cede power to a more streamlined model of administration – as we remarked in *Badfellas*, there is something of import in the old phrase "turkeys do not vote for Christmas" – but they do have the opportunity to respond positively to proposals that at least give FIFA the chance of regaining credibility as a responsible and ethical body representative of the interests of the multiple constituencies that make up the global football industry.

FIFA is fighting for its life, in need of more than a cosmetic makeover. And as shown above the FBI and the US Department of Justice have been clear that its investigations are not simply going to go away. But such external pressures can be the stimulus for change, as Sundar Katwala noted in 2000[15] when he observed that the reform of sport governance, in the hands ideally of an emergent generation of sport administrators, was most likely when stimulated by external pressures for reform. And FIFA has not lacked those in recent years.[16] But we should not leave the last word with the FBI and the US attorney general. It is FIFA, not the US or Swiss courts, that has banned Blatter and Platini from involvement in any football-related activity; it is the FIFA Ethics Committee that has banned the silver-tongued charmer, but proven liar, Jérôme Valcke from football, for life. Was it someone who had been silent for years, who, at the end of the summer in 2015, felt sufficiently emboldened to inform FIFA's ethics chambers that Blatter and Platini had struck a dodgy deal way back; or was it someone, a figure such as Valcke perhaps, who blew the whistle as form of revenge for their own suspension and fall? Either way, the ethics process now threw light on the joint and interdependent interests that had been shared by Blatter and Platini since 1998 as they became partners in the elevation of the French footballing legend to the UEFA presidency, as illustrated in *Badfellas* and further reaffirmed in *FIFA: The Men, the Myths and the Money*.[17] We are reminded, once more, of Jürgen Lenz's astute and reverberating observation, quoted in *Badfellas*, that "FIFA's now so corrupt that it no longer knows that it's being corrupt"; just two days before his suspension Michel Platini was protesting to anyone who would listen that he had in fact underclaimed – that he had invoiced CHF800,000 *less* than he was due. In early April 2016, the Panama Papers revealed details of the dealings of the law firm Mossack Fonseca with a multitude of offshore companies; Platini had:

> relied on Mossack Fonseca to help him administer an offshore company created in Panama in 2007 … Platini was given an unlimited power of attorney for Balney Enterprises Corp., which was still an active business as of March 2016, according to Panama's commercial register.[18]

Such offshore activity was not necessarily illegal or criminal, but far from the moral high ground that Platini had been claiming as the new and relatively young face of a more transparent FIFA.

Now that Blatter is gone, the reforms can be instituted by a new generation, the organization restructured and renewed, the excesses reviewed and reduced (including the president's salary; Blatter was paid £2.5 million in 2015), and the football delegates to FIFA from the confederations encouraged and supported to participate in meaningful dialogues. In March 2016 FIFA published its financial and governance report for 2015, confirming its first annual loss since the near-bankruptcy of 2002 – although the "negative result" of US$122 million was comfortably covered by its "healthy reserves".[19] The indictments would continue, and more badfellas would be weeded out and dealt with as the FIFA story continued to unfold in a never-ending narrative – FIFA seeking repayments from its former top men via legal action, securing new sponsors such as China's Wanda Group in the early weeks of Infantino's presidency, and prepared to cope with revelations emerging from the ongoing criminal investigations. However, with a wider range of voices at the table, and an authentic commitment to transparency and accountability, there is just a chance that FIFA could give the peoples' game the leadership and governance that it deserves. FIFA's future is in the balance though, and every move will be scrutinized, every past act evaluated by a vigilant and ravenous global commentariat. Gianni Infantino soon learned this just a few weeks into his presidency when the Panama Papers revelations threw up his signature from a 2006 deal when, as head of UEFA's legal division, he had countersigned a media rights deal in which the Panama-based company Cross Trading paid UEFA – via its partner TEAM Marketing – US$111,000 for Champions League TV rights, selling these on to Ecuadorian broadcaster Teleamazonas for $311,170. In 2007, Cross Trading bought the TV rights for the UEFA Cup and the UEFA Super Cup for US$28,000, selling the rights on, again to Teleamazonas, for US$126,000. Cross Trading is a subsidiary of a company, Full Play, owned by Hugo Jinkis, one of those indicted in the US intervention in May 2015.[20] The reach of the RICO actions is a long and enduring one, and this single administrative duty – or oversight – may prove expensive for the new FIFA president, potentially damaging to his reputation and image. Indeed Infantino lost his calm exterior and demeanour in his response to this diminutive profile in the Fonseca/Panama Papers.[21]

Albert Camus' *The Plague* (1947) reminds us that change does not come easily. Reflecting on the enduring power of institutionalized evil, which for him was embodied by Nazism, Camus wrote:

> [The] bacullus of the plague never dies or vanishes entirely, but it can remain dormant for dozens of years in furniture or clothing … it waits patiently in bedrooms, cellars, trunks, handkerchiefs and old papers, and … perhaps the day will come when, the plague will rouse its rats and send them to die in some happy city.

To reiterate, even in the Congress at which Gianni Infantino was elected president, delegates from national associations were lobbying to keep their committee positions despite the shrinking of the committee structure, and the talk was of the need for working groups, subcommittees and specialist commissions. And the likes of Jérôme Champagne, one of the Blatter fixers within the HBFD, retreating back to his base in the Canton of Zug, would still be looking to broker deals for the right fee, and mobilizing his diplomatic skills to feed a voracious media and public relations industry, whilst also keeping the appropriate skeletons locked in the most secure of cupboards, and tempting investigators and researchers with opinions and information as part of a tacit arrangement whereby his reputation would remain relatively unscathed: "a brilliant conman", as we have heard him described by some, or maybe a still-active relic of the HBFD?

In June 2016 the excesses of Blatter and his close cronies were further reaffirmed when FIFA's own lawyers, US firm Quinn Emanuel, who were immersed in a trawl of financial documents within the governing body, reported that Blatter, Valcke, and deputy secretary general Markus Rattner, had been awarded £55 million (CHF79 million) in dubious contracts and routinized forms of compensation. Bill Burck, of Quinn Emanuel, wrote that this "appears to reveal a coordinated effort by three former top officials of FIFA to enrich themselves through annual salary increases".[22] We showed in the first chapter of *Badfellas* how Julio Grondona sanctioned the opaque and crooked finances of Blatter's FIFA, and it is Grondona who is named as the signatory (with Valcke) for Blatter's bonus payments for/from the 2014 Brazil World Cup and the previous year's Confederations Cup (CHF 12million, approved 19 October 2011), and for/from the 2010 South Africa World Cup (CHF11 million, approved 1 December 2008). Grondona was the sole signatory to approve Blatter's "annual representation expenses" of CHF500,000 in 2008. Blatter was sole signatory in siphoning millions of Swiss francs to his general secretary, Valcke, and joined Valcke in signing off the monies that went Kattner's way. Just three months before the emergence of the detail of this enrichment strategy of FIFA's top three officials, Kattner himself had sat as acting general secretary throughout the Congress at which the FIFA reforms were accepted, and at which Infantino won the vote for the presidency; no wonder then that he could look so unflustered throughout the proceedings, knowing what he had pocketed before the reform process could take hold. Valcke and Kattner were even given (in a contract amendment dated 30 April 2011) severance terms guaranteeing full payment should their employment be terminated before the contract's end, including – astonishingly, brazenly, greedily beyond belief – an indemnification clause forcing FIFA to pay all legal fees and fines that might accrue should the employee incur "costs and losses" from "civil or criminal proceedings against him". This is an outrageous abuse of institutional responsibility and trust, a corrupt climax, part confession, part thieves' charter, to the embedded malpractices of a corruptible and exposed generation of FIFA personnel.

These financial irregularities occurred under the watch of FIFA's auditor KPMG, which, as we showed in the first chapter of *Badfellas*, had wriggled its way out of any responsibility for the ISL-related problems of FIFA's precarious finances in 2002. On 13 June 2016, KPMG Switzerland resigned its position as FIFA's auditor, and FIFA "welcomed" the change, stressing the need for its financial functions to be "thoroughly reformed".[23]

The Quinn Emmanuel "update" observed that the clauses secured by Valcke and Kattner were "provisions" that "appear to violate mandatory Swiss law". As collusion fuelled corruption, and malpractice became commonplace, the FIFA of Havelange and Blatter became a law unto itself, and such violations of the law had become normalized. But a FIFA fighting for credibility and survival had to act and move from within. And by the time of the Quinn Emanuel revelations, Kattner had already been sacked for "breaches of fiduciary responsibilities". FIFA itself now provided the evidence behind the revelations to the US and Swiss authorities, in this sense collaborating with those investigations so that the organization, as an injured party or victimized institution, would not be vulnerable to, and could continue to repel, the reach of the RICO and the flow of indictments. "The FIFA volcano is exploding", observed Blatter's adviser Klaus Stoehlker on FIFA's publication of these damning financial details, before scuttling away from the explosion and terminating his professional relationship with the increasingly discredited Swiss.[24]

Allegations, first circling in May 2016 in the *Frankfurter Allgemeine Zeitung*, were also getting louder, claiming that Infantino had "pushed for the removal of FIFA's Audit and Compliance chief Domenico Scala", related to the new president's refusal "to accept his $2 million salary on offer from the compensation committee headed by Scala".[25] Scala was dismissed by FIFA and accused Infantino of using the new FIFA Council effectively as a means of controlling purportedly "independent" appointments. Infantino was accused of ordering the destruction of records of meetings, and had to deal with leaked redacted memos as FIFA's reform process creaked forwards; he was learning fast the power and persistence of the bacchus of the plague released by the corruption and ethical vacuity of the HBFD. By mid-July 2016 Infantino was facing investigation by his ethics committee, relating to allegations concerning possible conflicts of interest in using private jets provided by a country bidding for the World Cup, appointing individuals without full checks on their eligibility, and claims for personal expenditure on laundry, an exercise machine, flowers, and mattresses. In this list of the trivial and the substantive we could see the tensions swirling around the rivalries and the turbulent dynamics of the post-HBFD organisation. By early August Infantino was cleared on all counts with no extended investigation, FIFA confirming that "no violation of the FIFA Code of Ethics has been committed". In his personal statement in this FIFA media release Infantino said that his and his administration's focus remained on "improving FIFA's governance and repairing its reputation, and restoring trust with its stakeholders. This critical work will continue." When Havelange's death was announced less than a fortnight later, from Rio de Janeiro during the Olympic Games, it was a reminder that such critical work would be facing questions for years to come concerning the long-term legacy of the HBFD.[26] So as Infantino's short honeymoon drew to a close it was business as usual up at the Home of FIFA, begging the question "when will Blatter and his disgracefully enriched coterie face the full force of criminal justice and receive custodial penalties commensurate with their gross misdemeanours"?

We ended *Badfellas*, in 2003, with a call to action: "See you in the trenches" was our rallying cry (as well as on the terraces). It is just possible that as we go over the top we will begin a new journey in which the lies have evaporated, the corruption has diminished, and FIFA can operate, genuinely, in the spirit of its slogan. "For the Game. For the World" could become a respected rationale rather than a laughing stock. If the respect is not restored a different body altogether might emerge to control the world game, the US agencies will have had the last word after all, and some of us will be re-imagining the future of world football all over again.

Notes

1 This chapter draws upon Alan Tomlinson, "Opportunity knocks", *When Saturday Comes*, No. 350, March 2016: 8; Alan Tomlinson, "FIFA and leadership: The fall of Sepp Blatter", January 2016, www.alantomlinson.typepad.com/alan_tomlinson/2016/01/fifa-and-leadership-the-fall-of-sepp-blatter.html; as well as observations and discussions by both authors in Zurich before, during and following the election of FIFA's ninth president in February 2016.

2 Alan Tomlinson, "Divide and rule", *When Saturday Comes*, Vol. 337, March 2015: 9.

3 See www.justice.gov/opa/speech/attorney-general-loretta-e-lynch-delivers-remarks-press-conference-announcing-law, accessed 4 December 2015.

4 See Alan Tomlinson, *FIFA: The Men, the Myths and the Money* (London and New York: Routledge, 2014), Chapter 6, "Cash cow".

5 *2016 FIFA Reform Committee Report (December 2, 2015)*, but considered at the ExCo before this, 27 November 2015: 1.

6 It may be rather ungracious, even shabby, to note that Hayatou had the previous year persuaded his confederation, CAF, to abolish the age limit for its presidents, so allowing him to continue beyond the age of seventy years old, and therefore be eligible for another shot at the FIFA presidency for at least a few years should the Infantino dawn prove to be a false one. FIFA has no stated retirement age for committee members, or the president, even in the 2016 reforms.

7 See "ADHRB files OECD complaint over Sheikh Salman FIFA candidacy", 11 February 2016, at www.adhrb.org/2016/02/adhrb-files-oecd-complaint-against-fifa/#_ftn2, accessed 5 March 2016. The OECD is the Organization for Economic Cooperation and Development.

8 See Mary Papenfuss and Teri Thompson, *American Huckster: How Chuck Blazer Got Rich From – And Sold Out – The Most Powerful Cabal in World Sports* (New York: Harper, 2016): 221.

9 John G. Ruggie, "For the game. For the world", *FIFA & Human Rights, Corporate Responsibility Initiative Report No. 68* (Cambridge, MA: Harvard Kennedy School, 2016): 36.

10 Ibid.

11 "United States of America against Jeffrey Webb, Defendant (Case 1:15-cr-00252-RJD-RML, Document 312-1, Filed 04/18/16)", Sealed Proceedings, 23 November 2015 (38 pages), United States District Court, Eastern District of New York, US Courthouse, Brooklyn, New York: 27.

12 Ibid.: 26.

13 See the draft of the revised statutes at www.resources.fifa.com/mm/document/affederation/bodies/02/74/76/37/draftfifastatutesextraordinarycongress2016en_neutral.pdf, accessed 28 March 2016.

14 Interview with Alan Tomlinson, Nyon, Switzerland, 24 April 2008. I am grateful to the British Academy for its support for this fieldwork (Award Number SG: 47220, "The construction and mediation of the sporting spectacle in Europe, 1992–2004", conducted 2007–10).

15 Sundar Katwala, *Democratizing Global Sport* (London: The Foreign Policy Centre, 2000): 90–2.

16 See Sylvia Schenk, *Safe Hands: Building Integrity and Transparency at FIFA* (Berlin: Transparency International, 16 August 2011). Just a few months after publication of this report, in early December 2011, Transparency International withdrew from its role as FIFA adviser and reform consultant, when Professor Mark Pieth was asked by FIFA to lead a group of independent

government experts and stakeholder representatives in a new Independent Governance Committee (IGC). Pieth soon expressed frustration with the factors constraining his role as chair of the IGC, though the committee stimulated the adoption of a new Code of Ethics the following year, alongside the procedural principles of the newly established investigative and adjudicatory chambers. See the *FIFA Governance Reform Project*, first report of the IGC (Basel: Basel Institute on Governance, 20 March 2012). Leaving this role at the end of 2013, Pieth himself then became, in effect, a source of external pressure. Both Transparency International and Pieth were nevertheless thanked for their contributions by François Carrard in the preface to the report of the FIFA 2016 Reform Committee.

17 Alan Tomlinson, *FIFA*, see Note 2 above.

18 Gary Rivlin, Marcos Garcia Rey and Michael Hudson, "Leak ties ethics guru to three men charged in FIFA scandal", *The Panama Papers*, 3 April 2016, The International Consortium of Investigative Journalists, pdf document: 8. This *Panama Papers* story also identified business links between Uruguayan lawyer Juan Pedro Damiani, a member of FIFA's Independent Ethics Committee, and three of those indicted by the US Department of Justice in May 2015: Uruguayan Eugenio Figueredo, former CONMEBOL president and FIFA vice-president; and Argentinean father-and-son businessmen Hugo and Mariano Jinkis (p. 3). Damiani had represented the Jinkis's offshore company Cross Trading, which was registered in the obscure island base of Niue. See also Owen Gibson, "Fifa: New crisis for football as inquiry launched into 'conflict of interest' ", *Guardian*, Monday 4 April 2016: 7.

19 See *Financial and Governance Report 2015, 66th FIFA Congress/Mexico City, 12 and 13 May 2016;* www.resources.fifa.com/mm/Document/AFFederation/Administration/ 02/77/08/71/GB15_FIFA_web_en_Neutral.pdf, accessed 31 March 2016; and "FIFA reports loss for 2015, but increases middle-term financial objectives", Media Release (FIFA.com), 17 March 2016, www.fifa.com/about-fifa/news/y=2016/m=3/news=fifa-reports-loss-for-2015-but-increases-middle-term-financial-objecti-2770880.html, accessed 31 March 2016.

20 See Note 25 in the previous chapter "Sequel: Badfellas on the Run"; see also Note 18 above on Jinkis's connections with a long-term member of FIFA's Ethics Committee.

21 For fuller accounts see Owen Gibson, "Panama Papers: FIFA president Gianni Infantino pulled into corruption scandal", *Guardian*, Wednesday 6 April 2016; and Keir Radnege, "Perception, perception, perception … Infantino in a flap over fallout to the 'Panama Papers' ", *World Soccer*, May 2016: 125.

22 FIFA, "Attorneys for FIFA provide update on internal investigation and detail on compensation for former top officials", Media Release, 3 June 2016, available at: www.fifa. com/governance/news/y=2016/m=6/news=attorneys-for-fifa-provide-update-on-internal-investigation-and-detail-2799851.html accessed 3 June 2016. On Infantino's early brush with the Ethics Committee, see www.fifa.com/about-fifa/news/y=2016/ m=8/news=statement-from-fifa-president-gianni-infantino-2819874.html, accessed 5 August 2016. On the allegations, see Richard Conway, "FIFA president Gianni Infantino to be interviewed by ethics committee", BBC Sport, 14 July 2016, www.bbc.com/sport/ football/36795446, accessed 14 July 2016.

23 FIFA, "FIFA statement on KPMG resignation", 13 June 2016.

24 Stoehlker was quoted in Luke Harding (and agencies), "Blatter, Valcke and Kattner awarded themselves £55m, say FIFA lawyers", *Guardian*, 3 June 2016.

25 Andrew Warshaw, "Infantino orders council tapes destroyed as FIFA's new culture of cover-up deepens", *Inside World Football*, 3 June 2016, available at: www.insideworldfootball .com/2016/06/03/infantino-orders-council-tapes-destroyed-fifas-new-culture-cover-deepens/ (accessed 12 July 2016).

26 On the lack of celebratory acknowledgement of Havelange's centenary, see Alan Tomlinson, "Happy Hundredth Havelange", http://alantomlinson.typepad.com/alan_ tomlinson/2016/06/happy-hundredth-havelange.html, 2 June 2016; for an obituary, Murad Ahmed, John Sugden and Alan Tomlinson, "João Havelange, world football chief, 1916-2016: FIFA president who became tainted by bribery findings", *Financial Times*, 17 August 2016, www.ft.com/cms/s/0/8d45ab96-349c-11e6-bda0-04585c31b153. html#axzz4IQqThaht, accessed 17 August 2016.

ACRONYMS

AFC	Asian Football Confederation
ASOIF	The Association of Summer Olympic International Federations
FIFA	Fédération Internationale de Football Association
CAF	African Football Confederation (Confédération Africaine de Football)
CBF	Brazilian Football Federation
CFU	Caribbean Football Union
CONCACAF	Confederation of North, Central American and Caribbean Association Football
CONMEBOL	South American Football Confederation (Confederación Sudamericana de Fútbol)
ExCo	Executive Committee (of FIFA)
FA	The Football Association (England)
FAP	Financial Assistance Programmes
FASA	Football Association of South Africa
FBI	Federal Bureau of Investigation
FCO	Foreign and Commonwealth Office
GAISF	General Association of International Sports Federations (rebranded as Sport Accord)
GOAL	GOAL development scheme
HBFD	Havelange-Blatter FIFA Dynasty
IAAF	International Association of Athletic Federations (formerly International Amateur Athletic Association)
IFAB	International Football Association Board
IOC	International Olympic Committee
IMG	International Marketing Group
ISL	International Sport and Leisure

MLS	Major League Soccer
NASL	North American Soccer League
NASSS	North American Society for the Sociology of Sport
OFC	Oceania Football Confederation
OCEANIA	Confederation of South Pacific Football Associations (OFC)
RICO	Racketeer-Influenced Corrupt Organisation
SANROC	South African Non-Racial Olympic Committee
SASF	South African Soccer Federation
TEAM	TEAM Marketing AG
TOP	The Olympic Programme
UEFA	European Union of Football Associations (Union des associations européenne de football)
UN	United Nations
UNESCO	United Nations Educational, Scientific and Cultural Organization
USSF	United States Soccer Federation

CAST LIST

This is a selective list. For a fuller listing of individuals featured in the book, see the general index.

The cast list is based upon two criteria: the named individual must appear several times within the text; and/or have contributed to the study, however directly or indirectly, through enabling access to sources, or via contact with the authors.

Each name in the list is followed by a résumé of the individual's position and profile in relation to connections with FIFA's political and economic apparatus during the period covered by our narrative in *Badfellas* and beyond.

Addo, Farah: b. 1935, d. 2008, Somalian sports administrator, and source of allegations that bribes were offered for votes in the 1998 election for the FIFA presidency. Banned from football-related activity for ten years by FIFA's disciplinary committee in 2004, for embezzlement in misusing funds intended for grassroots football development. Blatter had won a court injunction two years earlier to silence him in relation to the 1998 election.

Aigner, Gerhard: b. 1943, German football executive, general secretary/chief executive of UEFA 1989–2003.

Al-khalifa, Sheikh Salman bin Ebrahim: b. 1965, Bahraini football administrator, member of the ruling royal family of Bahrain. President of the AFC 2013 to present.

Aloulou, Slim: b. 1942, d. 2015, Tunisian football administrator and a lawyer by profession, represented CAF on the FIFA ExCo from 1998–2004. Banned by FIFA in 2010 for two years, for failing to report evidence of misconduct.

Bhamjee, Ismael: b. 1944, Botswanan football administrator. Banned by FIFA in 2010 for four years, for failing to report evidence of misconduct, and for taking bribes. Sent home by Blatter for selling on World Cup tickets at three times their face value at World Cup 2006 in Germany, he promptly resigned from his position on the FIFA ExCo.

Beckenbauer, Franz: b. 1945, German football prodigy who won the World Cup as both player and manager, and led Germany's successful bid to stage the event in 2006. A FIFA ExCo member, he was banned by FIFA from all football-related activity for ninety days, for lack of cooperation in its investigations into the 2018 and 2022 World Cup bids. He was placed under investigation by the Ethics Committee in October 2015, in relation to the finances of the 2006 World Cup.

Bell, Joseph Antoine: b. 1954, Cameroonian international football goalkeeper who played at the highest level in France and represented his country at three World Cups, the 1984 Los Angeles Olympics, and several CAF championships.

Bin Hammam, Mohamed: b. 1949, billionaire Qatari businessman and sport administrator, president of AFC 2002–11, member of FIFA ExCo. Major backer of Blatter for the presidency in 1998, and spent hundreds of millions of US dollars buying support for Qatar for its successful 2022 bid, acting at arms'-length from, but as the frontman for, the Qatar regime's ambitions to stage the World Cup. Suspended and banned by FIFA after offering bribes for votes for his presidential bid, administered in the Caribbean in 2011 by Jack Warner. Banned for life by FIFA in July 2012.

Blatter, Joseph "Sepp": b. 1936, Swiss sport administrator, joined FIFA in 1975, becoming general secretary in 1981 and elected as FIFA's eighth president in 1998. Elected for a fifth term in May 2015, before saying that he would resign a few months into that term; suspended by FIFA Ethics Committee in October 2015, then banned from football-related activity for eight years in December 2016 for dubious financial dealings with Platini.

Blazer, Chuck (Charles Gordon): b. 1945, US businessman and sport administrator, general secretary of CONCACAF 1990–2011, and on the FIFA ExCo from 1996–2013; chaired media/marketing committee. Informant for FBI from December 2011. In November 2013, confessed at a closed US court to a range of racketeering offences, implicating numerous co-conspirators.

Boyce, Jimmy: b. 1944, president of Northern Ireland's football organizing body the IFA (Irish Football Association) and member of the FIFA ExCo as representative of the British Associations (2011–15).

Cañedo, Guillermo: b. 1920, d. 1997, Mexican lawyer, business analyst, media entrepreneur and vice-president member of FIFA's ExCo from 1968 until his death. Chairman of FIFA's Media Committee from 1972, pioneering television deals spawned by FIFA's expanding event schedule and global portfolio.

Cavan, Harry: b. 1915, d. 2000, Long-serving Irish senior vice-president of FIFA, representing the British football associations on the FIFA ExCo up to 1990; president of the Irish Football Association 1958–94.

Champagne, Jérôme: b. 1958, French diplomat in diplomatic service 1983–98, diplomatic adviser to France 1998 World Cup, FIFA executive and president's adviser 1999–2010. Stood for the FIFA presidency himself in 2016, gaining a mere seven of the 207 available votes.

Charlton, Bobby, Sir: b. 1937, English footballer regarded as one of the greatest players in the history of the British game; ambassador for The Football Association in, for instance, World Cup bidding; and erstwhile businessman in coaching and development fields.

Chung, Mong Joon, Dr: b. 1951, South Korean businessman, politician and football administrator, scion of the industrial giant and FIFA sponsor, Hyundai; long-term member of FIFA's ExCo up to 2011, banned for six years by FIFA Ethics Committee in October 2015, on confidentiality and disclosure criteria related to the bidding process for the 2018 and 2022 World Cups, and so unable to pursue his bid for the FIFA presidency.

Coe, Sebastian, Lord: b. 1956, British athlete and sports administrator, elected as president of the IAAF in 2015. In 2006 became the first independent chair of FIFA's Ethics Committee, although there is scant detail of any specific contribution in that role.

Cooper, Keith: English communications professional and journalist, FIFA communications head in the 1990s, sacked by Blatter following the presidential election of 2002.

Dassler, Horst: b. 1936, d. 1987, German businessman and sports marketing pioneer, boss of Adidas and godfather of global sport marketing, working with FIFA and the IOC via his arm's-length marketing agency ISL. Mentor of Sepp Blatter.

Davies, David: b. 1948, English broadcaster, commentator and consultant, a former executive director of the Football Association.

Dempsey, Charles ("Charlie"): b. 1921, d. 2008, New Zealander hailing from Glasgow, Scotland, businessman and football administrator, general secretary then president of the OFC (OCEANA).

Diakité, Amadou: football administrator from Mali, member of the FIFA ExCo but suspended/banned by FIFA for two years in 2010–11, relating to accusations of bribery and his statements in a *Sunday Times* sting that African members of the FIFA ExCo were offered US$1–1.2 million for a vote for Qatar; and revelations in a British parliamentary enquiry that he'd been paid to vote for Morocco in the bidding process for the 2010 World Cup, which saw South Africa awarded the event.

D'Hooghe, Michel, Baron: b. 1945, Belgian doctor and football administrator, long-term chair of FIFA's Medical Committee and longest-serving member of its ExCo (1988 to present). Stalwart of numerous FIFA committees (pre-2016 reforms). Cleared by FIFA, in 2015, of any breach of ethics for accepting a valuable painting from a Russian representative in the build-up to the 2010 decision of the ExCo to award Russia the 2018 World Cup.

Eckert, Hans-Joachim: German lawyer, chair of the Adjudicatory Chamber of FIFA's Ethics Committee.

Erzik, Şenes: b. 1942, Turkish banker, project manager and football administrator, a UEFA vice-president from 1994 and member of the FIFA ExCo from 1996 to the present (its second-longest serving member).

Ganga, Jean-Claude: b. 1934, Congolese politician and sports administrator, Congo's ambassador to China, and activist and organizer against apartheid. Lobbyist in IOC circles and controversially open about the corruption that has characterized bid and election processes for the Olympics and FIFA events and positions.

Garcia, Michael: b. 1961, US lawyer, chair of the Investigatory Chamber of FIFA's Ethics Committee; resigned in 2014 over FIFA's dilution of his report into the 2018 and 2022 World Cup bid process, damning the "lack of leadership" in the FIFA hierarchy. Former US Attorney for the Southern District of New York (2005–2008) specialising in the prosecution of cases of public corruption and terrorism.

Granatkin, Valentin: b. 1908, d. 1979, Russian football and ice hockey international (goalkeeper), and sports administrator; a vice-president of FIFA from 1946, and senior vice-president under Havelange. Chairman of the USSR's football federation 1959–64 and 1968–73.

Grondona, Julio: b. 1931, d. 2014, Argentinean football administrator, chair of his country's football association 1979–2014, and a FIFA ExCo member/vice-president 1988–2014. As chair of FIFA's Finance Committee he was responsible for innumerable financial transactions including the undeclared remuneration for the president, Blatter, and the infamous "disloyal payments" at the heart of the Ethics Committee's charges against Blatter and Platini.

Havelange, João (Jean-Marie Faustin Godefroid), Dr: b. 1916, d. 2016, Brazilian industrialist and sports administrator, FIFA's seventh president, defeating England's Sir Stanley Rous in 1974. Condemned in FIFA report on financial dealings and bribes for contracts under his presidency, but his conduct described as "morally and ethically reproachable," resigned his honorary presidency of FIFA – and his life-membership of the IOC – just before publication of the report.

Hayatou, Issa: b. 1946, Cameroonian athlete, physical educationalist and sports administrator, chair of CAF 1988 to the present, and acting president of FIFA prior to the election of Infantino in February 2016. Long-term member of the IOC.

Hempel, Klaus: former ISL executive who left the company and co-founded TEAM; one of the architects of the UEFA Champions League.

Howell, Denis: b. 1923, d. 1998, British Labour Party politician and top-class football referee, was the country's minister for sport when England hosted the 1966 World Cup finals.

Infantino, Gianni: b. 1970, Swiss-Italian lawyer and football administrator, at UEFA since 2000, becoming general secretary of that organization in 2009. Elected as FIFA's ninth president in February 2016.

Jennings, Andrew: b. 1943, British investigative journalist, reporter, broadcaster and author of influential studies into corruption in the IOC and FIFA.

Johansson, Lennart: b. 1929, Swedish industrialist and football administrator, UEFA president 1990–2007. Lost to Blatter in the election for FIFA president in Paris in 1998, and to Platini for the UEFA presidency in 2007.

Jordaan, Danny: b. 1951, South African politician and sport administrator, prominent in South Africa's staging of the 2010 World Cup as chief executive officer of the organizing body of the event. He was an anti-apartheid activist and has held the position of mayor of Port Elizabeth.

Käser, Helmut: b. 1912, d. 1994, FIFA general secretary 1960–81, covering the presidencies of England's Arthur Drewry and Sir Stanley Rous, and the early years of João Havelange's regime. Succeeded as general secretary by Sepp Blatter.

Kelly, Graham: b. 1945, English football administrator who was secretary of the Football league from 1978–89, and chief executive of the Football Association 1989–98.

Kissinger, Henry, Dr: b. 1923, US diplomat and political scientist, controversially awarded the Nobel Peace Prize in 1973; sometime writer on "soccer" for US papers such as the *LA Times*, and lobbyist for the US as part of its challenge to host the Men's World Cup.

Koloskov, Viacheslav: b. 1941, Russian football administrator, FIFA vice-president and ExCo member 1980–96. A member of the organizing committee for Russia's successful 2018 World Cup bid, he was a lobbyist of the ExCo members/voters, presenting the ExCo veteran Michel D'Hooghe with a valuable painting whilst visiting him in Bruges.

Lacoste, Carlos, Vice-Admiral: b. 1929, d. 2004, Argentinean military/naval careerist and politician; briefly served as Argentina's president, and was a South American representative on FIFA's ExCo.

Lenz, Jürgen: Former Adidas employee, joint founder of marketing enterprise TEAM, and architect of the UEFA Champions League in its earlier formats.

Lynch, Loretta E.: b. 1959, US lawyer, from 2015 the Attorney General of the United States who spearheaded the investigations into FIFA corruption and the subsequent indictments. She had previously served as US Attorney for the Eastern District of New York (1999–2001 and 2010–15), leading the court actions against the informant Chuck Blazer.

Maradas, Emannuel: editor of *African Soccer*, and consultant on African soccer development.

Mayer-Vorfelder, Gerhard: b. 1933, d. 2015, German politician and football administrator, president of the German Football Association from 2000 to 2006.

Mifsud, Joseph, Dr: b. 1950, Maltese lawyer and football administrator, UEFA Executive Committee member and sometime member of the FIFA ExCo as European representative. Has had to answer questions concerning personal payments for arranging fixtures between a Maltese and a German club, when Germany was lobbying for the necessary FIFA ExCo votes that ultimately gained it the 2006 World Cup.

Milla, Roger: b. 1952, Cameroonian footballer and one of the first African footballers to make a major mark at World Cups, becoming the oldest goalscorer (at forty-two years of age) in World Cup history when scoring at the 1994 event.

Millichip, Bert, Sir: b. 1914, d. 2002, English lawyer and football administrator, chair of The Football Association 1981–96.

Mutko, Vitaly: b. 1958, minister of sport in the government of the Russian Federation; a voting member of the FIFA ExCo when the 2018 World Cup was awarded to Russia.

Nally, Patrick: b. 1947, British entrepreneur and marketing specialist who worked in journalism and public relations whilst pioneering the sport marketing industry. Founder of the West Nally group which included among its clients the IOC and FIFA. Responsible for FIFA's marketing partnerships, including the breakthrough deal with Coca-Cola during the early Havelange years.

Omdal, Per Ravn: b. 1947, Norwegian former president of his country's national football association, vice-president of UEFA from 1996, and a UEFA-nominated member of the FIFA ExCo 1994–2002.

Pound, Richard ("Dick"): b. 1942, Canadian lawyer, author and sports administrator, former competitive swimmer. Veteran of the IOC and first president of the World Anti-Doping Agency.

Rimet, Jules: b. 1873, d. 1956, French football administrator, FIFA's third, and longest-serving president, from 1921–54.

Rothenberg, Alan: b. 1939, US lawyer, businessman and sports executive who has championed the development of soccer/association football in the US sports landscape, including the staging of the men's World Cup in 1994.

Rous, Stanley, Sir: b. 1895, d. 1986, English physical educationalist, schoolteacher, international football referee and sports administrator. Secretary of The Football Association, 1934–62, FIFA's sixth president 1961–74.

Samaranch, Juan Antonio; b. 1920, d. 2010, Spanish (Catalan) sports administrator and minister of sports under the Franco regime; and Spanish ambassador in Moscow/USSR. President of the IOC 1980–2001, when the IOC was embroiled in corruption scandals on unprecedented scales.

Soosay, Alex, DAto': Malayasian football administrator, AFC general secretary 2009–15, having worked there since 1995; resigned in June 2015, following suspension by the AFC after investigation of allegations that he sought to obstruct an accounts audit that potentially linked him to Mohamed Bin Hammam's corrupt practices as AFC president.

Teixera, Ricardo: b. 1947, Brazilian football administrator, son-in law of Havelange, and president of the Brazilian Football Confederation 1989–2012. With Havelange, Teixera received, between 1992 and 2000, payments of CHF41 million from FIFA's marketing partner ISL (not, at that time, a crime in Switzerland).

Thompson, Geoffrey: b. 1945, former chairman of The Football Association, and vice-president at both UEFA and FIFA. Led England's unsuccessful bid to stage the 2018 World Cup. A member of the FIFA ExCo that voted in December 2010 for the hosts for the 2018 and 2022 World Cups.

Tognoni, Guido: Swiss sports administrator, who has worked for both FIFA and UEFA. Sacked twice by FIFA though in the second case with the incentive of the continuation, for two-and-a-half years, of his £150,000-a-year salary. Called, by reporter Andrew Jennings, "the most mercurial figure in world soccer".

Torres, Carlos Alberto: b. 1944, Brazilian footballer who captained Brazil to World Cup victory in 1970 in Mexico.

Ueberroth, Peter: b. 1937, US executive, businessman, and sports entrepreneur; Commissioner of Baseball from 1984–89, and the driving force behind the Los Angeles Olympic Games of 1984.

Valcke, Jérôme: French journalist, marketing specialist and football administrator, former general secretary of FIFA, suspended for selling on World Cup tickets and for misuse of expenses. In January 2016 he was banned for twelve years by FIFA's Ethics Committee, and sacked from his post.

Velappan, Peter, D'Ato: b. 1935, Malaysian physical educationalist and football administrator; general secretary of the AFC, 1978–2007.

Walker, Ernie: b. 1928, d. 2011, Scottish football administrator, secretary of the Scottish Football Association 1977–90. Active in UEFA and outspoken critic of FIFA practices.

Warner, Jack: b. 1943, Trinidadian schoolteacher, businessman and politician, CONCACAF president 1990–2011, when he resigned the position. Indicted by US Department of Justice in May 2015; in September 2015 he was banned for life by FIFA from any football-related activity.

Weah, George: b. 1966, Liberian footballer and politician who after retirement from football has dedicated his time to politics in Liberia, elected to the senate in 2014.

Weber, Jean-Marie: b. 1942, Swiss sports marketing executive and former chairman of Horst Dassler's creation – the marketing company ISL – that collapsed in 2001 with debts of £153 million. Known widely as FIFA's "bagman", who administered the bribes. He was charged with fraud, embezzlement and the falsification of documents by prosecutors in the canton of Zug, Switzerland, in 2008.

Will, David: b. 1936, d. 2009, Scottish lawyer and football administrator, president of the Scottish Football Association and active in UEFA and FIFA, a vice-president of the latter for fifteen years.

Winterbottom, Walter: b. 1913, d. 2002, English physical educationalist and footballer, first coach/manager of England's national football side, and influential director of coaching at The Football Association. Also served as general secretary of the Central Council for Physical Recreation, and was the first director of the UK's Sports Council.

Zen-Ruffinen, Michel: b. 1959, Swiss lawyer and football referee who worked his way up at FIFA from 1986, picked out by Blatter when the latter was general secretary. Became general secretary himself in succession to Blatter in 1998, but left after leading a failed challenge from within the ExCo against Blatter's dictatorial presidential style and mismanagement of both people and finances. Has since offered his consultative skills to high-paying clients and bidders for, say, the World Cup.

INDEX